MANY LAMPS, ONE LIGHT

Many Lamps, One Light

• •

LOUISVILLE PRESBYTERIAN
THEOLOGICAL SEMINARY

A 150th Anniversary History

Rick Nutt

WILLIAM B. EERDMANS PUBLISHING COMPANY
GRAND RAPIDS, MICHIGAN / CAMBRIDGE, U.K.

Published 2002 by
Wm. B. Eerdmans Publishing Co.
255 Jefferson Ave. S.E., Grand Rapids, Michigan 49503 /
P.O. Box 163, Cambridge CB3 9PU U.K.

Printed in the United States of America

06 05 04 03 02   7 6 5 4 3 2 1

Library of Congress Cataloging-in-Publication Data

Nutt, Rick.
Many lamps, one light: Louisville Presbyterian Theological Seminary:
a 150th anniversary history / Rick Nutt.
p.   cm.
Includes bibliographical references and index.
ISBN 0-8028-3913-4 (alk. paper)
1. Louisville Presbyterian Theological Seminary — History.
I. Louisville Presbyterian Theological Seminary.   II. Title.

BV4070.L6956 N88   2002
230′.07′35173944 — dc21

2002029472

www.eerdmans.com

For
The Louisville Presbyterian Theological Seminary
Community of 150 Years

Faculty, Students, Administration, Staff, Board, and Supporters

In honor and in memory of
Dr. Theodore M. and Bessie Greenhoe

CONTENTS

CONTENTS

PREFACE

L ouisville Presbyterian Theological Seminary celebrates its 150th anniversary in 2003. In 1853 a group of courageous Presbyterian leaders
launched the Danville Theological Seminary on the campus of Centre College. It was an inauspicious time to start a seminary, with sectional tensions growing and the prospect of war looming. The Danville Seminary,
like nearly every seminary, barely survived the Civil War and the period of
reconstruction that followed. In 1893, another Presbyterian seminary was
launched in Louisville. Of these two, the latter was related to southern
Presbyterians; the former, to northern Presbyterians. At a time when few
thought that cooperation between these two groups was possible, much
less desirable, leaders of the two seminaries joined forces in Louisville in
1901, creating the only Presbyterian seminary jointly sponsored by both
churches.

It thus became a bridge between North and South. The substance of
that metaphor has changed over the years; Louisville Seminary has since
been a bridge between theological differences, a bridge between the academy and the church, a bridge between races, and more. But building
bridges always means taking risks — spanning rivers, highways, or other
dangers.

Some things have changed over the course of Louisville Seminary's
history. But most impressing to me in reading this book were the continui-
ties — the steadfast commitment of the Seminary to the church, its focus
on preparing people for parish ministry, its perseverance in teaching and
writing in the light of Christian witness, its willingness to take some risks
for the sake of the gospel.

The author is Dr. Rick Nutt, Professor of Religion at Muskingum College. Dr. Nutt is a Louisville Seminary graduate and completed his Ph.D. in church history and ethics at Vanderbilt University. He has written a splendid account of the twists and turns, peaks and valleys of Louisville Seminary, and he has placed it within the larger context of American Christianity, theological education, and American culture. He was a logical choice to write the Seminary's history; he proved to be the best choice too. We are deeply grateful for the months he devoted to travel, research, and writing over the last several years.

The title of this book, *Many Lamps, One Light,* is taken from the motto adopted by Louisville Seminary early in the twentieth century and incorporated in Latin into the Seminary's first seal (see back cover). *Lampades Multae, Una Lux* has been an enduring way of expressing the Seminary's commitment to bring together people of diverse backgrounds and help them to unite as one light to illumine the path of our common pilgrimage.

May this book inspire you as well, so that we might better understand the providence of God, whose word is a lamp to our feet and a light to our path.

JOHN M. MULDER
President

INTRODUCTION

Milestones in our personal and corporate lives prompt reflection on the past and hopeful thinking about the future. So it is as Louisville Presbyterian Theological Seminary comes to the sesquicentennial anniversary of one of its predecessor institutions, the Danville Theological Seminary.

This history could have been written with any number of themes or from any number of approaches. One could organize the story around the Seminary's unique role as the sole point of contact between northern and southern Presbyterianism for the better part of a century, and that fact is a recurring element in this book. One could choose to build the history around the development of social justice ministries in the life of the Seminary, and that also plays a part in the current work. One could treat the institution, in its various manifestations, as the product of the will of key leaders, especially its presidents. The story is organized, to a large extent, around presidencies, but individuals are not treated as the final determinative force in the life of the institution. One could make use of the image of the Seminary as a bridge — between denominations, between academic and ecclesiastical life, between congregations and the church at large, between theological groups, and other ways. The reader will also find that a part of the story — explicitly so in the final chapter — but it serves as a subtheme at best. Finally, the history could take the form of a "lives of the saints" — a paean to the greatness of the people who made the Seminary tremendous beyond measure. But although this work is written with respect, even love, for Louisville Seminary and the people who have made, and continue to make, it the fine institution it is, the reader will find shortcomings and struggles a part of the story. (At this point I should note that uncounted people have been important to the life of Louisville Seminary. A reader's favorite person may be only briefly mentioned, or not at all. I can only hope those readers will understand the limitations under which such a work as this inevitably labors.)

There are two themes around which this history is organized. The first shows the ways in which Louisville Seminary reflected developments in American Christianity and American culture. I take it as axiomatic that the church and its institutions exist under the power of God and the influence of the societies in which they find themselves. The history of the Seminary demonstrates the economic, social, political, intellectual, and in one case even climatological forces of American society as they affected American Protestantism. Warfare, economic boom and bust, urbanization and industrialization, the rise of corporations, matters of racial justice, social change (especially for women), paradigm shifts in the understanding of how the world works, and other factors made an impact on the educational endeavor of Louisville Seminary. The ways in which this particular seminary responded to those forces can be informative for understanding developments in mainstream Protestantism as a whole.[1]

---

1. There have been a number of outstanding studies of seminaries and theological education in the recent past, and the reader who desires to understand even more of Louisville Seminary's reflection of trends in theological education and the influences of society on the work of seminaries and divinity schools than I could include in this work may consult them. See, for instance, Conrad Cherry, *Hurrying Toward Zion: Universities, Divinity Schools, and American Protestantism* (Bloomington and Indianapolis: Indiana University Press, 1995); Barbara G. Wheeler and Edward Farley, eds., *Shifting Boundaries: Contextual Approaches to the Structure of Theological Education* (Louisville: Westminster/John Knox Press, 1991); Alice Frazer Evans, Robert A. Evans, and David A. Roozen, eds., *The Globalization of Theological Education* (Maryknoll, N.Y.: Orbis Books, 1993); and Dorothy C. Bass, Benton Johnson, and Wade Clark Roof, "Mainstream Protestantism in the Twentieth Century: Its Problems and Prospects" (Papers presented to the 1986 annual meeting of the Council on Theological Education, Presbyterian Church [U.S.A.]). Good histories of non-Presbyterian seminaries are George M. Marsden, *Reforming Fundamentalism: Fuller Seminary and the New Evangelicalism* (Grand Rapids, Mich.: William B. Eerdmans Publishing Co., 1987), and Robert T. Handy, *A History of Union Theological Seminary in New York, 1836-1986* (New York: Columbia University Press, 1987). For histories of Presbyterian seminaries, some better than others, see William K. Selden, *Princeton Theological Seminary: A Narrative History, 1812-1992* (Princeton: Princeton University Press, 1992); James Arthur Walter, ed., *Ever a Frontier: The Bicentennial History of the Pittsburgh Theological Seminary* (Grand Rapids, Mich.: William B. Eerdmans Publishing Co., 1994); Howard Miller, "Seminary and Society: A Case Study of Their Interrelationship. David Leander Stitt and Austin Presbyterian Theological Seminary, 1945-1971" (A Report Submitted to the Lilly Endowment, 1987); J. McDowell Richards, *As I*

The second key theme is that, in the midst of changes in the way it educated people for ministry in the Presbyterian Church, Louisville Seminary remained constant in its vision and commitment to serve the church. When the 1810 General Assembly of the Presbyterian Church authorized the creation of denominational seminaries, it asserted that such institutions should be "nurseries of vital piety, as well as of sound theological learning, and to train up persons for the ministry who shall be lovers as well as defenders of the truth as it is in Jesus."[2] The reader will find that the responsibility of Louisville Seminary to the church, both ecumenical and Presbyterian, has always been foremost in its self-identity — not always articulated, but at times very plainly so. It is to this role that Louisville has self-consciously returned since reunion deprived it of its singular role as an institution of two Presbyterian denominations.

It has become obligatory for authors to render their thanks to those who have played a role in helping bring a work to fruition. Those who write know that the obligation ought not be fulfilled perfunctorily or out of a mere sense of propriety. That is especially true in this case, for this history would be much weaker without the help of others. Of course, the Seminary itself trusted me with the privilege of doing this work and made its completion possible with both financial and moral support. Debbie Ethridge assumed the onerous job of compiling the appendices and did a superb job. Melissa Nebelsick, Angela Morris, and Michelle Melton spent countless hours assembling the photographic insert. The library, through the person of its director, Joe Coalter, gave me special library privileges which greatly facilitated my research, and for that I am grateful. President John M. Mulder made the project possible and read the manuscript. Gene March, Ellis Nelson, L. C. Rudolph, Louis Weeks, and Al Winn read early drafts as well. Their insights have been invaluable. Centre College allowed me to have access to its archives, and the opportunity to work in that idyllic setting shall not soon be forgotten.

My own institution, Muskingum College, supported this project, not

---

See It: Columbia Theological Seminary, 1932-1971 (Decatur, Ga.: Columbia Theological Seminary Press, 1985); Thomas White Currie, Jr., *Austin Presbyterian Theological Seminary: A Seventy-Fifth Anniversary History* (San Antonio: Trinity University Press, 1978); and Ovid R. Sellers, *The Fifth Quarter Century of McCormick: The Story of the Years 1929-1954* (Chicago: McCormick Theological Seminary, 1955).

2. Cited in Steve Hancock, "Nurseries of Piety? Spiritual Formation at Four Presbyterian Seminaries," in Milton J Coalter, John M. Mulder, and Louis B. Weeks, *The Pluralistic Vision: Presbyterians and Mainstream Protestant Education and Leadership,* The Presbyterian Presence Series (Louisville: Westminster/John Knox Press, 1992), 72.

least by granting a special leave to accomplish the actual writing of the book. I owe a unique debt to my colleagues in the Religion and Philosophy Department for agreeing to let me have the year free of teaching, for it meant a hardship for them. Lilly Endowment, Inc., and the Rollin M. Gerstacker Foundation funded various portions of the research for and publication of this history, without which its completion would have been impossible. Dr. Theodore Greenhoe, for whom Louisville Seminary's Greenhoe Lectures are named, served on the Gerstacker Foundation's board and for many years as the pastor of the Memorial Presbyterian Church of Midland, Michigan. It is in his and his wife's memory and honor that this book is published. A special thanks goes to those people — over fifty in number — who opened their homes or offices or traveled to the Seminary campus in order to be interviewed. They gave of their time and insight so that this work could be richer in its portrayal of Louisville Seminary's story. It was an immense joy to visit with people, many of whom I did not know, and share a deep affection for the Seminary and learn of the role they had played in its life and the contributions they had made.

Finally, I thank my family for putting up with my extended absences from home during research trips, and Mary Gene for reading the first draft and saving me from some embarrassments. I trust all those who helped will think the finished product is worth their sacrifice.

Soli Deo Gloria.

· I ·

A SEMINARY OF THE FIRST CLASS

Danville Theological Seminary, 1853-1901

As Presbyterians migrated across the Appalachian and Allegheny Mountains into Kentucky at the end of the eighteenth and beginning of the nineteenth centuries, education was among their prime concerns. It was essential, they knew, to be able to prepare candidates for ministry in the newly formed congregations in Danville, Harrodsburg, and Lexington. Presbyterians were instrumental in securing a charter for Transylvania Seminary (College) in 1780. A Board of Trustees finally met in 1784; David Rice, the "father" of Kentucky Presbyterianism, who preached his first sermon in Kentucky at Harrodsburg in 1783, served as chair. Transylvania, a state school located in Danville, moved to Lexington in 1788 and there came under the influence of an anti-ecclesiastical Enlightenment rationalism (termed "French infidelity" at the time). It eventually became Transylvania University. Transylvania Presbytery was organized in 1785, and Presbyterians were so convinced of the need for Christian education on the frontier (especially given the apostasy at Transylvania) that they played a role in founding a number of other academies, colleges, and seminaries, all of which eventually failed. A solid footing for theological education did not emerge until the founding of Centre College in Danville in 1819. Although the Synod of Kentucky initiated the school's charter, the state legislature assumed control of Centre until 1823, when reorganization and a new charter placed it under Presbyterian control — as it remains today.[1]

---

1. There are a number of histories that chronicle the story of religious migration into the West of the early national period. A classic in the field is William Warren Sweet's multivolume *Religion on the American Frontier*. Of particular interest would be the second vol-

I

Why were Presbyterians so committed to the cause of education in the West? Their Reformed heritage, with its emphasis on an educated ministry and discerning laity who could read the Bible for themselves, played a large part. In the new nation, furthermore, Protestants in general feared the western wilderness — not just the physical wilderness, but also the spiritual wilderness they believed it fostered. Isolation, hard living conditions, the absence of institutions to organize and refine life, and the less-than-desirable character of some who moved west made many Christians in the East, and many who migrated, anxious for the spiritual health of the nation as people crossed the mountains into the Ohio and Mississippi Valleys. People held that Christianity was essential to civilization and refinement, and they believed that education constituted an indispensable element of faith. Consequently, denominational colleges were founded at a rapid pace in western Pennsylvania, Ohio, and Kentucky.[2]

Presbyterians were also concerned with establishing the means for raising up an educated ministry; after all, not just anyone could be given license to preach. In recognition of this need, the Presbyterian Church in the United States of America (PCUSA) General Assembly took steps to found a theological seminary west of the mountains. There was substantial competition for the seminary by Presbyterians in the West, and the 1827 General Assembly settled on Allegheny (now Pittsburgh), Pennsylvania, as the site for Western Theological Seminary. Not all supported that decision, though, and Presbyterians in Indiana began Hanover Seminary in 1827.[3] Cincinnati Presbyterians founded their own Lane Theologi-

---

ume, *The Presbyterians, 1783-1840. A Collection of Source Materials* (New York: Harper and Brothers, 1936). See also the first volume of Ernest Trice Thompson's *Presbyterians in the South* (Richmond, Va.: John Knox Press, 1963). Helpful accounts of the place of Presbyterianism in Kentucky can be found in Chapter I, "Beginnings," in Louis B. Weeks, *Kentucky Presbyterians* (Atlanta: John Knox Press, 1983); and I. S. McElroy, *The Louisville Presbyterian Theological Seminary* (Charlotte, N.C.: The Presbyterian Standard Publishing Co., 1929), 15-29. Clearly, although David Rice is justifiably identified with early Presbyterianism in Kentucky, many other faithful ministers and laypeople promoted the cause of Christ in the Reformed tradition with vigor; note that the Transylvania charter was secured prior to Rice's arrival in Kentucky.

2. One can see the anxiety over the West in the great Lyman Beecher's *A Plea for the West* (Cincinnati: Truman and Smith, 1835), in which he feared that Catholics would settle the West and dilute the United States' liberty, freedom, and civil institutions, and in Horace Bushnell's *Barbarism the First Danger: A Discourse for Home Missions* (New York, 1847).

3. Hanover Seminary moved to New Albany, Indiana, in 1840, then to Chicago, Illinois, in 1859, eventually to become McCormick Theological Seminary and pass into denominational control.

cal Seminary in 1832. Centre opened a theological department for the training of ministers in 1828. Presbyterians in the Synod of Kentucky supported Hanover, later known as New Albany, but the school suffered from a perpetual financial precariousness which eventually rendered it unsatisfactory to its constituents.[4]

In 1837 the PCUSA split apart. The denomination divided into the New School Presbyterians, with strength primarily in the North, and Old School Presbyterians, who were concentrated in the South.[5] The New School embraced the New England theology which modified the traditional Calvinist view of original sin and passive human role in the drama of salvation. New Schoolers also tended to support a variety of reform efforts, including plans for the eradication of slavery. The Old School, by contrast, maintained a traditional, even strict, Calvinist stance and tended to defend slavery. The differences were irreconcilable. Kentucky Presbyterians were overwhelmingly Old School in their allegiance.

In light of the schism, Lane and Western seminaries allied themselves with the New School. That left New Albany — supported by the Old School synods of the West — as the lone Old School seminary west of the mountains to serve the church in the Ohio and Mississippi Valleys.[6] The school's ongoing financial problems prevented it from providing the ministerial preparation the churches expected.

The Founding of Danville Theological Seminary

As a result of such an unsatisfactory state of affairs, in 1853 the Old School General Assembly received petitions from the synods supporting New Albany to found a seminary under Assembly control in the West. Alongside those petitions was a communication from the board of the New Albany seminary offering it to the General Assembly for denominational control, on the presumption that this would give it a firmer financial footing. It became clear that the Old School Assembly would have to take some decisive

4. For some of the work of Kentucky Presbyterians for ministerial education see Walter A. Groves, "A School of the Prophets at Danville," reprint copy from *Filson Club History Quarterly* in the Danville Theological Seminary Papers, Centre College Archives.

5. That Princeton Theological Seminary in New Jersey was the dominant center of Old School thought belies the inadequacy of identifying the denominations too closely with any one section of the nation.

6. The synods supporting New Albany were Indiana, Cincinnati, Kentucky, Missouri, Tennessee, Illinois, and Northern Indiana.

action on the matter of a western seminary to complement the role of Princeton, Union (Virginia), and Columbia in the East.

It is obvious that the Synod of Kentucky positioned itself at the Assembly to get the new seminary within its bounds at Danville. John C. Young, president of Centre College, was elected moderator of the Assembly that year. He called for a kind of "rump assembly" of the commissioners from the eleven western synods to develop a proposal for the Assembly's consideration on the question.[7] Kentucky had the most representatives in the ad hoc group, and W. C. Matthews of that state was elected as moderator. More importantly, Robert J. Breckinridge, pastor at Lexington, was among Kentucky's delegates to the Assembly that year. As Walter Groves wrote of Breckinridge, he "attended few meetings in his life which he did not dominate."[8] The heart of the recommendations this group submitted to the General Assembly suggested that the Assembly "establish in the West, under its own care, a Theological Seminary of the first class" in a location completely of the Assembly's own choosing, and that no other judicatory in the West should establish another seminary to rival that of the Assembly until it had a fair chance of success. Those suggestions seem innocent enough until one knows that the Synod of Kentucky had authorized the commissioners from its presbyteries to pledge the members and churches of the synod to provide $20,000 to pay for a professor's salary at any seminary in the West if the Assembly should act to found one, but to promise $60,000 for three professorships, ten acres of land, and the handling of legal proceedings to secure all charters and franchises from the state if the seminary were located in Danville.[9] This proposal came before the General Assembly alongside the committee's resolutions.

Before the General Assembly could consider the question, it had to refer the matter to its Standing Committee on Theological Seminaries. Moderator Young appointed Breckinridge to the chair of that committee. The "deck was stacked" as the committee voted to accept the recommendation of the ad hoc committee and received suggestions for places in which to locate the school. St. Louis, New Albany, Nashville, Cincinnati, and Danville were suggested, but the lucrative offer from the Synod of Kentucky simply precluded real consideration of any site but Danville. When the Assembly finally voted on the issue, New Albany received 33

---

7. The synods were Missouri, Nashville, Mississippi, Memphis, Illinois, Indiana, Northern Indiana, Cincinnati, Ohio, Arkansas, and Kentucky.

8. Groves, "School," 242.

9. The $60,000 pledge equals approximately $1,160,000 in 1999.

4

votes, St. Louis received 78, and Danville received 122. Breckinridge engineered every step of the process at the General Assembly and brought a new stage of theological education to Kentucky and the West. Despite the obvious political maneuvering at the 1853 General Assembly, Young later suggested that, looking back over the struggle for theological education in Kentucky, one could see the providence of God working toward the establishment of Danville Theological Seminary (DTS) through all the tensions and failed efforts. No human could have discerned God's purpose at the time, but in retrospect one might "admire and adore the hand of the Lord."[10]

As the Assembly's vote revealed, many opposed the choice of Danville. Danville Seminary was a blow to New Albany, and those close to the seminary fought to sway the commissioners to support the already-existing institution. Ill feelings lingered beyond the adjournment of the General Assembly; Breckinridge, never averse to polemic, denounced the "calumniators" who continued to issue "torrents of malignant slander" against Kentucky's new seminary.[11] Others believed the location of the Assembly's seminary in a slave state a mistaken idea and argued that candidates for the ministry from north of the Ohio River would not choose Danville. Young called those concerns groundless, and the presence of large numbers of northerners among the student body prior to the Civil War vindicated his stance.[12] Of forty-seven students at Danville in 1858, eleven were from clearly northern states. Indeed, the founders of the school hoped they could serve as a means of understanding between the North and South on the matter of slavery.

Danville Theological Seminary opened its doors on October 13, 1853, to a very promising start. Twenty-three students matriculated that first Fall, and much of the promised $60,000 was in hand; by the end of the school year the Kentucky churches had subscribed $65,000.[13] The faculty consisted of Breckinridge, professor of exegetic, didactic, and polemic the-

10. John C. Young, "Address," 4, in "Addresses Delivered at the Inauguration of the Professors in the Danville Theological Seminary, October 13, 1853" (Cincinnati: T. Wrightson, 1854), Box 1, Danville Theological Seminary Papers. For the story of the General Assembly see pp. 242-43; McElroy, *Louisville Presbyterian Theological Seminary*, 35-41; and Robert Stuart Sanders, *History of Louisville Presbyterian Theological Seminary, 1853-1953* (Louisville: Louisville Presbyterian Theological Seminary, 1953), 14-16.

11. Robert J. Breckinridge, "The Inaugural Discourse of Robert J. Breckinridge, D.D., LL.D.," 43-46, in "Addresses Delivered at the Inauguration."

12. Young, "Address," 18-20.

13. Groves, "School," 244.

ology; E. P. Humphrey, professor of biblical and ecclesiastical history; and Joseph G. Reasor, instructor in oriental and biblical literature. The last was appointed after two others elected by the General Assembly, the famous Benjamin M. Palmer of New Orleans and Phineas B. Gurley, declined appointment. Stuart Robinson, who later achieved fame as pastor of Second Presbyterian Church in Louisville and an opponent of Breckinridge, served on the faculty from 1856-1858. Stephen Yerkes, who would play a pivotal role in Danville's history, joined the faculty in 1857.

In the days before seminary presidents, Breckinridge was the undisputed leader of Danville Seminary. Born in 1800 in Fayette County, Kentucky, Breckinridge studied law and from 1825-1828 served as state legislator from his home county. Illness in 1828 led to a conversion experience and ministry, no small transformation for Breckinridge. Robert Stuart Sanders has written that "Mr. Breckinridge had been very worldly until his conversion. It was said that he was the best hunter, the best dancer, and the best stump speaker in Kentucky when he accepted Christ as his Saviour."[14] Breckinridge began to read divinity under ministerial tutelage (a common style of professional education at the time), became a candidate for ministry in 1831, and by 1832 was installed as pastor of Second Presbyterian Church in Baltimore, Maryland. In 1845 he became president of Jefferson College in Pennsylvania, then pastor of First Presbyterian Church in Lexington, Kentucky, in 1847, whence he created Danville Seminary. His ability and influence in the Old School are further manifested by his election as General Assembly moderator in 1841. Louis Weeks has written of Breckinridge, "Without doubt the most important pastor during the period [immediately preceding, during, and after the Civil War] was Robert J. Breckinridge. He also proved the most irascible, the most frequent party leader in whatever fight divided Kentucky Presbyterians."[15] Breckinridge possessed a superior intellect, and in its first years Danville offered a solid theological education in the Old School tradition. The student body grew to thirty-seven the second year and, by 1859-1860, to fifty-three students. It was an auspicious beginning.

14. Sanders, *History of Louisville Seminary,* 20. Breckinridge was, like Charles Finney, an early "second-career" ministerial candidate.
15. Weeks, *Kentucky Presbyterians,* 59.

The Educational Ethos

Danville Seminary existed for the sole purpose of educating young men for ministry — specifically the Presbyterian ministry, but the founders stated their willingness to accept students from other denominations.[16] To make the institution available to any candidate for ministry there was no tuition charged for classes. The education, aside from approximately $90 per year for room and board, was "gratuitous" to all.[17] The Board of Directors and faculty argued that education for ministry was unique. As training for a profession, the most rigorous academic standards and expectations should exist. Yet a seminary should provide more than just an intellectual education; it should also educate a person's character. Observed Breckinridge of the ministry:

> As a profession extremely peculiar and infinitely momentous in the subject matter of its course, its training demands a corresponding exaltation. As a profession, in which the personal character and intimate life of the person himself, is a fundamental element not only of his success, but of his very right to pursue his profession at all, a new and altogether singular element is introduced into the required system of training. And finally, as a profession combining duties and employments, widely different in their character — the teacher and the administrator of religion, both in one — the preacher of the gospel and the ruler amongst the flock — that rarest of all combinations in earthly things, high theoretical skill, and great practical success — the training that can fit one for all this, is liable to still higher and more peculiar modifications.[18]

Over two decades later, at his installation as professor of didactic and polemic theology, new hire Jonathan Edwards was admonished to remem-

---

16. "Plan of the Danville Theological Seminary, under the care of the General Assembly of the Presbyterian Church in the United States of America" (Louisville: Morton and Griswold, 1854), 6, Box 1, Folder 1, Danville Theological Seminary Papers. Presumably the Seminary would accept students only from other "evangelical," or Protestant, denominations.

17. "Plan of the Danville Theological Seminary." The absence of any tuition charge was not an unusual practice at the time.

18. Breckinridge, "Inaugural Discourse," 32. The school's "Plan," 7, described the education of a seminarian as "Not only that which is social and public — but also that which is private and personal; not only study and instruction — but discipline and practice; not only growth in knowledge, but growth in grace also; everything is to be embraced, according to its importance in the future career of a minister of the blessed Gospel."

7

ber that "your work divides itself into two departments — to furnish your students with a knowledge of the Holy Scriptures, and by all possible appliances to bring their hearts into cordial submission to their authority — their heads with sound learning, and their hearts with grace."[19] This effort to educate for both piety and knowledge, for both the practical and theoretical, would guide Danville and its successor seminaries into the twenty-first century. That purpose played a central role in the criteria for those called to teach at the Seminary. For faculty appointments the board would only make suggestions to the General Assembly of Presbyterian ministers in good standing who had been "statedly engaged as such, in some employment immediately connected with the cure of souls — for at least five years, preceding [their] election."[20] As Hal Warheim, professor at Louisville Presbyterian Theological Seminary, noted of the faculty until after World War II, they "seem to have been chosen not as theological experts, and certainly not as specialized scholars, but as outstanding examples of the G[eneral] P[ractitioner] minister who was at once scholar, teacher, preacher, pastor and Christian Gentle*man;* professional 'text-books' incarnate; role-models for the next generation of Preachers of the Gospel and male leaders of the church."[21] The students learned not only the content of faith and Holy Writ, but devotional practice and pastoral identity as well.

Danville Theological Seminary designed its curriculum to achieve that lofty goal. The course of study was divided into four areas: Exegetical, Didactic, and Polemic Theology; Biblical and Ecclesiastical History; Biblical and Oriental Literature; and Church Government and Pastoral Theology. The Bible was seen as the primary text in every area of study because, in good Calvinist fashion, the faculty understood all theology, morality, and church practice to grow directly out of Scripture. For example, in pastoral theology courses students read primarily the Pastoral Epistles, and

19. A. C. Dickerson, "Charge to the Professor Elect," 4, in "Addresses Delivered at the Inauguration of Rev. Jonathan Edwards, D.D., LL.D., as Professor of Didactic and Polemic Theology in Danville Theological Seminary, April 17, 1878" (Danville, Ky.: 1878), Box 1, Inaugural Addresses Folder, Danville Theological Seminary Papers. Edwards was a graduate of the Presbyterian Theological Seminary of Chicago (McCormick) and held a number of pastorates in the Midwest and in Philadelphia and Baltimore. From 1866-1868 he had been president of Washington and Jefferson College. He left DTS in 1880 to become pastor of Seventh Presbyterian Church in Cincinnati, Ohio. He was not related to the famous eighteenth-century theologian of the same name.

20. "Plan of the Danville Theological Seminary," 13.

21. Hal M. Warheim, "The History of a 'First-Class Dream' (Facts and Fantasies about Curriculum at Louisville Presbyterian Theological Seminary, 1853-1981)," 9. Emphasis in the original. Manuscript copy in author's possession.

church history defined the deviation or faithfulness of various ideas, movements, and individuals in terms of Calvinistically interpreted biblical doctrines.

Danville Seminary instituted a unique method of instruction beginning with its first session. The school eschewed the "Princeton Plan" of education, in which the student body was divided into three classes of middlers, juniors, and seniors. Instead, there were no classes at all, except for instruction in Hebrew, which had a first and second level. All students studied together in every course each year, which meant that every professor taught every student for at least one hour each day. All students studied the section of each department offered each year, covering each field in its entirety over three years. The faculty, rather than offering the same courses each year, covered their fields on a three-year rotation. Exams and various exercises tested the students' comprehension of a given subject, regardless of whether it took less or more than three years to master. Breckinridge, who seems to have devised the plan, explained that the principle behind it was "the thing aimed at, being not the amount of time consumed, but the amount of progress made."[22] Of course, students of the day were confronted with nothing resembling a modern curriculum containing its variety of courses from which to choose, perhaps with a few required core courses. The curriculum was prescribed for the student from start to finish. Electives did not exist.

Of course, education never happens in the classroom alone; this is especially true at a seminary. Danville Seminary provided a number of co-curricular means of preparing its students for ministry. Above all, the students worshiped. Each day began with a service that included reading of Scripture, prayer, and hymns.[23] Students held prayer meetings each day, and on Sunday the students and faculty attended worship *en masse*. Monthly meetings among the students examined their spiritual state, and faculty and students gathered each Sabbath for "a familiar conference upon subjects relating to spiritual training for the Christian ministry, its

22. Breckinridge, "Inaugural Discourse," 34. See also Sanders, *History*, 18, for a description of the plan, as well as DTS catalogues from the period (e.g., "Sixth Annual and Second Triennial Catalogue of the Officers and Students of the Theological Seminary of the Presbyterian Church, at Danville, Ky., 1858-59" (Louisville: Hull and Brother, 1859), 15, in Danville Theological Seminary Papers. One might also note that seminaries offered no degrees until later in the nineteenth century, and seminaries had trouble keeping students enrolled for the full three years of study. This curriculum is interesting for the student of LPTS history because, as we shall see, in the 1960s a curriculum with some of the same goals was introduced.

23. One should note that classes met Monday through Saturday.

duties, trials, &c."[24] This ethos of Calvinist devotion persisted until the Seminary's merger in 1901.

Students prepared not only their intellects and spirits for ministry, but developed their practical skills as well. Field education did not exist, and students were only rarely allowed to fill vacant pulpits during the school year. Practical skills for ministry developed, first, through weekly gatherings of the Seminary community in which students presented "skeletons of sermons and critical exercises on portions of the original [that is, Greek and Hebrew] Scriptures, and deliver[ed], without using notes, popular lectures and sermons in the presence of all the Professors and students. They also had similar exercises with the Professor of Pastoral Theology."[25] Since the school year ran from the beginning of October until early May, the students had long summer periods in which to engage in ministry in some form, and this provided them with at least some field experience. The Seminary proudly announced that a student could locate "useful employment, as teachers, colporteurs, &c, during the summer, . . . combining the advantages of pecuniary emolument with experience in efforts to do good, and a knowledge of the great domestic missionary field, in the heart of which the Seminary is planted."[26] Two points in that assertion should be noted. First, summer employment provided the opportunity not only to practice ministry but also to earn money to defray the cost of seminary education. This was important, for the scholarships the Seminary provided students in need constantly threatened to drag the school into debt. Second, a mission mentality was present from the beginning at Danville. In the 1854-1855 year a student licensed to preach offered himself to the Board of Foreign Missions for service abroad.[27]

In its early years Danville Seminary had no dormitories, and consequently students boarded with families in town. The school made of this a virtue with implications for the student's ministerial preparation: "In pre-

24. "Annual Catalogue of the Theological Seminary of the Presbyterian Church, at Danville, Ky., 1878-79," in Danville Theological Seminary Papers. In the early years of the seminary the faculty and students held their own worship each Sunday. (See, e.g., "Sixth Annual and Second Triennial Catalogue," 15.

25. "Annual Catalogue, 1878-79."

26. "Second Annual Report of the Board of Directors of the Danville Theological Seminary, to the General Assembly of the Presbyterian Church," *Minutes of the General Assembly of the Presbyterian Church in the United States of America* (Philadelphia: Presbyterian Board of Publication, 1855), 337. This fieldwork, or field experience, was not field education in the post-World War II sense of supervised practice of ministry.

27. "Second Annual Report."

paring for a profession, one of whose chief elements of success must consist in the power to mingle pleasantly, and to live in sympathy with the people, it is manifestly no unimportant consideration, that so far as consistent with faithful study, the student should keep up his connection with, and as far as possible increase his knowledge of, the every-day interests and moving impulses of human life."[28]

The education at Danville was, as its Old School affiliation would indicate, decidedly conservative.[29] Breckinridge ensured that Old School Calvinism, with its strict adherence to scholastic Reformed theology, would be vigorously promoted by the school. When the faculty, under Breckinridge's leadership, began to publish the *Danville Quarterly Review* in March, 1861, the articles reflected that traditionalist Calvinism. The first article, "The Relative Doctrinal Tendencies of Presbyterianism and Congregationalism in America," was a defense of the division of the church into Old and New Schools in 1837 and an excoriation of the ongoing Congregational and New School heresies regarding Scripture and the nature of sin.[30]

The priority of the Bible in every area of knowledge was assumed and affirmed at Danville. Scripture served as the basic text for each course of instruction, and the Seminary expected professors "to instruct the class in those portions of the text which are directly related to their several depart-

28. "Fourth Annual Catalogue of the Officers and Students of the Theological Seminary of the Presbyterian Church at Danville, Ky., 1856-1857" (Louisville: Morton and Griswold, 1857), 17, in Danville Theological Seminary Papers. This comment is again interesting, in that many people who knew LPTS at its 109 E. Broadway location thought one disadvantage of the move to Cherokee Park was the removal of the students from the immediacy of life experienced downtown. But the downtown could be too immediate, as L. C. Rudolph noted: "The level of noise and dirt in that splendid but unregulated old building made normal instruction all but impossible. My office and classroom had open windows in Spring — Summer — Fall onto First Street. All traffic squeaked to a stop at that 1st and Broadway light and gunned engines to roar away again." Rudolph to the author, May 30, 1999.

29. Weeks, *Kentucky Presbyterians*, 67-77, demonstrates the overwhelmingly Old School allegiance of Kentucky Presbyterianism. The churches supported the abrogation of the Plan of Union with the Congregationalists and the division of the church into Old and New School denominations. The sympathy of the Old School to slavery undoubtedly helps to explain the stance, although Kentucky pro-slavery sentiment was generally more moderate than that of the Deep South.

30. "The Relative Doctrinal Tendencies of Presbyterianism and Congregationalism in America," *Danville Quarterly Review* I (March 1861): 1-23. The articles were unsigned, so one cannot be sure of authorship — although this particular article bears the marks of Breckinridge's polemic.

ments."[31] The entire system of Calvinist theology grew directly out of Scripture; indeed, the essential purpose of God's written revelation was to enable one to study it scientifically and discern its doctrinal teaching. As a result, the curriculum of the Seminary consisted of imparting to students the same doctrinal system through a variety of means. Exegetical (what would later be called Biblical) Theology was essentially the same as Didactic (Systematic) Theology, achieved by an examination of the theological facts of Scripture arranged into a system that, not surprisingly, proved thoroughly Reformed. By the same token, Biblical and Ecclesiastical History comprised a unit, beginning with the "Old Testament Church" as people of Israel such as Abraham and Jacob manifested faith and as events in Israel's life anticipated typologically the coming of Christ and the church. Polemic Theology (Apologetics) demonstrated the inadequacy of any but the Christian understanding of reality and truth.[32]

Danville Seminary came into existence not only in the wake of the New England theology and its modification of strict Calvinism but also as new developments in biblical criticism challenged traditional understandings of Scripture and Darwin's exposition of evolutionary theory led many to question the nature of inspiration and revelation in the Bible. Predictably, Danville rejected the claims of reason over revelation and any attempt to weaken the authority of the Bible.

The Enlightenment assertion that all truth was rational and discernible by human intellect (rendering revelation superfluous) and that the universe existed by immutable natural law (rendering miracle unnecessary) met stiff resistance by the Old School. Presbyterians valued the use of reason, of course, and expected the intellect to be trained for the most acute understanding. Yet reason could only be correct when acknowledging the priority of revealed truth: "But when she [philosophy] oversteps the line,

31. "Annual and General Catalogue of the Officers and Students of the Theological Seminary of the Presbyterian Church, at Danville, Ky., 1874-75" (Danville: 1875), 17, in Danville Theological Seminary Papers.

32. Breckinridge, who taught theology, used as a text in Didactic Theology his magnum opus in two volumes: *The Knowledge of God, Objectively Considered, Being the First Part of Theology Considered as a Science of Positive Truth, Both Inductive and Deductive* (New York: R. Carter and Brothers, 1858) and *The Knowledge of God Subjectively Considered, Being the Second Part of Theology Considered as a Science of Positive Truth, Both Inductive and Deductive* (New York: R. Carter and Brothers, 1859). This Old School theology, which has acquired the name Princeton Theology because of the leading role in its formulation played by Archibald Alexander, Charles Hodge, and Benjamin Warfield of that institution, is the subject of Mark Noll, *The Princeton Theology, 1812-1921: Scripture, Science, and Theological Method from Archibald Alexander to Benjamin Warfield* (Grand Rapids: Baker Book House, 1983).

and undertakes to perform the functions of a judge where she should occupy the position of a humble disciple; and ventures not only to mingle her speculations with the holy utterances of God, but to palm them off as of equal importance, and even to ignore some of his plainest and most imperative announcements; she must expect to be treated as an intruder."[33]

Worst of all, in the minds of Old School Presbyterians, rationalism had infected the church — most plainly seen, first, in the higher criticism that proposed the documentary composition of the Pentateuch and separated the Jesus of history from the Christ of faith, and, second, in the New School theology that denigrated the majesty of God. Such false Christianity denied miracles, founded itself on reason (obviously de-emphasizing revealed truth), undercut the Bible's authority in faith and practice, and thereby injured the cause of morality. The greatest danger to true faith in the church came not from without, but from those "shamelessly sucking the breasts of the mother which nurtured them, while endeavoring with parricidal hand to deal her a death blow."[34] Nor did Danville waver from its defense of the traditional faith after eventual reunion of the Old School "North" with the New School in 1870 or the approach of the new century. When John M. Worrall was called to the faculty in 1892, he declared the faith of the church under assault by a system of thought which called itself higher criticism but was, in fact, destructive. Its strong rationalism opposed the idea of revealed truth, Worrall asserted, but more importantly its effect was to "discredit the Bible, and to shake the confidence of the people in its divine origin, its truthfulness and its authority."[35]

---

33. "The Relation which Reason and Philosophy Sustain to the Theology of Revelation," *Danville Quarterly Review* 1 (March 1861): 37.

34. "The New Gospel of Rationalism," *Danville Quarterly Review* 1 (September 1861): 367.

35. John M. Worrall, "Our Theological Seminary," 24, in "Inaugural Services of John M. Worrall as Professor of Ecclesiastical History and Church Government" (Danville: N.p., 1893). The exposition of Worrall's thought is found on pages 20-25.

The American Protestant response to the challenge of the intellectual revolution in the last half of the nineteenth century is discussed in Arthur M. Schlesinger, Sr., "A Critical Period in American Religion, 1875-1900," reprinted in John M. Mulder and John F. Wilson, eds., *Religion in American History: Interpretive Essays* (Englewood Cliffs, N.J.: Prentice-Hall, 1978); Lloyd J. Averill, *American Theology in the Liberal Tradition* (Philadelphia: The Westminster Press, 1967); Paul A. Carter, *The Spiritual Crisis of the Gilded Age* (DeKalb, Ill.: Northern Illinois University Press, 1971); Kenneth Cauthen, *The Impact of American Religious Liberalism* (New York and Evanston, Ill.: Harper and Row, 1962); William R. Hutchison, *The Modernist Impulse in American Protestantism* (Oxford and New York: Oxford

Danville Theological Seminary and the Civil War

The Civil War proved a watershed in the nation's history and devastated Danville Seminary. Its strong beginning was disrupted after eight short years by the onset of the conflict. Breckinridge tied the school to the Union cause, a course of action with irreversible consequences.

The situation in Kentucky at the beginning of the war defies easy assessment. Kentucky was, of course, a slave state, but there existed a significant amount of moderate anti-slavery sentiment that rejected both the indefinite perpetuation of slavery and abolitionism. Rarely did the defense of slavery reach the fervency found in the Deep South. Robert Breckinridge himself advocated a moderate anti-slavery stance.[36] That helps explain why, despite the presence of slavery in Kentucky and the state's technical neutrality, it appears that the majority opinion was Unionist — including among Presbyterians. With the election of Lincoln and the subsequent secession of southern states, Breckinridge, always absolutely certain of the truth of his convictions, vigorously promoted the Union cause.

Breckinridge found both the North and South at fault in the crisis of the Union, but he put the prior blame on the North. When the northern states chose to disregard the fugitive slave laws so important to the slaveholding states, and when a vocal minority in the North constantly agitated for immediate abolition of slavery, they were guilty of unwarranted assaults on the sovereignty of the slave states on anarchic principles (an horrific social idea for a strict Calvinist). Anarchy begets more anarchy, and the southern states began to secede. Writing before the events at Fort Sumter, Breckinridge posited that if the North would allow the South to have slavery — slavery was clearly allowed by God, being a condition of human fallenness — perhaps the unionists in the slave and border states could prevail against further secession, and the Confederate states could rejoin the Union.[37]

Lest anyone suppose that Breckinridge would defend secession because he held the North more accountable for precipitating the national dilemma, it is clear he plainly rejected it. The sovereignty of the individual

---

University Press, 1976); and George M. Marsden, *Fundamentalism and American Culture: The Shaping of Twentieth-Century Evangelicalism, 1870-1925* (New York and Oxford: Oxford University Press, 1980).

36. Weeks, *Kentucky Presbyterians*, 61-67, describes the ambiguity of the state of affairs in Kentucky at the time.

37. "Our Country — Its Peril — Its Deliverance," *Danville Quarterly Review* 1 (March 1861): 73-115.

states did not exist apart from the Union, he argued, for the nation came into existence as a unified entity with its own ideals and principles. The Declaration of Independence gave voice to America's national identity prior to statehood and the Constitution framed and ordered it. Unity did not depend on the consent of the states. Thus Breckinridge could say, "What sovereignty did Kentucky ever have except the sovereignty that she has as a State of the United States. . . . We became a State and we became of the United States at the same moment."[38] In the midst of the war, Breckinridge asserted powerfully that at independence the colonies "recognized that Union, and their duty of allegiance to it, as already existent realities, not by virtue of any act of voluntary league or confederacy on their part, but from the very manner of their origin and native relations to each other. . . . The Constitution did not create the Union."[39]

Just as momentous as national division was the split of most Protestant churches North and South.[40] The slavery issue rent the Methodist Church in 1844 and the Baptist Convention in 1845. The New School Presbyterians divided in 1857; the southern group took the name United Synod of the South, and eventually became a part of the Presbyterian Church in the United States (PCUS). The Old School held together until the 1861 General Assembly approved resolutions from commissioner Gardiner Spring that enjoined allegiance to the United States on members of the denomination. Many in the Old School held tightly to the doctrine of the "spirituality of the church," which had been formulated most fully by James Henley Thornwell.[41] The doctrine asserted that the

38. "Discourse of Dr. R. J. Breckinridge Delivered on the Day of National Humiliation, January 4, 1861, at Lexington, Ky.," *Danville Quarterly Review* 1 (June 1861): 327. This political speech was unabashedly intended to keep Kentuckians in the Union camp. Students of U.S. religious history will recognize Breckinridge as a proponent of the idea of a Christian America with a special calling to lead the world to God. One reason the Union was important was that "there is the blessing of our glorious example to all nations and all ages; there is the blessing of irresistible power to do good to all peoples, and to prevent evil over the face of the whole earth; there is the blessing of an unfettered Gospel and an open Bible and a divine Saviour, more and more manifested in our whole national life as that life deepens and spreads . . . overflowing and fructifying all peoples besides" (321).

39. "The Union and the Constitution," *Danville Quarterly Review* 3 (September 1863): 346.

40. C. C. Goens, *Broken Churches, Broken Nation: Denominational Schisms and the Coming of the Civil War* (Macon, Ga.: Mercer University Press, 1985), demonstrates that church divisions actually contributed to the split of the nation.

41. For a complete treatment of the doctrine see Ernest Trice Thompson, *The Spirituality of the Church: A Distinctive Doctrine of the Presbyterian Church in the United States* (Richmond, Va.: John Knox Press, 1961).

church as the church could not properly involve itself in social or political matters, although it was incumbent on individuals to be active Christian citizens. The Gardiner Spring Resolutions flew in the face of that concept and became the occasion for the Old School to divide into the Presbyterian Church in the U.S.A. and the Presbyterian Church in the Confederate States of America. At the end of the war the latter church, still restricted to the South, took the name Presbyterian Church in the United States.

Many argued that the General Assembly had no constitutional basis for such a political pronouncement, but Breckinridge refuted that position. He affirmed the spirituality of the church and declared that if a nation became immoral or unjust, the church was obligated to submit, even to the point of suffering — although individual Christians could rebel against such a government under certain circumstances. Yet it was also appropriate for civil affairs to come before a church court in extraordinary cases, and Breckinridge believed a pastoral letter on the current rebellion (i.e., the Spring Resolutions) fell within the General Assembly's purview. He did think the Spring Resolutions were a mistake. In effect, they incited Presbyterians in the Confederacy to rebellion against their government. It would have been better to delineate the rights of both church and Christian citizens in their relation to the civil power, the duty of subjection, and the limits to the right of rebellion.

Still, the right of the Assembly to pass such a resolution seemed plain to Breckinridge. Occasionally political conditions — especially those which pitted Presbyterian against Presbyterian in civil war — arose which required moral and political pronouncement from the church on the basis of God's law as the church could discern it. After a survey of Presbyterian declarations during the War for Independence, Breckinridge wrote that "It is *safe, scriptural, constitutional, and in accordance with the practice of the fathers,* for the General Assembly to decide the question of allegiance, or of obedience to the civil power. . . ."[42] The separation of southern Presbyterians was, then, improper. The Old School Presbyterian Church was not heretical or unsound in doctrine, nor unscriptural or oppressive in the use of discipline.[43] Breckinridge, who always believed it was important to defend points of principle to their full extent, proposed a resolution to the 1862 General Assembly which opposed both the secession of states and

---

42. "The Late General Assembly — Church and State," *Danville Quarterly Review* 1 (September 1861): 509. Emphasis in the original.

43. "The Late General Assembly," 521-523.

the withdrawal of Presbyterians in the South to their own denomination. It passed after extensive debate.[44]

The turmoil of war took its inevitable toll on the fortunes of Danville Seminary. The school, which had over fifty students in attendance for the 1859-1860 school year, had only eleven students appear for the fall 1861 term — and only two of those were new students.[45] Conditions did not improve during the course of the war and actually deteriorated with the peace at Appomattox.

The majority of the Presbytery of Louisville was fervently pro-Confederacy; in fact, Breckinridge carried on a heated public debate with his former faculty colleague Stuart Robinson, pastor of Second Church in Louisville, who was forced into Canadian exile from 1864-1866 for his defense of the South.[46] When the 1865 Old School General Assembly directed all of its presbyteries, particularly in the border states, to examine new and incoming ministers on their opinions regarding slavery and their loyalty to the Union, the Presbytery of Louisville passed a "Declaration and Testimony against the Erroneous and Heretical Doctrines and Practices which have Obtained and been Propagated in the Presbyterian Church during the Last Five Years." The 1866 General Assembly in turn directed the Synod of Kentucky to exclude from its meeting any signers of the "Declaration and Testimony," which Breckinridge sought to do by resolution when synod met in 1866. The resolution was soundly defeated, precipitating the division of the synod.[47] Those who supported the "Declaration and Testimony" eventually found their way into the Presbyterian Church in the United States, or "Southern Presbyterian Church." The minority, including Breckinridge and Danville Seminary, remained in the

44. "The General Assembly of 1862, of the Presbyterian Church in the United States of America," *Danville Quarterly Review* 2 (June 1862): 305-15. For a more complete treatment of Kentucky Presbyterianism during and immediately after the Civil War, see Weeks, *Kentucky Presbyterians.*

45. "Danville Theological Seminary. Annual Report of the Board of Directors," *Minutes of the General Assembly of the Presbyterian Church in the United States of America* (Philadelphia: Presbyterian Board of Publication, 1862), 661-62.

46. The 1862 General Assembly informally exonerated Breckinridge of any wrongdoing in his conflict with Robinson, who charged him with improper use of a seminary professorship for political causes. No doubt both protagonists were guilty of undue vitriol. See "The General Assembly of 1862," 352-70.

47. Weeks, *Kentucky Presbyterians,* 88-92, shows that the Gardiner Spring Resolutions and the self-righteousness of the General Assembly regarding slaveholders galvanized this sentiment against the Old School. Weeks also presents a more complete chronicle of this episode, which involved vehement conflict at both the synod and General Assembly levels.

northern Old School. E. P. Humphrey, also at DTS, concurred with Breckinridge in supporting the Union and attempting to excise the "disloyal" Presbyterians from the synod.[48]

The decision of Danville Seminary to stay within the northern Old School denomination proved the death of the institution, although thirty years lapsed before the burial. There remained no natural constituency for the school, and the reunion of the Old School and New School General Assemblies in 1870 (both denominations by then almost exclusively northern) brought Danville into competition with Lane Theological Seminary, only a little more than one hundred miles away in Cincinnati. To some extent, Danville Seminary also competed with the Theological Seminary of the Northwest (McCormick) in Chicago. The devastating effect of both ecclesiastical and civil wars and their aftermath resulted in the closing of DTS for the 1866-1867 school year. The school was reorganized in 1867, reducing the board of fifty-four by half[49] and making the school year run during the summer months, from the beginning of May to the beginning of November. This shortened the year by two months.[50] The General Assembly directed the Seminary to return to a conventional school year in 1870.[51]

Down to Consolidation

Through all of its exigencies, Danville Theological Seminary struggled on diligently. In 1875 the student body, at the direction of the General Assembly, was reorganized into classes. The curriculum underwent few substan-

48. Weeks, *Kentucky Presbyterians,* 88-92; "To the Presbyterian People of Kentucky," printed letter in Danville Theological Seminary Papers; "Rev. Dr. Wilson's Reply to the Address of Rev. Dr. E. P. Humphrey," in Danville Theological Seminary Papers.

49. "Danville Theological Seminary. Annual Report of the Board of Directors," *Minutes of the General Assembly of the Presbyterian Church in the United States of America* (Philadelphia: Presbyterian Board of Publication, 1867), 412-13. The reason given for the reduction was that the members of the board were too scattered geographically and suspicions that some were "not in hearty sympathy" with the Seminary.

50. "Annual Report of the Board of Directors." The closing of the school this year, and again in 1872-1873, technically prevented Stephen Yerkes from being second in years of faculty service. Without them he would have served continuously for thirty-nine years. He is tied for third-most years of service with C. R. Hemphill, who taught at LPTS from 1893-1930. A. B. Rhodes, who taught continuously at LPTS from 1944-1982, is second in years of service at thirty-eight years. David Steere, 1957-1996, is first with thirty-nine years of service.

51. "Danville Theological Seminary. Annual Report of the Board of Directors," *Minutes of the General Assembly of the Presbyterian Church in the United States of America* (New York: Presbyterian Board of Publication, 1870), 149-51.

tive changes. To supplement the standard course of study, the faculty invited renowned pastors, denominational leaders, or ministers engaged in special ministries to lecture to the Seminary community. By the 1890s the lists of lectures revealed the attempt by these traditional Calvinists to address contemporary issues and new areas of learning. In the 1896-1897 school year, for instance, the students heard presentations on "Christianity and Socialism" and "The New Psychology."[52]

The faculty underwent more extensive changes, although the conservative nature of its Calvinism remained. Upon Breckinridge's death in 1869, Stephen Yerkes, who joined the faculty in 1857 as professor of biblical and oriental literature, replaced the DTS founder as its leading figure. He became professor of biblical literature and exegetical theology, then in 1892 New Testament Literature and Exegesis. Yerkes was an appropriate successor to Breckinridge, for after he graduated from Yale in 1837 he prepared for the ministry by reading theology under Breckinridge in Baltimore. The faculty members always came out of the parish — often prestigious pulpits — and were leaders in the church. Nathan Rice, professor of didactic and polemic theology from 1874 until his death in 1877, held a number of prominent pastorates, including Fifth Avenue Presbyterian Church in New York. Rice also served as editor of a series of journals, taught at Lane, helped found McCormick Seminary, and was president of Westminster College in Missouri when called to Danville Seminary.[53] Rice and five other teachers at DTS served as moderators of the General Assembly: E. P. Humphrey, Stuart Robinson, Joseph T. Smith, Robert Livingstone Stanton, and William C. Young.[54] That number is all the more remarkable considering only twenty-five people taught as professors or instructors in the Seminary's forty-eight-year history.[55]

However, even such a noteworthy and diligent group of faculty could not stem Danville's decline. When the school returned to a conventional schedule in 1870, there was a contingent of four faculty but only six students. The student population crept up to twenty-two for 1876-1877, only to drop again to eight in 1879, rarely climbing above thirty full-time students again.[56]

---

52. "Annual Catalogue of the Theological Seminary of the Presbyterian Church at Danville, Ky., 1896-1897," 7, in the Danville Theological Seminary Papers.

53. McElroy, *Louisville Presbyterian Theological Seminary*, 23-24.

54. McElroy, *Louisville Presbyterian Theological Seminary*, 24.

55. See Appendix B for a list of DTS faculty.

56. In the 1890s there were some students enrolled at both Centre College and the Seminary.

The decline in student numbers corresponded to a decline in financial health. The solid beginning of $65,000, plus land and some buildings, did not lead to the growth many thought it promised. Even before the war the Seminary repeatedly broadcast that it received virtually no gifts which originated outside the Synod of Kentucky and beseeched the General Assembly to make Danville truly a seminary of the entire denomination. If it were, and if theological education in the West concerned the denomination, support should come from every quarter of the church. Anti-slavery sentiment north of the Ohio played a role in this problem, of course.[57] The Board of Directors believed the Seminary needed an additional $75,000-$100,000 to endow permanently the salary of a fourth professor, provide minimal facilities, and yield sufficient income to supply aid for students in need.[58] During breaks professors repeatedly traveled, particularly to the East, soliciting gifts for the Seminary. The endowment of the school did grow, up to approximately $170,000 by 1867 — but little more through the remainder of the century. The General Assembly of 1880 observed that Danville Seminary, "though not yet relieved from complicated embarrassments, with which it has struggled since the separation of the Northern and Southern Churches, is holding on its way, 'faint yet pursuing.'"[59] Even so, in 1893 the school proudly opened the new Breckinridge Hall (still in use at Centre College) with dormitory rooms in one end and classrooms, library, and lecture halls in the other. This allowed the school to move from its inadequate downtown location next to the college on the edge of town.

Faculty turmoil increased the trauma through which DTS periodically labored. After the Seminary reopened following the 1866-67 closing and returned to a standard year in 1870, three professors — Yerkes, George Archibald, and Samuel McMullen — tendered their resignations in the spring of 1872. Nathaniel West, who taught Didactic and Polemic Theology, apparently did not resign. The reason for the resignations was not given, but Danville had made amendments to its charter — probably to deflect suggestions that the General Assembly move the institution to the West Coast because of its financial problems. Perhaps these developments played a role in the faculty resignations; most likely they hoped to force the

57. See especially the "General Statement" in the "Sixth Annual and Second Triennial Catalogue."

58. "First Annual Catalogue," 31-32. As we shall see, helping students meet the cost of seminary education never ceased to be a problem and was a consistent cause of budget woes.

59. *Minutes of the General Assembly of the Presbyterian Church in the United States of America* (New York: Presbyterian Board of Publication, 1880), 59.

Assembly's hand on the matter of the move. At any rate, the Seminary again held no session for the 1872-1873 year.[60]

In 1873 the board, undoubtedly wanting to strengthen the Seminary against further attempts at removal, again elected Yerkes, Archibald, and McMullen to the faculty. West was now gone. Since Yerkes alone accepted the position, he was the sole teacher for the two students who enrolled. The next year Archibald accepted re-appointment, and Nathan Rice and John Hays joined the faculty to put the school at full strength. The school's standing slowly improved, and students numbered in the twenties until another crisis struck in the 1880s. The faculty was down to Yerkes, Archibald, and Hays for 1882-1883 (and only seven students), but the last two resigned. Yerkes again labored on alone from 1883-1886 because the board could not hire any others, teaching one student in 1883-1884 and 1884-1885, and two in 1885-1886. Beginning in 1886 the Seminary offered classes taught by members of the Centre faculty, a practice that persisted to the close of the century. This could hardly have been what the founders envisioned when they sought a seminary of the first class.[61]

Toward Consolidation

Although the 1872 General Assembly declined the proposal to remove the Seminary to the far West, the school's troubles resulted in other schemes to reorganize, move, or merge Danville with some other seminary. In 1883, not coincidentally the year the board elected to keep Yerkes alone on the faculty, a joint PCUSA and PCUS committee was formed to study the possibility of cooperation by the two denominations in the areas where both existed. At the same time some members — not a presbytery or synod — of the PCUS in Kentucky requested that Danville Seminary be transferred to control of their denomination. In 1884 a recommendation of joint "occupancy" was devised with an equal number of representatives on the board,

---

60. *Minutes of the General Assembly of the Presbyterian Church in the United States of America* (New York: Presbyterian Board of Publication, 1873), 531 and 594.

61. One can keep track of the rising and falling fortunes of DTS with a survey of the annual reports to the General Assembly. Also of interest are the Seminary's catalogues, especially the "Annual Catalogue of the Theological Seminary of the Presbyterian Church, at Danville, Ky., 1886-1887," 7-8, in the Danville Theological Seminary Papers. With Yerkes on the faculty the school added Claude Martin full-time and used Ormond Beatty and John McKee of Centre — these to teach ten students. The catalogue called it an encouraging return from the brink of extinction.

an equal number of professors, denominational control of any money it raised for the school (in case the joint venture should end), and moving the Seminary to Louisville. The PCUSA Synod of Kentucky approved the plan, but the PCUS synod, noting that the northern synod in Kentucky had no authority to act on the matter since the Assembly controlled the Seminary, declined any action. Nonetheless, the joint committee sent its proposal to both General Assemblies in 1885. The PCUSA approved the plan, but the PCUS voted in the negative because of "insuperable practical difficulties." Apparently the PCUS would have had no share in the already-existing endowment or assets of Danville Seminary. The failure of this project prompted the board to redouble its efforts to strengthen the school as it again expanded the faculty beginning in 1886.[62]

Thus ended the final realistic attempt to save Danville Seminary in the nineteenth century. The failure to bring it within the PCUS led to the founding of another school in Louisville as DTS clung to life through the 1890s. Our narrative now turns to that other seminary, which marked another step toward the goal of a seminary of the first class in the Ohio and Mississippi Valleys.

---

62. See McElroy, *Louisville Presbyterian Theological Seminary,* 43-48, and *Minutes of the General Assembly of the Presbyterian Church in the United States of America* (Philadelphia: Presbyterian Board of Publication, 1884), 67-68.

• II •

THIS NEW AND VIGOROUS FOUNDATION
OF THEOLOGICAL LEARNING

*Louisville Presbyterian Theological Seminary
and Seminary Merger, 1893-1920*

The division of Kentucky Presbyterians left the PCUS without a seminary in the state — or the lower Mississippi Valley. Southwestern Presbyterian University (now Rhodes College in Memphis, Tennessee) at Clarksville, Tennessee, added a divinity school in 1885. Although the school performed "admirable work, it was the judgment of many that only a separate institution, not related to any college or university, and situated in a large city, could hope to secure the support of all the Synods in this region and render the service required by this great and growing constituency."[1] Consequently, an effort, based in central Kentucky, emerged to establish a seminary in the western bounds of the PCUS.

The Movement to Found Louisville
Presbyterian Theological Seminary

In 1874 the PCUS Synod of Kentucky opened Central University in Richmond, and in 1889 the synod voted to begin raising funds for an institution of theological education. I. S. McElroy left his pastorate, moved to Lexington, and took on the task of soliciting money for that purpose. Cen-

---

1. Charles R. Hemphill, "The Origin and History of Louisville Seminary," *The Register* 7 (April, May, June 1918): 5.

tral University had dental and medical schools located in Louisville, and the possibility existed that the theological school would be placed there also. McElroy later observed that he had a two-fold task in his fundraising: to build interest in a seminary among the churches and actually to solicit gifts. The first proved the more difficult task, for many still thought the two synods of Kentucky would eventually agree to make Danville a joint seminary. Others believed improvements in rail service and safety made Union Seminary in Virginia easily accessible. Still others did not see an urgent need for a theological seminary and doubted that money could be raised because Central University required so much financial support from Kentucky Presbyterians. However, L. H. Blanton, Chancellor of Central, helped McElroy make the case for a seminary with his steadfast support of the effort.

McElroy raised funds through the use of evangelistic meetings. He preached over nine hundred sermons, and more than five hundred members were added to church rolls in Kentucky during his campaign. Only after preaching did he present the case for a seminary and ask for money. He found that "[w]hen the meetings were most fruitful in spiritual blessings the subscriptions were most liberal for the Seminary."[2]

In 1891 funds sufficient to hire one professor had been raised, and T. D. Witherspoon taught courses in Bible at Central University and comprised the entire theological school. The curators of the university still urged the synod to push on with plans for a full theological institution to be established in the Southwest (Central's effort lasted but one school year). The synod that year invited the Synod of Missouri and the five synods participating in the support of the Divinity School at Southwestern (Nashville, Memphis, Alabama, Mississippi, and Arkansas) to join Kentucky in creating an independent seminary in the Southwest. The synods would agree beforehand that the school should be located in a city — either Nashville, St. Louis, or Louisville. The seminary would bear the name "The Theological Seminary of the Southwest." The school should open with suitable buildings and a minimum of $100,000 in endowments. If deemed best to locate the school in Nashville or St. Louis, the Synod of Kentucky would urge its constituents to support it fully. If Louisville were chosen, the synod itself pledged sufficient buildings and the endowment, plus whatever the other synods would contribute, with representatives from every synod on the Board of Directors. All the synods except Mis-

2. I. S. McElroy, *The Louisville Presbyterian Theological Seminary* (Charlotte, N.C.: The Presbyterian Standard Publishing Co., 1929), 52-58.

24

souri declined the offer of this new venture, and Louisville became the agreed-upon site. The founders decided on the more familiar Louisville Presbyterian Theological Seminary as the name of the new institution.[3]

Why did the Synod of Kentucky believe there was a need for a seminary in the Southwest? The only two PCUS seminaries (Union and Columbia) stood on the Atlantic seaboard, too far removed from the Ohio and Mississippi valleys to address the peculiar needs of the people there. Second, Presbyterians in the region were losing their candidates for ministry to seminaries of other denominations or to seminaries out of the region — from which they might not return upon graduation. Third, the synod noted the growing prosperity of the Southwest and argued that Presbyterians should be able to fund a seminary without injury to other benevolence needs. Finally, they believed a school was needed to prepare Presbyterian ministers of the region to "stand as a bulwark against the tide of heterodoxy and rationalism that is sweeping in upon the Church."[4]

With the synods of Kentucky and Missouri in agreement, the 1893 General Assembly approved and welcomed "most cordially this new and vigorous foundation of theological learning. . . ."[5] That foundation had been the work of many people, especially those who would become essential to the life of Louisville Seminary. L. H. Blanton of Central University has already been mentioned as a key force behind the drive for a theological seminary in Kentucky. W. T. Grant, a lay member of Second Presbyterian Church in Louisville, opened his home repeatedly for meetings to plan for the founding of the Seminary once Louisville was determined as the site. He subsequently became treasurer and a major benefactor of LPTS. Colonel Bennett H. Young, prominent Louisville attorney and church figure, saw to the legal matters of incorporation and securing the charter. Thomas W. Bullitt was another layman who took keen interest in the establishment of the school. Charles R. Hemphill, pastor of the large and wealthy Second Presbyterian Church, proved indefatigable on behalf of the Seminary. All of these men served on the charter Board of Directors, which had twelve representatives each from the synods of Kentucky and Missouri.[6] Such were some of the leading lights who inspired others to en-

3. A more complete treatment of this effort can be found in Synod of Kentucky [PCUS], Minutes 1890-1899. (N.p.), 350-52; 406-9; and 449-51; Hemphill, "Origin," 5; and McElroy, *Louisville Seminary*, 59-67.

4. Synod of Kentucky, Minutes, 407-8.

5. Quoted in Hemphill, "Origin," 6.

6. For some of those responsible for the founding of LPTS, see Synod of Kentucky, Minutes, 477-88; Robert Stuart Sanders, *History of Louisville Presbyterian Theological Semi-*

sure that Louisville would accomplish the successful establishment of a seminary for the "education and training of young men as ministers of the Gospel" according to the standards of the PCUS.[7]

Gifts supporting the new seminary arrived from every quarter of the Synod of Kentucky (unfortunately, little money was forthcoming from Missouri), and the city of Louisville was saved to the last for a canvass of the churches. The planners expected generosity from the Presbyterians of the city sufficient to proceed with the purchase of land and buildings to house the seminary. Unfortunately, the Panic of 1893 gripped the nation and extra benevolent giving became a difficult idea to sell. McElroy, still fundraiser for the project, called the first meeting in the city with key leaders of the church in order to present his case. Young, who had already given substantial moral and legal support for the school, had been bankrupted by the depression and refused to attend out of embarrassment. McElroy knew that Presbyterians throughout the state looked to Young for leadership and compelled him to attend, arguing that his presence alone was important. After a presentation of the needs of the Seminary and its place in the life of the church, Young declared he had some land valued at $2,500 (his only remaining asset) which he would give to the school. His sacrificial example inspired others to give generously. H. B. Haldeman, owner of the *Courier-Journal,* gave the largest initial gift of $10,000. With the work of such laypeople and the solicitations of the city's clergy, the money to open LPTS was soon in hand.[8]

Louisville Presbyterian Theological Seminary opened its first session on October 2, 1893. The founders had exceeded their goal of $100,000 almost by half ($147,000, approximately equal to $2.45 million in 1999 dollars), and within a year had another $100,000 in hand by a gift of A. J. Alexander. Student enrollments which exceeded expectations required annual giving above the original estimates, but people such as the Grants, Youngs, and Haldemans responded to help meet student financial need. As at Danville, students attended Louisville Seminary without cost and

---

nary, 1853-1953 (Louisville: Louisville Presbyterian Theological Seminary, 1953), 26 and 34; T. M. Hawes, "Memories and Hopes," *The Register* 7 (April, May, June 1918): 13. For Grant specifically, see Minutes of the Board of Directors, Presbyterian Theological Seminary of Kentucky (1901-1920), October 1, 1901. Louisville Presbyterian Theological Seminary Archives (hereinafter LPTS Archives).

7. Charter of the Louisville Presbyterian Theological Seminary, May 3, 1893, in the Records of the Board of Directors, Louisville Presbyterian Theological Seminary (1893-1901). LPTS Archives.

8. McElroy, *Louisville Seminary,* 76-81, tells this story firsthand.

roomed for free — with an incredible $12 per month for board! Even at that, many students required financial aid, which was informally considered a loan to be repaid once a graduate was installed in a church. By 1899 the Seminary could offer ten scholarships of $100 for students who had their college degrees and would perform mission work in the city — in a sense, the first field education.[9]

Louisville Seminary owned very little in the first two years of its existence — exactly one house on Second Street to house students, near the Second Church manse. The Seminary rented another house for students, and others followed. The houses were aging and the accommodations spartan, making courage an asset for the resident. Lindsey McNair, class of 1895, recalled, "My beloved roommate and I found some trouble in getting all the rest we wanted because of the assembly of so many rats making merry and once or twice greeting us with a bite as we tried to sleep. But what did this matter?"[10]

Seminary classes met in the Sunday school rooms of Second Church, which also provided most of the necessary supplies and equipment for the Seminary. In 1899, in recognition of the generosity and support of Second Church in housing the Seminary and paying the salary of one professor for six years, the board named Hemphill's position the "Second Church Louisville Chair of New Testament Exegesis."[11] In 1895 LPTS received a gift of property at First and Broadway from W. H. Haldeman.[12] A large home, the Barrett Mansion, stood on the property, in which classes met that fall. Stables on the lot were converted to accommodate a few student rooms and a refectory. Later renovations to the third floor of the house provided more dormitory rooms. The site, with the mansion eventually replaced by a neo-Gothic campus, would be Louisville Seminary's home for almost seven decades. The very location of the Seminary in the heart of a large city (Louisville's population was approximately 200,000 at the time) raised questions

9. McElroy, *Louisville Seminary,* 69-72, is again the most thorough and convenient source for fundraising information. On student finances in the early years see, among others, the Annual Announcement of the Louisville Presbyterian Theological Seminary (1893-1894), 29-30; and the Annual Announcement of the Louisville Presbyterian Theological Seminary (1899-1900), 30.

10. Cited by Sanders, *History of Louisville Seminary,* 37.

11. Records of the Board (1893-1901), May 2, 1899, in LPTS Archives. See also John M. Vander Meulen, "A Review of the Past Ten Years of the Louisville Presbyterian Seminary, 1920-1930," 7-8, manuscript, LPTS Archives.

12. LPTS also received property in Chicago valued at $75,000, which was the bulk of the $100,000 gift from A. J. Alexander. Hemphill, "Origin," 8.

for some. Many wanted LPTS in a suburb of Louisville, against the judgment of those who held it should stand downtown. For a time this sentiment enjoyed a great deal of popularity. The original plan, however, was that the Seminary would move out of the city center as soon as possible.[13]

One problem in facilities that would affect LPTS down to the present appeared — surprisingly — in its very first year: housing for married students. In 1893 six married students moved to Louisville with their families. Three found apartments to rent, but three men and their wives took up residence in the rented dormitories. The faculty held that the presence of the women provided an undue distraction and improper temptation to students.[14] Consequently, they petitioned the board to urge married students to leave their families at home to be cared for by relatives or a church. Failing that, the students should find housing in the city — but definitely not live in dormitories.[15]

That first session saw thirty-one students enrolled at LPTS. Four students, who had previously completed two years of study elsewhere, graduated the next spring.[16] That was more students than any expected; in the 1894-1895 school year the number leapt to sixty, and by the fourth year the student population peaked at sixty-seven.[17] From that high, numbers declined to the turn of the century, with thirty-one again for 1899-1900.

A global vision for ministry marked Louisville from its very first student body. Among the students in attendance were Isaac Yonan, a Persian Christian who returned to his homeland upon graduation and accepted a position as a professor in Urmia College, and William Beattie, a Canadian whose father, Francis Beattie, served on the faculty. R. E. McAlpine, a missionary to Japan on furlough in the United States, enrolled as well.[18] Of the 1896 class, the first to attend LPTS for three years (sixteen in number), several became missionaries, according to William Crowe.[19] Apparently an ecumenical witness in the Seminary's work began with the matriculation

13. McElroy, *Louisville Seminary*, 144. Southern Baptist Theological Seminary stood just down the street from LPTS and moved out of downtown before the Presbyterians.

14. This latter point was only circumspectly made, with all due modesty.

15. Faculty Meeting Minutes (1893-1901), April 30, 1894, in LPTS Archives.

16. McElroy, *Louisville Seminary*, 74.

17. McElroy, *Louisville Seminary*. McElroy places the count of 60 students in the 1895-1896 school year (which was correct), but the report to the General Assembly gives that number the previous year also. *Minutes of the General Assembly of the Presbyterian Church in the United States* (Richmond, Va.: Presbyterian Committee of Publication, 1894), 242.

18. Sanders, *History of Louisville Seminary*, 36.

19. Sanders, *History of Louisville Seminary*, 37.

in 1895 of special student Frank E. Lewis, a minister of the Methodist Episcopal Church, South.[20] Another student of note was James H. Taylor, class of 1897, who was Woodrow Wilson's pastor during his presidency. Taylor conducted the late President's memorial service.[21]

Students in 1893 encountered a faculty of six to prepare them for ministry. All six of the men were leaders of the denomination and had wide experience in both the pulpit and classroom. Faculty appointments and responsibilities were: Thomas D. Witherspoon, professor of pastoral theology, homiletics, and biblical introduction; William Hoge Marquess, professor of Old Testament exegesis and English Bible; Hemphill, professor of New Testament exegesis; Francis R. Beattie, professor of systematic theology, the Standards, and apologetics; Edwin Muller, professor of church history and polity; and Thompson M. Hawes, professor of elocution. The only change to the faculty until 1901 occurred with the death of Witherspoon in November of 1898. John Sprole Lyons replaced him for the remainder of the school year, after which the other professors took on Witherspoon's courses.[22]

Witherspoon, a descendant of John Knox, graduated from Columbia Theological Seminary, served in the Civil War, held a series of pastorates (including First Presbyterian in Louisville), and won election as moderator of the General Assembly in 1884. He served as the faculty of the short-lived theological department at Central University before his call to Louisville Seminary, and while in Louisville he filled the position of the synod's superintendent of evangelistic work. Marquess claimed a distinguished ancestor as well. His great-grandfather was Moses Hoge, a leader of Virginia Presbyterianism and key figure in the early life of Hampden-Sidney College and Union Seminary in Virginia. His ministry prior to LPTS was in Missouri; the last eight years there he was both pastor in Fulton and president of Westminster College. At Louisville Seminary he also filled the pulpit of the Crescent Hill church for a number of years. Marquess had the unusual ability to read at least seven languages.

Charles Hemphill was a rare professor for the time because he went to parish ministry only after filling a series of academic positions. After graduating from Columbia Theological Seminary in 1874, he was Hebrew instructor at the school, then held a Greek fellowship at Johns Hopkins

20. The Annual Announcement of Louisville Presbyterian Theological Seminary (1895-1896), 9.

21. Sanders, *History of Louisville Seminary,* 38.

22. See Appendix B for a list of LPTS faculty members from 1893 to 1901. The following faculty descriptions are all from McElroy.

University, whence he joined the faculty at Southwestern Presbyterian University and subsequently Columbia Seminary. In 1885 he was called to the pulpit of Second Church in Louisville, simultaneously holding his faculty position at Louisville Seminary from 1893-1899 (the church continued Hemphill at full salary; he was not paid by the Seminary). Hemphill contributed more than any other single person in creating LPTS in both his devotion to the school and the responsibilities he was given — chair of the faculty until 1910 and first president, 1910-1920. Like the other professors, Hemphill's service to the church was broad and effective. Elected moderator of the General Assembly in 1895, in 1896 he also represented the PCUS on the General Council of the Reformed Churches throughout the World holding the Presbyterian System, forerunner of the present World Alliance of Reformed Churches.

Francis Beattie, a Canadian by birth, graduated from Knox Theological College and was the only member of the faculty with a Ph.D. That was a rare credential in those days of the pastor-theologian as seminary professor. After two pastorates in Canada, Beattie taught apologetics at Columbia Seminary from 1888 (at which point he joined the PCUS) until his call to LPTS in 1893. He added the position of associate editor for the *Christian Observer* when it moved to Louisville in 1896, and he held the post until 1906. Edwin Muller, pastor at Westminster Presbyterian in Louisville beginning in 1888, continued to serve the church while he taught at the Seminary from 1893-1901. Like Hemphill, he received no pay from the Seminary for the first few years of teaching.

Thompson Hawes, born in Indiana, held no seminary degree but received his ministerial education under Witherspoon, E. O. Guerrant (renowned missionary in the Appalachian Highlands), Dwight L. Moody, and John Broadus (respected president of Southern Baptist Theological Seminary). In 1884 he began to teach elocution and public speaking at Southern Baptist Seminary. In 1893 he was ordained to the ministry by the Presbytery of Louisville, installed as pastor of Highland Presbyterian Church in the city, and called to teach elocution at Louisville Seminary while continuing at the Baptist Seminary. Hawes filled all three positions with skill until his death in 1919; he taught without pay from Louisville Seminary for the last eight years.[23] Hawes was known as a singularly humorous man, making him a fitting predecessor to another Highland pastor, Henry P. Mobley. Robert Stuart Sanders wrote, "Some of us still remember a day in

23. Louisville Presbyterian Theological Seminary Board of Directors. Minutes (1920-1939), May 4, 1920. LPTS Archives.

his church when four members of a family, sitting near the front, fainted one after the other. Dr. Hawes remarked later that 'that's the way I mow 'em down.'"[24] Nor was the faculty only committed to teaching; they accepted other responsibilities as well. Muller served as secretary of the faculty; Witherspoon was the first librarian; Beattie was intendant — overseeing the housing of students, maintenance, and related duties.

Although there were no changes to the original faculty except for Witherspoon's death, the Seminary added others periodically to supplement the curriculum. For 1894-1895 Robert L. Dabney — former professor at UTS-Va., founder of Austin Seminary, strict Calvinist, unreconstructed former Adjutant-General to Thomas "Stonewall" Jackson until his death, and (by the time of his arrival in Louisville) blind — held the position of lecturer in Christian ethics. The same year the Seminary secured the services of Clement Stapleford of the University of Louisville School of Music to offer a class in reading music, singing, and hymnody to LPTS students, a practice which continued with periodic interruptions under different lecturers for many years.[25] It was upon Witherspoon's death in 1899 that the board divided his work between Hemphill and Marquess and called them to full-time service on the faculty, with pay.[26] In February, 1901, as the Seminary made its transition to merger with Danville Seminary, Muller resigned his post to accept a call to First Presbyterian Church in Lexington, Kentucky.

As at Danville, the faculty members were models of the kind of pastor the Seminary hoped to produce: hardworking, conservative pastor-theologians. They took an intense and pastoral interest in their students, pushing them to be studious and striving to enhance their piety. While there was a clear distance between teacher and student, at the same time the faculty became friends to the students, who respected them and regarded them with deep affection. Lindsay McNair remembered the first group: "To sit at the feet of such men was a rare privilege. They were great scholars; they were magnificent teachers; they knew how to preach."[27] In short, they exemplified the kind of pastor the students hoped to become. The faculty's memorial on the occasion of Marquess's death could well have been offered for any of the group: "He was a man of the Book, all his

24. Sanders, *History of Louisville Seminary,* 55.

25. See, for instance, Annual Announcement (1894-1895), 4, and Annual Announcement (1898-1899), n.p., both in LPTS Archives.

26. See Records of the Board (1893-1901), May 2, 1899.

27. Cited in Sanders, *History of Louisville Seminary,* 37. This feeling toward LPTS faculty has remained constant over its history.

life long an eager, reverent and unwearied student of God's Word; mighty in the scriptures, saturated with their spirit, able expositor and unsurpassed teacher of the heavenly Truth they contain. He was a man of prayer."[28]

Life at Louisville Seminary

Louisville Seminary constantly emphasized its goal of "training men for the practical work of the ministry."[29] To accomplish that purpose the faculty organized the curriculum into "schools of instruction" (e.g., Old Testament Exegesis, New Testament Exegesis, Church History, and Preaching), which comprised four groups or departments: Bible, Theology, Church History, and Practical Theology. When the middle two are combined, one sees that the general organization of the curriculum that exists today was already in place at the school's opening. As at Danville Seminary, instruction in the Bible was considered paramount and made the greatest claim on the student's time. The Seminary assumed that a student came to school with a classical liberal arts education and a thorough knowledge of Greek, but soon had to provide a class for those with "defective" preparation in the language.[30] Students were expected to work hard. Although the school year remained, as at Danville, shorter than later practice (October to May), the only holiday was Christmas Day. Usually, however, that break was generously extended by one or two days, and the faculty regularly "suspended exercises" on Thanksgiving so students could attend worship in area churches. Classes met Monday to Saturday, with a lighter schedule on the first and last days of the study week.[31]

The course selections were few in number, designed "to give unity and system" to the three years, and left little freedom for a student's choice (e.g., three year-long courses in both Old Testament and New Testament exegesis and systematic theology). Yet some leeway was given to students in planning their course of study. Faculty did suggest a three-year plan for the degree-seeking student as early as 1899, but it was not mandatory.[32]

28. Cited by McElroy, *Louisville Seminary,* 99.

29. Annual Announcement (1893-1894), 11.

30. Annual Announcement (1896-1897), 29. Seminaries expected a classical education of even those students who had not completed or attended college.

31. See Faculty Meeting Minutes (1893-1901), throughout.

32. Annual Announcement (1899-1900), 10-11, and subsequent catalogues. Undoubtedly the Seminary began this practice earlier; this year marked its first publication.

The Seminary also sought to address changes in types and methods of ministries emerging at the end of the century. The impact of urbanization and industrialization, discussed more fully below, created new institutions and practices in American Protestantism. Urban evangelism, epitomized by Dwight L. Moody; urban missions to reach the unchurched, especially immigrants and African-Americans; growing reliance on Sunday school to socialize young people into church membership; and Christian social and evangelistic organizations such as the Young Men's and Young Women's Christian Associations all made an impact on the Protestant churches. Louisville Seminary reflected that. When Hemphill added pastoral theology to his teaching responsibilities in 1899, he expanded the description to emphasize his special attention to "Sunday schools; young people's societies; methods of work; missions in city and country; the evangelist; the missionary pastor; the conduct of public worship." The course also included a section on selection and use of hymns. One can only speculate regarding the impact on theological education of "gospel hymns" promoted by Moody's songleader Ira Sankey, Billy Sunday's songleader Homer Rodeheaver, and Fannie Crosby as they spread in popularity among the churches.[33]

The new ministries and groups required not only pastors trained in different methods of ministry but also trained laypeople. The YMCA and YWCA depended on lay leadership, as did the Student Volunteer Movement, a mission recruiting body. Consequently, from the beginning Louisville made its courses available to pastors who desired to further their education and training and to "Ruling Elders and other Christian men who wish to fit themselves for practical work in the Sunday-school, in the Young Men's Christian Association, or other lines of Christian activity."[34] To further that end, in 1896 the school added a few advanced courses for pastors doing "post-graduate" study (i.e., continuing education) and upper-level students. In the first year those courses included "Messianic Prophecies," "The Old Testament in the Light of Modern Research," and "The Philosophy of Religion."[35] The faculty, in its first report to the board in 1894, proposed that they offer special courses in the summer to students, ministers, church officers, and other Christian workers. The board applauded the idea but declined to approve the request for financial rea-

33. Annual Announcement (1900-1901), 19-22.
34. Annual Announcement (1893-1894), 11. This policy was frequently reiterated in the Seminary's publications.
35. Annual Announcement (1896-1897), 30.

sons. Still, it further illustrated the Seminary's desire to serve the whole church in creative and innovative ways.[36]

Since not all students were seeking or eligible for a degree, LPTS had a variety of means for recognizing achievements of scholarship. A certificate was granted if a student successfully completed study in a department in one of the "schools"; a diploma signified graduation from one of the schools; and a B.D. indicated graduation from all the schools in the Seminary curriculum.[37]

The LPTS charter, under the aegis of the synods of Kentucky and Missouri, stipulated that all professors in the school be members of the PCUS and subscribe to an oath, and not teach contrary to, the standards of the church as they embodied the system of doctrine found in Scripture.[38] Accordingly, the Seminary education manifested a distinctly conservative Old School theology which defended a strict Calvinism. The theology of the Old School vigorously taught that Calvinism was merely the discernment and systematic ordering of doctrines revealed by God in Scripture. The study of the Bible, which dominated the curriculum, primarily had as its goal the discovery of the theology God meant to reveal to humankind and the discernment of the progressive revelation that led to the incarnation of Jesus the Christ and brought people to belief in him. Conversely, other areas of study, such as systematic, apologetic, or philosophical theology, or church history, or practical theology, explicated the Scripture's doctrinal bases for the subject.[39] This explains how faculty could move from one area of teaching to another with a minimum of effort; each was primarily doctrinal, so the shift to a new discipline simply required one to adjust the starting point of the approach.[40]

However, no seminary in the 1890s could ignore, or remain unaffected by, the intellectual revolution wrought in the previous two centu-

---

36. Sanders, *History of Louisville Seminary,* 42.

37. Annual Announcement (1893-1894), 25.

38. Charter, in the Records of the Board of Directors (1893-1901).

39. Many courses looked very different than they would today, of course, in part because of this doctrinal emphasis. In Church History, for example, the "History and Development of Doctrine" was stressed — to the exclusion of external political, economic, sociological, and cultural developments which affected the church and its theology. The Annual Announcement of the Louisville Presbyterian Theological Seminary (1898-1899), 20.

40. I do not mean to suggest that all areas of study simply covered the same material or did the same thing. The principles of study and approach governing different subjects of the curriculum demanded variety of the teachers and students. The point here is to emphasize again, as in the previous chapter, the doctrinal nature of the Old School understanding of faith and its practice within clearly defined first principles.

ries. The Enlightenment had promoted the concept that all truth was rational and could be grasped by the use of human reason alone. The growth of
scientific methodology as the measure of truth — that is, only that was
true which could be verified by testing and quantification — led to changes
in the understanding of human behavior and history. The fields of sociology, anthropology, literary criticism, history, and psychology began to rev-
olutionize the way people thought about life and human existence. The
most unsettling development proved to be the application of literary criticism to the study of the Bible. In its most thoroughgoing forms, usually
among the German scholars, this higher criticism of the Bible threw open
the question of the inspiration of Scripture's writers. If the Bible were not
revealed truth from God, of course, then the system of doctrine derived
therefrom might collapse. In particular, assertions that Moses did not
write the Pentateuch but that it came from the redaction of a series of doc-
uments coincided with Charles Darwin's proposition of biological evolution to make the divine inspiration of the Bible a flashpoint for conservative defense of traditional theology.

Course descriptions indicate the nature of the theology that students
who attended LPTS carried away with them. In "Biblical Introduction," in
which the questions of authorship, historical setting, and literary sources
of the books of the Bible were discussed, Thomas Witherspoon faced
higher criticism directly: "The proper sphere and limitations of the Higher
Criticism are defined; its legitimate work is recognized; the unsound principles, fallacious methods, and rationalistic spirit of what are known as its
more advanced schools, are pointed out, the invalidity of their conclusions
shown, and the true theory of literary criticism suggested." He asserted
that geographical matters — topography, history, and customs of the people — would not be presented so much for the purpose of informing questions of exegesis, "but more particularly in view of their formative influence in determining the character of the human element in revelation."[41]
Apparently, however, Witherspoon's conservatism did not tend to what
would later be called Fundamentalism. There was an open investigation of
the claims of higher criticism and some of its conclusions embraced. In
short, while defending the revelation of God in Scripture and carefully defining the human role in the Bible's composition, there was an air of mod-
eration in propounding the "faith once for all delivered to the saints."[42]

41. Annual Announcement (1893-1894), 12.
42. That phrase from Jude 3 was a common way of intimating that Old School
Presbyterianism was ancient — really, biblical — in its content.

Marquess presumably took that approach as well, for he retained the course description when teaching it fell to him.

The extant records reveal the most about Beattie's theology. Course descriptions for Systematic Theology note that the Westminster Standards guided the material and that textbooks were those of James Henley Thornwell, Dabney, and Charles Hodge of Princeton Theological Seminary — three of the most traditional of the Old School theologians.[43]

More interesting is the outline of Beattie's lectures for Apologetics, printed and bound for distribution to the students.[44] Beattie defined apologetics as "a reasoned defense and vindication of the essential truth, supernatural origin, divine authority, and inherent sufficiency of the Christian system of doctrine, worship, ethics, and redemption, together with systematic refutation of all opposing theories."[45] The use of the word "reason" was an intentional repudiation of both the Enlightenment assertion that religious belief constituted mere "superstition" and the accommodation of liberal Protestantism to Darwinism. Beattie thought that liberal Protestantism capitulated to science by declaring that science and Christianity address different realms of human knowledge. Faith, they held, was a matter of an inner experience of the risen Christ.

Following the lead of Charles Hodge, Beattie considered theology itself a science that utilized the only true scientific method. He declared that both nature and intellectual truth were rational and could only be brought into harmony by postulating the existence of a Mind which organized "both the laws of thought and the laws of nature. They find unity in God."[46] Beattie's theology combined a kind of idealism with Scottish Common Sense Philosophy, which rejected the form of empiricism which said one can only know the properties of an object but not the object in itself. Human beings have, he argued and demonstrated, certain innate ideas or capacities which can only be explained by the existence of a loving, purposeful Creator. Reflection on the world and reasoning based on one's inner consciousness lead to the idea of God. A person can trust what she observes of life because there is not a sharp distinction between an object's attributes and its essence — when one knows about an object one also knows the object in its essence. Consequently, the role of the theologian is

43. The Annual Announcement of the Louisville Presbyterian Theological Seminary (1898-1899), 18-19. LPTS Archives.

44. Francis R. Beattie, "Apologetics: Outline of Lectures," 1899. (N.p., n.d.). LPTS Archives.

45. Beattie, "Apologetics."

46. Beattie, "Apologetics: Course I. Fundamental. Lecture XVI."

like that of the scientist: observe the facts and laws governing life, put them in logical relation, and draw the conclusions to which one is led. One inductively moved from the particular to the general hypothesis or law.

The most important source of facts for that scientific theological enterprise was the Bible, which made its veracity and authority of utmost importance. Higher criticism had to be refuted because, first, it was unscientific (it ruled out the Bible as specially inspired literature without examining the Bible's own evidence) and second, it questioned the Bible's authority. After a survey of the development of higher criticism, Beattie leveled two charges against it. First, higher criticism assumed that only natural rational principles could govern the composition and critical study of Scripture. Beattie countered that an honest assessment of the Bible yielded the conclusion that it could best be explained by revelation. Second, higher criticism assumed that religion and morality unfolded throughout history by evolutionary advancement. Beattie argued that the history of religion manifests not progress but decline, due to the rejection of true faith in history. Such a declension would explain the ongoing presence of the world's myriad primal religions. In short, Beattie defended the historicity and infallibility of Scripture and, consequently, the full divinity of the historical Jesus against those who, in the quest to find the Jesus behind the gospel accounts, would make him less.[47]

When considering the relationship between natural science and Christianity, Beattie assumed there could be no contradiction because all truth came from God. Speaking specifically of evolution, Beattie held that all theories of the origin of life which were "abiogenetic" (i.e., that organic or living matter arose out of inorganic matter) are patently wrong and unscientific, for no experiment or observation had ever shown it. Life could only come from life ("biogenesis") — actually, pre-existent life (that is, God). The only real question was whether some kind of first genus or germ was created from which all life developed — organic evolution — or whether there was a creation of species so that all members of them descended by natural generation — special creation. Organic evolution (in effect, Darwinism) remained unproven and had serious evidential difficulties to overcome, Beattie asserted, but added that he "would not close the case, but leave it open for future discovery and more light."[48]

---

47. Beattie, Apologetics: Course II, and *Radical Criticism: An Exposition of the Radical Critical Theory Concerning the Literature and Religious System, of the Old Testament Scriptures* (New York: Fleming H. Revell Co., 1894). This book was a compilation of a series of articles Beattie published in *Christian Observer*.

48. Beattie, Apologetics: Course III.

Still, Beattie was confident that the origins of humanity could not be explained by evolution; it did not address the facts and flew in the face of the plain testimony of Scripture that all humans originated in "race unity" in Adam and Eve. The variety of races in the modern era could not be explained by progressive evolution but by race degeneration as people wandered further from God.[49] Although one should be cautious about inferring too much from the theology of one professor, it is safe to say that this survey of Beattie's approach to apologetics indicates the generally conservative education the LPTS faculty offered students and expected them to communicate to the laity of the PCUS.

The course descriptions for the School of Homiletics and Pastoral Theology serve as reminders that Louisville Seminary meant to educate students for ministry. Students in Elocution publicly presented homilies and lectures in chapel the first Thursday of each month in addition to the writing and preaching of sermons in classes. The description of the course in pastoral theology, which met three hours each week for a full year, reveals the understanding of the pastoral office out of which it grew. Later questions of counseling, psychology, and administration, which influence the curriculum today, were absent. Instead, the issue turned on the pastoral identity, devotion, and conduct of the minister. One hour each week found the student involved in the study of the Pastoral Epistles (in Greek) to learn their instruction in "the pastoral office and care."[50] The prospective minister would study "the pastor in his personal character and spiritual life; in his settlement over a charge and entrance upon his work; in his study; in his closet [i.e., devotional prayer]; in his pulpit; in the prayer-meeting; in the Sabbath-school; in the homes of his people; in revival meetings; in inquiry meetings; in the chamber of sickness; in the courts of the Church, etc."[51] Attention was even given to those characteristics and skills necessary for domestic or global mission work.

The extra- and co-curricular life of students reinforced the goals of the academic program. The LPTS faculty closely regulated student behavior, and students submitted to that supervision by subscribing to the following oath: "Deeply impressed with the sense of importance of improving in knowledge, prudence and piety preparatory to the gospel ministry, I solemnly promise, in reliance on Divine grace, that I will faithfully and diligently attend all instructions of this Seminary, and that I will conscien-

---

49. Beattie, Apologetics: Course III. The racism of that assertion is not at all subtle.
50. Annual Announcement (1898-1899), 22.
51. Annual Announcement (1898-1899), 21-22.

tiously and vigilantly observe all the rules and regulations specified in the Constitution, and also obey all lawful requisitions and readily yield to all wholesome admonitions of the professors. . . ."[52] The Seminary assumed that personal faith and a life of prayer were important for a pastor. As a result, professors led devotional services every morning in chapel, at which the entire student body was expected. Further, the students conducted their own "family prayer" in the dormitories both morning and evening, and held weekly prayer services as well.[53] All was not work and prayer, however. Louisville Seminary received a gift of gymnastic equipment to alleviate the sedentary student life and the YMCA stood nearby.

Although field education did not exist in the formal, credit-bearing and remunerated form it later assumed, students did gain practical experience in ministry during the school session. Every student was appointed to a church in the city to carry out some part of the church's program — church school, young people's societies, evangelistic work in mission stations, and so on. This work was always conducted under the "consent and direction of the Faculty, and is to be made an integral part of the training given by the seminary."[54] The faculty noted the students' work in organizing Sunday schools and leading prayer meetings, perceiving a real benefit to them in their practical skills for ministry and to Presbyterianism in the city as expanded ministries became possible.[55]

The opportunity for students at Louisville Seminary to engage in ministry in the city proved an important development in the PCUS. The importance of the city in the growing nation could not be ignored, and Protestantism began to emphasize ministry in the city. The era between the Civil War and the end of the nineteenth century transformed the U.S. The industrial revolution led to rapid urbanization. As jobs increasingly located in cities, urban areas swelled with people moving in from the surrounding towns. At the same time, middle- and upper-class residents of the cities (mainly white Protestants) began to move out of the city center to the suburbs as transportation became easier. Areas of poverty developed where the unemployed or working poor lived.[56] Immigrants, mainly

---

52. Constitution of the Louisville Presbyterian Theological Seminary, in the Records of the Board of Directors, Louisville Presbyterian Theological Seminary (1893-1901). LPTS Archives.

53. Annual Announcement (1893-1894), 28.

54. Faculty Meeting Minutes (1893-1901), October 31, 1893. LPTS Archives.

55. Faculty Meeting Minutes (1893-1901), April 30, 1894.

56. One should remember that workdays were twelve or fourteen hours long, six days a week, even for women and children.

from eastern and southern Europe, arrived in remarkable numbers. They accelerated the growth of cities, especially those in the eastern U.S., and exacerbated the social needs of the cities. In southern cities the immigrants were more likely African-Americans moving from rural areas in search of work.

Protestantism, in spite of the presence of large, "tall-steeple" urban churches, thought in terms of a morality and a church life that grew out of a small-town ethos with a heavily individualistic ideology. The growth of industry and large corporations, the problems and demands of labor, the enormity of urban social ills, and the tendency to individual anonymity in modern society all presented an unprecedented challenge to Protestantism in the U.S. Protestants began efforts to evangelize and assimilate immigrants, who were usually poor and had different cultural and religious patterns than northern European Protestants. They also initiated mission work among the "Freedmen." In addition to new organizations for the cities (such as the "Y"), "institutional churches" emerged to provide not only worship but social services to the inner city. Some Protestants even initiated a movement eventually known as the Social Gospel. Mainline Protestants had only limited success with their efforts among the unchurched of the city centers, but they expended great energy in ministry. Mission efforts by existing congregations planted many new churches in the developing suburbs of the cities.[57]

Louisville Seminary was founded at the height of this changing situation. The planners wanted to place the Seminary in a large city in order to have the resources a city could afford and to provide sufficient opportunities for students to gain practical training for ministry. The desire for the students, predominantly small-town in their upbringing and experiences, to see the needs of cities and learn the styles of ministry appropriate for serving there motivated the decision for a city as well. LPTS threw stu-

57. The literature treating American Protestantism's response to urbanization and industrialization is extensive. See chapters 3, 4, and 5 of Robert T. Handy, *A Christian America: Protestant Hopes and Historical Realities,* 2nd ed (New York and Oxford: Oxford University Press, 1984); Henry F. May, *Protestant Churches and Industrial America* (New York: Harper and Brothers, 1949); Aaron Ignatius Abell, *The Urban Impact on American Protestantism, 1865-1900* (Hamden and London: Archon, 1962); Paul A. Carter, *The Spiritual Crisis of the Gilded Age* (Dekalb, Ill.: Northern Illinois University Press, 1971); Donald K. Gorrell, *The Age of Social Responsibility: The Social Gospel in the Progressive Era, 1900-1920* (Macon, Ga.: Mercer University Press, 1988); C. Howard Hopkins, *The Rise of the Social Gospel in American Protestantism, 1865-1915* (New Haven: Yale University Press, 1940); and Ronald C. White and C. Howard Hopkins, *The Social Gospel: Religion and Reform in Changing America* (Philadelphia: Temple University Press, 1976).

dents directly into an unimpeded experience of life in the city as they worked among both civic and church leaders and those for whom life was a constant struggle at best. Within a stone's throw of the school one could encounter alcoholics, transients, and prostitutes. The professors observed in 1895 that for the students "very many and very great advantages attended the prosecution of their studies in the midst of life and activities of city life and that no harmful results were noticeable."[58] LPTS was the only PCUS seminary located in a large city, and McElroy writes that W. W. Moore, president of Union Seminary at the time, used Louisville's success as an argument for moving his school from Hampden-Sydney to Richmond, Virginia.[59]

Another powerful movement had an impact on the co-curricular education at Louisville Seminary from its start. In the 1880s the Student Volunteer Movement for Foreign Missions (SVM) organized to place the claim of global ministry before college and seminary students, recruiting missionaries and raising money for denominational boards. Millennial expectations fed the renewed desire to preach the gospel around the globe, and the urgency of the attempt was expressed in the motto: "Evangelize the World in this Generation."[60]

At the second meeting of the faculty Witherspoon and Beattie were appointed to a committee to discuss "the question: — how to promote the missionary spirit in the seminary." One day each month was set aside for hearing mission lectures, or student presentations on issues in mission or the needs of some domestic or global mission field.[61] The Seminary re-

---

58. Records of Board of Directors (1893-1901), April 30, 1895.

59. McElroy, *Louisville Seminary*, 81-85. At the time Columbia Seminary, later located in Decatur, Georgia, was still in Columbia, South Carolina.

60. For studies of the American mission effort, see Henry Warner Bowden, "An Overview of Cultural Factors in the American Protestant Missionary Enterprise," in R. Pierce Beaver, ed., *American Missions in Bicentennial Perspective* (South Pasadena, Calif.: William Carey Library, 1977); John K. Fairbank, ed., *The Missionary Enterprise in China and America* (Cambridge, Mass.: Harvard University Press, 1974); Charles W. Forman, "A History of Foreign Missions Theory in America," in Beaver, op. cit.; Kenneth Scott Latourette, *Christianity in a Revolutionary Age: A History of Christianity in the Nineteenth and Twentieth Centuries*, 5 vols. (Grand Rapids, Mich.: Zondervan Publishing House, 1969); Stephen Neill, *The History of Christian Missions* (London and New York: Penguin Books, 1986); and Clarence P. Shedd, *Two Centuries of Student Christian Movements: Their Origins and Intercollegiate Life* (New York: Association Press, 1934). The outstanding recent work is William R. Hutchison, *Errand to the World: American Protestant Thought and Foreign Missions* (Chicago and London: The University of Chicago Press, 1987).

61. Faculty Minutes (1893-1901), October 3 and 17, 1893.

peatedly noted in the catalogue that some courses included the relationship of the subject to mission and the practical experience in mission available in a large city. For a time the Hospital College of Medicine and Louisville Medical College both offered scholarships to seminary students intent on mission careers who also sought some medical training.[62] The students organized their own mission "band" on campus that met weekly, discussing matters of mission concern, usually with literature published by the SVM.[63] Lecturers often hit the theme as well; in 1894 the Seminary heard a lecture on the "Methods of Evangelistic Work" by the famed Appalachian missionary E. O. Guerrant.[64] Some of the work done by students in the city bore visibly lasting results. Student preaching and teaching in Sunday school missions of area churches resulted in the formation of new churches — Bardstown Road Church grew out of a Highland Church mission staffed by seminarians, for example.

Perhaps the most prominent and significant seminary enterprise was the John Little Mission, which led to two Presbyterian churches and the ongoing Presbyterian Community Center. It shared the concern and some of the techniques of the settlement house movement, which emerged in some cities just before the turn of the century.[65] In November 1897 the Home Mission Committee of the Students' Missionary Society voiced a concern to work among the "coloreds" in the city of Louisville. Soon afterward A. L. Phillips, Secretary of Colored Evangelization for the PCUS, encouraged the students in such an endeavor during a visit to Louisville. As a result, six students (G. V. Dickey, E. P. Pillans, E. H. Moseley, H. McDowell, Daniel Little, and John Little) rented a former lottery building on Preston Street, visited in the neighborhood, and on the afternoon of Sunday, February 4, 1898, taught twenty-three children in Sunday school. The students also led worship every Wednesday and Sunday evening. Soon, between forty and fifty children attended each week.[66]

As the seminary students taught the children, they got an education of a different sort themselves. When they would call on absent students or canvass the neighborhood, the young mission workers "were appalled as they saw the poverty of their wards, the dens of iniquity in the neighborhood, the saloons and gambling holes, and became conscious of the fact that there was little effort being made by the Christian forces of the city to

62. Annual Announcement (1898-1899), 13.
63. Annual Announcement (1898-1899), 30.
64. Faculty Minutes (1893-1901), November 13, 1894.
65. The best known of the settlement houses was probably Jane Addams' Hull House.
66. John Little, "Our Colored Work," Christian Observer 89 (December 25, 1901): 9.

minister to the needs of this particular section."[67] Under those conditions, little wonder the students despaired that it took seven years for their preaching to gain its first church member or that they had to abandon any printed curriculum and write their own simplified material at the start, "from the Bible itself, beginning with God as the Creator of their spirits. . . ."[68]

The students planned to end the work at the end of the school year, but Daniel Little decided to maintain it through the summer, enlisting a number of women from area churches to teach. Lucy Belknap of Second Presbyterian Church, whose family had a growing hardware business, was among the first volunteers. Other prominent women in Louisville such as Louise Speed, also of Second Church, later joined in the work of the mission. The students returned to take up the work at the start of the 1898-1899 year and the volunteers remained as part of the expanding program. One of the children who frequently attended pled importunately with the seminarians to open another mission in the Smoketown area, about one mile south of the first mission. He eventually overcame their hesitancy and Louisville Seminary missionary society took up a collection, secured some money from the faculty, and rented a building for five months in Smoketown in April 1899. That Sunday school opened with thirty-five students.

The work of the mission grew rapidly, meeting a great need for the African-American community in Louisville and providing invaluable experience for the students. The Seminary leadership was impressed with the work being done. John Little supervised the work through the summer of 1900, at which time the faculty decided that the work had so grown that the cause of the mission should be placed before presbytery for its supervision. The presbytery accepted the challenge and called Little, who had graduated, to oversee the work. Little valued the support of the faculty in the work, crediting Beattie with persuading him to stay with the mission

67. John Little, Material Prepared by Rev. John Little for a book of history of the Presbyterian Colored Missions. Ca. 1936, 2, Folder 2, Box 5, Presbyterian Community Center Papers, University Archives and Records Center, University of Louisville. John Little received another education, as well. "Our first landlord was a saloon keeper and each month it was my duty to go to his saloon and pay the rent. He wrote out a receipt and handed it to me and then according to his custom he asked me, 'What will you have to drink?' I explained I did not drink. He urged, 'I have some very fine wine, won't you try some.' Again I thanked him. He then brought out a box of cigars. When I explained that I did not smoke he seemed perplexed and finally said, 'Do you drink buttermilk?' This time I accepted and the next morning he presented me with a bottle he ordered brought in from his farm." Folder 10, n.p.

68. Little, Material Prepared, Folder 10, n.p., and Folder 2, 2.

and personally visiting churches with him to present the cause for their support. The faculty all contributed financially to the mission and preached there on occasion.[69]

The impact of this work was singular and lasting. Eventually the missions were able to purchase their own buildings, and in 1902 they provided the only public playground for African-American children in the city. Sewing classes began just after the turn of the century, and Belknap and Speed soon persuaded Beattie's wife to begin teaching a cooking class. The mission on Preston Street developed into Hope Presbyterian Church of the PCUS, and the Smoketown mission became Grace Presbyterian Church of the PCUSA. They later united to form Grace-Hope Presbyterian Church. William Sheppard, famed PCUS missionary to the Congo and the first African-American to serve abroad, received a call to Grace Church in 1912 and worked closely with the Little Mission. Countless Louisville Seminary students gained experience in evangelism and urban ministry at the missions and learned lessons in self-sacrifice from observing Little — whom they called "The Bishop."[70] When Little looked back on the work forty years later, he observed that both missions still existed and had their doors open seven days a week. Two institutional churches were joined to each one, offering "classes in sewing, cooking, shoe repairing, recreational clubs for both boys and girls, public bath house, nursery school, playground, and boy scout troops together with a religious program on Sunday which included preaching both morning and evening, two Sunday schools and Vesper service for the young people."[71]

Like settlement work as whole, the Little Mission reflected progressive attitudes for the period in which it began. There is no escaping the fact that this work had racist and paternalistic overtones that sought to make African-Americans more like white middle-class Protestants. Still, many people received and accepted the gospel of Christ who might otherwise have had only the slightest exposure to it, and they were offered a place of refuge from social conditions that were often dangerous and debilitating. Boys who learned woodworking at the mission frequently secured jobs in

69. Little, Material Prepared, 12, Folder 9. See also "Our Colored Work," 9.

70. Sanders, History of Louisville Seminary, 47.

71. Little, Material Prepared, 3, Folder 2; 8, Folder 3; Norman A. Horner, Kim Smith King, and Louis B. Weeks, "Evangelism and Mission at Louisville Seminary," 3-4, manuscript copy in author's possession; and Weeks, Kentucky Presbyterians, 137-39. The work of the mission had a demonstrable impact on the workers as well. Paul Tudor Jones said Little and the mission transformed his understanding of race relations. He later became important in the Memphis civil rights movement.

carpentry. The first supervisor of sewing classes in the Louisville public schools was a product of the Little Mission sewing classes who went on to graduate from Hampton Institute. Little wrote of one girl who went through the cooking classes and landed a job cooking for a family in the city: "Two members of this family have purchased their own homes. The lessons of thrift and personal economy had been instilled into the life of a child."[72] One can wish, in retrospect, that the mission had been more forward-looking in addressing questions of racism and urging the children to aspire to more than tasks appropriate to "their place." Yet, the seminary students were products of their time, and within that context they offered a liberating word of faith and life to those they served.

Toward Merger

At the end of the 1893-1894 year the Louisville faculty expressed its desire "[t]o recognize the goodness of God in the large measure of blessing which has rested on the seminary during the year. In the large numbers of students in attendance; in the good health vouchsafed both to the Faculty and students; in the diligence of the students in their work; and in the good results reached in study, there is much to make all connected with the institution thankful and hopeful."[73] However, the solid beginning of the school soon began to suffer. Already by January 1896 the endowment income proved to be less than expected (the effects of the Panic of 1893 lingered), and the churches failed to give annual amounts sufficient to meet the budget. The main drain on the school's finances was the scholarships promised to help students meet their expenses — student numbers remained so far above predictions that more money was a constant need. In 1896 and 1897 the board took loans on property the Seminary owned, and in the spring of 1897 the faculty recommended that aid no longer be offered to students.[74] Applications declined with that decision, as did the student population. For 1897-1898 there were forty-one students, down twenty-six from the previous year. By 1899-1900 thirty-one students enrolled, and the year after only twenty-eight.[75] In the face of

72. Little, Material Prepared, 2, Folder 5, and 8, Folder 3.
73. Faculty Minutes, April 30, 1894.
74. Some of the scholarships were restored the following year.
75. See Records of the Board of Directors (1893-1901), Executive Committee Minutes, January 2, February 21, April 29, 1896; March 22, 1897; and April 26, 1898; Annual Announcement (1898-1899), 10-11; Annual Announcement (1900-1901), 7; and Faculty Minutes

that reality LPTS began to explore the possibility of consolidation with that other struggling Kentucky seminary, Danville. The negotiations soon bore fruit.

"No Bar to Such Consolidation"

As the nineteenth century became the twentieth, both Danville Theological Seminary and Louisville Presbyterian Theological Seminary struggled to remain financially afloat. Danville clearly stood in greater danger than did Louisville. It appeared obvious that divided Presbyterianism in Kentucky could not maintain competing schools. Many supporters of each believed that something had to be done to stave off closing, and informal discussions began concerning a merger of the two institutions. (The merger also included the consolidation of the PCUS' Central University and the PCUSA's Centre College at Danville, under the name of the former; eventually the name reverted to Centre.) The talks resulted in a plan of consolidation, which both boards approved in the spring of 1901. The LPTS board approved the plan unanimously, although B. H. Young stated his judgment that the plan was "not satisfactory or wise."[76]

The plan called for joint ownership and control of the new seminary — located in Louisville and named the Presbyterian Theological Seminary of Kentucky — by the PCUS synods of Kentucky and Missouri and by the PCUSA General Assembly. The Board of Directors would have twenty-four members. The PCUS Synod of Kentucky would elect six members, the PCUS Synod of Missouri would elect six, and the PCUSA Synod of Kentucky would elect twelve — that is, twelve members from each denomination. Since the PCUSA synod did not have to elect people who were members of the synod, that meant that the school could receive wider ownership.[77] The plan of consolidation anticipated the objections of those who might object to the merger on theological grounds by noting that both seminaries existed for the same purpose of educating people for ministry according to the standards of each denomination. Furthermore,

---

(1893-1901), April 25, 1898. In this last the faculty noted that the drop in students could not be attributed completely to the difficulty of student aid. The numbers of candidates were down throughout the PCUS and the Missouri and Kentucky colleges graduated only one candidate for the ministry in June 1897.

76. Records of the Board of Directors (1893-1901), April 5, 1901.

77. Records of the Board (1893-1901), and John M. Vander Meulen, Seventh Annual President's Report, May 3, 1927, LPTS Archives.

"the Confession of Faith and Catechisms of said churches are the same, and their other standards are nearly the same."[78] The PCUSA synod approved the consolidation easily. There was some opposition in the PCUS Synod of Kentucky (but little or none in Missouri), apparently mostly from people in the Richmond area who did not want to lose the college in their city.[79]

The PCUSA General Assembly voted in favor of consolidation without incident. However, the proposal generated substantial opposition in the PCUS from those who feared cooperation with northern brothers and sisters who were considered more liberal theologically and socially. They reasoned that the Old School Calvinism of the PCUS could be compromised by the joint control of the training of ministers.[80] The *Christian Observer* responded that both the corporate and theological interests of the PCUS were protected by the plan. Currently, the General Assembly had the right to veto only professors at Louisville Seminary, not members of the board. Now it would have that control also — and not only board members elected by the PCUS synods, but by the PCUSA synod as well. Further, no grounds existed on which to fear doctrinal change in the PCUSA (there was a movement afoot to modify some clauses in the Westminster Confession of Faith), for the only doctrinal or confessional changes allowed in the governance of the Seminary would be those approved by both General Assemblies. The safeguards to protect the traditions of the PCUS were sufficient.[81]

When the PCUS General Assembly met in 1901, the Committee on Theological Seminaries, by a vote of six to five, recommended in its majority report that the denomination not approve the consolidation of Danville and Louisville Seminaries. The minority report recommended approval. The majority reported that they sympathized with the difficulty of Louisville and Danville Seminaries working in a divided Presbyterianism for funds and students, but thought recruitment would only be more difficult if the Seminary were put under control external to the synod. Further, the agreement "expressly excludes the teaching of the distinctive principles of our Church." Finally, the committee argued that cooperation would inevi-

78. Minutes of the Synod of Kentucky, Called Meeting, April 23, 1901, 7, and Records of the Board of Directors (1893-1901), April 5, 1901.

79. Minutes of the Synod of Kentucky, Called Meeting.

80. See especially comments of the *Central Presbyterian* cited by Ernest Trice Thompson, *Presbyterians in the South* (Richmond, Va.: John Knox Press, 1973), 3:199-200.

81. "Educational Movements in Kentucky and Missouri," *Christian Observer* 89 (May 1, 1901): 3.

tably work toward union of the denominations. The debate over the issue lasted for almost two days.[82]

S. L. Morris, chair of the committee, expanded on the majority report on the floor of the General Assembly. He asserted that the two denominations differed doctrinally, especially where the PCUS held to "distinctive" doctrines. (This was the PCUS code word for the spirituality of the church, by which the southern denomination believed it followed a more biblical and constitutional principle of separation of church and state by staying out of politics and social issues. That meant that the PCUS, by its passive attitude, offered no critique of, and *de facto* endorsed, prevailing racial and cultural practices of the society in which it existed.) In a consolidated school, Morris argued, the ideas of the North would influence ministers of the PCUS, diluting the conservative outlook of the PCUS. Graduates of such a seminary would surely go forth to preach union of the denominations.[83]

Col. Thomas W. Bullitt, Judge Shackelford Miller (both prominent Louisville Presbyterians, strong supporters of the Seminary, and members of the LPTS board), and Beattie all spoke on behalf of merger. Bullitt argued that the agreement provided sufficient safeguards against any doctrinal deviation in the PCUS. He asserted further that since the standards of the denominations were the same, the PCUS had no distinctive doctrines. In response, Thomas Cary Johnson, professor at UTS-Va., said the spirituality of the church was a distinctive doctrine — not in the standards themselves but in their interpretation. The latitude with which the PCUSA treated Calvinism showed that it was "infested with rationalism of the most extreme type."[84] Johnson also feared that if one denomination vetoed the election of a board member or professor from the other, the friction could lead to lawsuits which could mean the loss of the seminary or some of its assets to the PCUSA. (Some legal disputes after the Civil War had resulted in the courts granting ownership of churches or institutions to the PCUSA.) The consolidation carried too much risk, Johnson opined: "It is immensely more important to know that our students shall be taught aright than to proceed to a questionable gain brought about by consolidation."[85]

82. "Consolidation of the Kentucky Seminaries," *Christian Observer* 89 (May 29, 1901): 26.

83. "Consolidation"; Thompson, *Presbyterians in the South,* 200.

84. "Consolidation," 27.

85. "Consolidation." The *Christian Observer* showed its prejudice by granting that those on the side of the majority report "earnestly advocated" their stance, while Bullitt and the others defended merger with "consummate ability."

The issue came to a close when a substitute motion which included approval of the merger passed by a vote of 120 for, 56 against, and 12 absent and not voting. In what was hardly a ringing endorsement, the General Assembly declared,

> That while the Assembly may not wholly approve the wisdom of the consolidation of the two seminaries, yet, in view of the fact that there was practical unanimity in the Synods of Kentucky and Missouri as to the measure, and because of the safeguards thrown about the compact, this court hereby imposes no bar to such consolidation, but gives its assent thereto, leaving the entire responsibility thereof to the Synods of Kentucky and Missouri.[86]

Two protests were filed against the vote to merge the schools (the first signed by twenty-six commissioners, the second by five), reflecting the arguments made during the floor debate. Thus, Danville Seminary and Louisville Seminary were joined, one seminary under the control of both the PCUSA and the PCUS.[87]

The General Assembly's vote launched a unique experiment in the history of the two largest Presbyterian denominations in the U.S. The Presbyterian Theological Seminary of Kentucky was, as one person put it, the window through which the two denominations could see and learn of one another. It may have been more important for the PCUS in learning of the PCUSA, for the PCUSA extended into the South. The Seminary showed that the students, faculty, and board members from both denominations could work together and that the differences between the two were negligible.[88] In retrospect, one thing must be granted the opponents of

---

86. *Minutes of the General Assembly of the Presbyterian Church in the United States* (Richmond, Va.: Presbyterian Committee of Publication, 1901), 38, 60-61, and 95-100.

87. For the story of the merger and issues surrounding it, see, in addition to the sources cited above, "The General Assembly," *Christian Observer* 89 (May 29, 1901): 2-3; and McElroy, *Louisville Seminary,* 121-30.

88. This point has been made by many, but especially by Henry Pope Mobley and Paul Tudor Jones (Interview, April 26, 1992). Later in the century — especially after World War II, when LPTS became a more national seminary — people would note that the Seminary's location was such that it was nobody's place. Of the people who attended, those from the East were coming West; those from the West, going East; those from the North, going South; and those from the South, going North. Louis Weeks thought that was a helpful pedagogical tool, for it meant students had a kind of openness to new things by their very choice of LPTS. See Clinton Morrison Interview, March 16, 1993, and Louis Weeks Interview, March 15, 1993.

merger. They were certain that a joint seminary would inevitably lead to church reunion, and proponents of the merger denied that. The Seminary constantly declared for years that it would not advocate or work for re-union. Eventually, however, the Seminary became pivotal in efforts at re-union of the two denominations and its graduates living witnesses to and proponents of their compatibility.[89]

There had been other merger attempts previously, and others would follow. The successful consolidation of Danville and Louisville in 1901 prompted another attempt surprisingly soon. In 1909 the General Assembly of the PCUSA moved to establish the Presbyterian Seminary of the South in Lebanon, Tennessee. The school had a feeble existence from the beginning, and already in 1910 the board proposed a merger to the board of the Presbyterian Theological Seminary in Kentucky. The proposal would have added faculty and, it was hoped, students and money to the Louisville institution, but the Louisville seminary did not feel it was in the financial condition to accept the merger. The Seminary of the South was soon absorbed by Lane Theological Seminary in Cincinnati.[90]

Building a Campus

The newly-created Presbyterian Theological Seminary of Kentucky continued to occupy the buildings of its Louisville predecessor. The relationship with the PCUSA brought new Louisville churches into close contact with the Seminary; for instance, initial board meetings were held at Warren Memorial Presbyterian Church, instead of Second Church as before. The board soon made the erection of a campus at First and Broadway a priority and began raising money to that end. The decision was made that the campus should have Neo-Gothic stone architecture, built in three wings to create a quadrangle. The plant would be built in sections, as money became available. Peyton Hoge, pastor of the Pee Wee Valley church, who

---

89. This decision for cooperation between the two denominations came just at the beginning of the great twentieth-century ecumenical movement. An ecumenical missionary conference was held in New York City in 1900, followed by the 1910 international missionary conference in Edinburgh, which became one of the greatest forerunners of ecumenism as it developed in twentieth-century Christianity.

90. *Minutes of the General Assembly of the Presbyterian Church in the United States of America* (Philadelphia: Office of the General Assembly, 1909), 82-83; and Minutes of the Board of Directors, Presbyterian Theological Seminary of Kentucky (1901-1920), May 7, 1910. LPTS Archives.

served on the board from 1899 until his death in 1940 — almost all of that time on the executive committee — supervised the design of the campus and, more than any other, was responsible for its utility and beauty.

The first stage of the building would house the refectory and contain dormitory rooms. The cost for that hall was estimated at $40,000, and the board would not proceed without $25,000 in hand. Money was slow in coming until, early in 1903, the Seminary was able to use some of the estate left to the school by W. N. Haldeman of Second Presbyterian Church to start the erection of what became Haldeman Hall on the east wing.[91] The refectory, which created a corner with Haldeman Hall, was completed at the same time in 1904 with a substantial $5,000 gift from Lucy Belknap. When her mother contributed an equal amount in 1907 it was named the Belknap Refectory. A $25,000 gift from board member James R. Barret, longtime elder of First Presbyterian Church in Henderson, Kentucky, in memory of his wife, made possible the Lucy Stites Barret library next to the refectory. The library was the centerpiece of the campus and was crowned by a bell tower.

A couple who played a remarkable role in the building of the 109 East Broadway campus was W. T. Grant and his wife. Grant had been born in Scotland, and despite his mother's desire to see him enter the ministry, he never felt called to that vocation. Grant came to the United States, became financially successful and, like Haldeman, joined Second Presbyterian Church, where Charles Hemphill played no small role in their generosity to the Louisville Seminary. Grant eventually married a niece of Stuart Robinson, who joined him in his support for the Seminary. Grant's will left his entire estate of approximately $300,000 (approximately equal to $5.1 million in 1999) to the school, at the time the largest gift to Presbyterian theological education in the history of the South. Most of the money went to the endowment, but some was used to erect Grant-Robinson Hall. The hall, finished in 1907 and comprising almost the entire west wing of the quadrangle, contained living quarters, faculty offices, and classrooms. The remaining quadrangle buildings were Harbison Chapel, just west of the library; the Annex, which completed the west wing and connected Grant-Robinson to the chapel; and Todd Memorial Hall, which completed the east wing. Entrance to the grounds was gained through the Cooper Memorial Gateway. By the time work was completed, the cost of the campus buildings and grounds totaled just over $218,000.[92] Churches and in-

91. Minutes of the Board (1901-1920), June 19, 1903.
92. *Minutes of the General Assembly of the Presbyterian Church in the United States*

dividuals were solicited to take on the expense of furnishing a dormitory room, which many did — especially in Missouri and Kentucky, of course.[93] The Louisville seminary was judged to be among the best facilities for theological education in the U.S. for its location, its practicality, and the beauty of its architecture.[94]

The Continuing Conservative Theological Outlook

The control of the Seminary by two denominations had no effect on the conservative, traditionalist approach it offered to biblical and theological study or theological education as a whole. After all, both Danville Seminary and Louisville Seminary had been proudly Old School prior to the merger, and this stance remained. The catalogue announced to prospective students that "chief emphasis is laid upon studies having a direct relation to the Holy Scriptures, and there is allotted to these studies a little more than half of the hours of the whole course."[95] The Bible, which anchored the students' education, was understood as God's Word in such a way that human agency in the process of revelation was seen in its "full value," without lowering the believer's "conception of its Divine origin and infallible character."[96]

Jesse Cotton, inaugurated as chair of Old Testament upon William Hoge Marquess's death, maintained his predecessor's outlook. Cotton asserted that although many believers were shaken by the claims of modern rationalistic biblical scholarship (with its elimination of the supernatural from any role in the composition of the Bible), their fears were ungrounded. The Bible itself testifies it is from God, Cotton argued, and Jesus himself used the Old Testament as of God's authority.[97] Nor did Cotton eschew the doctrinal approach to the study of Scripture. His course in

(Richmond, Va.: Presbyterian Committee of Publication, 1910,) 125. The cost of construction would equal approximately $3.45 million in 1999.

93. Minutes of the Board (1901-1920), May 2, 1905.

94. See Minutes of the Board (1901-1920), October 1, 1901; May 5, 1908; May 3, 1910; and Sanders, *History of Louisville Seminary,* 41. The campus at "109" can still be seen, exterior intact, as one site of the Jefferson County Community College.

95. The Annual Announcement of the Presbyterian Theological Seminary of Kentucky (1903-1904), 13. LPTS Archives.

96. The Annual Announcement of the Presbyterian Theological Seminary of Kentucky (1902-1903), 17. LPTS Archives.

97. Jesse L. Cotton, "The Christian Minister and the Old Testament," *The Record* 1 (January 1912): 5-13. LPTS Archives.

English Bible and Biblical Theology explicated the way in which the entire Christian Bible presented the history of redemption.[98]

William Beattie, who died in 1906, was replaced in 1908 by Robert A. Webb. Webb modified somewhat the course in Apologetics, but the approach and content did not change. Indeed, Beattie's books were required reading in two of his courses.[99] Webb's own strict Calvinism manifested itself in his book, *The Theology of Infant Salvation*.[100] The book was published at the height of controversy in the PCUSA over adding an explanatory note to the Westminster Confession of Faith on the salvation of those who die in infancy. Webb surveyed what he termed false understandings of salvation: "Pelagian," which teaches humans are sinless in their nature; "Semipelagian" (Arminian), which teaches the universality of Christ's atonement, as opposed to High Calvinism's assertion that atonement was for the elect only; "Romish," which placed salvation in the acts of the church; and "Mystic" (Pantheistic), which taught salvation through the soul's unity with Christ. Only Calvinism, he offered, taught salvation through the free receipt of Christ's righteousness. After an exegesis of biblical passages dealing with children and infancy (particularly "Suffer the little children" in Mark 10:13-16, which he said demonstrated that children were in the heavenly kingdom), Webb forcefully defended the doctrine of election and concluded that only elect infants die. Certainly, not all infants were elect — predestination precluded that — but all who died in infancy were. Webb's stance was that damnation is a penal judgment of God, the justice and meaning of which turn on a person's recognition of wrongdoing. An infant, not yet capable of moral conclusions, would be bereft of such awareness. It would suffer punishment — rightly so, given its original sin — but not know why. Therefore, Webb reasoned, God must allow the reprobate to grow to an age of moral accountability, and the death of an infant stands as proof of its election.

Clearly, then, Webb was a strict Calvinist. He only agreed to the call to Louisville after assurances that the school stood for cooperation between the PCUS and PCUSA, not organic union, and upheld the PCUS standards.[101] His teaching style was equally rigorous. Classes were for lecture and discussion. Webb "did not allow the student to take notes, but re-

---

98. The Annual Announcement of the Presbyterian Theological Seminary of Kentucky (1909-1910), 21. LPTS Archives.

99. Annual Announcement (1909-1910), 16-17 and 23-24.

100. Robert A. Webb, *The Theology of Infant Salvation* (Richmond, Va.: Presbyterian Committee of Publication, 1907).

101. *The Register* 8 (July, August, September, 1920), 14. LPTS Archives.

quired him to write out the lecture after leaving the class-room, a most admirable mental discipline."[102] Students respected and liked him, however, and his reputation in the PCUS was such that five presbyteries overtured the 1920 General Assembly to publish a volume of his work following his death in 1919. The result was the release of *Christian Salvation: Its Doctrine and Experience* in 1921.[103]

The curriculum, which remained essentially unchanged after consolidation, revealed the understanding of ministry that guided theological education in Presbyterianism in the late nineteenth and early twentieth centuries. The minister was conceived to be the conveyor of biblical and theological truth and the means of grace, whose job was to expound that truth and counsel people to an experience of salvation. The practice or methods of ministry were believed to grow out of the possession of that truth — that is, ministry was the fruit of intellectual knowledge applied to life. That is why there were no courses in the practical conduct of ministry besides homiletics and the one course in pastoral theology that encompassed both evangelism and Sunday school. That also explains why no single faculty member had responsibility for pastoral theology courses. Each faculty member taught an academic area and, in addition, some pastoral course. That arrangement undoubtedly achieved, to some extent, a laudable integration of learning and practice in the Seminary education, but it also grew out of the assumption that the practice of ministry emerged naturally out of biblical and theological learning.[104]

There was also validity to the Seminary's claim that the curriculum was designed "to give unity and system" to the whole — much more so than would be true later in the century. Unity in the curriculum was achieved through the prescription of a stringent course of study that allowed for few electives and which almost everyone took sequentially. Further, as noted above, a unity existed between disciplines because of their essentially doctrinal purpose — Bible, theology, and church history all, in some manner and degree, taught the truth of Reformed doctrine. The understanding of each discipline as a special field of knowledge with its own methodologies was present, but not in the modern sense, which did not begin to take root until the 1920s.

The consolidated Seminary continued the practice of Louisville to

102. *The Register* 8, 15.

103. Robert Alexander Webb, *Christian Salvation: Its Doctrine and Experience* (Richmond, Va.: Presbyterian Committee of Publication, 1921).

104. This line of thought was suggested to me by Warheim, "The History of a 'First-Class Dream,'" especially pages 15-16.

offer special advanced courses, intended primarily for the continuing education of area ministers. Course titles reveal that the purpose of those offerings was to keep people abreast of new developments in religion and the world: "Science and Religion" and "Studies in Religious Experience" (based on William James's work) offered by Beattie and "Higher Criticism of the Old Testament" taught by Marquess serve as examples.[105] Outreach on the part of the faculty to make the Seminary a school of the entire church, not only for ministerial education, met with approbation from all quarters. The board commended faculty "for bringing in Sunday School and other practical Christian workers to deliver series of addresses to the students, and that they be authorized to introduce similar courses whenever in their judgment it may be for the best interest of the Institution."[106]

The faculty, undoubtedly encouraged by such support, requested and received approval to allow women to take regular Seminary classes if they were enrolled in a proposed Women's Missionary Training School. Some women who desired to train for Sunday school work did take classes during the 1908-1909 year, but plans for the training school were suspended until the school's financial situation would warrant its founding. Records indicate that teaching women in the classroom passed out of practice as well.

Nor did the faculty teach exclusively in the Seminary. In 1914 the board applauded the extra labor of the faculty in teaching courses to women, in the YMCA, adult Bible classes, and one to young attorneys in the city. This, of course, was in addition to the supply preaching in which the faculty were constantly engaged. The board was pleased that the faculty was "extending the influence of the Seminary in all such fertile fields."[107] The sponsoring of lectures for the community and offering of special classes both on and off campus was the origin of a long tradition of lay education to the church at large and continuing education for ministers, both practices that continue at the Seminary to this day.

The most significant curricular development of the period came with the 1914-1915 school year. At that time the Seminary added to its offerings four courses that marked a distinct expansion of the practical preparation

---

105. *The Register* 6 (January, February, March 1917): 16; Annual Announcement (1902-1903), 28; Annual Announcement (1904-1905), 25; Annual Announcement (1906-1907), 26. LPTS Archives.

106. Minutes of the Board (1901-1920), May 7, 1907.

107. Minutes of the Board (1901-1920), May 5, 1908, and May 5, 1914; Presbyterian Theological Seminary of Kentucky, Minutes of the Faculty (1909-1914), Faculty Report for 1909-1910. LPTS Archives.

for ministry. To accommodate the additions the third year of both Hebrew and Greek were made optional. The courses were in Christian sociology, Christian ethics, religious education and Sunday school, and Christian missions. The additions were clearly designed to broaden the seminary student's practical preparation for ministry and to respond to contemporary developments in American Protestantism and its milieu. The course in sociology addressed the "problems of poverty, capital and labor, the family, wealth, etc." with reference to the Prophets and New Testament — testimony to the idea that the practical was founded on the scriptural and doctrinal.[108] In the same way, the description of the religious education course noted the changing approaches to the field and the consequent need for a separate course to train ministers for their role in the educational ministry of the church.[109] Its attention to trends in the field of pastoral ministry was evident already in the first year of the course, when John M. Vander Meulen, pastor at Second Presbyterian Church and former professor of psychology at Hope College in Holland, Michigan, gave a series of lectures on educational psychology to the religious education class.[110] The Seminary's interest in mission work carried on the tradition of both Danville and Louisville Seminaries.[111] Both the PCUSA and PCUS participated in the great mission movement of the day, and the Seminary sought to instill mission interest in both those who would choose to go abroad or into the domestic field and those in churches who could pique the interest of the laity, whose support for mission workers was vital. In addition to lecturers on campus, already in 1911 church history professor Henry Dosker offered courses in "The Missionary Pastor" and "Missions in City and Country," although they were not listed in the catalogue. Dosker taught the 1914 course in mission and was made professor of mission in 1919. With the addition of these courses the Seminary had taken a stride into the realm of practical training, the first of many far-reaching changes in that area of seminary education.[112]

The completion of one's college education is so taken for granted today that it is difficult to remember that less than a century ago admission to sem-

---

108. *The Register* 4 (January, February, March 1915): 26.

109. Handy, *A History of Union Theological Seminary,* 96, notes that at the turn of the century electives began to appear at Union, the start of a trend. Selden, *Princeton Theological Seminary,* 97-100, makes the same observation.

110. Handy, *Union.* See also Warheim, "First-Class Dream," 12-13.

111. See the discussion above for some of the literature regarding the mission movement.

112. Handy, *Union,* 27; and Horner, King, and Weeks, "Evangelism and Mission," 3-4.

inary could be much more flexible — and often was. One story, unusual in some respects and common in others, illustrates particularly well the differences between the past and present. Christopher McCoy Franklin was born in 1889 in the mountains of western North Carolina. His father, who had no formal education, experienced educated people as those who took advantage of him and his neighbors, and so he prohibited his children from attending school. Somehow the younger Franklin acquired a desire for education and, when he turned twenty-one, left home and went to Berea School in Kentucky. In his first year he passed from the first to the eighth grade. Eventually, with two years of college at Berea, Franklin felt called to ministry and made his way to Louisville to seek admission to the Presbyterian seminary there. He was admitted in 1916 as a special student who could not receive a B.D. degree without a bachelor's degree from a college or university. Franklin decided to take courses at the University of Louisville simultaneously with his work at the Seminary. He earned his B.D. from the Seminary and later received his Bachelor of Education degree from the university. He went on to a long ministry in North Carolina and east Tennessee, with an especially long service in Madisonville, Tennessee, and as principal of the nearby Bachman Memorial Home and School.[113]

Although Franklin's story is remarkable in terms of the particulars of his own life situation, it was relatively common for the Seminary to admit to full-time study students who had not completed college. Their degrees were not granted until the college degree was completed. One well-known Louisville Seminary graduate who had one course to complete in college before he received his B.D. was Frank Hill Caldwell.

Students continued to have the opportunity for out-of-class instruction, primarily through guest lectures and work in local churches and missions. Some lectures addressed the needs of ministry and pastoral identity in a changing world. Such topics as Sunday school, church development, church finance, and stewardship were broached. Vander Meulen's lectures in educational psychology have been mentioned. Other notable addresses included "How I Prepare My Sermons" by Dunbar Ogden; "The Proper Place of Ambition in Ministry" by E. Y. Mullins, president of Southern Baptist Seminary; two lectures on "City Church Problems" by Charles Stelzle, PCUSA pioneer in the field of labor and Christianity; "The Successful Minister" by E. O. Guerrant; and "The Ministry and Our Time" by John Grier Hibben, president of Princeton University. A highlight of the 1911-1912

---

113. See the list of the 1919 graduating class in *The Register* 9 (January, February, March 1920). The story was told to me by Franklin's son, M. McCoy Franklin, May 4, 1994.

school year was an address by William Jennings Bryan at Warren Memorial Church during a meeting of the Men and Religion Forward Movement.[114]

Of course, lectures on mission continued to be emphasized by the Seminary. In 1912, William Sheppard assumed the pastorate of Grace Presbyterian Church. As a former missionary to the Congo who achieved fame for his defiance of King Leopold over human rights abuses, Sheppard regularly gave presentations on global mission.[115] Special lecturers such as I. M. Yonan, LPTS graduate from Persia; C. H. Pratt, former missionary who eventually joined the faculty; and Samuel Zwemer, renowned expert on Arabia and Islam, helped students and church members understand global Christianity. Perhaps the most famous lecturer was Robert Speer, PCUSA leader of the mission and ecumenical movements, who spoke at Southern Baptist Seminary at the close of World War I on "Our Debt to the Pioneers of Modern Missions," "The Missionary Motive Today," and "Our Aims in the War and the Aims of Foreign Missions."[116]

Some lectures dealt specifically with places where current mission interest was concentrated. For example, with the coming of China's revolution in 1911 the Euro-American mission community, led by people such as John R. Mott, Sherwood Eddy, and Fletcher Brockman (all of the International YMCA), believed it was a special moment of opportunity for a mass movement of Christianity in that great land.[117] From 1912-1914 the Louisville Seminary heard at least five lectures on China, with titles such as "The China of Today," "The Political Conditions in China," and "The Needs and the Opportunities in the China of Today."[118] Not surprisingly, World War I

114. Minutes of the Board (1901-1920), September 15, 1914; *The Record* 1 (January, 1912): 16; *The Register* 8 (January, February, March 1919): 6; the Annual Announcement of the Presbyterian Theological Seminary of Kentucky (1910-1911), 5; and *The Register* 5 (January, February, March 1916): 5. LPTS Archives.

115. See, for example, *The Register* 5 (January, February, March 1916): 5.

116. The Annual Announcement of the Presbyterian Theological Seminary of Kentucky (1902-1903), 4; *The Register* 1 (March 1912): 5; Annual Announcement (1910-1911), 5; and *The Register* 8 (January February, March 1919): 6. LPTS Archives.

117. For that sense of hope see James C. Thomson, Jr., Peter W. Stanley, and John Curtis Perry, *Sentimental Imperialists: The American Experience in East Asia* (New York: Harper and Row, 1981); Kenneth Scott Latourette, *A History of Christian Missions in China* (New York: Russell and Russell, 1967); Latourette, *The Twentieth Century Outside Europe,* vol. 5 in *Christianity in a Revolutionary Age;* and Rick Nutt, *The Whole Gospel for the Whole World: Sherwood Eddy and the American Protestant Mission* (Macon, Ga.: Mercer University Press, 1997), 76-92.

118. *The Register* 2 (January, February, March 1913): 5; and 3 (January, February, March 1914): 6. LPTS Archives.

also prompted a few lectures; Speer's are an excellent example. James Buswell, a military chaplain, spoke on "Religious Work in the Camps," and A. T. Trawick of the YMCA War Service Department described the "Evils Resulting from the War and Ways of Meeting Them." The shock of seeing Christians killing one another in perhaps the most brutal war in history left Robert Webb asking, "Has Christianity Failed?"[119]

Presbyterians at this time shared mainstream Protestantism's passion for, and attitudes about, mission. An element in mission work at the turn of the century was the belief that not only did people in places such as Africa and Asia need to receive the gospel of Christ, but that they needed, in large measure, to become more like western Christians. The idea was especially widespread that political and cultural institutions — ideas of freedom, representative government, individualism, and industrial progress — which had developed within Anglo-American society were the most advanced in the world and helped explain English and U.S. world prominence. As a result of that belief, the missionary service often took on an air of arrogance and, as William Hutchison called it, "cultural imperialism."[120]

Many workers in the field questioned that approach to mission. They began to urge that the mission enterprise develop indigenous leadership to whom the direction of the work of the church could be transferred and to urge exploration of the ways in which the gospel could be presented in such a way that it spoke to and within the local culture, not over against it. The World Missionary Conference held at Edinburgh, Scotland, in 1910 reflected that growing attitude, particularly in the address of V. S. Azariah of India — even though it was dominated by European and American Christianity. The general Christian populace in the United States retained the attitude of superiority in mission. It comes as no surprise, then, that in the 1905-1906 school year the Seminary received D. L. Leonard for ten lectures on "The Anglo-Saxon as a factor in the World's Redemption." Eight years later J. S. Sibley, a minister in Louisville, spoke about "America's Opportunity for Christ."[121]

Mission needs within the United States also received attention. At

119. *The Register* 7 (January, February, March 1918): 6; and 8 (January, February, March 1919): 6.

120. William R. Hutchison, *Errand to the World.* See also Robert T. Handy, *A Christian America,* chapters 4 and 5.

121. Annual Announcement (1905-1906), 6, and *The Register* 3 (January, February, March 1914): 6. The Seminary's fervent attention to global mission bore demonstrable fruit. Three members of the class of 1915 alone went abroad — Edward Caldwell, Walter Dolive, and Richard Dosker, son of the faculty member. See *The Register* 4 (April, May, June 1915).

least four presentations each year kept those issues before the students and churches. Ministry among rural churches was particularly addressed because of Louisville's location, as in "Missions among the Appalachian Mountaineers."[122] In an effort to take advantage of the Seminary's urban location there were also presentations on "Social Ethics" and, by John Little, "The Negro Problem" (Little frequently made presentations on the topic).[123] Interestingly, during the 1919-1920 school year Rabbi Joseph Rauch spoke on "The Place of the Jew in the Future," perhaps prompted by Britain's Balfour Declaration regarding the Middle East.[124] Again, students responded to the call. The work of Christopher Franklin in Appalachia has been noted. A classmate of his from Spain, Henry Blanco, went to New Mexico to work among the Spanish-speaking people there.[125] The faculty often were role models of concern for church growth and evangelism. In 1915 the PCUSA presbytery in Louisville formed a committee to battle apathy about church extension among its members. The three-person committee were all faculty at the Seminary — Henry Dosker, Jesse Cotton, and Edward Warren.[126]

The education of seminary students also took place in extra-seminary settings. In 1906 the faculty, on petition of the students, adjusted classes to allow students to attend a convention of the SVM meeting in Nashville from February 28 to March 3. In 1911 a Sunday school conference met in the Seminary on January 20-21. Again, class schedules were altered so that students could participate. The Committee on Theological Seminaries of the International YMCA held a meeting of western and southwestern seminaries in Louisville in 1916 at the invitation of Southern Baptist Seminary and the Presbyterian Theological Seminary of Kentucky. Both students and faculty were a part of the proceedings and of framing recommendations for theological education. Resolutions from the group asked seminarians to push for the recruiting of more candidates for ministry and, given the world war, to promote the study of internationalism and world peace. One suggestion for seminaries sounded very familiar: press-

122. *The Register* 2 (January, February, March 1913): 5; and 5 (January, February, March 1916): 5.

123. *The Register* 9 (January, February, March 1920): 8.

124. *The Register* 9 (January, February, March 1920): 8.

125. *The Register* 8 (April, May, June 1919). The Seminary also learned of a nascent ecumenical spirit when Thornton Whaling, president of CTS, lectured on the "Federation of American Presbyterianism." *The Register* 3 (January, February, March 1914): 6.

126. H. E. Dosker, J. L. Cotton, and Edward L. Warren, "To the Members of the Presbyterian Church (U.S.A.) Louisville." November 6, 1915. LPTS Archives.

ing forward the missionary needs of the world through one day each month set aside for special study.[127]

The Seminary community thought of itself as a close family, a kind of model of what fellowship in Christ could be. Periodically, faculty members lived in rooms on campus; Webb was one. That, along with the continuation of morning prayers, worship, the missionary day each month, dining together, and informal contact of students with faculty, built a relationship important to the entire ethos of seminary life and education. The faculty even joined the students in exercise after a bowling alley was installed in the basement of Grant-Robinson Hall.[128] Faculty entertained the students in their homes or at social gatherings on campus. (That the Seminary was bound to the racial insensitivities of the day, to say the least, was shown at one of these gatherings when Hemphill gave "inimitable readings from Uncle Remus.")[129] The students' field work continued as an important part of their training. The faculty closely supervised the progress of students in that work, and at times even participated as preachers in mission stations.[130]

Changes at the Presbyterian Theological Seminary of Kentucky

The faculty at the opening of the new seminary retained Hemphill, Marquess, Beattie, and Hawes from the previous Louisville Seminary and brought Clarence Crawford and Claude Martin from Danville Seminary. John Worrall of DTS was given emeritus status and a $1,200 per year pension. Some teaching assignments were adjusted from those prior to the merger, but the educational approach and content saw little change.[131] Faculty salaries were set, if the budget permitted, at $3,000[132] for all professors except Hemphill. He was to receive $3,500, because the board felt ob-

127. Minutes of the Faculty of the Presbyterian Theological Seminary of Kentucky (1902-1909), February 6, 1906; Minutes of the Faculty of the Presbyterian Theological Seminary of Kentucky (1909-1914), January 3, 1911; *The Register* 5 (July, August, September 1916), n.p. LPTS Archives.

128. Minutes of the Board (1901-1920), May 7, 1907.

129. *The Record* 1 (January 1912): 15.

130. In 1908, for example, both students and faculty accepted the responsibility for preaching at the Bardstown Road mission. Faculty Minutes (1902-1909), March 26, 1908.

131. Minutes of the Board (1901-1920), April 23, 1901, and July 16, 1901; and Annual Announcement (1901-1902), 4.

132. That salary would approximately equal $51,000 in 1999.

ligated to pay him what he had received from Second Church prior to joining the faculty full-time. Hemphill declined the higher salary in the interest of equity among the faculty — and set a precedent for faculty concern about relative parity in salaries that still exists.[133]

The faculty of the Louisville Seminary underwent significant changes up to 1920. The addition of Cotton and Webb after the departures of Marquess and Beattie has been noted. J. Gray McAllister replaced Crawford upon his departure in 1909. One of the most interesting faculty hires was Henry Dosker. The role of LPTS over the years as a bridge between the PCUS and PCUSA is a conspicuous element of the Seminary's life to any person with even a passing acquaintance with the school. Less acknowledged is the ongoing relationship of Presbyterianism with its Dutch Reformed brothers and sisters in the Seminary. When the seminaries were consolidated, Dosker, a well-known and esteemed pastor in the Dutch Reformed Church, was teaching at Western Theological Seminary in Holland, Michigan. Upon Claude Martin's death in 1902 Dosker was elected professor of church history by the Seminary board, but he declined. The Seminary failed to find another satisfactory candidate, so Dosker was offered the position again in December of the same year. He accepted and became a mainstay of the Seminary in the fields of church history, practical theology, missions, and — for a period — apologetics. Thus began a relationship with the Dutch Reformed Church in the upper Midwest that included notable Seminary people such as John M. Vander Meulen, Peter Pleune, and John Olert (all joined the Presbyterian church, although Dosker retained his Dutch accent until his death).[134]

The bringing together of faculty from two — even three — denominations to a site which had been the location of one predecessor seminary might have caused problems of ego, theology, resentment, or power. However, no such issues seem to have afflicted the Presbyterian Theological Seminary of Kentucky in its transition period. Sanders wrote in his history that "these united groups of teachers and students worked together amicably and efficiently. One never heard church union advocated, yet the Seminary was an eloquent demonstration of 'how good and pleasant it is for brethren to dwell together in unity.'"[135]

133. Minutes of the Board (1901-1920), July 16, 1901, and October 22, 1901.

134. For some references to Dosker and the Dutch connection see Minutes of the Board (1901-1920), June 12, 1902, and December 18, 1902; Annual Announcement (1906-1907), 15-23; and Mobley and Jones Interview. Still later, Craig Dykstra and John Mulder would continue this tradition.

135. Sanders, *History of Louisville Seminary*, 47.

A major step in the operation of the Seminary was the initiation of the office of president. At its founding, administration of the Seminary was vested in the chair of the faculty, which passed from person to person. By 1907 the board was convinced of the need for a president to manage Louisville's affairs but did not think the financial condition of the school would allow it. The next year they revised the constitution to provide for a president without taking any steps to call someone to the post. Finally in 1910 the board turned to Charles Hemphill, the natural leader of the faculty (a tutor for New Testament Greek was hired to release him from that portion of his teaching load). He served as president until 1920.[136]

The administrative need for a president was underscored in a telling manner at the very same meeting at which Hemphill was elected to the position. E. W. C. Humphrey proposed, and the board approved, that a budget be prepared each year by the president and executive committee of the board, "giving an estimate of the expected revenue and expenditure of the coming year, with recommendations concerning any deficit and how the same should be met."[137] The absence of an annual budget exposed the virtual absence of administration of the Seminary. The day-to-day affairs of the institution were overseen by the faculty chair, the intendant, and, after 1902, a part-time librarian. Faculty members and (to a limited degree) the board were expected to place the importance of the Seminary before prospective students and donors as they had opportunity. In 1907 the board recorded its approval of the practice of sending students and faculty to colleges for recruiting.[138]

As with many church-related institutions of the time, the administration of Louisville was so loose that no accounting record was maintained on campus. The books were kept by the treasurer of the board at his office in a local bank. The intendant and faculty chair disbursed and received money without knowing whether the Seminary had cash on hand, a practice which continued long after Hemphill's presidency. Clearly, a major part of Hemphill's job was to raise money for the annual fund on a consistent basis. In 1917 the board hired French Thompson as Extension Secretary to relieve Hemphill of some of that burden, but this first experiment at having a development officer was short-lived.[139] The shoestring style of

---

136. Minutes of the Board (1901-1920), January 29, 1907, and May 5, 1908; *The Register* 2 (January, February, March 1913): 4. LPTS Archives. This event was an early sign of what we shall describe as the incorporation of Protestantism in the U.S.

137. Minutes of the Board (1901-1920), May 3, 1910.

138. Minutes of the Board (1901-1920), May 7, 1907.

139. Minutes of the Board (1901-1920), May 1, 1917.

Seminary operations was obvious in the library. Edward Warren was librarian from 1902-1927, after which he was granted emeritus status. The first catalogue of holdings was done by Louise Conn in the 1930s. Until then one was not perceived as necessary, for the entire library holdings and their locations were indelibly etched in Warren's memory.[140] In this situation an enormous task fell to Hemphill, and he gave sacrificially of his energy, time, and intellect to move the Seminary forward.

The dedication of the board of directors in the Seminary's operation deserves mention. The board only met once each year, but the executive committee — comprised until the 1970s of people who lived in the immediate Louisville area — met frequently and took an active role in decision-making. The board had a heavy representation of ministers, often from large churches and prominent in their synods. With few exceptions, board members gave of their money and of their time to the Seminary, and often to the church at large. Humphrey, a prominent Louisville lawyer, served on the PCUSA committee which wrote the revisions to the Westminster Confession of Faith just after the turn of the century and actively participated in the Alliance of Reformed Churches throughout the World holding the Presbyterian System.[141] The Seminary enjoyed a good relationship between the board and faculty, a rapport which persists to the present day.

Despite hard work on the part of everyone associated with the Seminary, the financial difficulties that had plagued both predecessor institutions persisted. The board initially set aside $3,000 for student scholarships, but apparently could have made use of much more. Students paid $90 for room and board, and the administration judged a student could live for $160-$190 a year "with due economy."[142] The Seminary often operated on a deficit, and faculty salaries were frequently in arrears. Honoraria from pulpit supply, editorial work, or other service were given to the Seminary.[143] The deficits for some of the years under consideration seem small ($7,700 in 1908-1909, $17,000 in 1909-1910), but they represented a frightening percentage of the budget of approximately $60,000.[144] The encouraging sign was that the endowment and assets of the Seminary con-

140. Sanders, *History of Louisville Seminary*, 71-72.

141. Minutes of the Board (1901-1920), May 1, 1917.

142. Minutes of the Board (1901-1920), May 6, 1902; and Annual Announcement (1919-1920), 34.

143. Sanders, *History of Louisville Seminary*, 49.

144. Minutes of the Board (1901-1920), May 4, 1909, and May 3, 1910. The budget of $60,000 would have been approximately $950,000 in 1999 dollars; the $17,000 deficit was equal to approximately $270,000.

tinued to grow. The problem was that the endowment income, combined with annual giving, was insufficient for the ongoing needs of the school. The new campus meant higher utility and maintenance costs, and the student body — the numbers of which remained relatively high, though fluctuating — required more aid.

Louisville sought to address its financial needs in a number of ways. In 1907 an alumni association was formed. It was hoped that, among other benefits and purposes, the association would be the means for graduates to support the school with their gifts and direct church members of means to do the same. One should remember that, until the Sixteenth Amendment to the Constitution established a national income tax in 1913, there was no financial benefit to charitable giving.[145] In 1904, Crawford was sent east for one month to raise ten scholarships of $2,500 each for student aid and to visit colleges for recruitment. In 1905, when student numbers were lower than usual, the Seminary rented some dormitory rooms to the University of Louisville.[146]

After Hemphill's election to the presidency, the board directed the faculty to address the problem of annual giving by securing at least fifty people willing to pledge a minimum of $100 per year for three years.[147] Only three years later Hemphill received a mandate to develop a plan for increasing the endowment by $200,000 — if annual giving were inadequate, then the interest-producing notes would be increased to produce more income. The result was an intense campaign in 1915. The Seminary received a $50,000 matching challenge grant from a Mrs. John Kennedy of New York City, so they hired Philo Dix, State Secretary of the Kentucky YMCA, to canvass the churches. The campaign operated much like a church stewardship drive. The Seminary was the central location from which teams went out to churches and individuals. Lasting from May 13 to May 18, the Louisville phase of the campaign raised $65,000, with the synods of Missouri and Kentucky to follow. The effort fell short of $200,000 but was considered successful nonetheless.[148] The faculty missed just one event that might have been the occasion for raising money. In 1903 the board solicited from the faculty its thoughts on a celebration of the fiftieth anniversary of the founding of Danville Seminary. The faculty doubted a

145. Annual Announcement (1909-1910), 34.
146. Minutes of the Board (1901-1920), May 2, 1904, and September 21, 1908.
147. Minutes of the Board (1901-1920), May 2, 1911.
148. Minutes of the Board (1901-1920), May 5, 1914; and *The Register* 21 (July, August, September 1915), 2-8.

commemoration would be of value, but they volunteered to make arrangements if the board wished to proceed.[149]

The student body grew as a result of the Seminary's recruiting efforts, rising to seventy students for the 1914-1915 year. The students included a range of international students from such lands as Canada, England, Scotland, Japan, Persia, and Australia. During these years Louisville Seminary enrolled what must have been its first non-Christian student; Hugo Taustine, preparing for the rabbinate, was admitted to a course in Hebrew. Despite its traditionalist Calvinism, the Presbyterian Theological Seminary of Kentucky could exhibit a kind of ecumenical spirit that extended not only to other Reformed Christians but beyond the church itself. One also notes that, in 1919, the faculty decided women could enroll in any course they chose and, upon successful completion of the course, receive a certificate verifying the achievement. However, "This action was not intended to give them technical enrollment in the Seminary as professional students of the institution."[150]

The United States' entry into World War I hindered the fortunes of the Seminary further. In May 1918 the board was already contemplating the possibility they could only pay three professors' salaries the next year, although the decision instead was to relieve Hemphill of all teaching for the spring semester for fundraising (other professors distributed his course work).[151] With young men off to military service, the student body dropped to forty-three for 1918-1919 and thirty-eight the next year.[152] With fewer students the Seminary was able to offer some of its rooms in Grant-Robinson Hall for soldiers, which helped ease financial distress.[153] Additionally, the famous influenza epidemic of 1918-1919 affected the Seminary. The school closed for one month in the fall of 1918, on orders of the Board of Health, although the dormitories and refectory remained open. Other less serious disruptions due to influenza came the following February.[154]

All of this did nothing to bolster the economic health of Louisville

149. Faculty Minutes (1902-1909), March 6, 1903.
150. Minutes of the Faculty of the Presbyterian Theological Seminary of Kentucky (1914-1925), January 31, 1917, and April 24, 1919.
151. Minutes of the Board (1901-1920), May 7, 1918, and Faculty Minutes (1914-1925), February 8, 1919.
152. Unless specified, numbers of students in this work refers to B.D. or (later) M.Div. students.
153. Sanders, *History of Louisville Seminary,* 54.
154. Faculty Minutes (1914-1925), October 17, 1918; and February 1 and 8, 1919.

Seminary. For 1917-1918 the school ran an $11,000 deficit and made plans to increase the endowment even further and increase annual giving from synods and alumni. The spirit of the faculty manifested itself in the trial when they volunteered to preach more in order to receive more money to give the Seminary and to solicit donors. Even more, each of the six professors gave a gift of $100 — taken from salaries that were already too low.[155] Another interesting development was the formation, conceived by Hemphill, of a Seminary League, intended to develop a group of friends of the Louisville Seminary who were willing to pledge an annual amount to the school. The aim was to make annual income steadier and more reliable. This proved yet another precursor of an idea that again emerged later in the life of the institution.[156]

So Louisville struggled financially but grew stronger in its legacy, its curriculum, its service to the church, and its place in the world and the Louisville community. The new Synod of Appalachia (PCUS) joined as a controlling body of the Seminary in 1918 (the PCUS representation was now distributed as Kentucky, 7; Missouri, 3; and Appalachia, 2).[157] This extended the Seminary's constituency into the mountain portions of Virginia, West Virginia, North Carolina, and Tennessee. Still, it would take ceaseless work to carry the Presbyterian Theological Seminary of Kentucky ahead. Hemphill concluded he was advancing too far in age to maintain the burden of the presidency, and in 1920 he stepped down — to the relaxing job of professor and academic dean. When John M. Vander Meulen was installed as president in 1920, a new era in the Seminary's life began.

155. Faculty Minutes (1914-1925), May 3, 1918.
156. Minutes of the Board (1901-1920), May 6, 1919.
157. Minutes of the Board (1901-1920), May 7, 1918.

THE OLD ORTHODOXY IN TERMS OF
MODERN LIFE AND EXPERIENCE

*The Presidencies of John Vander Meulen
and John R. Cunningham, 1920-1936*

A s Charles Hemphill stepped down from the presidency of Louisville
Presbyterian Theological Seminary[1] to return to teaching, the United
States and its churches entered a time of monumental change. The economic boom of the 1920s and the subsequent Depression; the populariza-
tion of intellectual developments in the biological sciences and the social
sciences, especially psychology; the ongoing impact of earlier immigra-
tion, urbanization, and industrialization; and the aftermath of World War I
all affected American culture. Religion and religious institutions — including those responsible for theological education — responded to these and
other forces in a variety of ways. LPTS felt the impact of both economic
prosperity and decline and changes in American thought and social organization. While the Seminary remained conservative in its attitude and
theology, there were also changes deemed necessary to keep theological
education abreast of changes in church and society. These were days of difficulty and transition.

---

1. The Board of Directors of the Presbyterian Theological Seminary of Kentucky
voted in 1927 to change the name of the school back to that of the PCUS predecessor, Louisville Presbyterian Theological Seminary. Technically, the name change did not become effective until 1928, for a change to the Seminary charter required a vote at two consecutive
meetings. This chapter will use the renewed name, which continues in use to the present,
throughout to refer to the school. Minutes of the Board of Directors of Louisville Presbyterian Theological Seminary (1920-1939), May 3, 1927, and May 1, 1928. LPTS Archives.

Growth and Struggle under
John Vander Meulen, 1920-1930

When Hemphill tendered his resignation to the board in 1920, he had already laid the groundwork for hiring a successor — undoubtedly fearful that the board would persuade him to continue in his duties until a replacement was found. He presented the board with a letter from Brainerd Lemon, a local jeweler and committed member of Second Presbyterian, offering to pay $6,000 for the salary of a new president and increase the salary of each professor by $1,000 if the board elected John Vander Meulen.[2] (The offer of an increase to the professors' salaries was especially needed.) The board accepted the offer, and Vander Meulen became the second president of Louisville Seminary.

Vander Meulen was a man of broad experience and exceptional reputation who continued the Second Presbyterian Church and Dutch Reformed connection of Louisville Seminary. Reared and educated in the Reformed Church in America, Vander Meulen had been pastor of Second Presbyterian Church in the city from 1912-1917, during which time he had served on the LPTS board and lectured to the Seminary community. From that position he had gone to the First Presbyterian Church in the Chicago suburb of Oak Park, Illinois, whence he was called to the Seminary presidency. In addition to his duties as president, Vander Meulen would teach in the area of religious education until 1924, to which he added homiletics in 1923. Vander Meulen was particularly suited for teaching Christian education, as it had been one of his central duties during a stint in home missions in the Oklahoma Territory, and he had been a college professor of educational psychology for six years. Still later Louisville would call on him to teach theology.[3]

As had been the case in the past, from 1920-1936 the Seminary's B.D. student population fluctuated — now even more dramatically than previously. From a low of thirty-four students in 1920-1921, the Seminary numbers climbed rapidly to a high of 102 in 1924-1925. The number of students declined slightly the next few years; enrollment suffered considerably with the onset of the Depression, but never again dropped as low as thirty-four.[4]

2. Minutes of the Board (1920-1939), May 4, 1920.

3. In addition to McElroy's and Sanders' accounts of Vander Meulen's election and background, see Minutes of the Faculty of the Presbyterian Theological Seminary of Kentucky (1914-1925), March 12, 1918; *The Register* 10 (April, May, June 1921): 4-5; and Vander Meulen, "A Review of the Past Ten Years," 1.

4. This coincided with what Robert T. Handy called "The American Religious De-

Married students posed a renewed housing problem in the early 1920s. This was, presumably, due in part to the attendance of young men who had delayed ministerial training for military service in World War I. The board noted the situation as early as May 1920, but did not act until the next year, when it rented apartments for housing married students. Because the expense for the students exceeded what they would have paid for seminary rooms, Louisville Seminary bore some of the cost.[5] In 1926 LPTS purchased the "Gheens property," a large house directly behind the Seminary on Gray Street, for married student housing. That acquisition alleviated the problem for a few years, but in the 1930s married students were also occupying dormitory rooms in the main campus.[6]

Aside from the B.D. students and local ministers who continued their learning by taking the special graduate courses, Louisville Seminary expanded its constituency in other ways. From November 1921 to February 1922, LPTS ran a "Bible College" for sixty-five laymen and -women (many more of the latter than the former) from the Louisville area. Courses offered to the lay workers included English Bible, Christian Education, Sunday School Programming, and Church Organization and Efficiency. The faculty were pleased with the program, but it proved financially unworkable.[7] If it seemed curious to see women in the hallways and classrooms on campus, it would not be long until Louisville would admit women as students in regular classes — albeit only as special students. The 1929-1930 school year found two women enrolled in seminary courses, apparently the first women to attend regular seminary classes in LPTS history. At least one, Mrs. Frederick Olert, was a student's wife.[8] The following year other women joined these two, one a woman of particular interest. A Mrs. Miller, licensed to preach by the Cumberland Presbyterian Church, was admitted by the faculty to the regular course of study leading to the B.D., but informed that she would not be granted the actual degree.[9] Change surely came to LPTS, but incrementally.

---

pression, 1925-1935," reprinted in John M. Mulder and John F. Wilson, eds., *Religion in American History: Interpretive Essays* (Englewood Cliffs, N.J.: Prentice-Hall, 1978).

5. Minutes of the Board (1920-1939), May 11, 1920, and June 3, 1921.

6. Minutes of the Board (1920-1939), Executive Committee, March 22, 1926, and Fannie Caldwell Interview.

7. *The Register* 11 (January, February, March 1922): 39-40. LPTS Archives.

8. *The Register* 19 (January, February, March 1930): 19.

9. *The Register* 20 (January, February, March 1931): 22, and Minutes of the Faculty of the Presbyterian Theological Seminary of Kentucky (1925-1932), October 30, 1930. LPTS Archives.

There was significant faculty turnover between the world wars. Many of those added would be central to the life of the Seminary into the 1960s, which made their hiring momentous. When Vander Meulen assumed the presidency in 1920, the late Robert Webb's professorship in apologetics, systematics, and ethics remained vacant. Louisville Seminary was able to persuade Thornton Whaling, president of Columbia Seminary, to accept the position in 1921. Vander Meulen called Whaling the most outstanding teacher of those subjects in the PCUS. He took pains to stress that Charles Hemphill did not originate the idea of approaching Whaling, even though the two men were brothers-in-law.[10] Whaling's stature in the denomination was manifested by his election as moderator of the 1924 PCUS General Assembly, which dealt with matters of theology in a delicate fundamentalist-modernist atmosphere.

One of the Seminary's most providential additions came in 1925. Lewis J. Sherrill, an LPTS graduate serving in Tennessee and directing that synod's Christian education program, was called as instructor in religious education, young people's work, and church efficiency. Sherrill held only a B.D. at the time but immediately proceeded to pursue his doctorate at Yale University under Luther Weigle, the leader in the field. Sherrill was to wield tremendous influence in the area of theological and Christian education, not only at Louisville but throughout the denomination and in Protestantism as a whole. He held the deanship at Louisville Seminary for two decades; was one of three founders of the forerunner to the current Association of Theological Seminaries, which helped initiate standards and accreditation processes for theological schools; and wrote extensively in the field of Christian education. In witness to his ability, in a year of leave from LPTS to complete his doctorate, Yale made Sherrill a visiting lecturer, and Weigle chose him to teach one of his seminars during a semester's absence. Vander Meulen noted in 1930 that Princeton Seminary had already repeatedly sought Sherrill with a lucrative salary, but Sherrill chose to remain with his alma mater. Clearly he was to be an authority in the field.[11] His addition to the faculty was one of a collection of moves during these years that began to make Louisville stand out in the practical area of theological education — the area for which it has been best known and most distinctive.

10. John Vander Meulen, "The Members of the Board of Directors in the Presbyterian Theological Seminary of Kentucky" [President's Report for 1921], 10-12. LPTS Archives.

11. Minutes of the Board (1920-1939), November 5, 1924; Vander Meulen, President's Eighth Annual Report, May 1, 1928; Vander Meulen, President's Tenth Annual Report, May 6, 1930; and *The Register* 14 (January, February, March 1925): 6. LPTS Archives.

In 1924 Charles Pratt joined the faculty in the newly-created department of mission and evangelism. A former missionary of the PCUS to Africa, Pratt was a beloved teacher and, by all accounts, a man of remarkable spirit. Andrew Rule, a colleague, testified to Pratt's care for others when he related that occasionally he would put an arm around Rule's waist and say, "Andy, I love you." Pratt's character was such that neither he nor Rule were embarrassed by the open display of affection, for it seemed natural.[12] Rule was Henry Dosker's successor; the latter died in 1926, and Vander Meulen said his twenty-three years of service as a professor of church history were of a quality unequaled in any Presbyterian seminary in the country.[13] Rule had a B.D. from Princeton, where he had been an adherent of the arch-conservative Benjamin Warfield, and a Ph.D. from the University of Edinburgh. That made him only the second faculty member in the Seminary's history with an earned doctorate. His arrival precipitated a shifting of teaching responsibilities. Rule took up church history from Dosker, but pastoral theology was reassigned to Pratt. Rule added apologetics, leaving Whaling with systematics and ethics.[14]

Further faculty changes came quickly. William Douglas Chamberlain, studying for his Ph.D. at Southern Baptist Seminary, became instructor in New Testament exegesis and Greek in 1928. He assisted Hemphill, who had exceeded the biblical "three-score years and ten" and reduced his teaching load. Julian Price Love moved from Lane Theological Seminary as it closed and began a long tenure in English Bible and Biblical Theology. Frank Hill Caldwell was called from McComb, Mississippi, to teach homiletics in 1930, as Vander Meulen moved to systematic theology. Whaling retired to emeritus professor and John Rood Cunningham became president. By the 1931-1932 school year LPTS had nine full-time faculty, the highest number yet — and more who had earned doctorates, or were pursuing them, than ever before.[15] This faculty was the most theologically di-

12. *The Register* 39 (June 1950), n.p. LPTS Archives. At Pratt's arrival Dosker relinquished his work in missions, teaching only church history and practical theology.

13. *The Register* 16 (January, February, March 1927): 3, and Vander Meulen, Fifth Annual President's Report, May 5, 1925, manuscript copy. LPTS Archives.

14. *The Register* 17 (January, February, March 1928): 9, and *The Register* 16 (April, May, June 1927): 2-3. Academic doctorates, as opposed to the honorary D.D., began to be expected of LPTS faculty. When Sherrill earned his Ph.D. from Yale, he was the third to do so. Pratt earned a Ph.D. from SBTS in 1932, and Julian Price Love, added to the faculty in 1930, held his from the University of Cincinnati. The increasing professionalization of the faculty did not diminish the expectation of their role as examples of ministerial identity, however.

15. For these, and other, faculty hirings and changes, see Minutes of the Board (1920-1939), Executive Committee, May 24, 1928; *The Register* 18 (January, February, March 1929):

verse in the Seminary's history. Sherrill subscribed to a liberal interpretation of Calvinism, while the others were conservative (Rule and Vander
Meulen perhaps most so) to moderate. However, records suggest that they
worked in relative harmony.

Another Louisville Seminary "institution" came to work at the
school in 1929. Robert Veazey, alumnus of the Seminary, became instructor in music and organist for worship and other gatherings. Because
Veazey was blind, LPTS gave him a room in the dormitory where he lived
until his retirement. Veazey's attitude and faith touched the lives of generations of seminary students; many testified that they first learned from him
that a person with a physical disability was not necessarily handicapped.

The administrative structure at Louisville first moved toward modern organization under Vander Meulen and Cunningham. The first change
was an expansion of the Seminary's controlling synods and, consequently,
the number of directors. The series of events that led to those changes
demonstrated the ways in which even seminaries are touched by, and participate in, ecclesiastical politics.

In his first year as president, Vander Meulen learned of a proposed
plan to revive the divinity school at Clarksville, Tennessee, which had
suspended operations in 1917, and merge it with Columbia Seminary.
The plan would place the new seminary in Memphis and secure the control of the Alabama, Arkansas, Louisiana, Mississippi, Tennessee, and
Texas synods. That would, of course, seriously challenge Louisville's
ability to recruit students and raise money in the PCUS. Partially to prevent the execution of the plan, Vander Meulen sought to bring Whaling
from Columbia's presidency to Louisville. He knew Whaling favored a
consolidation of some kind and would be a key figure in the success of a
Memphis seminary. At Vander Meulen's and Hemphill's initial conference with Whaling he suggested a merger of Louisville and Columbia
Seminaries with the revived Southwestern Divinity School in Memphis,
creating one seminary for the lower Mississippi Valley — really, all of the
Deep South. The LPTS president and dean said that would be impossible
given their current commitments and endowment restrictions. Convinced that Louisville needed to expand its constituency by adding the
synods south of Kentucky as controlling synods, Whaling suggested a

---

9; *The Register* 19 (January, February, March 1930), 31-41, 65-66; and Minutes of the Board
(1920-1939), May 6, 1930. The 1930-1931 year was unique in that the Seminary had four presidents on its faculty simultaneously: Hemphill, now with emeritus status, Vander Meulen,
new president Cunningham, and future president Caldwell.

merger of Columbia and Louisville in Louisville. Consultations with the Columbia Seminary faculty came to naught. In essence, the Columbia faculty did not feel they could leave the seaboard area. Whaling agreed to accept the theology professorship at LPTS if the Seminary strengthened itself by expanding its synods as he deemed necessary for its long-term health.[16]

Louisville Seminary made overtures to the synods of Tennessee, Alabama, Mississippi, and Louisiana — the very synods Columbia wanted to add to its sphere of influence. With Whaling gone to Louisville Seminary, William McPheeters of the Columbia Seminary faculty wrote the synods to dissuade them from supporting LPTS. His argument was two-fold. First, he said that Kentucky Presbyterians had always opposed Benjamin Palmer's plan for one great university and divinity school for the Mississippi Valley of the PCUS. They were still trying to thwart Southwestern. More seriously, McPheeters asserted that Louisville Seminary was theologically unsound because of its ties to the PCUSA. The liberal doctrines and incorrect political role of that denomination infected LPTS, and the cooperation of the denominations in the school pointed inevitably to church union.

Vander Meulen responded by noting that the General Assembly of the entire denomination had voted against Palmer's proposal when it came before that body. Nor were Kentucky Presbyterians committed only to Louisville. He reminded the synods that Louisville Presbyterians had been willing to have the Seminary located in St. Louis or Nashville at its founding in 1893. Vander Meulen answered the second charge by asserting that LPTS had always been conservative — he himself was a student of Benjamin Warfield — and that the most traditional members of the faculty were often from the North. Nor had the Seminary ever supported or promoted reunion of the PCUS and PCUSA. Robert Webb would not have taught at Louisville if it had. Not only that, but Vander Meulen revealed that Whaling would not come to Louisville Seminary until the PCUS representation on the board was changed from one-half to two-thirds. In 1921 the membership of the board changed from twenty-four to thirty-six, and the PCUSA Synod of Kentucky elected one-third of the board and the PCUS synods of Kentucky, Missouri, and Appalachia two-thirds. The result of this maneuvering (and each seminary dispatched representatives to all the synod meetings) was that the Synod of Alabama joined in control of LPTS in 1923 and the Synod of Tennessee in 1924. This last effectively

16. Vander Meulen, President's Report for 1921, 10-12.

killed the chances of a divinity school at Southwestern when it moved to Memphis.[17]

There were more telling administrative changes at Louisville which involved the daily affairs of the school. For example, the library had always been informally run on a shoestring budget. Its collection was comprised of donations from pastors, usually at their deaths,[18] and the acquisitions the librarian (E. L. Warren) could secure with the $100 budgeted annually. In 1924 Mattie Witherspoon was hired as assistant librarian and the budget grew to $150 for books and $25 for periodicals. This began to address the inadequacy of the library, a weakness later consistently cited by accrediting agencies.[19] Warren retired in 1927 and the position remained vacant until Louise Conn was hired in 1929. She created the first card catalogue for the school.[20]

More important, Witherspoon undertook the responsibilities of bursar. The board created a committee to oversee the investment of the endowment, rather than the board as a whole making those decisions. Witherspoon, as bursar, would now have the checkbook and accounts, previously maintained by the board treasurer, at her desk. That allowed the president and dean to know the Seminary's ongoing financial status. Witherspoon held the position until 1949.[21] The bursar made administration of the Seminary easier for the president and dean. Administrative tasks grew with the student body and faculty, making Witherspoon's work all the more important. The fundraising function of the presidency in-

17. For this story, see Vander Meulen, President's Report for 1921; *The Register* 10 (October, November, December 1921), n.p.; *The Register* 13 (April, May, June 1924), n.p.; Vander Meulen, "The Seminary at Louisville and the Southern Church," April 14, 1923; Vander Meulen, "To the Members of the Board of the Presbyterian Theological Seminary at Louisville," manuscript, 1923; Minutes of the Board (1920-1939), May 3, 1921; October 10, 1921; May 1, 1923; and May 6, 1924. A few years later merger discussions with Xenia Theological Seminary in St. Louis raised the possibility that LPTS would become a seminary of three denominations, not two — the PCUS, PCUSA, and the United Presbyterian Church in North America (UPCNA). Faculty Minutes (1925-1932), October 19 and 25; November 1 and 8; and December 6, 1928.

18. One of the largest such gifts came from Stephen Yerkes to Danville Seminary upon his death, and the White Library still displays a plaque commemorating the bequest.

19. Minutes of the Board (1920-1939), May 5, 1924; May 6, 1924; May 5, 1925; and Executive Committee, December 9, 1922.

20. *The Register* 19 (January, February, March 1930): 11; Sanders, *History of Louisville Seminary,* 71-72.

21. "The Department of Investment and Finance," in Minutes of the Board (1920-1939); also Sanders, *History of Louisville Seminary,* 71-72. Witherspoon also served as something of an intendant of the campus.

creased. Consequently, in 1923 Louisville hired S. W. McGill, who had done fundraising and worked with the YMCA in Tennessee, as executive secretary for one year. In that role he was to relieve Vander Meulen of some administrative and development work. He only stayed six months.[22] One further sign of organizational modernization and professionalization of the Seminary was the institution of mandatory retirement at age seventy for faculty. Since no pension was in place, the Seminary would guarantee payment of salaries to retirees.[23] Then, in 1930, the board voted to place all professors in the pension plan of either the PCUSA or PCUS — ten percent of salary and housing allowance, with the Seminary paying three-fourths of the cost. The structure and management of the Seminary was slowly becoming more complex.

The growth of Louisville Seminary was made possible by, and required, expanding financial resources. LPTS operated at a deficit and drew money out of the endowment capital each year when Vander Meulen arrived, and he set out to end that practice. The income from endowment fell $21,000 short of the annual budget; that was the amount in annual giving required to operate in the black.[24] He resolved to accept invitations to preach at churches only if they agreed in advance that he could make a plea for gifts to the endowment and receive a collection for the operating budget. He came to believe this idea was the "leading of Divine Providence."[25] He went first to the church in Greenville, Kentucky, where board member W. G. Duncan was a member. That church of eighty-six members gave over $1,000 to the operating budget, and Duncan pledged $100,000 for the endowment.[26] By 1923 Vander Meulen reported that Duncan had paid most of that pledge and that the endowment had increased approximately $200,000 in the last year — partly as a result of a joint campaign by the two synods of Kentucky. That pushed the total endowment over $700,000, and for 1923-1924 the school escaped a deficit in spending. The endowment grew another $100,000 in 1924-1925.[27] The fi-

22. Minutes of the Board (1920-1939), May 1, 1923, and November 24, 1923.

23. Minutes of the Board (1920-1939), May 5, 1925, and May 1, 1928. Technically, retirement was already set at 70, but a professor could be re,-hired annually — and usually was. Now, effective 1930, that policy ceased.

24. Vander Meulen, President's Report for 1921, 3.

25. Vander Meulen, President's Report for 1921, 4.

26. Vander Meulen, President's Report for 1921, 4-5.

27. Vander Meulen, "To the Members of the Board of the Presbyterian Theological Seminary at Louisville," manuscript copy, 1923; Fifth Annual President's Report, May 5, 1925. Manuscript copy. LPTS Archives. *Minutes of the Sixty-third General Assembly of the*

nancial outlook grew sufficiently positive that in 1924 Louisville added a housing allowance to faculty salaries.[28]

Another noteworthy gift came to the Seminary in 1927. The board became anxious to fulfill the original desire of placing the LPTS campus out of the city center, and in 1927 appointed a committee to acquire a new site. The site "should contain an ample campus with quiet and beautiful surroundings and yet be so accessible to the churches and other advantages of the city that the students could take advantage of these for inspiration and service to their spiritual profit."[29] One motivating factor in the desire to move was surely the smog in Louisville. Alumni report that on some fall and winter days people drove automobiles with their lights on until after noon and that white shirts would turn gray from the fallout. The Seminary's huge coal furnace undoubtedly contributed its fair share to the pollution.[30]

In the meantime, Charles Pratt of the faculty had become close to R. S., C. K., and A. D. Reynolds of the Reynolds Aluminum company. Pratt, with their guidance, profited from the stock market boom of the 1920s. Together they bought a twenty-acre plot of land on Cannons Lane, near Seneca Park on the city's East side, and gave it to LPTS. The land came to be called the Pratt-Reynolds Campus. The board, understandably elated over such a gift, wanted to move the Seminary to the new site as soon as possible, with the Oxford Gothic structure downtown moved stone-by-stone to the suburban location to serve as the heart of the new campus. In 1930, just months after the stock market crash, Vander Meulen suggested they wait a while longer. The move would be expensive, requiring a financial campaign — it was obviously not an opportune time for that — and required the sale of the old campus, which should wait until real estate came out of its "present slump."[31] It would take three more decades to effect the move.

However, the financial growth under Vander Meulen did not prevent further struggle. When he first arrived on campus, the Seminary had nowhere to house the Vander Meulen family. With his low salary and with rental limited in the city, the president of LPTS lived in a second-story

---

Presbyterian Church in the United States (Richmond, Va.: Presbyterian Committee of Publication, 1923), 102-3.

28. Minutes of the Board (1920-1939), May 16, 1924.

29. McElroy, *Louisville Presbyterian Theological Seminary,* 145.

30. Henry P. Mobley, "The Administration of Louisville Presbyterian Theological Seminary, 1930s to the 1990s." Draft manuscript, 1992. Copy in author's possession.

31. Mobley, "Administration of LPTS," 145-46; Minutes of the Board (1920-1939), May 7, 1929, and May 6, 1930.

apartment on South First Street. One wonders why he declined an offer to teach homiletics at McCormick two years later.[32]

The growth in the endowment and annual giving that Vander Meulen achieved could not keep pace with rising expenses most years. In 1927 he noted that annual giving remained the most urgent financial need of Louisville Seminary, for the growing student body and faculty required more money for financial aid and faculty salaries and housing. The "supporting" synods generally were not providing support as governing bodies: LPTS received nothing from the Synod of Appalachia and the PCUSA Synod of Kentucky, nor from Alabama or Tennessee, although the school received gifts from individuals.[33] The financial pressure led Vander Meulen to ask the board in 1928 to allow him to resign. He observed that the key to the office now was fundraising, and he had increased the endowment over $500,000 in eight years. Annual giving was harder. Union Seminary received $19,000 and Columbia Seminary $16,000 annually from their controlling synods; Louisville Seminary received only $5,000. "The logical inference is that it is up to the President of the Seminary," Vander Meulen wrote. "For this failure of our controlling Synods adequately to support us makes it necessary, if the Seminary is to make ends meet and not to eat into permanent funds, which is suicidal, to conduct a constant solicitation of small gifts for current expenses among private individuals and the burden of this naturally falls on the president."[34]

Vander Meulen could only meet the obligation by repeatedly appealing to friends in Louisville, his former church in Oak Park, which had no direct interest in LPTS, and other places. To be a friend of his meant that one "may expect to pay for it by being solicited for the Seminary." Further, Vander Meulen did not believe his talents were "executive" but in the classroom, and he wished to return to full-time teaching.[35] The stress manifested itself in 1926, when his doctors ordered absolute rest and Vander Meulen dropped his administrative and teaching duties for approximately two months.[36] The board accepted his resignation, effective upon electing a replacement. That took two years.

Life at Louisville had an intimate character, due in part to the campus

32. Vander Meulen, President's Report for 1921, 14, and "To the Members of the Board," 1923.

33. Vander Meulen, Seventh Annual President's Report, May 3, 1927.

34. Vander Meulen, Eighth Annual President's Report, May 1, 1928.

35. Vander Meulen, Eighth Annual President's Report.

36. Minutes of the Faculty of the Presbyterian Theological Seminary of Kentucky (1925-1932), March 19, 1926. LPTS Archives.

arrangement, which joined living, study, worship, and office space, and due in part to intentional efforts to build fellowship in the community. The faculty continued to exercise a keen interest in and oversight of the lives of their students. *The Register* for March 1936 announced that the following school year would begin with a two-day retreat of faculty and students — a practice maintained into the 1960s.[37] The retreat was an opportunity for upper-class students to help entering students get acclimated to Seminary life and learn what they could expect. It was also a period when the participants, especially the faculty, talked about their lives of faith and pastoral identity. Again, the faculty exhibited the idea of the pastor-theologian, and the outing closed with a worship service that included Communion. Daily chapel continued at the Seminary, as did the special days for mission and student prayer groups.

In 1923 the students themselves described life at the Seminary. They related the usual information regarding study and devotional life, emphasizing the close-knit nature of the Seminary community. There were also social outlets, through dances at the YWCA and athletics at the YMCA. A quartet formed which sang at church meetings, picnics, prisons, mission stations, and occasionally out of town. A small Seminary orchestra sprang up as well.[38] By 1926 there was even a basketball team that toured the Upper South and played against church-related colleges. Their record was 4-2.[39] Perhaps the most concrete illustration of the spirit of caring that obtained at LPTS occurred in 1931. A student's mother died what faculty minutes called a "tragic death," and the young man was so devastated that his roommate accompanied him home at the Seminary administration's suggestion. Students donated one-half of the cost and the faculty provided the rest so this friend could console his bereaved roommate. The giving is even more touching when one recalls that this came in the deepening of the Depression.[40] Vander Meulen seemed correct to describe LPTS to prospective students as a school where one could gain a broader sense of church cooperation and catholicity, be intellectually challenged, and experience an environment which enlivened the student's spiritual life at the same time.[41]

---

37. *The Register* 25 (March 1936): 4. LPTS Archives.

38. "Where and How at the Seminary" (n.p., 1923). This was a promotional pamphlet for prospective students written totally by Seminary students. LPTS Archives.

39. *The Register* 15 (January, February, March 1926): 40-41. LPTS Archives.

40. Faculty Minutes (1925-1932), November 5, 1931. Such examples of caring within the Seminary community could be multiplied many times over, from each era of the school's history.

41. *The Register* 19 (April, May, June 1930): 3-4. LPTS Archives.

During the inter-war period the Seminary community took its first steps (excepting Breckinridge's Civil War activities) into social ministry, albeit very cautiously. Protestantism had, from the earliest days of the new nation, addressed social problems through a web of voluntary societies. Slavery, war, dueling, alcohol, prison conditions, and women's rights only begin to suggest the range of reforms undertaken. With notable exceptions, however, when Protestants dealt with social ills they and their churches did so in the conviction that one changed social conditions by transforming — really, regenerating — individuals. It was only at the end of the nineteenth century, with the coming of urbanization and industrialization, that the Social Gospel movement emerged to argue that there exist social structures of sin that require changes to the systems and institutions in which people live.

Given the denomination's "distinctive doctrine" of the spirituality of the church, the Social Gospel made little headway in the PCUS. That, combined with the generally conservative nature of Louisville Seminary, prevented a social witness from developing there — although it was clear that, within its individualistic limits, the Seminary took an active role in meeting the social needs of the city (witness, for example, the John Little Mission).[42] The PCUSA had undertaken a social witness through its Bureau of Social Service under Charles Stelzle in 1911, but it operated against substantial opposition. Only in the 1930s did the PCUS establish its Committee on Moral and Social Welfare. Louisville Seminary, then, was acting roughly in concert with the denominations, although its social stances did not address economics.[43]

In 1930 a Mr. Richmond, identified as a "colored pastor" in Louisville, sought to begin work at the LPTS with a view to receiving his B.D. A faculty committee studied what might be done. Pratt reported back that, of course, Kentucky law forbade integrated classes in educational institutions, so that Richmond could not be admitted to regular classes. A possi-

---

42. The Seminary would also speak out when it believed that intrusions were being made into the religious life of the city or its people. Note, for instance, that in 1930 the faculty issued a protest to a proposal to hold a dance to raise money for the Community Chest when it learned the dance "would in effect be entirely on Sunday." Faculty Minutes (1925-1932), February 13, 1930.

43. Donald K. Gorrell, *The Age of Social Responsibility,* examines the work of the PCUSA in social ministry, especially through the work of Charles Stelzle, but says nothing of the PCUS. For the PCUS see Thompson, *Presbyterians in the South,* vols. 2 and 3, and, to a lesser extent, Joel L. Alvis, Jr., *Religion and Race: Southern Presbyterians, 1946-1983* (Tuscaloosa, Ala.: The University of Alabama Press, 1994).

ble solution was for the faculty to work privately with Richmond but not to enter it into the records of the Seminary. That clearly precluded the granting of a degree. Vander Meulen suggested that John Davis, long-time board member and attorney who provided much free legal work for Louisville Seminary, be consulted to determine whether it would be possible to conduct separate classes for African-Americans on campus. There is no further mention of the matter in Seminary records, so the entire discussion presumably came to naught. Perhaps Richmond, faced again with the indignities of segregation and prejudice, dropped the affair.

Louisville Seminary was not yet ready to defy Jim Crow, although there did seem a genuine concern for serving the educational needs of African-Americans. Julian Price Love, for example, led a Bible study for the Ministers' Alliance of Colored Ministers of Louisville during 1933-1934.[44] Further, the faculty definitely opposed violence against African-Americans and was willing to take a public stance. At its January 25, 1934, meeting the faculty responded to the lynching of a man in Hazard, Kentucky, with a telegram to the governor which it also released to the *Courier-Journal:* "Deeply deplore yesterday's lynching in our state. The Faculty of the Louisville Presbyterian Seminary would express to you its concern in this matter and respectfully urge that you give statement through the press to the country at large, expressing for yourself and for our citizenship strongest disapproval of such lawlessness."[45]

Pratt appears to have been the most interested in social application of the gospel. In 1933 he asserted in a book review that the social gospel was the gospel of Jesus, for he taught one gospel with an individual and social dimension. The church should involve itself in economic and industrial issues, for the "law of love, human brotherhood, [and] the obligation to live unselfishly" were all central to Jesus' teaching. Love, reviewing the same book, was lukewarm regarding the book but enthusiastic about its ideas.[46] Pratt also held membership in an unnamed "commission" trying to halt the lynching of African-Americans. In a lament that missionaries had offered up for decades, he declared that "America stands condemned in lands such as India and China for group sadism and every minister of the gospel should speak in no uncertain terms from the pulpit so as to create a Christian public sentiment that will make lynching no more."[47]

44. Faculty Minutes (1925-1932), September 25, 1930, and March 1, 1934.

45. Minutes of the Faculty of the Louisville Presbyterian Seminary (1932-1940), January 25, 1934. LPTS Archives.

46. *The Register* 22 (July, August, September 1933): 13-15. LPTS Archives.

47. *The Register* 22 (October, November, December 1933): 19. LPTS Archives.

The horror of World War I, combined with revelations of profiteering by U.S. weapons manufacturers, manipulative propaganda on the part of the Allies as well as the Central Powers, the absence of any evidence that the war had made conditions in Europe better, and the failure of the war to achieve its idealistic goals (that is, to be "the war to end all wars" and "to make the world safe for democracy") led to a widespread movement of opposition to war in the 1920s and 1930s. A number of denominations pledged never again to support war, and a broad movement of pacifists, socialists, and varieties of antiwar activists mobilized to promote disarmament and the settlement of international disputes without resort to arms. Perhaps the apex of the effort came with the ratification of the Kellogg-Briand Treaty by over two dozen nations, agreeing they would not make war.[48]

Young people, especially in the churches, often joined in the sentiment to stop war. In 1931 nineteen Louisville Seminary students petitioned the faculty to offer a course on "Peace and Disarmament,"

> in view of the forces in this nation which make for excessive armaments and for war, in view of the need for public sentiment and Christian conscience in the face of possible war . . . in view of the close and vital implications which are contained in our Christian religion on the question of war and peace, and in view of our felt need for thinking through these implications and examining the evidence available on the subject. . . .[49]

The petitioners all promised to enroll in the course if the faculty offered it. The faculty decided to make the course available, to be taught by President

---

48. The definitive attack on the attitudes of Christians in the United States during World War I was Ray H. Abrams, *Preachers Present Arms: The Role of the American Churches and Clergy in World Wars I and II, with Some Observations on the War in Vietnam*, rev. ed. (Scottsdale, Pa.: Herald Press, 1969). His conclusions have been modified by John Piper, *The American Churches in World War I* (Athens, Ohio.: Ohio University Press, 1985). There are a number of studies of the interwar peace movement and the attempt of American Protestants to come to grips with the fascist designs of Germany and Italy. See, for instance, Peter Brock, *Twentieth-Century Pacifism* (New York: Van Nostrand Reinhold, 1970); Charles Chatfield, *For Peace and Justice: Pacifism in America, 1914-1941* (Knoxville: University of Tennessee Press, 1971); Charles DeBenedetti, *Origins of the Modern American Peace Movement, 1915-1929*, KTO Studies in American History (Millwood, N.Y.: KTO Press, 1978); and Donald Meyer, *The Protestant Search for Political Realism, 1919-1941*, 2nd ed. (Middletown, Conn.: Wesleyan University Press, 1988).

49. Faculty Minutes (1925-1932), November 19, 1931.

Cunningham with the help of Love and Pratt.[50] It may have been taught as an extra course, for it was never listed in any Seminary publications. Three years later the local Peace Action Committee in the city asked the faculty to write to Kentucky's senators opposing the Vincent Navy Bill, which would have increased the size of the Navy and military spending for it. The legislation had already passed the House. The faculty decided in this instance to act on the matter as each member felt led, but they would not act as a body.[51] One should note in this regard that Love was known within and without the Seminary for his opposition to war and was often referred to as a pacifist. He did not call himself a pacifist, but did oppose militarism. Precise definitions aside, Love clearly sympathized with the movement to prevent war and endured the denunciations of others for his stance.[52]

Louisville's first steps into the social arena were obviously tentative. This undoubtedly arose from the fundamentally conservative approach of the faculty and students and a concern to stay alert to the sentiment of the people on whom the Seminary depended for its financial well-being. This was reinforced in 1932 when Vander Meulen reported to the faculty that he had counseled on their behalf with Carl Winters, a Th.M. student, "to investigate the possible tendency to over emphasis of the social gospel." He said that Winters took the "warning and advice of the Faculty kindly."[53] One also notes that in 1936 the board passed a resolution to "direct the faculty to admonish the students from time to time, as occasion may require, regarding their participation in political and social activities, urging upon them the imperative necessity of refraining from activities which shall reflect unfavorably on the Christian ministry."[54] The minutes give no indication regarding what student action prompted the board's comment.

Both the ethos and purpose of theological education at LPTS began to receive particular scrutiny from the faculty. They became concerned about their role in the preparation of their students for ministry. Was the Seminary's function primarily the academic and intellectual education of candidates for the ministry, or were they to judge the students' fitness for ministry and Christian life? At the close of the 1925-1926 school year Vander Meulen noted that Louisville had dismissed three students "whose

50. Faculty Minutes (1925-1932), December 10, 1931.

51. Faculty Minutes (1932-1940), February 15, 1934.

52. For a discussion of Love's attitude on the subject, see Rick Nutt, *Toward Peacemaking: Presbyterians in the South and National Security, 1945-1983* (Tuscaloosa, Ala.: The University of Alabama Press, 1994), 54.

53. Faculty Minutes (1925-1932), March 31, 1932.

54. Minutes of the Board (1920-1939), May 5, 1936.

conduct did not seem to us to commend them as candidates for the ministry. More and more, it has borne in upon us that only the Seminary can stand between the Church and an unworthy ministry. The presbyteries cannot be trusted to do this, perhaps partly because they do not have sufficient access to the facts and partly because of their commendable joy that a young man should offer himself for the gospel ministry."[55] To some extent, at least, the faculty perceived itself as a gatekeeper to the ministry in more than just academics.

The faculty continued to wrestle with the question. Love raised it in 1933, and the faculty minutes recorded his query in a pointed fashion: "Dr. Love raised the question whether our graduating the men involves our judgment merely as to their academic fitness or as to their general fitness for the ministry."[56] Apparently the faculty could not fully resolve the dilemma, for in 1935 they asked the board to define "more fully than has been done in the Constitution the basis upon which students shall be graduated from the Seminary." The faculty suggested four criteria: "evidence of Christian character"; personal attributes that promised "usefulness" in the ministry; fulfilling all academic requirements; and a faith sufficiently evangelical (by which they meant Reformed). The faculty would devise a method of conference with students to determine their status on all but the third point.[57] There is no record of a response from the board.[58]

The faculty took their proposal seriously. When approving the graduates for the class of 1935, one student prompted extensive discussion. There was no question of the student's academic achievement, but some professors had doubts regarding his theology and commitment and wondered if they should recommend him to the board for a degree. They decided to meet with the student and recommended him for the B.D. following "a clear and emphatic statement of his evangelical faith and purpose."[59] This was just one more way in which the Seminary manifested its self-identity as an institution of the church, with responsibility for the work of its graduates in the church, and as a place of caring and mutual upbuilding of the candidates it educated.

---

55. Vander Meulen, Sixth Annual President's Report, May 4, 1926. Manuscript copy. LPTS Archives.

56. Faculty Minutes (1932-1940), January 12, 1933.

57. Faculty Minutes (1932-1940), October 17, 24, and 31, 1935.

58. This question of the tension between the necessity of scholarly academic preparation of students and the responsibility to the church for preparing students for ministry is treated by Cherry, *Hurrying Toward Zion,* chapter five, "Two Yokes of Responsibility."

59. Faculty Minutes (1932-1940), May 7, 1935.

Theology and Theological Education

Although Protestantism in the United States underwent disturbing theological conflict during the 1910s and 1920s, LPTS remained relatively untouched by the dispute and its theology continued to be conservatively Calvinistic. That is all the more remarkable given the intensity of the fundamentalist-modernist battles waged in the PCUSA and the prominence of such Presbyterians as J. Gresham Machen and William Jennings Bryan in the debate as a whole. Records of the Seminary indicate no turmoil regarding the issue.[60]

Henry Dosker, the Dutch Calvinist who taught church history, remained as traditional as ever. Indeed, he may have been the most sympathetic to fundamentalism of all the faculty, for at his death his children established a fellowship in his name to be given to an outstanding graduate in church history who could affirm the principles for which Dosker "valiantly contended": the deity of Jesus, the historicity of the virginal conception, the physical resurrection of Jesus, the doctrine of the substitutionary atonement, and other basic tenets of Presbyterianism.[61] In 1925 the faculty began to review books for *The Register,* rendering a service to pastors and alumni. Often the reviews revealed as much about the reviewers as they did the books. Dosker's assessment of A. C. McGiffert's *The God of the Early Christians* was that it was a "ruthless handling, in a most rationalistic vein, of one of the greatest mysteries of the faith."[62]

In theology, the legacy of Breckinridge, Beattie, and Webb made itself felt. Thornton Whaling reviewed YMCA evangelist Sherwood Eddy's *New Challenges to Faith.* Eddy, a popularizer of theological trends, undertook to demonstrate how the church could acknowledge the truth of scientific methods and discoveries, especially in the field of psychology, and reformulate Christian belief in terms that would appeal to a generation

60. On the fundamentalist-modernist controversy in the PCUSA, see Lefferts A. Loetscher, *The Broadening Church: A Study of Theological Issues in the Presbyterian Church since 1869* (Philadelphia: University of Pennsylvania Press, 1954); Marsden, *Fundamentalism and American Culture;* and Bradley J. Longfield, *The Presbyterian Controversy: Fundamentalists, Modernists, and Moderates* (Oxford: Oxford University Press, 1991).

61. List of Bequests and Endowments of Louisville Presbyterian Seminary together with Known Conditions Attaching to Them. Folder "Finances: General," Box "President's Office, 1966-1967," LPTS Archives.

62. *The Register* 14 (October, November, December 1925): 10-11. McGiffert, a well-known historian at Union Seminary in New York, was among the liberals who sought to recast theology in concepts informed by the intellectual and scientific developments in the nineteenth and twentieth centuries.

reared in a scientific worldview. Whaling noted Eddy's achievement of his goal and recommended it for study by pastors and students as an example of modernist thought and where it erred. He then rejoiced at the re-release of Dabney's *Systematic and Polemic Theology* and hoped it would prompt a re-issue of James Henley Thornwell, Breckinridge, Beattie, and others. That would provide a Presbyterian counterweight to the popular Eddy and Harry Emerson Fosdick, who were "theological pygmies" by contrast.[63]

Andrew K. Rule, called in 1927 to teach church history after Dosker's death, took on apologetics when Whaling retired in 1929. A student, even devotee, of Warfield, Rule would offer three decades of conservative theological instruction at LPTS. His conservatism, however, was of an open, intellectually honest, and irenic faith commitment that sought common ground rather than contention.

Rule's treatment of science bespoke his style of conservatism. As the discipline of physics confronted the world with the theory of relativity and its consequent paradigm shift in how the universe could be understood, he took up the task of relating physics to faith.[64] Rule argued that a minister had to be aware of changes in science and the scientific worldview in order to have any hope of preaching the gospel with relevance in the contemporary context. The most important recent changes had been in the field of physics; new discoveries had thrown into question the Newtonian mechanistic physics that reduced the world to laws of cause and effect. First, the theory of relativity posited that nothing could be measured absolutely, but only relatively, as time became the fourth dimension. Werner Heisenberg added to Einstein's work the principle of indeterminacy, taken up in the realm of sub-atomic physics by Arthur Eddington and James Jeans. Christians, Rule suggested, could use the argument of indeterminacy to refute a positivistic or mechanistic view of the world that precluded the guiding hand of God. To build Christian theology on it, however, would be a mistake, for indeterminacy would eventually lead to chaos and was therefore not scriptural. The Christian could further take heart in a growing humility by many scientists, who as a group had hitherto overreached in their claims for scientific methodology and explanations of the world.

Science itself was beginning to hint at teleological, rather than

63. *The Register* 16 (July, August, September 1927): 12-13, and 16 (October, November, December 1927): 11-12. Eddy and Fosdick were popularizers of others' work. While important and intelligent liberals, they were hardly the leading theologians of that school of thought.

64. Andrew Rule, "Some Thoughts on the Spiritual Significance of Recent Changes in the Science of Physics," *The Register* 22 (October, November, December 1933): 3-13.

mechanistic, evidences in nature. Eddington and Jeans used the language of mind to describe the essential nature of reality; the atom looked more and more like an organism (that is, a society of electrons, protons, and neutrons) and not a simple unit of inert matter; and biology and chemistry were showing a "teleological fitness of the inorganic world." Science might be returning to an appreciation of the spiritual, and in that the Christian could take heart.[65] Rule kept an open mind on the question of evolution, provided it was theistically grounded. He argued, in fact, that the religion-science controversy of the day was not that at all, for science properly conceived had no conflict with faith. The dispute was between two rival philosophies: theistic and naturalistic. Rule sought a mediating stance, positing that "there have been self-sacrifice and self-interest on both sides; obscurantism and the pure love of truth on both; a consistent adherence to one's own proper business and a readiness to stray into other fields on both."[66]

In the 1930s Rule and Vander Meulen offered a class on Modern Tendencies in Theology. The course concentrated on the emergence of liberal theology from the beginning of the nineteenth century to the fourth decade of the twentieth. The course introduction made clear the approach the instructors would take. Modern theology has been dominated by the "humanistic mood," they observed, by which they meant an emphasis on the dignity and inherent goodness of the individual, an emphasis on "brotherhood" which "tends to run into Sentimentalism," and a tendency to abandon a description of reality to science and reduce religion to the realm of ethics.[67] Central to understanding liberal theology was that, in accepting the empirical scientific worldview, it separated fact and value. Only that could be accepted as fact which could be quantified or verified by testing. Yet empiricism, most theologically influential in the work of Immanuel Kant, undercut the confidence that human beings can know things in themselves. All humans can know is what we perceive of the reality external to us. Thus, religion cannot properly speak about reality in itself, but only human relations in it; religion was reduced to speaking about value. Liberalism, following that lead, made Christianity, in effect, an ethical system. Rule and Vander Meulen rejected such an epistemological limitation of the faith:

65. Rule, "Some Thoughts."
66. *The Register* 24 (April, May, June 1935): 7.
67. Rule and Vander Meulen, "First Semester Course in Modern Tendencies in Theology (Liberal)." Manuscript, ca. 1933. LPTS Archives.

Obviously, we are a part of the world-system of which these external objects are also a part; and, if it is properly called a system at all, the parts of it are harmoniously related. The knowledge-relation between our minds and external objects is surely no accident.... It would follow, would it not, that the laws whereby our minds bring order into the raw materials of the senses are the same as the laws of the things themselves. The external objects are not distorted in the process of being known. We do, or can come to, know things as they are.[68]

The professors traced the development of humanist-liberal theology from its beginnings in the work of Kant, whose emphases were taken up by Friedrich Schleiermacher, followed by Albrecht Ritschl and Adolf von Harnack. They also surveyed, through a study of Albert Schweitzer's *The Quest of the Historical Jesus,* the course of New Testament study in such people as David Strauss, Johannes Weiss, and, of course, Schweitzer's own understanding of Jesus' messianism. Rule's and Vander Meulen's assessment was the standard conservative view of liberal Protestantism: in giving in to scientific and humanistic presuppositions about the nature of reality and human being the liberals denied the supernatural basis of Scripture, abandoned the idea of original sin, and sacrificed the majesty and transcendence of God for an emphasis on God's immanence. Most seriously, liberal New Testament studies denied the deity of Jesus and Jesus' own messianic awareness. Therefore, they were wrong.[69] Against the liberals, the course commended to the students the work of Warfield, W. Douglas MacKenzie (in particular *The Christ of the Christian Faith,* 1933), and Geerhardus Vos (*The Self-Disclosure of Jesus,* 1926). The first and last of those evangelical theologians, Vander Meulen believed, were "simply crushing" to liberalism. What they demonstrated, among other points, was the clearly messianic self-consciousness of Jesus that disclosed Jesus' divinity and work of redemption. Vander Meulen also spoke favorably of the work of Rudolf Otto, whom one would not consider a conservative, whose *The Idea of the Holy* made a strong argument for the reality and existence of God as an objective truth.[70]

The end of the course included a discussion of the "Theology of Crisis" emerging under the influence of Karl Barth and Emil Brunner. The teachers welcomed their move away from liberalism but urged caution before one embraced it wholesale. Rule, for example, had only begun to read

68. Rule and Vander Meulen, "First Semester Course."
69. Rule and Vander Meulen, "First Semester Course."
70. Rule and Vander Meulen, "First Semester Course."

Barth, but thought that he reacted too strongly to liberalism with his rejection of the possibility of any natural theology. There were also points at which Barth and Brunner differed from orthodox theology — that is, from Calvinist conservatism. First, Barth adopted the use of a higher criticism that rejected the doctrine of the plenary verbal inspiration of Scripture, suggesting the Bible is the Word of God only in an existential moment of experiencing the Eternal. Second, Barth would speak of God only as Wholly Other, in essence unknowable except in relation to creation. He thought orthodoxy made of God too much an object of our knowing. Finally, Rule questioned Barth's denial of orthodox "historism." Barth argued that the orthodox conservative built too much on historical facts, when in fact history is too relative as a proof of the absolute. Faith and theology, Barth argued, must be based on the eternal. Historical events, above all the resurrection, were central to Christianity, Rule held.[71]

These course lectures reveal that students at Louisville in the early 1930s received an exposure to key figures of modern Protestant theology: Schleiermacher, Harnack, Otto, Barth, and so on. The treatment was limited and filtered through the convictions of conservative instructors. The students did not, apparently, read the work of the theologians themselves, nor were they yet learning about the work of the Niebuhr brothers on the American scene. A study of the theology taught in Presbyterian seminaries in the twentieth century by John M. Mulder and Lee Wyatt holds that Barthian, or neo-orthodox, thought began to appear by the 1930s.[72] Louisville was not yet a school where neo-orthodoxy was taught (that occurred with the arrival of Hugh T. Kerr, Jr., in 1936), but it was addressed and acknowledged. Mulder and Wyatt also found that at this time historical theology began to appear alongside purely systematic or dogmatic theology — that is, theology treated as it grew out of and changed with historical contexts over against a set of doctrines existing eternally and absolutely.

71. Rule and Vander Meulen, "First Semester Course."

72. John M. Mulder and Lee A. Wyatt, "The Predicament of Pluralism: The Study of Theology in Presbyterian Seminaries Since the 1920s," in Milton J Coalter, John M. Mulder, and Louis B. Weeks, *The Pluralistic Vision: Presbyterians and Mainstream Protestant Education and Leadership,* the Presbyterian Presence Series (Louisville: Westminster/John Knox Press, 1992). The leading neo-orthodox writers in the United States were the brothers Reinhold and H. Richard Niebuhr. They profoundly affected theology in the nation through such books as Reinhold's *Moral Man and Immoral Society* (New York: Charles Scribner's Sons, 1932) and *The Nature and Destiny of Man,* 2 vols. (New York: Charles Scribner's Sons, 1941) and H. Richard's *The Kingdom of God in America* (Chicago and New York: Willett, Clark and Co., 1937) and *Christ and Culture* (New York: Harper and Brothers, 1951).

Rule specifically resisted that trend. He referred often to Willard L. Sperry's *Yes, But — The Bankruptcy of Apologetics.* Sperry, a chastened liberal in the aftermath of World War I, said that, even though liberalism had been proven faulty, the day of the older apologetics was past. Religious truth, he argued, was not a system received "once for all" via revelation, but a process of discovery that rendered no doctrine final. Rule rejected that assertion.[73] Thus, the enormous theological shifts occasioned by the horror and disillusionment of World War I were making only the smallest impact on Louisville Seminary.

The historical-critical study of Scripture made no greater inroads at Louisville than did liberal theology. The understanding of the Bible as a theological text was giving way in much of biblical scholarship to one in which the Bible reflected the historical situations in which its books were written. But biblical theology continued to dominate at LPTS. The acquisition of a collection of Palestinian pottery illustrates the point well. Melvin Grove Kyle, president of Xenia Theological Seminary in St. Louis and a leading biblical archaeologist, discovered the collection of 400 pieces, which dated from pre-Abrahamic to early Christian times.[74] Kyle believed it would be the premier collection in the United States, a claim given credence by its use by James Pritchard in his *The Ancient Near East in Pictures* and the request of a professor at Hebrew University in Jerusalem to have pictures of some pieces for classroom use. Brainerd Lemon, LPTS board member, bought the artifacts in 1929 for the Seminary and gave money to endow a Department of Palestinian Archaeology which would offer lectures and classes on the subject. The antiquities, now displayed in the Seminary library, were named the Lemon Collection. Kyle became the Permanent Lecturer in the department.

The aim of archaeology for the Seminary became clear in Kyle's first lectures, which defended the Mosaic authorship of the Pentateuch and the archaeological testimony to the reliability of the Old Testament.[75] Indeed, Vander Meulen was glad to have the Lemon Collection precisely because it "corroborates and establishes in a wonderful way the historical accuracy and reliability of the Old Testament. The students of the seminary will have the visible evidence before them of the trustworthiness of the Bible.

---

73. Rule, "Introduction to Apologetics," class notes of Thomas A. Schaefer. Ca. 1941. LPTS Archives.

74. Xenia Seminary had moved to St. Louis, and would subsequently move to Pennsylvania to help create Pittsburgh-Xenia Theological Seminary.

75. See *The Register* 45 (Winter 1956): 6-7; Minutes of the Board (1920-1939), May 6, 1930; and *The Register* 19 (January, February, March 1930): 41. LPTS Archives.

The destructive higher criticism of the Bible has been largely speculative and theoretical. The science of Archaeology has proved to be the concrete and practical refutation of the speculations of the higher critics."[76] Shortly after Vander Meulen's declaration, Cotton reviewed a book which, among other assertions, placed the book of Daniel in the Maccabean period and much of the Psalter in the post-exilic era. He disliked the assumptions on which the study was based, calling it the "ripened fruit of the Graf-Wellhausen theory."[77]

Louisville Seminary, then, maintained its conservative theological and biblical orientation. However, it seems self-consciously to have eschewed the stridency of fundamentalism, as had the PCUSA as a whole in its debates of the 1920s. Vander Meulen wrote of the Seminary that "it refuses to be tagged by any such names as Fundamentalist or Modernist. But it makes no secret of the fact that it holds to the conservative and evangelical, not the 'liberal' view of theology."[78] Perhaps Thornton Whaling best expressed the LPTS stance in an article, "The Crisis of the Presbyterian and Reformed Churches."[79] The *Presbyterian Standard* had asserted that progressive theology was making inroads in the PCUS. Whaling urged readers to remember 2 Timothy 2:24-25, which exhorts believers to patience and meekness in teaching those who oppose them. With that in mind Whaling noted that ordination in the PCUS required one to accept the standards' "system of doctrine" with liberty in many particulars. Whaling suggested that people might generally follow the lead of the Presbyterian and Reformed Churches of America, which had agreed that the Westminster Confession and Catechisms, Belgic Confession, Heidelberg Catechism, and the Canons of the Synod of Dort constituted, in essential agreement, different expressions of the same system. If there were those who could not accept historical Reformed theology, he suggested they be allowed to withdraw to another denomination with charity.

Whaling then argued that the so-called progressive theology was, in fact, antiquated. Liberalism bore the marks, he asserted, of Neo-Platonism, Gnosticism, and Pantheism. The church needed to exercise better oversight

76. Vander Meulen, President's Ninth Annual Report, May 7, 1929. LPTS Archives.

77. *The Register* 19 (July, August, September 1930). LPTS Archives. The Graf-Wellhausen Theory, also known as the Documentary Hypothesis, asserts that the Pentateuch was not written by Moses, but rather assembled by different redactors over time.

78. Vander Meulen, "Friendly Chat Number Two," *The Register* 19 (April, May, June 1930): 3. See also page 5. LPTS Archives.

79. Whaling, "The Crisis of the Presbyterian and Reformed Churches," *The Register* 12 (July, August, September 1923): n.p.

of its colleges and seminaries to ensure that the standards were taught, and the church should be ready to try for heresy those who strayed.[80] In retrospect the contradictions of Whaling's thoughts stand out, but as a whole may also represent a true indication of Louisville's position through the first half of the century: definitely conservative, sometimes rigidly so, but generally moderate, cautious, and usually charitable when confronted by differing opinions.

In the same article in which Vander Meulen declared Louisville Seminary's conservatism he noted that, in a rapidly changing world, the church had to find appropriate language and new forms to communicate the gospel.[81] It was in the 1920s and 1930s that LPTS began to develop more fully the practical area of theological education for which the Seminary has most distinguished itself.[82]

In 1921 W. G. Duncan began to pay on his pledge of $100,000 for the Mary Hamilton Duncan Memorial Fund. Of the pledge, $80,000 was to endow a chair in "Church Efficiency, the Sunday School and Young People's work, or like subjects," and the other $20,000 funded a lecture series and library acquisitions in the field. Vander Meulen was the first person to hold the professorship, which eventually came to be called the Mary Hamilton Duncan Chair of Religious Education.[83] Duncan continued to give money for the library to purchase works in Christian education ($700 for 1926-1927); according to Vander Meulen, that enabled LPTS to amass the best library in the field of any Presbyterian seminary.[84] The endowment of a chair in the field points up the growing importance not only of the Sunday school itself but also the emphasis on organization and methods of education that would make a church's program most appealing and effective.

The changing focus of Christian education as a discipline became clearer in 1925 when Vander Meulen vacated the Duncan chair to fill the

---

80. Whaling, "The Crisis."

81. Vander Meulen, "Friendly Chat Number Two," 3.

82. As this history will show, the Seminary has had a series of leading teachers of Christian education: Lewis Sherrill, Ellis Nelson, and Craig Dykstra to name only three. It has pioneered in field education under C. Morton Hanna and its program of Congregation-Based Ministry in the 1970s-1980s. David Steere moved the Seminary into a renowned program in pastoral care. And preaching, historically, has been a strength at LPTS.

83. Minutes of the Board (1920-1939), Executive Committee, February 15, 1921, and plenary board, May 6, 1930; Vander Meulen, "Review of the Past Ten Years," 5. Duncan felt called, as a youth, to ministry, but the death of his father prevented it. He took a keen lifelong interest in theological education.

84. Vander Meulen, Seventh Annual Report.

Herrick Johnson chair in homiletics, where his true enthusiasm lay. The search for a replacement proved difficult. The most qualified people with experience, according to Vander Meulen, were all adherents of liberal theology, which rendered them unacceptable. This was the point at which Lewis J. Sherrill, who was a pastor in Tennessee and already directing that synod's education program, was hired. Upon coming to the Seminary to fill the Duncan chair in 1925, he began to pursue a doctorate at Yale under Luther Weigle, teaching all his courses in the spring semester and studying at New Haven in the summer and fall.[85]

This marked the beginning of the application of psychology (especially what today would be called developmental psychology) to the understanding of education. How should a church divide its children into classes? What material should be introduced and when? No longer was Christian education the memorization of the catechism and Bible stories. One notes, for example, that the first two Duncan lecturers — Weigle and William McDougall of Duke University — titled their presentations "The Psychological Bases of Christian Education" and "Modern Materialism in the Light of Psychology."[86] Sherrill's career confirmed the wisdom of choosing him for the position. Renowned as an innovator and leader in the field, he became Executive Secretary of Religious Education in the PCUS in 1929 and the Executive Secretary of the Conference of Theological Seminaries in the U.S. and Canada. Sherrill was central in developing accreditation practices for seminaries and wrote extensively, all in addition to holding LPTS' deanship for two decades. Sherrill finished his career at Union Seminary in New York, where he moved in 1950.[87]

Not only was education becoming more important to the curriculum, but the practical experience, or fieldwork, of the students received a more formal structure. The Seminary found that student preaching created problems, although its lure seemed obvious: students needed money and vacant churches required preachers. The faculty held, however, that student preaching should be closely monitored lest it lead to sloppy habits (writing sermons too hurriedly, most often) and detract from proper semi-

85. Vander Meulen, Sixth Annual Report, manuscript copy. LPTS Archives. Handy, *A History of Union Theological Seminary*, 125, observes that the early years of the twentieth century saw a distinct emphasis on Christian education emerging in theological education. Weigle was renowned in the field.

86. *The Register* 15 (January, February, March 1926): 6; and 18 (January, February, March 1929): 11.

87. Minutes of the Board (1920-1939), May 7, 1929, and Faculty Minutes (1932-1940), April 11, 1935.

nary study — not only reading class assignments but the "collateral reading" the seminarian should accomplish. In effect, Charles Pratt was asked to assume the duties of the first director of fieldwork in 1925. A survey of other seminaries found that they all struggled with the issue, so LPTS devised a policy that generally reflected the informal practice of the past. All students were assigned to a site for one-to-three hours of volunteer work each week. The theory was that the work would be good for the students' spiritual lives and provide experience proclaiming the gospel in some way. Later, in 1934, rather than performing volunteer work, juniors were assigned to work in churches throughout the city — learning through an apprentice relationship with their pastors.[88] Further, it was decided that juniors would not fill vacant pulpits at all, and middlers and seniors only with permission of the faculty, presumably in the person of Pratt. Significantly for the formation of a pastoral identity, the students initiated a plan by which the student body was divided into groups, with a professor for each group providing spiritual, academic, and vocational guidance.[89]

In 1930 the field education possibilities expanded a little more when Sherrill offered credit for a summer practicum in religious education. Seminarians did not organize or conduct church education programs, but analyzed the ways in which a particular congregation carried out that ministry and then returned to campus for meetings to reflect on what they had learned, how they might make use of it, and how the congregation could benefit from their observations. There was also a practicum in teaching religion which involved teaching in a church and reflections with Sherrill and other students.[90] Evangelistic work by students also continued to happen informally. By the mid-1930s the students had formed a Religious Work Council which organized services for the jail and workhouse, sponsored street preaching on Saturday nights, and volunteered at the various missions in the center city, the YMCA, local hospitals, Union Gospel Mission, and the Old Ladies' Home.[91]

The inauguration of courses in church efficiency further evidenced the changing nature of the area of practical theology. Originally part of the purpose of Duncan's gift, in 1923-1924 LPTS held a course in church

88. Cunningham, President's Annual Report, May 7, 1935. LPTS Archives.

89. *The Register* 14 (October, November, December 1925): 5-8. LPTS Archives.

90. *The Register* 19 (January, February, March 1930): 37, and Faculty Minutes (1914-1925), April 23, 1925. LPTS Archives. Chapter six will discuss a program that was much like these which emerged during Ellis Nelson's presidency, called Congregation-Based Ministry. So the old became new again.

91. *The Register* 24 (October, November, December 1935): 7-9. LPTS Archives.

efficiency with J. V. Logan as lecturer, taken up the following year by Sherrill upon his arrival.[92] The course was administrative in its orientation: how to organize programs, defining the purpose of programs, the relation of the local congregation and pastor to the larger church, stewardship and fiscal management of a congregation, and church advertising. Mainstream Protestantism, closely allied with the corporate economic system that developed after the Civil War and with lay membership that, generally speaking, helped formulate and profited from that system, increasingly came under the influence of organizational and management practices of the corporate model.

Louis Weeks has shown that business methods and concepts of organization were adopted not only at the level of the General Assembly of the Presbyterian denominations as they grew but also by congregations. The role of the pastor was in the early stages of a transition toward an understanding of one who organized programs and ran an administratively efficient church. Perhaps the easiest symbol of that metamorphosis was the pastor's study becoming the pastor's office. Elders became less the spiritual leaders of the congregation and more a "board" to oversee the work of the church. Other church roles became more specialized and, in some cases, professional — the advent of music directors, for example.[93] Not only was this trend reflected in course work, but in the lectures delivered on campus. During the 1924-1925 school year Nicholas Dosker, Vice-President of the National Bank of Kentucky and son of the seminary professor, spoke on "The Minister and the Laws of Business." Three years later the Seminary and Louisville community learned about "The Pastor as Executive," "The Daily Life of the Pastor," "How to Succeed in the Ministry," and "Important Aids in the Ministry."[94]

Even the oldest staple of practical theology, homiletics, changed. The homiletics course had always been spread over all three years of a student's study. The first year's course was given over to learning how to prepare and preach a sermon. The second year was the history of preach-

---

92. *The Register* 13 (January, February, March 1924): 5. See also the course descriptions in *The Register* 14 (January, February, March 1925): 26-37.

93. Louis B. Weeks, "The Incorporation of the Presbyterians," in Coalter, Mulder, and Weeks, eds., *The Organizational Revolution: Presbyterians and American Denominationalism,* the Presbyterian Presence Series (Louisville: Westminster/John Knox Press, 1992). In the same volume see Craig Dykstra and James Hudnut-Beumler, "The National Organizational Structures of Protestant Denominations: An Invitation to a Conversation."

94. *The Register* 14 (January, February, March 1925): 8; and 17 (January, February, March 1928): 11.

ing, in which one read, analyzed, and discussed sermons of the great preachers of the past. The third year showed the most influence of the new educational ideas, for the class studied the psychology of the hearer and methods of persuasion in preaching. The changes in and expansion of the practical theology courses were all reflections of growing trends in theological education and the church. At LPTS doctrinal and biblical content and methods were assumed to stay the same, but how one applied the faith to life and how a pastor filled the ministerial role were in transition.

One can detect the growing professionalization of the pastoral office, the expansion of the role of the pastor beyond those of the study and the pulpit, and the specialization of fields of knowledge and methodologies of study. This also manifested itself in the professionalization of the faculty itself, suggested by the increase of those holding the earned doctorate. By 1931-1932, of nine full-time faculty members, including the president, four held the Ph.D and others were working toward theirs. It was during this period that the Seminary also began its program in the Masters of Theology, a one-year post-graduate degree. Students could specialize in Church History and Theology, Bible, or Practical Theology. That brought some new and more specialized courses into the curriculum, such as "The Synoptic Problem," "The Philosophy of Religion," "Problems of Modern Missions," and "History of the American Church."[95]

Missions, which had always held a prominent place in life at Louisville Seminary, took a larger place in the curriculum at the same time its presence in the co-curricular experience of the Seminary retreated. The monthly mission days continued through the 1920s and lectures often addressed both domestic and global mission. Dosker was granted a sabbatical for the 1919-1920 year, during which he traveled throughout Asia learning about the church there — and visiting his son, Richard, who served in Japan. The next year he spoke twice on "Lights and Shadows in Japan." One year L. Nelson Bell, a medical missionary to China who was Billy Graham's father-in-law and became moderator of the PCUS in 1972, made a presentation. It must have been particularly interesting to hear Mohammed Ali, a convert from Islam (not the famous boxer from Louisville), deliver "My Conversion and Attending Persecutions." The Seminary continued to hear about "Colored Missions," primarily from John Little. People such as Warren Wilson kept the needs of the rural and mountain church

95. *The Register* 15 (January, February, March 1926): 25, and *The Register* 16 (January, February, March 1927): 26-36.

before the Seminary community.[96] Of course, Dosker continued to offer his course on missions.

Mission study in the curriculum took a major step forward in 1924. R. S. Reynolds, of Reynolds Aluminum and one of the brothers with whom Pratt would donate the tract of land to LPTS, provided the money to endow a chair in missions. This was the first chair of missions in any Presbyterian seminary in the nation and one of the earliest of any denomination (Southern Baptist Theological Seminary had the first missions chair).[97] Pratt was the person called to fill the position.[98] Eminently qualified to teach missions, he had served as a missionary in Korea and then come back to the U.S. to hold the position of Secretary of the PCUS Executive Committee of Foreign Missions. Obviously, the addition of a person to teach in the field full-time allowed for growth in the courses of study.

In place of Dosker's one course in missions Pratt offered three. The first course studied the Bible as a mission text. How did it demonstrate God's plan of redemption from the beginning, and how were God's people to present it to others? The second course surveyed the history of mission work, with a special emphasis on the modern period of the Protestant mission endeavor of the nineteenth and twentieth centuries. The third course was in comparative religions, insofar as global mission work forced the church to face squarely the relationship of Christianity to other faith systems.[99] Pratt also taught two courses on evangelism which addressed the practice of evangelism by pastors and the history of evangelistic methods from the New Testament to the present. It was logical that oversight of student fieldwork fell to him. Andrew Rule later asserted that Pratt laid the groundwork for the program of rural fieldwork for which the Seminary became known under the leadership of C. Morton Hanna.[100]

Pratt proved an exemplary choice not only because of his skill and dedication, but because he knew the developments of modern mission work and theory very well. The great missionary movement of Anglo-American Protestantism at the turn of the century gave rise to significant changes in the understanding of missions and global Christianity. First was the ecumenical movement, given impetus in the World Missions Con-

96. *The Register* 10 (January, February, March 1921): 6; 11 (January, February, March 1922): 6; 12 (March 1923): 7; 13 (January, February, March 1924): 7.

97. Many other schools would follow with departments of mission, including courses in the sociology of religion and world religions. See Cherry, *Hurrying Toward Zion*, 70.

98. Minutes of the Board (1920-1939), May 6, 1924.

99. *The Register* 14 (January, February, March 1925): 26-37.

100. *The Register* 39 (June 1950): n.p. LPTS Archives.

ference at Edinburgh in 1910, which gave rise to the International Missionary Council. The Faith and Order and Life and Work conferences became precursors to the World Council of Churches. Not only did missions provide the primary drive for the ecumenical movement, but also the understanding of the mission enterprise was in transition. The recognition that mission was often tied, wittingly or unwittingly, to the colonial power of Europe and the U.S. forced missionaries to address the sense of superiority with which the gospel was often presented to people of other faiths and cultures. Consequently, missiology began to explore the extent to which the gospel had been bound to European thought, how the gospel could be communicated across cultures, and how the gospel could be enculturated without crossing over into an improper syncretism — a question asked of European enculturation of the gospel as well. There also arose an emphasis on the development of indigenous leadership for the church in each nation and the growth of national churches around the world.

Pratt was conversant with these developments in the field. Norman Horner, who served as a missionary and later taught mission at Louisville Seminary, observed that "[h]is personal acquaintance with the developing ecumenical movement, his specific attention to Eastern Orthodoxy and Roman Catholic worship and work, and his passion for the great international conferences on Faith and Order, Life and Work, and Missions leading to the World Council of Churches gave students a broad perspective for that time."[101] Pratt added an elective "Seminar in Cooperative Movements in Modern Christianity" in 1929.[102] Aside from Pratt's classes, mission days brought ecumenism before the students also. For example, S. H. Chester, a minister in Nashville, spoke on "The Stockholm Conference" on Life and Work of 1925, which he had attended.[103] Of course, students participated in a small corner of the ecumenical movement simply by virtue of their attendance at LPTS.[104]

Pratt also exposed students to the changing face of mission. With the onset of the Th.M. degree and expansion of graduate and elective courses, he offered a course in the "Problems of Modern Missions." The students would examine the questions of "missions and politics, race problems,

101. Norman Horner, Kim Smith King, and Louis Weeks, "Evangelism and Mission at Louisville Seminary," 5. Unpublished manuscript, copy in author's possession.

102. *The Register* 18 (January, February, March 1929): 31. LPTS Archives.

103. *The Register* 15 (January, February, March 1926): 8. LPTS Archives.

104. For the ecumenical movement see Ruth Rouse and Stephen Neill, eds., *A History of the Ecumenical Movement, 1517-1948* (London: SPCK, 1954), and Stephen Neill, *A History of Christian Missions,* 2nd ed. (London and New York: Penguin Books, 1986).

world peace and economic contacts with non-Christian peoples."[105] In 1929 Pratt changed the first course in mission from "The Bible as a Mission Text" to "Foreign Missions in a Changing World." The class involved a study of the question of autonomous churches around the world and the rising spirit of nationalism affecting missions and indigenous churches since World War I. A course in comparative religions, taught for many years as part of the missions department, became "The History of Religions" as an elective. Among the graduate electives was listed "Missions in the Light of the Jerusalem Conference" (this was the 1928 meeting of the International Missionary Council).[106]

The growing belief that attitudes about the developing nations and methods of mission needed to change lest the receiving nations eventually reject missions and Christianity altogether took concrete form in a published proposal titled *Re-Thinking Missions: A Laymen's Inquiry after One Hundred Years.*[107] The work of a study commission chaired by Harvard philosophy professor William Hocking, it became known simply as the Hocking Report. The report urged that mission work by the Western nations emphasize philanthropic work such as education and medical service, eschewing direct preaching or evangelistic work and thinking of missions as a temporary project that sought to build autonomous and locally-led churches in every nation. The commission's further suggestion that the churches work toward a unified world religion that was not necessarily Christian was its most distinctive and controversial feature.

In response to its release Pratt gave a 1933 presentation on the book at a lengthened chapel service to which local ministers and Seminary friends

---

105. *The Register* 16 (January, February, March 1927): 34. LPTS Archives.

106. *The Register* 18 (January, February, March 1929): 31-32. LPTS Archives.

107. The Commission of Appraisal, *Re-Thinking Missions: A Laymen's Inquiry after One Hundred Years* (New York and London: Harper and Brothers, 1932). The mission community had begun to confront questions about how Christianity in the West should encounter and relate to the non-European world and other religions before the turn of the century. By the 1920s enough questions had been raised about traditional mission strategies to prompt the Hocking Report. See Pearl S. Buck, *Is There a Case for Foreign Missions?* (New York: The John Day Co., 1932), and Daniel Johnson Fleming, *Whither Bound in Missions* (New York: Association Press, 1925). The field of missiology arose out of those discussions and ecumenical conversations, giving rise to a body of literature analyzing the cultural embodiment of Christianity and how it is transmitted across cultures. Two of the leading works in that area are David J. Bosch, *Transforming Mission: Paradigm Shifts in Theology of Mission* (Maryknoll, N.Y.: Orbis Books, 1991), and Lamin Sanneh, *Translating the Message: The Missionary Impact on Culture,* American Society of Missiology Series (Maryknoll, N.Y.: Orbis Books, 1989).

were specifically invited. The content of his remarks does not survive, but given the conservatism of Louisville Seminary he must surely have stood foursquare against the disavowal of Christianity as the world's supreme religion. Still, the Seminary community was abreast of the current issues in missiology.[108] Later, during a curriculum revision in 1932, Pratt described his course, "Introduction to Modern Missions," as discussing possible reasons for the post-war decline in mission interest. "This leads to a study of the present place and work of missions in the various countries," he wrote. "An effort is made to discover just to what extent there is a living Church in each land, free from missionary control and showing ability to carry forward the work of evangelizing its own people. International-mindedness and the teaching of Jesus regarding race and industry are stressed."[109] In the 1931-1932 year Robert Speer lectured to the community on "The Triumph of Missions."[110]

As the presence of mission study multiplied in the curriculum, its cocurricular profile declined. Beginning with the 1933-1934 school year Louisville Seminary announced in its catalogue that one day was set aside for mission emphasis regularly — no longer monthly. It turned out that mission day was observed once each semester.[111] It was still marked by lectures, sometimes by familiar or famous missionaries. In 1931 the Seminary heard again from alumnus Isaac Yonan, who delivered three lectures on "The Mohammedan World."[112] Toyohiko Kagawa, the famed Japanese convert to Christianity who maintained an untiring sacrificial work among the poor in the city of Kobe, spoke in chapel on March 13, 1936. This was of special interest to the Seminary community, for according to *The Register* in 1931 it was Harry Myers, class of 1897 and missionary to Japan, who won "Kagawa to an acceptance of Christ as his Savior and [guided] him into a life of . . . deep consecration and useful service."[113]

In 1930, after a two-year search, the board finally found a person to succeed Vander Meulen as president. As Vander Meulen reflected on the last decade of the Seminary under his leadership, he outlined an expansive and active success. Internally, the Seminary had begun to build its staff;

---

108. Faculty Minutes (1932-1940), February 2, 1933.

109. *The Register* 22 (January, February, March 1933): 43-44. LPTS Archives.

110. *The Register* 22 (January, February, March 1933): 12. LPTS Archives.

111. *The Register* 23 (March 1934): 47, and Faculty Minutes (1932-1940), October 24, 1935.

112. *The Register* 20 (January, February, March 1931): 12. LPTS Archives.

113. Faculty Minutes (1932-1940), March 12, 1936, and *The Register* 21 (January, February, March 1932): 10.

had expanded the faculty; raised salaries; provided a housing allowance for faculty members; added lectureships; initiated fellowships for graduates; strengthened the library; tripled the student body from his first year; added the Th.M.; and raised admission standards, so that virtually no students entered the Seminary in 1930 without an undergraduate bachelor's degree. Externally, the number of controlling synods had grown, although that did not yet bear the financial fruit for which Vander Meulen hoped, the Seminary had acquired a new site, and the endowment had risen just over $650,000 to total assets of $1.36 million.[114]

None could dispute that Vander Meulen's had been a productive tenure that had moved LPTS ahead financially and academically in a singular way. He continued to hope that the Seminary would create an atmosphere where its students learned "such an inner life of devotion and prayer and communion with the risen Christ that they will have the strength and inspiration of a first-hand, not a second-hand, Christian life." Further, as he returned to teaching he had a vision of Louisville Seminary as a school which would promote the "old faith in a supernatural redemption for a lost world," although in a changing world he believed that "new weapons" would have to be created to address modern forms of unbelief.[115] The board, although it regretted Vander Meulen's resignation, rejoiced that he would remain on the faculty "to translate the old Gospel into the language of the present day, to bring the old orthodoxy to young men in terms of modern life and experience."[116] The future of LPTS seemed brighter than ever.

The Presidency of John R. Cunningham

After an extended search for Vander Meulen's successor, the Seminary turned to a graduate of Westminster College in Fulton, Missouri, and a member of Louisville's class of 1917, John R. Cunningham. Following graduation, Cunningham had served churches in Grenada, Mississippi, and Gainesville, Florida, and was called to the Seminary from First Presbyterian Church in Bristol, Tennessee. Cunningham presided over some of the most difficult years the Seminary would face.

114. Vander Meulen, "A Review of the Past Ten Years of the Louisville Presbyterian Seminary, 1920-1930." Sanders, *History of Louisville Seminary,* 57-67, recounts the accomplishments of the decade also.
115. Vander Meulen, "A Review."
116. Minutes of the Board (1920-1939), May 6, 1930.

Early in Cunningham's tenure the Seminary underwent major curricular revisions. In 1924 Robert L. Kelly published *Theological Education in America: A Study of One Hundred Sixty-One Theological Schools in the United States and Canada.*[117] Kelly criticized seminaries in North America for "inadequate numbers of faculty, a paucity of research libraries, scanty finances, students with deficient college training, and faculty reliance on outmoded teaching methods."[118] Most Protestant seminaries retained too much emphasis on the Bible and biblical languages in their curriculum, ignoring the use of social sciences that marked theological education at some university divinity schools.[119] All of those criticisms applied, in lesser or greater degree, to Louisville Seminary.

The Kelly study resulted in a movement to establish standards for theological education in North America. In the 1930s the recently formed American Conference of Theological Schools, in which Louisville Seminary dean Sherrill played a key role, conducted a comprehensive study of theological education in the U.S. and published its findings and recommendations in four volumes titled *The Education of American Ministers.* Sherrill had received an advance copy of the report and initiated the Seminary's reconstruction of its program in accord with the report's suggestions and, significantly, began to address many of the concerns raised by Kelly. It appears that he wrote most of the new plan himself. Put into effect in the fall of 1932, it was well received by the board, faculty, and students. A joint board-faculty committee called it a "vast step forward" and Vander Meulen thought it "represented the best theological thinking in the ministry along pedagogical lines." It received commendation from external assessment committees.[120]

The new curriculum and requirements gave the seminarian's course of study a contemporary format. Describing the new plan in its first year of application, Louisville Seminary reassured the church and prospective students that neither the biblical-theological content nor the core study imperative for ministry had been cast aside. Rather, the faculty recognized that in

---

117. Robert L. Kelly, *Theological Education in America. A Study of One Hundred Sixty-One Theological Schools in the United States and Canada* (New York: George H. Doran Co., 1924).

118. Cherry, *Hurrying Toward Zion,* 13.

119. Howard Miller, "Seminary and Society," I.18, emphasizes this point.

120. Miller, "Seminary and Society," 1932; J. R. Cunningham, President's Annual Report, May 3, 1932; Frank H. Caldwell, "Louisville Seminary Looks Around and Ahead" (n.p., n.d.). Ca. 1940. LPTS Archives. Sanders, *History of Louisville Seminary,* 73-74, emphasizes the modernity of the curriculum.

some regards the needs of all seminarians were the same, while students also had differing aptitudes and interests. Consequently, the students would no longer have a rather strictly prescribed course of study for two years with a few electives possible in the third, but a set of core courses to complete (fifteen out of thirty units) and fifteen units of distribution requirements with a specialization in an area of interest. The curriculum was divided into three groups: A, Biblical; B, Historical and Doctrinal; and C, The Church at Work. Those divisions remain in place to the present, giving students a great deal of independence in devising their seminary careers. Flexibility extended even to the biblical languages, for now work in only Hebrew or Greek was required, but the expansion of offerings in each allowed a more thorough study of either than previously possible.[121]

In addition to meeting the standard course requirements, other steps were instituted to lead up to the B.D.: senior seminars and comprehensive examinations. At the end of each year juniors took an exam in Bible content, middlers took a test covering basic knowledge in each of the three curriculum groups, and seniors demonstrated special competency in their area of specialization. This curriculum saw the beginning of the required senior sermon. Additionally, although it was not a requirement, it is interesting that juniors had one hour each week of the first semester for a "President's Conference," designed to "help the students to become oriented to the whole field of seminary training. Practical topics relating to personal conduct and spiritual life will be discussed."[122]

The subjects and content of courses changed little, and not many courses were added to the curriculum. Still, this was an innovative step in theological education. Hal Warheim accurately described it as an attempt at balance. The Seminary strove to encompass both old and new educational material and methods, academic and practical preparation for ministry, and the general knowledge required of a minister and mental rigor and satisfaction attendant to achievement in an area of personal interest.[123] A further goal was to lead the students into learning as a lifelong endeavor and to help them learn to think theologically about life and ministry. The faculty hoped to "emphasize the larger content in factual knowledge rather than the mere detail, and to lead the student to think of all factual knowledge as a tool to apply rather than an end in itself."[124]

121. *The Register* 22 (January, February, March 1933): 25-44. Warheim, "The History of a 'First-Class Dream,'" 19-20, gives a good description and analysis of the curriculum.

122. *The Register* 22 (January, February, March 1933): 29-30.

123. Warheim, "First-Class Dream," 19.

124. Faculty Minutes (1932-1940), October 27, 1932.

This change in the curriculum came in the midst of the greatest and most dangerous issue the Seminary had to face during Cunningham's presidency — the Great Depression. For institutions dependent on interest earned on investments and charitable giving, the Depression proved a threat of monumental proportions. The problem was accentuated by the expansion of the budget during the 1920s, occasioned by the addition of some staff and faculty and salary increases for the latter. Fannie Caldwell recalled the failure of the bank in which LPTS had placed its money, even before her husband received his first paycheck.[125] During the Depression, the highest level of income from all sources came, not surprisingly, in 1930: $79,557. The lowest was the 1936-1937 school year: $57,235. Already by 1933 Cunningham was reporting a $14,000 annual drop in endowment interest from the year 1929-1930, almost a 25% loss. Some notes held by the Seminary were not paid, and giving was down. Donations from individuals fell from $12,000 to under $2,000 per year.

The budget was reduced from $80,000 at the start of the Depression to $68,500, but Louisville could not avoid deficit spending, often in the range of $10,000 per year. The Pratt-Reynolds campus, the mortgage of which was being paid by the donors, was lost when Pratt and his friends, who had placed everything in the stock market, were bankrupted. The Pratts even lost their home and moved into Seminary housing (later bought by A. B. and Lela Rhodes).[126] Drastic times evoke drastic measures. The faculty, beginning in 1932, voluntarily accepted a 10% reduction in salary. They were joined by Mattie Witherspoon and Miss Rutledge, the president's secretary, starting in 1933. Salaries remained at that reduced level at least until 1936.[127] In 1932 the board authorized the president and treasurer of the board to borrow up to $50,000 (approximately equal to $550,000 in 1999) to meet the needs of the Seminary, using securities Louisville held as collateral.[128] Trying to defray the deficit in even small ways, LPTS for the first time assessed students a $25 registration, or tuition, fee. Board charges rose $3 per week in 1932, followed by another $2 for room and board in 1934. Students could still attend Louisville Seminary for $200-$300 per

125. Fannie Caldwell Interview.

126. Minutes of the Board (1920-1939), May 3, 1932; Cunningham, President's Annual Report, May 3, 1932, and May 2, 1933, manuscript copies, LPTS Archives; Mobley, "The Administration of Louisville Presbyterian Theological Seminary"; and Sanders, *History of Louisville Seminary,* 69-70; Mobley and Jones Interview.

127. Seminary histories show that this was not an unusual step during the Depression.

128. Minutes of the Board (1920-1939), May 3, 1932; September 30, 1932; and May 2, 1933.

year, a struggle for most in the economic crisis. The board even suspended the awarding of senior fellowships in order to use the investment income for regular operating expenses in those cases where living donors would give their consent.[129] Nor was the toll on the Seminary only financial. The numbers of students fell from an average of 90-100 at the start of the decade to the mid-40s by 1936. Of the students who attended, it became more difficult to find them summer placements and field experiences which helped them meet expenses through the school year. Once they graduated, it grew increasingly difficult to place them in churches.[130]

However, all the news was not bad. Despite the diminishing returns on the endowment, it grew through the untiring efforts of Cunningham, the faculty, and the board. During the 1933-1934 year the endowment increased $79,000, primarily due to a gift of $67,000 from the Patterson estate. This gift did not directly provide financial relief, but funded the Patterson Scholarships and Patterson Fellowships that, over time, were instrumental in bringing promising students to LPTS.[131] The next year the endowment increased another $30,500. In all, through the heart of the Depression, Cunningham was able to add almost $250,000 to the endowment — a sum approximately equal to $2.7 million in 1999, a feat even more remarkable given that his tenure was only six years.[132] Through budgetary cutbacks, financial sacrifice on the part of personnel, and diligent fundraising, Louisville Seminary was able to keep its doors open. In 1935 the faculty passed a resolution of thanks to God for the leadership of the board and the president. Many institutions had closed during the Depression, and of those still operating many had reduced the faculty or services. At LPTS, "economies have been affected, but these have been handled in

129. *The Register* 22 (January, February, March 1933): 48; Minutes of the Board (1920-1939), May 3, 1932, and May 2, 1933.

130. Cunningham, President's Annual Report, May 3, 1932. In 1932 the PCUS again addressed the question of the number of seminaries the small denomination was supporting, brought to the fore once again by the Depression. An Ad Interim Committee on the Training of the Ministry and the Reduction in the Number of Its Seminaries was appointed in 1932, which led, yet again, to merger discussions with CTS. Both schools were favorable to the idea, but CTS did not feel they could leave Atlanta and the LPTS faculty believed its work as a joint seminary was distinctive and they should not leave Louisville, on the border of North and South. So again the discussions came to naught.

131. The Patterson Scholarship was available to students who had completed four years of Greek or Latin at the undergraduate level.

132. Cunningham, President's Annual Report, May 1, 1934, and May 7, 1935; Minutes of the Board (1920-1939), May 2, 1933; and Faculty Minutes (1979-1982), August 29, 1980. LPTS Archives.

such a way as not to impair the educational efficiency of the seminary."[133] Only those who experienced the Depression could fully fathom the emotional and physical toll those years exacted, as well as the sacrifice and labor it took to maintain the Seminary's existence despite the perpetual running of deficits.

The faculty's expression of appreciation for the leadership of the board and president in difficult times was also a veiled vote of confidence in the midst of some problems Cunningham experienced with two faculty members, Vander Meulen and Rule. The first sign of the problem in the records comes in minutes of the executive committee of the board in May 1935, which note a "certain lack of harmony" in the faculty. The board subsequently voted its full confidence in Cunningham.[134] The exact nature of the problem between the men is lost in history, but it appears to have been primarily a clash of personalities.

In the spring of 1931, at the close of Cunningham's first year as president, an automobile hit Vander Meulen as he crossed the street; both of his legs were broken. There were those who believed the injuries resulted in a changed personality in him, perhaps even occasioned by some brain trauma.[135] For whatever reason, Vander Meulen disagreed with some of Cunningham's administrative decisions, a problem exacerbated by his status as immediate predecessor in the post. Witherspoon and Rutledge, bursar and president's secretary respectively, reportedly were devoted to Vander Meulen and relayed to him information they obtained in their administrative relationship to Cunningham. Others accepted Vander Meulen's claim that he sought only to help Cunningham by carrying out some administrative tasks.[136] There are hints that the dispute may have been more than just a dif-

133. Faculty Minutes (1932-1940), April 25, 1935.

134. Minutes of the Board (1920-1939), May 7, 1935.

135. This idea was held by Peter Pleune, pastor at Highland Presbyterian Church in Louisville at the time and part of the Dutch connection at LPTS. Dosker had been instrumental in bringing Vander Meulen to campus, who in turn helped Pleune receive a call to the church in Paducah, Kentucky, whence he was called to Highland. Vander Meulen and Pleune had a very close friendship, even owning houses next door to one another in Holland, Michigan. Pleune believed the damage in the accident changed Vander Meulen and rendered him unable to let Cunningham be president on his own terms. Mobley and Jones Interview. Anne Caldwell, daughter of Frank Caldwell, had the same impression about the effects of Vander Meulen's injuries. Al Winn remembered that Frank Caldwell told him that, at the commencement just after Vander Meulen's accident (but which Mrs. Vander Meulen attended), Cunningham failed to mention the accident as the cause of Vander Meulen's absence, at which both Vander Meulens took offense. Winn Interview.

136. Frank A. Nelson to Frank H. Caldwell, April 21, 1952. Copy in author's possession.

ference in personalities, but only hints. In a letter to the board in July 1935, Cunningham wrote: "I trust that you will not be aroused by reports regarding insurmountable curriculum difficulties, or of unorthodoxy among our faculty and recent graduates. I am forced to the conclusion that the recent unpleasantness has been largely personal."[137] Perhaps Rule and Vander Meulen had disagreed with the extensive curricular revisions of 1932, and perhaps these two disciples of Warfield questioned the theological soundness of some Seminary instructors. It was probably not a coincidence that in 1936 Dosker's heirs requested the return of their bequest for the Dosker Fellowship and received it.[138]

At any rate, the focus of the controversy turned on Vander Meulen's relationship to Cunningham. Through a long and painful series of meetings through the summer and fall of 1935 involving the board, faculty, and administration in various combinations, Rule defended Vander Meulen's position. Despite diligent efforts, no resolution of the issue emerged. Matters came to a head at a special meeting of the board on February 4, 1936. The board interviewed every faculty member to discern the state of the conflict, after which they expressed their full support of Cunningham and began the process to amend the by-laws of the Seminary to give the president "complete administrative authority." A letter to Vander Meulen and Rule directed them to limit themselves to teaching and avoid any administrative activities, to ensure that Louisville Seminary kept the "favorable opinion and support of its constituency and be not made the subject of unfounded rumors," and to work with the president as sole administrator and to cease "factional differences" in the faculty.[139] This rebuke, as Vander Meulen referred to it twice in a response, pained him deeply; he pledged his submission.[140]

137. Cunningham to the Members of the Board of Directors, July 25, 1935. Copy in author's possession.

138. Minutes of the Board (1920-1939), Executive Committee, May 15, 1936. There also exists, in Cunningham to Frank Hill Caldwell, May 21, 1936, a reference to theological matters surrounding a bequest to the Seminary, in which he mentions Vander Meulen. Such references are hints of a theological problem, but not enough to allow one to draw conclusions.

139. "Resolutions from the Minutes of the Louisville Presbyterian Seminary Board Meeting of February 4, 1936, Which Pertain to Faculty Relationships." This is part of a packet of photocopied materials relating to the Vander Meulen-Cunningham affair in the author's possession. This action of the board was expunged from the minutes at a meeting in 1952 to remove this embarrassment to the record of service of Drs. Rule and Vander Meulen to LPTS.

140. Vander Meulen to Gentlemen of the Board of the Louisville Seminary, February 10, 1936.

Cunningham, undoubtedly wearied by the strain of keeping the Seminary afloat in the Depression and addressing conflict within the faculty, announced his resignation on February 10, 1936, to accept the call to the pulpit of First Presbyterian Church in Winston-Salem, North Carolina. Sherrill was named acting president as the search for a successor began. The situation on campus remained unsettled; matters were only complicated when a severe illness left Vander Meulen debilitated.[141] In April the executive committee of the board unanimously agreed "that the present situation in the faculty would make the securing of a president impossible." Therefore, the step was taken to retire Vander Meulen at the end of the 1935-1936 year with emeritus status at his salary of $3,600 for life and to retire Rule at the end of the school year with salary continuation until the end of November. In short, both men were fired; Vander Meulen's health made it unnecessary in his case. Then, on May 5, the executive committee rescinded that action, placing Vander Meulen on leave and restoring Rule to the faculty. The full board, at the same meeting, granted the executive committee the power to do with the office of bursar what they felt was necessary for the good of the institution. Vander Meulen died soon thereafter, and Rule went on to two more decades of service to the institution. In Vander Meulen's case it was a very painful, sad, and regrettable end for one who had so sacrificially and ably led the Seminary to a new stage of existence.[142] It had been a time of hard controversy which left many with bitter feelings. With some order brought to the school, the presidency was offered to Frank Hill Caldwell, who accepted and began his duties with the 1936 school year.

141. For Cunningham's resignation, see Minutes of the Board (1920-1939), Executive Committee, February 10, 1936; for Vander Meulen's illness see the same for February 25, 1936.

142. In addition to the sources already cited, see in the packet regarding this affair excerpts from Minutes of the Board (1920-1936) and Executive Committee Minutes for May 7, May 14, May 20, and June 20, 1935; and May 5, 1936. Henry Cady Wilson to Harold F. Brigham, February 13, 1936; John Vander Meulen to Brigham, May 13, 1935; and Andrew K. Rule to the Executive Committee of the Board of Directors, May 13, 1935.

• IV •

INTO HARMONY WITH THE WILL OF GOD IN INTELLECTUAL INTEGRITY

The Presidency of Frank H. Caldwell, 1936-1964

The middle decades of the twentieth century were unusually turbulent. The Depression, seemingly interminable to those in the midst of it, eventually gave way to World War II. The war, in turn, brought carnage at a level never before experienced in human history and the inauguration of the nuclear age. The end of that war began another, dubbed a Cold War but continually heating up in places such as Korea. The postwar United States boomed in many ways: numbers of people, economically, suburban growth, claims for equality, and so on.

American Protestantism was affected by those changes and underwent others of its own. In theological seminaries what came to be called the neo-orthodox theology of Karl Barth, Paul Tillich, and Reinhold and H. Richard Niebuhr became much more influential than it had been before the war; in some quarters it dominated the theological scene. Historical-critical methods of biblical study triumphed in all but the most conservative seminaries. The understanding of the identity and role of ministry continued to change. Mainstream Protestant denominations became more involved in social justice ministries, especially with the advent of the civil rights movement. Louisville Seminary reflected those changes in American society and its churches. The Seminary initiated new programs in field education, continued to venture tentatively into social applications of the gospel, began to move beyond its tradition of defending conservative Calvinism, and — finally — made a move out of downtown Louisville. In all its changes, LPTS sought ways to remain theologically sound as it explored

God's leading into new forms of ministry in a changing world. Or, as the Seminary's popular motto of that time affirmed, it strove to prepare students to "preach the ancient gospel to a modern world."

Frank Caldwell Elected to the Presidency

As the turmoil surrounding the controversy between Vander Meulen and Cunningham came to some resolution with the former's death and the latter's resignation, the board faced the task of naming a successor to Cunningham. Some wanted Sherrill in the post, given his strong leadership in the Seminary and in theological education in the nation, but he declined to pursue the opportunity. Everyone agreed that the other strong candidate was Frank Caldwell, and the board quickly proceeded to elect him president of the Seminary. Henry Mobley has written that there is "strong evidence" Caldwell had been the choice for a period of time since Cunningham's resignation, but that he had refused while the conditions on the faculty remained so unsettled.[1] Caldwell would have a long tenure in office, and few presidents have shaped an institution as thoroughly as he did over the course of twenty-eight years.[2]

Caldwell's was an interesting sojourn to the presidency. A native of Mississippi, in 1919 he began his college studies at the United States Military Academy but had to withdraw when he could not successfully complete his mathematics course. As Caldwell put it, Douglas MacArthur, who was then superintendent at West Point, "didn't appreciate my creative treatment of mathematics problems because the answers didn't agree with the ones in the back of the book."[3] He returned to the University of Mississippi, where a sermon by Vander Meulen on a recruiting tour convinced him he was called to ministry. Although his father tried to dissuade him

1. Minutes of the Board (1920-1939), May 5, 1936, and Mobley, "The Administration of Louisville Presbyterian Theological Seminary." The depth of the problem for the faculty must have been greater than records can indicate, for Anne Caldwell said, "It was so bad that mother had told me several times that when Daddy came home and said he had been elected president, she wept. She wept!" Anne Caldwell Interview. Caldwell himself later joked that he was only elected because he had been on sabbatical and people could not tell on which side he stood. Mulder, "Memorial Minute," copy in author's possession.

2. A number of presidents at Presbyterian seminaries served long tenures as contemporaries of Caldwell. J. McDowell Richards held office at Columbia from 1932-1971; David Stitt was at Austin from 1945-1971; and John Mackay served Princeton from 1936-1959.

3. "Liberal Cleric in the South: Frank Hill Caldwell," *New York Times* (April 13, 1966). Photo of news clipping. LPTS Archives.

from going off to that "half-breed Yankee seminary," Caldwell left for LPTS before he finished his B.A. at Ole Miss and completed his work for the B.D. in 1925.[4] The faculty awarded him the Edward P. Humphrey Fellowship, but he could receive neither his degree nor the fellowship until he completed his baccalaureate degree. He served a group of PCUSA mission churches in the Bradsfordsville, Kentucky, area and received his B.A. from Centre College in 1926. In September Caldwell married Fannie Wells, and they spent the 1926-1927 school year at the University of Edinburgh where he pursued a Ph.D. in homiletics with the Humphrey Fellowship. He spent the summer of 1927 as assistant to President Vander Meulen, who took an extended trip to the Holy Land. Caldwell maintained the administration of the Seminary in the president's absence. The 1927-1928 year found Caldwell as acting professor of Bible at Centre, and then he went to the Presbyterian church in McComb, Mississippi, from 1928-1930. In 1930 he was called to Louisville Seminary to teach homiletics with the provision that he complete his doctoral work at Edinburgh, which he did in 1935. Then he became president in 1936, in the midst of the most serious conflict in the Seminary's history and the heart of the Depression. It was a formidable, even monumental, task, and few could have met the challenge as ably as Caldwell did.[5]

The Seminary to the End of World War II

The student population of the Seminary remained low through the remainder of the Depression and World War II. The numbers fluctuated between forty and fifty, dipping as low as thirty-eight in 1945-1946. The war touched the Louisville Seminary community in many ways, of course. As of July 21, 1942, nineteen alumni were known to be military chaplains. Eric Rule, Andrew's younger brother, was a pilot in the British Royal Air Force. Earl Bloxham left seminary at the end of the first semester in 1941-1942, just after Pearl Harbor. He eventually was a part of the D-Day invasion at Normandy Beach and led a task force that liberated the prisoners at Buchenwald. Bloxham finished his B.D. after the war and became a chaplain during the Korean War. Edwin P. Elliott, class of 1942, remembered

4. Fannie Caldwell Interview.
5. Not surprisingly, summaries of Caldwell's life abound. See Sanders, *History of Louisville Seminary,* 77; Fannie Caldwell Interview; and Mulder, "Memorial Minute." For some specific references in Seminary records prior to his election as president, see Minutes of the Board (1920-1939), May 5, 1925; May 3, 1927; May 2, 1933; and May 7, 1935.

that Sam Lee, a Korean-American student, returned from preaching in the field over Pearl Harbor weekend to find that federal agents had made an inspection of his room. Of course, the cost of war persisted for a long time and in many ways. An unnamed veteran who had enrolled at LPTS was told that he should withdraw from the Seminary because of his inability successfully to do his work. The faculty believed he should re-examine his call and seek counseling from a government agency to enable him to make a "better adjustment to civilian life."[6]

The Depression continued to take an enormous toll on Louisville's finances. Caldwell managed to keep the deficit for his first year down to $2,700, but that made the accrued deficit for the Depression up to that point approximately $49,000.[7] In the midst of the 1940-1941 school year, as the nation was beginning to come out of the Depression thanks, in large part, to increased production related to the war already underway in Europe, investment interest lagged $6,000 behind the previous year and LPTS had already borrowed $3,000 for the operating budget.[8] Caldwell labored to increase the endowment and contributions, obviously goals capable of only limited success under the circumstances. Economy measures instituted during Cunningham's presidency were maintained. Caldwell proposed selling approximately $165,000 in real estate that generated virtually no income for the school, but that had to wait until the market regained some of its value.[9]

Two additional steps made more money available for meeting operating expenses. Caldwell created a "League of Support" among friends of the Seminary, much like the program Hemphill had tried. The intent was to create a core of people committed to giving to LPTS each year and, perhaps, through bequests. That would provide the school a more consistent income on which it could depend. Even more, the League formed a core of people who would support Louisville not just with their money, but by spreading the news of its work and mission. The second step was an in-

---

6. For this last, see Faculty Minutes (1940-1951), April 29, 1948. See also Edwin P. Elliott's remembrances in "Life at Louisville Revisited," October 1992; *The Register* 31 (July, August, September 1942): 10; and *The Register* 41 (June 1952): 7. LPTS Archives. For a study of American Protestantism during World War II see Gerald L. Sittser, *A Cautious Patriotism: The American Churches and the Second World War* (Chapel Hill: University of North Carolina Press, 1997). Lee later endowed a scholarship.

7. That deficit would be approximately $500,000 in 1999 dollars.

8. Minutes of the Board (1920-1939), May 18, 1937; Minutes of the Board of Directors (1940-1960), February 7, 1940. LPTS Archives.

9. Minutes of the Board (1920-1939), May 18, 1937.

crease in tuition in 1938. Once the original fee had been assessed earlier in the decade, tuition, room, and board had been raised until it reached $175 per year. A summer meeting of the (PCUS) Conference of Seminary Representatives at Montreat made the recommendation that total fees for PCUS seminaries be made $250. The motivation for the step was more psychological than financial; divinity schools such as Yale and others with good reputations charged more than the Presbyterian seminaries, and by raising the amount the PCUS hoped to counter the possible impression that a lower cost equaled a lower quality of education. Louisville Seminary made the new charge effective in the 1940-1941 year, charging the student only $50 of the $75 increase — the remaining $25 was met with increased aid.[10]

The Presbyterian Church in the U.S.A. made plans in 1939 to conduct a Sesquicentennial Fund Campaign to raise $10 million for educational purposes throughout the denomination. The Seminary board agreed that LPTS needed a financial campaign but decided to carry one out independent of the PCUSA, focusing on its special needs with its own constituency. The board retained a New York firm to manage the effort, which was set to begin on October 1, 1940. The faculty pledged the impressive sum of $2,500 and Caldwell asked the board to join them. He obviously believed Louisville's future was in jeopardy, for he told the board that "we who are close to the seminary must undertake this campaign in the spirit of a crusade at personal sacrifice."[11] The campaign targeted the Seminary's controlling synods; it would begin in the two synods of Kentucky, hoping to raise $200,000 there. But even though the nation was beginning to emerge from the Depression, its effects prevented the kind of success for which LPTS hoped. Only a little over $50,000 was received in all. That was certainly helpful, but not enough to make much of an impact on the operating budget. It was partly in response to this disappointing campaign that Caldwell formed the League of Support.[12]

In January 1937, still in Caldwell's first year, the Seminary confronted a very different and dangerous crisis in addition to its financial woes. Three weeks of rain throughout the Ohio Valley caused the Ohio River and its tributaries to flood. By Saturday, January 24, much of downtown Louis-

10. Minutes of the Board (1920-1939), Executive Committee, October 14, 1938, and Minutes of the Board (1940-1960), Executive Committee, February 7, 1940.

11. Minutes of the Board (1940-1960), May 14, 1940.

12. Minutes of the Board (1940-1960), May 14, 1940; Minutes of the Board (1920-1939), May 2, 1939; *The Register* 30 (October, November, December 1941): 2-3; Mobley, "The Administration of Louisville Presbyterian Theological Seminary."

ville — the West End in particular — was flooded and water began to rise in the basement of the Seminary campus. It eventually came within two feet of the basement door on First Street. City officials evacuated downtown, and the students were told they could go home or be taken out to Highland Presbyterian Church, where Pleune would place them in members' homes. A few students chose to stay at the campus, as did the families of four servants the Seminary employed and some married students in Bingham Hall. Caldwell and Sherrill packed clothes and went down to stay for the duration.

At 8:30 Saturday night a group of 73 were brought to the Seminary by the Red Cross. They were to have been evacuated to the Highlands area but could not make it. The interracial group had taken refuge in the West End at the 23rd and Broadway Baptist Church; they included the church's pastor, E. N. Wilkinson, and his family. The Seminary building had no heat, of course, so the kerosene heaters, blankets, and food which the Red Cross provided were essential. People clustered together in rooms to sleep. Caldwell described that first night with the homiletician's flare and a pastor's care:

> But as I made my rounds with a flashlight at 2:30 A.M. to see that kerosene heaters and candles were all right and to check up on sick people, the most impressive sight was the chapel, with both negroes and white people rolled in blankets, with overcoats on top, trying to sleep on the chapel benches. . . . The light from around the bottom of the heater just revealed bundles of cold, exhausted humanity. The light which filtered through the top of the heater barely illumined the angels painted on the apse, and directed my thoughts anew to the familiar inscription — "Thy Word is Truth." I wondered what particular "Word" was especially appropriate "truth" for circumstances like those, unless it was the 107th Psalm. I felt that the chapel was being in a particular way reconsecrated that night, and I think I shall never be able to worship there again without a renewed sense of the relation between worship and service.

The danger outside was very real. The current on Broadway was so strong that only boats with large motors could navigate it. Even still, some capsized and a number of deaths were reported. Finally on Tuesday the weather broke and the Ohio River crested at 57.1 feet, more than 29.1 feet above flood stage. On Thursday the National Guard moved the Seminary guests to the Highlands, and the initial stage of the ordeal ended. In the midst of a remarkable and, for the entire city of Louisville, terribly destructive episode, those stranded for almost four days at LPTS helped one another, worked together, and formed a bond of fellowship across denominational and racial lines.[13]

The Depression put all seminaries in financial straits, of course, and enrollment remained exceedingly low. Consequently, the PCUS appointed a committee to survey the denomination's four seminaries. The study team gave Louisville high marks for its standards of admission — admitting students on probation or requiring work at the University of Louisville if a student had inadequate preparation in the pre-seminary curriculum; its curriculum; quality of faculty; and general educational program. Its weaknesses, not surprisingly, lay in the endowment and library.

The most challenging recommendation of the study was to reduce the number of PCUS seminaries from four to two. The committee gave three reasons for the suggestion. Financially, two seminaries could be supported more fully than four. Educationally, two seminaries could be served by quality faculty throughout and better libraries assembled. Finally, two seminaries were sufficient for the number of candidates the church had to educate. The two seminaries should be located in Richmond, Virginia, and Nashville, Tennessee. The former seminary, Union, would serve the seaboard states, where most southern Presbyterians lived. The latter would serve the western PCUS. Previous efforts showed that it was not realistic to join Columbia and Louisville Seminaries in one of their locations, nor to merge either of them with Austin. Consequently, the committee thought it best to have all three unite in Nashville, in proximity to the libraries and opportunities afforded by Vanderbilt University, the Peabody School for Teachers, and Scarritt College for Christian Workers (a Methodist equivalent to the Presbyterian School of Christian Education). The seminary should have a relationship with both the PCUS and PCUSA.[14]

Austin Seminary rejected the plan immediately. Columbia, again, expressed its willingness to merge with Louisville Seminary in Decatur, preferably without a tie to the PCUSA. Under those circumstances Union en-

13. The definitive, and by far the most compelling, description of the flood at LPTS is Frank Caldwell, "Notes on the Louisville Flood," manuscript, LPTS Archives. See also Sanders, *History of Louisville Seminary,* 79-80, and Fannie Caldwell Interview. She remembers having student Norman Horner, two other students, and the Seminary housemother staying at her house and keeping a large pot of soup continuously on the stove to feed anyone who stopped by in need of warmth and nourishment.

14. Given the facilities in Nashville, the study also suggested the Presbyterian Historical Foundation be transferred to the new seminary.

tered into discussions with Louisville regarding a merger of those schools in Richmond with joint denominational identity. Although Louisville Seminary was willing to make the move to Nashville, it declined to unite with Union. The board and faculty would leave Louisville if it were justified by the reduction of the number of seminaries and if the new institution would maintain and strengthen the work being done in Louisville. A new seminary in Nashville could do that, but they did not think merger with Union would; the Mississippi and Ohio valleys would lose their one seminary. Further, LPTS doubted the PCUSA would approve a move so deeply into the South. That Louisville seriously considered sacrificing its own existence for the cause of theological education was attested by a PCUSA Special Committee on Seminaries which lauded "the vision and initiative of President Caldwell and the Louisville Seminary in willingness to sacrifice the identity of the Seminary if necessary to promote a consolidation of seminaries."[15]

What neither the PCUS committee nor the leadership of LPTS could foresee were the changes and prosperity that would accompany the post-war era. There were a number of helpful developments during the war itself. With empty dormitory rooms due to low numbers of students, Louisville Seminary rented rooms to students from the nearby dental and medical schools. On weekends, dorm rooms and the basement of Grant-Robinson Hall were leased to the USO and YMCA to house and entertain soldiers who came to the city on leave from Fort Knox, a practice which continued until the peace. The Seminary instituted a summer school, apparently because they believed that draft boards expected year-round study to justify a ministerial deferment from military service. Although the school did not advise students to take summer classes because they wanted them to use the time for field experience, they were offered nonetheless. Due in part to those measures and increased interest income, by the 1942-1943 school year LPTS had a $3,000 surplus and enjoyed its best financial health since the start of the Depression.[16]

15. Minutes of the Faculty of the Louisville Presbyterian Theological Seminary (1940-1951), May 16, 1944. The most complete description of the merger discussions is *The Register* 32 (April, May, June 1943): 2-16. See also Survey of the U.S. Seminaries Works' Committee. 1942 Manuscript copy; "The Louisville Presbyterian Seminary and Proposed Consolidations of Presbyterian Seminaries" (n.p., ca. 1943); and Minutes of the Board (1940-1960), Executive Committee, March 3, 1943, and April 20, 1943, and full board, May 16, 1944. LPTS Archives.

16. See a number of references to summer courses during the war years in Faculty Minutes (1940-1951). For financial and space use issues see Minutes of the Board (1940-

In 1944 the Seminary received a gift to underwrite a person "to make special research in the fields of applied psychology, sales marketing, advertising, etc." William A. "Bennie" Benfield, who taught Old Testament and Hebrew, moved in 1944 from that position to vice-president and professor of practical theology. His task was to do research in modern advertising and marketing techniques to learn how better to present Louisville Seminary's mission to its constituency in recruitment and fundraising, thereby relieving Caldwell of some of that responsibility. Henry Mobley remembered Benfield as very intelligent and charismatic and an outstanding pulpiteer who, in addition to his own work, brought in committed business, advertising, and public relations laypeople to work with the Seminary. His job was, in fact, a precursor and early example of what a good development program would eventually become. Benfield, a graduate of Davidson College, also proved to be an exceptional recruiter who persuaded many students from Virginia and the Carolinas, traditionally areas of Union and Columbia influence, to attend LPTS. Indeed, owing at least in part to his influence, Mobley says those schools conferred with Louisville and verbal agreements were reached "that the seminaries should more or less honor the 'turf' established over the years."[17] Benfield was an effective promoter of the Seminary until his departure after the war.

Benfield was one of a number of changes to the faculty around this time. After Vander Meulen's death Hugh T. Kerr, Jr., taught doctrinal theology until called to Princeton in 1940. He was followed for two years by Glenn Maxwell, a former missionary to Brazil, who subsequently gave way to Walter Groves, who had taught at Alborz College in Iran for fifteen years before filling the doctrinal post at LPTS. Old Testament studies suffered a similar lack of continuity following Jesse Cotton's retirement. The longest any one person taught in that department was Benfield, 1940-1944. The faculty parade ended with his removal to the vice-presidency and practical theology, which led to the hiring of Arnold Black Rhodes in 1944. Rhodes became a constant presence on the faculty, serving from 1944 until 1982; until surpassed by David Steere, he held the record for longest service at the Seminary.[18] Rhodes taught Latin and history at Chamberlain-Hunt Academy in Port Gibson, Mississippi, for two years after his 1936

1960), Executive Committee, April 7, 1943, and June 23, 1943; *The Register* 32 (April, May, June 1943): 1-2; and Sanders, *History of Louisville Seminary*, 86-88. LPTS Archives.

17. Mobley, "The Administration of Louisville Presbyterian Theological Seminary"; and Minutes of the Board (1940-1960), November 30, 1943, and Executive Committee, April 26, 1944.

18. Rhodes served thirty-eight years, in five different decades, from 1944-1982.

graduation from Davidson College. His friend from Davidson, Benfield, wrote him about the Patterson Scholarship, and he chose LPTS for his seminary education in 1938. Rhodes and his wife, Lela, remembered the situation for married students at the First and Broadway campus: they lived in a two-room apartment in the east wing that required going into the hall for access from one to the other, and shared a common kitchen in the basement. By 1944, well on the way to his doctorate, Rhodes gave stability to the position in Hebrew and Old Testament.[19]

Although the education at LPTS at the time was conservative in nature and given to rather limited training in the Reformed tradition, the faculty was very intelligent and classically educated. Mobley and Jones tell of a game that Dr. and Mrs. Chamberlain played. He would translate some passage from English to Greek; she would then translate from Greek to Hebrew; he would go from Hebrew back to Greek; then she would finish by returning from Greek to English, and see how close their final translation was to the original English.[20]

Other changes were taking place with regard to faculty. By the end of the 1930s all seven full-time professors held earned doctorates, and those subsequently called without them earned doctorates while teaching. In 1939 Louisville Seminary instituted a program of sabbatical leaves. Sabbaticals had been granted in the past, but only sporadically on petition of a faculty member pursuing a particular project. Initially the leave was for a full year with pay, and they were granted on the basis of seniority. Sherrill had the first, followed by Rule. In short, the professionalization of the faculty was proceeding apace.[21] The Seminary had survived the Depression and World War II, even thriving in some ways. Few could have predicted the growth that peace would bring.

The Post-War Era to the Early Sixties

The trickle of people entering the ministry during the Depression and war turned to a flood soon after the peace was signed. Some of the reasons for

19. For faculty changes, see *The Register* through these years; Minutes of the Board (1940-1960), May 16, 1944, and Executive Committee, May 30, 1944; A. B. and Lela Rhodes Interview, May 9, 1992. LPTS Archives. See also Sanders, *History of Louisville Seminary*, 77-78.

20. Mobley and Jones Interview.

21. Minutes of the Board (1920-1939), May 2, 1939, and Minutes of the Board (1940-1960), Executive Committee, October 28, 1942.

that are not difficult to divine. The financial trials people faced during the Depression had made the cost of a seminary education, bargain though it was, prohibitive for many. The war had diverted people into military service or, in the case of some, the alternative service required of conscientious objectors. The end of the war sent those who had delayed ministerial education into the seminaries almost all at once.

Other reasons are less tangible. The Cold War, which heated up in Korea and in lesser conflicts through the 1950s, then later again in Vietnam, led many people to identify the United States with faith over against the atheistic Soviet Union. That contributed to a remarkable surge in church and synagogue membership and building, further spurred by the post-war "baby boom." Perhaps the spirit of the age led some people to perceive a call to ministry that they might otherwise not have detected. Further, this generation of young adults had lived through the worst economic and military experiences in history. Some turned to God to find meaning, strength, and comfort for the ordeals through which they had come.[22]

Louisville Seminary drew students for a number of reasons. College students headed for the ministry would hear faculty members or, more likely, Caldwell, preach in chapel services (this was the main recruitment method for seminaries) and be impressed with their contact.[23] Of course, the influence of home pastors had always been and continued to be important in candidates' choice of seminary. The Seminary's dual identity attracted those students interested to make contact with Presbyterian "cousins" about whom they knew little. Sometimes students from the PCUSA chose Louisville because it had a reputation for conservatism since it was a PCUS seminary, and sometimes students from the PCUS chose it because it had a reputation for liberalism because it was a PCUSA seminary. Whatever the precise causes, seminary enrollments skyrocketed in the decade after World War II, and LPTS shared in the growth.

The rising enrollments first became noticeable in 1948-1949, when the number of B.D. students reached fifty-six. However, the next year the number was seventy-eight, leaping thirty-four more to 112 for 1950-1951.

22. For an insightful analysis of the religious revival of the 1950s see James Hudnut-Beumler, *Looking for God in the Suburbs: The Religion of the American Dream and Its Critics, 1945-1965* (New Brunswick, N.J.: Rutgers University Press, 1994).

23. Thomas Duncan (Interview, February 2, 1992) is one who remembers being persuaded to attend LPTS rather than Union by his personal contact with Caldwell at Southwestern College, who also made him aware of the Patterson Scholarships — which he received for three years in college, during seminary, and to earn a Th.M. at Princeton.

That made a growth of seventy-four B.D. students in just five years. The number of students peaked at 141 in 1955-1956, numbers that would not be seen again until the late 1960s. Student enrollment settled back to the 120s for the rest of the decade. One curiosity was that the Centennial Class of 1953 counted three faculty sons among its numbers: Paul Love, Edwin Hanna, and Kenneth Foreman Jr. the last receiving his Th.M.[24] The 1953-1954 school year marked a milestone of sorts for Louisville Seminary — among the Presbyterian students there were a few more from the PCUSA than the PCUS. Although LPTS enjoyed dual denominational control, it had always — despite the presence of strong northern faculty members and Vander Meulen's presidency — had a southern feel about it and drawn more students from the PCUS than the PCUSA. But the Seminary was gaining a reputation for liberal leaning in the PCUS and was especially identified with the burgeoning movement for reunion with the PCUSA, so some PCUS students chose to go elsewhere. The number of PCUSA and PCUS students were approximately equal through the 1950s, but by the end of the 1960s the PCUSA dominated as the PCUS had previously.

The drawback to the influx of so many students was that it strained the Seminary's faculty, income, and facilities to accommodate them. The crunch in married students' housing made previous problems in that area seem minor by comparison. The students of the war generation were older than the traditional student coming out of college, and many had already married. Of the eighty-one students enrolled in 1948, fifty-eight were married, and the problem did not abate. The start of the school year in 1956 had 166 students enrolled in all degree programs, of whom 126 were married.[25]

The dilemma had been apparent by the spring of 1946 when the Seminary remodeled Grant-Robinson Hall into married student housing, gaining ten apartments. This necessitated the termination of the lease agreement with the USO for housing soldiers on leave. But the change provided only a very temporary stopgap and presented couples with less-than-ideal conditions. When George and Jean Edwards arrived in 1947, they had a room on the third floor with their bathroom on the second, and the com-

24. Minutes of the Board (1940-1960), June 5, 1953. Winn, who knew Foreman Jr. as a classmate at UTS-VA, writes that he came to LPTS after serving in west China under the PCUSA mission board, where he was held for a time by the Communist government as a suspected spy because of his fluent Chinese. His Th.M. thesis was on Marxist anthropology, titled "Red Man." Ernest White wanted all theses bound in black, but Foreman insisted that his be bound in a red cover. Winn to the author, May 31, 1999.

25. Minutes of the Board (1940-1960), Executive Committee, October 7, 1948, and November 9, 1956.

mon kitchen for married students in the basement.[26] In 1948 the board made plans to purchase an apartment building to make room for the expansion of married students, reasoning that they could rent the rooms once again to dental and medical school students to offset the cost of the apartment building. That did not become a reality until 1953 with the purchase of a building they named Marshall Hall. However, the apartments would hold only ten couples. It is no surprise that this problem became a major impetus for moving to a new location.[27]

The student bodies of the 1950s and early 1960s also provided harbingers of developments to come: the presence of women as regular students. Mary Keith Dosker, granddaughter of the late professor, and Mrs. Walter Swyers attended as special students in 1953 and 1956 respectively, as other women had done.[28] The first regular student was Judy O'Bannon, a Louisville resident who commuted to classes beginning in 1957. O'Bannon graduated Phi Beta Kappa from Indiana University and received a Rockefeller Theological Scholarship. As the first full-time, degree-seeking woman, she found the Seminary had difficulty adjusting to her presence on campus, as would other schools in the late 1960s and early 1970s.[29] O'Bannon chose to leave LPTS after her first year; in the 1990s her husband, Frank, was elected governor of Indiana.

The first woman to graduate from Louisville Seminary was Dora Pierce, who entered LPTS in 1958. The United Presbyterian Church in the United States of America, created by the union of the PCUSA and the smaller United Presbyterian Church in North America in 1958, voted to allow the ordination of women as ministers in that year. Pierce had graduated from Scarritt College, taught elementary school and worked in business before enrolling at LPTS. She graduated in 1961 to become the first woman in the history of the school to receive a degree, and in April 1999 the board created the Dora E. Pierce Professorship of Bible in her honor.[30]

26. Minutes of the Board (1940-1960), March 13, 1946, and George R. Edwards, untitled recollections of LPTS, 1993, in author's possession.

27. Minutes of the Board (1940-1960), Executive Committee, October 7, 1948, and September 2, 1953.

28. Louisville Presbyterian Theological Seminary. Minutes of the Faculty (1951-1962), September 14, 1953, and January 12, 1956. LPTS Archives.

29. Electronic mail from John M. Mulder, January 25, 2000. See also William Young Interview, May 4, 1944. LPTS Archives.

30. On Pierce, see the picture of the entering class in *The Register* 48 (spring 1959); *The Register* 50 (spring 1961): 68; *Seminary Times* 4 (September 17, 1958); and Delia Collins Interview, March 16, 1994. LPTS Archives.

A few women soon followed Pierce, usually not completing the degree. In treating the expanding role of women in the life of seminaries, one also notes that in 1959 Louisville brought the first two women members of the Board of Directors into service. Mrs. John McCabe was installed at the called meeting of January 6, 1959, followed on April 7, 1959, by Mrs. Robert B. Martin.[31] The women's movement would bring profound changes in this regard in the 1970s.[32]

The post-war years brought changes to the administrative and financial management of the Seminary. The distribution of representatives on the Board of Directors changed when two additional PCUSA synods joined in control of the Seminary in 1947. The PCUSA Synod of Kentucky had ten members, the Synod of the Mid-South one, and the Synod of Florida one, for one-third of the board. The PCUS synods of Kentucky, Missouri, Tennessee, Appalachia, and Alabama were given three each, and nine places were given over to the PCUS at large.[33] The board had always been comprised mostly of ministers, with some businesspeople present — mainly to see to financial matters. Caldwell believed it was important to get more committed laypeople and used this reorganization to expand the geographical and professional makeup of the board, which presidents of Louisville Seminary have always given high marks for collegiality, faithfulness, diligence, and wisdom. This trend away from a predominance of ministers on the board accelerated in the 1970s and after.[34]

As the board changed so did its investment practices. In 1941 it named a new treasurer, L. Owsley Haskins.[35] Soon thereafter the Kentucky Trust Company was named the assistant treasurer, in fact through the persons of board member Henry Offutt and J. Van Dyke Norman, who were named investment counselors for the account.[36] As befit generally conservative and cautious Presbyterians, the money was housed in safe investments — mostly bonds and securities, with some money in reliable

31. See the Minutes of the Board for those two dates.

32. For example, Harriet Robinson entered in 1960 (*The Register* 49 [spring 1960]: 72) and Jean Willis in 1963 (*The Register* 53 [spring 1964]: 46). For the story of the role of women in the Presbyterian church see Lois Boyd and R. Douglas Brackenridge, *Presbyterian Women in America* (Westport, Conn.: Greenwood Press, 1983).

33. Minutes of the Board (1940-1960), May 6, 1947.

34. Fannie Caldwell Interview.

35. Since DTS and LPTS consolidated there had only been two treasurers: Judge John Stites, president of the Louisville Trust Co., from 1901-1937, and Alex M. Forrester from 1937-1941. Sanders, *History of Louisville Seminary,* 91.

36. Sanders, *History of Louisville Seminary,* 91.

stocks. In 1950 the executive committee of the board, acting on their counselors' advice, moved a larger percentage of the endowment into the stock
market. At the same time the decision was made that, of the annual investment income, up to three and three-fourths percent of the endowment's
book value could be used for current operations. That figure suggests the
cautious nature of the investments historically and the relatively low, but
steady, rate of return they generated.[37] This policy of investment, coupled
with Caldwell's superlative fundraising ability, increased the endowment
over $500,000 from 1943-1953.[38]

The growing health of the Louisville Seminary enabled the board to
improve salaries, which had been stagnant for years. Faculty salaries
climbed slowly after the war, until by 1956 a professor at LPTS earned
$6,500, plus housing allowance and pension. Still those salaries were low
compared to similar seminaries, so for 1957-1958 the board proposed to
add $1,000 to them. That increase was contingent, however, on increased
giving, especially from the PCUSA's Council on Theological Education,
which was responsible for allocating money budgeted for the seminaries
of that denomination. Louisville felt it deserved a larger portion than it received.[39] Another change was instituted when, upon Chamberlain's death
in 1958, George Edwards became professor of Greek and New Testament
(he had earned his Ph.D. at Duke University after graduating from LPTS,
and had been named instructor to relieve some of Chamberlain's load
since 1956). Now professors could choose between living in seminary-
owned housing and buying their own homes with financing from the
Seminary. Salaries improved until, in the early 1960s, Caldwell's salary

37. Minutes of the Board (1940-1960), Executive Committee, June 23, 1950.

38. Sanders, *History of Louisville Seminary,* 91.

39. Minutes of the Board (1940-1960), Executive Committee, May 6, 1946, and July
27, 1956. Two items are notable in this regard. First, the ethos of community at LPTS was
such that the faculty did not have a rank of salaries. All were paid equally, it being a matter of
principle that faculty members were equally valuable. Even later, when salaries went up in
the 1960s and after there were assistant, associate, and "full" professors, salary differences
were small compared to many schools. Second, LPTS was in a curious situation for funding.
In the PCUS, seminaries were related to synods, and governing body money came from
them (giving by individuals and congregations was the other source of annual income, apart
from investments). In the PCUSA, seminaries were related to the General Assembly
through the Council on Theological Education (later the Council on Theological Seminaries), which allocated money budgeted for seminaries by the General Assembly. LPTS often felt like a "step-child" in both denominations, for they did not think the synods gave what
they should because they received money from the PCUSA, nor that the Council budgeted
what it should, for they received money from the PCUS.

was $12,000 and the salaries for the faculty ranged from $8,000 to $9,500.[40]

Administratively, the Seminary remained very sparse in personnel. Delia Collins, hired to work in the library in 1949, remembered that there were only seven administrative staff members in the entire Seminary when she began.[41] Mattie Witherspoon, the bursar, saw to all the ongoing financial accounting of the Seminary and had primary oversight of the buildings and grounds until G. Leonard Fels came as business manager and Director of Public Relations in 1949 (by which time Benfield had left his post as vice-president).

The PCUS study that cited Louisville for its library weaknesses prompted the Seminary to divert more of its attention there. In 1945 Ernest White, who held both theological and library science degrees, came on as director of the library. Louise Conn, who had filled that role for a number of years, became assistant; Delia Collins succeeded her and gave long years of service to LPTS. More money was allocated for library acquisitions. Under White's leadership the library grew into a fitting theological research facility. Holdings were updated and expanded in all fields of study; periodicals, an important and growing area of religious publishing, received special attention. White made the facilities more suitable and raised their organization to a new level. Gradually the library, later named for White, became a stronger and more modern resource for theological education.

The Seminary administrative staff could remain as small as it did because Caldwell took on much of the work himself, sometimes by necessity. By the early 1950s there were nine homiletics courses listed in the Seminary catalogue, only one of which Caldwell routinely taught: "Preparation and Delivery of Sermons." Adjunct faculty were brought in to teach other courses. There were occasions when Caldwell would teach two or three classes in one semester, leaving him free to travel for recruitment and fundraising during the other. Toward the end of the 1950s and in the early 1960s recent graduates were hired as assistants to the president to manage the day-to-day affairs of the Seminary because Caldwell was on the road so much.[42] The day was not too distant when the growth of Louisville Seminary would require more staff to administer its work.

40. Minutes of the Board (1940-1960), Executive Committee, December 17, 1957, and "Louisville Seminary — Salaries and Wages." Folder "Finances: General," Box "President's Office, 1966-1967." LPTS Archives.

41. Delia Collins Interview.

42. See *The Register* and Minutes of the Board for these years for Caldwell's teaching schedule and for those (Pleune and Benfield, e.g.) who picked up the slack in homiletics.

The post-war years marked a period of relative stability and growth in the faculty. The hiring of Kenneth Foreman Sr. from the Bible and Philosophy Department at Davidson College in 1947 settled the situation in doctrinal theology until his retirement in 1960.[43] Charles Pratt's retirement in 1948 led the Seminary to call Norman Horner, class of 1938, who had served as a missionary in west Africa for ten years, to teach missions and evangelism beginning in 1949.[44] Sherrill's acceptance of a position at Union Seminary in New York resulted in the move of Harry Goodykoontz, who had been with the PCUS Board of Christian Education before his call as Director of Students at the Seminary from 1945-1950, to the faculty in 1950 to succeed him.[45] L. C. Rudolph became assistant to the president and instructor in church history in 1954, and George Edwards arrived in New Testament in 1956. David Steere was called in the area of pastoral care in 1957, Kenneth Phifer in homiletics in 1959 (it was clear Caldwell needed full-time support in that field), and Albert Curry Winn in doctrinal theology in 1960. Sam Keen, the first person called to teach at LPTS who was not ordained to the ministry, arrived in 1962 to teach philosophical theology, replacing Rule. Harold Warheim also came in 1962 to teach in the field of Christianity and society. This flurry of hirings at the turn of the decade reflected two things: still further changes in the content and method of theological education, and the encroaching passing of the "old guard" of faculty.

Rule, Love, Pratt, Chamberlain, Hanna, and Foreman, stalwarts of the faculty during the 1940s and 1950s, all retired or died during the post-war years. When Rule retired in 1962 he had the second-longest continuous term of service — thirty-five years — in the school's history. Love retired in 1964 with thirty-four years of service. Although the faculty through the late 1950s continued to teach a relatively conservative Calvinism and did not expose students to the latest in biblical and theological scholarship, the students from those years speak of their teachers with nothing but the deepest affection. Students of those years recall Love's booming voice and masterful prayers at the beginning of class; Hanna's excellent instruction in the realities of ministry — visitation, interpersonal communication, and matters of pastoral care in general; Foreman's rigor in the classroom and his challenges to students to think through theologi-

---

43. Foreman, who loved the railroad and had an affinity for those who worked hard, retained his membership in, as Edward Farley (class of 1953) put it, the "railroader's union." Edward Farley in "Reflections," a collection of remembrances in 1993.

44. Norman Horner Interview, April 23, 1993.

45. Harry and Betty Goodykoontz Interview, May 16, 1992. LPTS Archives.

cal issues; Sherrill's astute mind to guide students into the psychological issues to be considered in education; and Caldwell's ability to refrain from forcing students into one model of preaching and instead identify a person's strengths and develop them into an individual preaching style. The faculty, in short, brought their entire faith and intellect into the classroom. One unnamed alumnus related a story about Foreman that characterizes the faculty as a whole. The graduate told Foreman during a visit, "'You have had a tremendous impact on my Christian life. I think you are a genius. Of all the men I have ever met you have the most creative mind.' He glanced at the floor silently for a moment and then replied, 'Well, all I can say is: you must have a very limited acquaintance.'"[46]

Theological Education

The continuity of the faculty meant that there were few changes in education at Louisville Seminary before and shortly after the war. A survey of the period reveals more far-reaching developments as the 1950s became the 1960s. Graduation requirements remained fairly constant after the new curriculum began in 1932; the junior Bible exam continued to be remembered as a true challenge. Students were given a syllabus at the start of the year and prepared for the test independently, in addition to their class work.[47] The senior area examinations persisted as well, although middler comprehensives came and went. In 1937, for instance, the exam was abandoned, and middlers received a list of Christian classics to read over the course of the year and on which to prepare reports.[48] The faculty became dissatisfied with that project, however, and in 1942 a middler exam over the Presbyterian standards (Westminster Confessions, Form of Government, Book of Discipline, and Directory for Worship) reappeared.[49] The junior Bible exam was abandoned in 1954.[50]

The faculty, increasingly concerned that graduates be prepared to confront the rapidly changing world following the war, eliminated the group examination for seniors in their area of specialization. In its place

46. *The Register* 56 (summer 1967): 7-8. LPTS Archives. This was a memorial issue on the occasion of Foreman's death.

47. John Olert Interview, March 15, 1992. LPTS Archives.

48. Faculty Minutes (1932-1940), March 11, 1937, and April 15, 1937.

49. Faculty Minutes (1940-1951), May 8, 1942, and *The Register* 40 (March 1951): 20. LPTS Archives.

50. *The Register* 43 (March 1954): 20-21. LPTS Archives.

they required a creative senior seminar, "The Minister and the Isms He Will Face," starting in the 1951 school year. The idea behind the seminar was that a minister would meet, or be questioned about, any number of religious and political movements making their presence felt in the nation and the world. About some movements there existed misinformation or hysteria; about others people might know very little. How could Christian thought and work be brought to bear on modern movements and worldviews? The seminar would be led by one faculty member from each area of the curriculum. The course addressed these "isms": Fundamentalism, Adventism (the Seventh Day variety), Dispensationalism, and Perfectionism among the "biblical" isms; Judaism, Roman Catholicism, Denominationalism and Ecumenism, and Healing Sects among the isms both "biblical and cultural"; and Totalitarianism, Fascism and Communism, Racism, Naturalism, Scientism and Modernism, and Secularism among the "cultural" isms.[51] This course remained until replaced by a Seminar on Evangelism in the early 1960s.

College and seminary faculties seem constantly driven to evaluate their programs and the goals they hope to accomplish. That accounts for the frequent, though relatively minor, tinkering with the curriculum by the LPTS faculty. The 1950s and early 1960s saw a flurry of studies of theological education, the most famous directed by the brilliant Yale theologian H. Richard Niebuhr. The faculty minutes of March 7, 1960, mention seven different studies by various organizations. They prompted the faculty once again to think through the purpose of its curriculum. Although few changes in course offerings resulted, some interesting conclusions were drawn. The task of a minister, they reasoned, entailed relationships and communication, for the purpose of mediating effectively "between God and the Gospel on the one hand, and modern man in the mid-twentieth century on the other." Three years was an insufficient length of time for students to learn all that was necessary for ministry. A core selection of courses could introduce students to the principles of ministry and fundamental knowledge a pastor required, however, and the use of electives allowed for a more rigorous application of thought to more difficult material and specialization in a preferred area of study. The faculty summarized its understanding of its task: "Manifestly, we cannot in three short years teach a student everything he needs to be, know, or do, though he ought to have a

51. Faculty Minutes (1940-1951), December 15, 1950; *The Register* 40 (March 1951): 20; and Arnold Black Rhodes, ed., *The Church Faces the Isms* (Nashville and New York: Abingdon Press, 1958).

clear self-concept of the minister's role by the time he leaves seminary. THE MINISTER MUST BE A LEARNER FOR THE REST OF HIS DAYS."[52]

Louisville Seminary hoped to provide a certain amount of information deemed essential to the ministerial vocation, but even more to develop in students the ability to think, analyze situations, and apply biblical and theological understandings of life to the world. No doubt they had been stung by an observation of Niebuhr's that looked too much like the curriculum in place at LPTS. H. Richard Niebuhr said of the average seminary curriculum that "it impresses the observer as a collection of studies rather than as a course of study. . . . [One's] impression is verified by the manner in which requirements for graduation are mathematically calculated and distributed among departments. The lack of unity is also indicated in the efforts that are made to provide for 'integration' by adding examinations, theses or interdepartmental courses which will insure that students will combine in their own minds what has been fragmentarily offered them."[53]

By World War II the biblical and theological conservatism of the Louisville faculty began to give way to a broader Calvinism. However, one would still characterize the Seminary as conservative into the late 1950s.

Robert Ogden, who taught Old Testament from 1938-1940, marked the first clear public break with Louisville Seminary's rejection of historical-critical study of the Bible. He introduced a third-year elective, "The Historical Development of Old Testament Criticism," in which the student examined efforts to understand the Hebrew scriptures "as they have been unfolded through the church's history. . . . The student will be thus enabled to work out his own estimate of the critical theories of Old Testament Interpretation." A second course, "The Present State of Old Testament Studies," covered the problems raised by the most recent scholarship in the field.[54] Julian Price Love knew critical theory and exposed students to it.[55] In *The Gospel and the Gospels,* published in 1953, Love asserted positively some conclusions of New Testament critical study; for instance, he accepted the priority of Mark among the gospels and the two-source hypothesis as the solution to the synoptic problem. He further referred to the gains in understanding the origins in biblical material that had come through the most recent school of thought, form criticism. At the same

52. Faculty Minutes (1951-1962), April 4, 1960. Emphasis original.

53. H. Richard Niebuhr, *The Purpose of the Church and Its Ministry: Reflections on the Aims of Theological Education* (New York: Harper and Brothers, 1956), 99.

54. *The Register* 29 (April 1940): 34. LPTS Archives.

55. McAtee Interview.

time, in footnotes he suggested that Rudolf Bultmann was too radical in his conclusions and made assertions that ignored questions raised by many scholars. For example, he often used sayings of Jesus as if he assumed they were all authentic.[56]

The acceptance of a moderate historical-critical understanding of Scripture advanced after the war. Rhodes and Chamberlain added "Introduction to the Bible," a course required of all students, in 1951. Now all students would be exposed to an interpretation of Scripture that was non-inerrantist and presented modern biblical criticism in a positive light.[57] In 1959, John Knox Press of the PCUS began to publish The Layman's Bible Commentary, of which Rhodes was an associate editor. The first volume was an introduction to the study of the Bible. Foreman's essay, "What is the Bible?" made a clear statement of his move away from the traditional understanding of Scripture which had reigned at LPTS earlier in the century. The Bible, Foreman argued, is literature, and human beings had an active role in writing it. Since it is also ancient, the Bible must be interpreted to the modern context. Is the Bible true? Yes, because it is the Word of God, by which Foreman meant that the Word or Truth of God's revelation was conveyed to the reader as the Holy Spirit acted in his or her heart and mind. The Bible is revealed truth — truth from God. The inspiration of the writers Foreman described as an urge-to-write that engulfed them as they apprehended God's revelation.

This was a plain rejection of the idea of plenary inspiration, which held that every word in Scripture was written by human agents, but in such a way that they rendered God's word without error. Foreman bluntly said the Bible contained errors of history and science.[58] Thomas Duncan, a student in the 1940s, remembered that he learned basic biblical criticism from Love, Rhodes, and the others. It was not, however, in an extreme form at all; for example, he does not recall any presentation of Bultmann. Al-

---

56. Julian Price Love, *The Gospel and the Gospels* (Nashville: Abingdon-Cokesbury Press, 1953).

57. *The Register* 41 (March 1952): 25. LPTS Archives.

58. Foreman had made the argument while still at Davidson College in a well-known article in the *Union Seminary Review*. Kenneth J. Foreman, "What is the Bible?" in Balmer H. Kelly, ed., *Introduction to the Bible,* vol. 1, The Layman's Bible Commentary (Richmond, Va.: John Knox Press, 1959). Jack B. Rogers and Donald K. McKim, "Pluralism and Policy in Presbyterian Views of Scripture," in Coalter, Mulder, and Weeks, eds., *The Confessional Mosaic: Presbyterians and Twentieth-Century Theology,* Presbyterian Presence Series (Louisville: Westminster/John Knox Press, 1990), note Foreman's *Union Seminary Review* article, which created a stir in the PCUS at the time of its publication.

though the Bible was not treated as without error, there was never any question of the authority of Scripture in Christian faith and life.[59] Louisville Seminary thus demonstrated the giving way of the inerrantist understanding of Scripture that Jack Rogers and Donald McKim have shown took place in all PCUS seminaries during the 1930s and 1940s. They show that "the biblical departments of the southern seminaries gradually added professors who did not believe that a conservative view of the Bible as the Word of God was necessarily bound to a belief in inerrancy."[60]

George Edwards brought the full range of New Testament studies to LPTS when he arrived in 1956. Edwards said it was not until he began doctoral study at Duke that he really discovered current New Testament scholarship in people like Bultmann, Ernst Käsemann, and C. H. Dodd. His presentation of the New Testament made extensive use of form criticism and the "demythologization" of the literature pursued by Bultmann. By 1964 he added an advanced course in New Testament that, beginning with Schweitzer's *The Quest of the Historical Jesus,* dealt with the issues of the historical reliability of the gospels and Jesus' messianic self-consciousness (that is, did Jesus know himself as messiah, and if so, when?).[61] Love's retirement brought Ulrich Mauser to the faculty, who shifted the field of biblical theology from a more doctrinal to a more historical understanding of the ideas in Scripture. There was less of a sense that the thought of the Bible was unified in a plan of redemption and more that it was given to fits and starts as the history of God's people unfolded.[62]

The study of the Bible at Louisville Seminary was of an entirely different nature by 1960 than it had been forty, or in some ways even twenty, years before. Gone was the inerrantist stance, which believed the Bible to be the final arbiter not only of faith and life but also science and history as well. In all Presbyterian seminaries the study of the Bible as God's revelation of a precise (Reformed) system of doctrine that rejected historical criticism gave way to modern literary, textual, sociological, and historical analysis. The secret, so to speak, was out, and it could not be put away again.[63]

59. Thomas Duncan Interview, March 23, 1992.

60. Rogers and McKim, "Pluralism and Policy," 39.

61. Edwards Interview; *The Register* 48 (spring 1959): 26-27; and 53 (spring 1964): 29. LPTS Archives.

62. *The Register* 53 (spring 1964): 30.

63. See John M. Mulder and Lee A. Wyatt, "The Predicament of Pluralism: The Study of Theology in Presbyterian Seminaries Since the 1920s," in Milton J Coalter, John M. Mulder, and Louis B. Weeks, *The Pluralistic Vision: Presbyterians and Mainstream Protestant*

Theological studies underwent a similar transition. Rule continued to teach apologetics and church history from his traditionalist stance — in 1954, for example, he added a new course in church history titled "Christianity and Culture in the Nineteenth Century." He described it as a "careful historical, apologetic and theological appraisal of the impact of the prevailing cultural trends of the West on the thought and life of the Christian Church during the nineteenth century. The appraisal will involve a comparison with historic [read: orthodox and true] Christianity, and with developments in the present century."[64] Hugh Kerr can probably be said to have laid the groundwork for the transition. He offered a course in the 1930s, "Present Trends in Theology," in which students read Barth, Brunner, and representative British and American theologians. Presumably the course included the Niebuhrs, although probably not Paul Tillich, who was only beginning to be known in the U.S.[65] His departure for Princeton delayed for a few years Louisville students' exposure to current theology.

Foreman, although certainly of a broader view than Rule, was still moderate in his theology and expected students to learn and accept Calvinist doctrine. In 1954 he published in book form a series of twelve articles that had appeared in *Presbyterian Outlook* which dealt with the vexing Calvinist problem of predestination and human free will. Foreman argued that, logically and experientially, God must be sovereign and organize all life within God's foreordaining will. Yet it was also true, logically and experientially, that human beings must be free. The Christian was left to affirm both of those contradictory statements, Foreman argued, regarding the problem as ultimately insoluble. In the final chapter he wrote that the best he could say was that

> God, the omnipotent, all-wise and all-loving, decided . . . to limit his Power in giving to his creatures, or to some of them, a measure of freedom. That he may have limited his knowledge, too, is possible. At all events, knowing all possibilities, he did not so limit himself that the control of the universe would ever be wrested from his hands. Why he gave to man the terribly dangerous gift of freedom, knowing (at least) that it could be used to man's destruction, I do not know. . . .
>
> So I have to believe both in the absolute foreordination of God — that God's will includes all things; I am not prepared to say that God's

Education and Leadership, The Presbyterian Presence Series (Louisville: Westminster/John Knox Press, 1992).

64. *The Register* 43 (March 1954): 29. LPTS Archives.
65. *The Register* 27 (March 1938): 38. LPTS Archives.

will literally and deliberately *makes* everything happen that does happen. That way, you get the puppet-universe. . . . I believe in the sovereignty of God but that for me (as for my church) does not mean that God leaves no freedom whatever to man. To believe that nothing whatever occurs except that God wills it, would involve me in Calvin's view that God's private will often goes against his public commands; a view of God which makes him into a kind of hypocrite.[66]

Clearly, Foreman's was a thoroughly Calvinist theology but of a moderate and critical sort. His review of Tillich's *Dynamics of Faith* shows that he was not given to a very speculative or philosophical theology. The book provided, he thought, an excellent introduction to the theology of Tillich and was very helpful for understanding faith in human life, but he disapproved of some of Tillich's key ideas. When Tillich argued that one should not speak of God as *a* being who acts in space and time, but rather as "being itself" or the "ground of being" which undergirds all reality, Foreman responded, "One can see from this one small book why many able minds cannot classify Tillich's thought as basically Christian. He is actually confused about Christian theology."[67] Al Winn, who replaced Foreman, also stood solidly within the Reformed tradition.

The major shift in theology at Louisville Seminary occurred with the hiring of Sam Keen. Called to succeed Rule, Keen did away with the apologetic approach to theology. The field, which Rule had changed from apologetics to "The Philosophical Interpretation of Theology" in Group B of the curriculum, was changed to "Philosophy and Christian Faith." That subtle shift in name signaled Keen's intent to examine how faith could be held, understood, and propounded in light of contemporary intellectual, scientific, and philosophical assertions — and to eschew a defense of Christian thought over against other systems.[68] Keen took that approach out of his own understanding of faith, but also because he had come out of a fundamentalist background and had rejected a theological style that expected acceptance of doctrine without wrestling with its implications. He brought that conviction to the classroom, where he actively challenged students to think about and reevaluate their beliefs.[69]

The metamorphosis taking place in biblical and theological study at

---

66. Foreman, *God's Will and Ours: An Introduction to the Problem of Freedom, Foreordination and Faith* (Richmond, Va.: Outlook Publishers, 1954), 60-61.

67. *The Register* 48 (winter 1959): 7. LPTS Archives.

68. *The Register* 52 (spring 1963): 33. LPTS Archives.

69. Young Interview.

Louisville proved notable, but the most far-reaching changes were again in Group C, or the practical field. In his Sprunt Lectures at Union Seminary in Virginia in 1945, published as *Guilt and Redemption,* Sherrill continued to apply the discoveries of psychology to Christian faith. He believed there was a growing belief that Christianity provided the only sufficient answer to guilt, but that there was an inadequate understanding of the depth of guilt because of an inadequate awareness of the depth of sin. Humans live in conflict, portrayed mythologically, philosophically, and religiously as a battle of irrationality against rationality, body against soul, or evil against good. Whatever the image, he argued, humans know they are not what they should be, and Christians know that humans themselves are responsible for sin through failure to obey God, and psychology can help explain how guilt manifests itself in a human's life.[70] In *The Struggle of the Soul,* after arguing that religion's role is to bring peace but also to disturb humans into deeper faith, Sherrill characterized the Christian view of life as a pilgrimage in which a person tries to understand life's crises and struggles within the purpose of God. In developmental psychology fashion, he explored how one can grow in faith through the five stages of childhood, adolescence, young adulthood, middle age, and old age.[71]

World War II evoked some new courses and the elimination of others in mission. Pratt dropped his courses on the ecumenical movement, the history of Presbyterian mission, and modern mission and the pastor, which dealt primarily with how a congregation could remain informed of mission work and support it. Two new courses emerged that showed the impact of the war. "Foreign Missions in the World of Tomorrow" asked, "What will be the effect of the war on the rising younger churches of mission lands? Equally important, what lands will be closed to missions? What new ones opened? . . . What effect will war have on the giving of the churches and offering of life for missionary service?" The "Seminar on the Church and World Order" focused more thoroughly on the political, economic, and cultural questions that would rise out of the war and the international organization it was assumed the nations would create. "What modifications will be made in the doctrine of absolute national sovereignty or the god-state of recent years? . . . How far are the motives to war economic? Access to sources of raw materials and international tariffs and currencies and national monopolies must be faced. . . . What has Christianity to say? How can it make its voice heard? Is a World Council of

---

70. Sherrill, *Guilt and Redemption* (Richmond, Va.: John Knox Press, 1945).
71. Sherrill, *The Struggle of the Soul* (New York: The Macmillan Co., 1951).

Churches the answer? How far can it come? Can Christians make themselves decisive in post-war councils?"[72]

Charles Pratt retired in 1948, to be replaced by Norman Horner in 1950. Horner restored some historical, practical, and ecumenical courses to the curriculum and added one that reflected the context of the Cold War: "The Church and Communism." Students studied communism, the challenge it posed to Christianity, and the church's responsibility to the underprivileged of the world.[73] Horner also changed the course in world religions from a reading course, taken only by student request, to a regular elective, and in 1952 added "The Sociology of the Expansion of Christianity," a course informed by the missiological questions of Christianity and culture.[74]

The most significant and telling development in Group C — indeed, in the entire curriculum — came with the introduction of pastoral counseling. If one compared a seminary's course offerings from before World War II to those of the late 1950s, perhaps the most striking difference would not be in biblical or theological studies but the absence in the earlier period of the contemporary field of pastoral care. Certainly psychology as a field and as a means of understanding human thought and behavior made itself felt early in the century. Understanding the psychological and emotional development of humans informed the teaching of religious education and homiletics as early as the 1920s (as we saw in the last chapter). Pastoral theology, however, remained primarily the study of the pastoral office and identity and, increasingly, the pastor as manager and administrator. How to comfort people in moments of bereavement, illness, and personal crisis constituted the minister's counseling role.

After World War II, psychology led to the development of a more "therapeutic" culture. If a person had emotional problems or behaved in ways harmful to the self or others, there was a growing tendency to assume not that the person had character flaws or was willfully immoral or sinful, but that there were psychological issues that, with therapy, could be addressed and healed.[75] This led to an attempt to apply the insights of psychology to the role of the pastor, especially as one dealt with people in crises of

72. *The Register* 31 (March 1942): 42-43. LPTS Archives.
73. *The Register* 39 (March 1950): 33. LPTS Archives.
74. *The Register* 40 (March 1951): 33, and 41 (March 1952): 35. LPTS Archives.
75. The reader will recognize that I am posing the pre- and post-therapeutic outlooks in stark and exclusive forms. Of course, in real life they are neither. Still, the post-war period has seen a clear expansion of understanding human being and behavior in psychological or psychotherapeutic terms.

one sort or another. By the early 1950s, Harry Goodykoontz taught, in addition to the earlier courses on psychology and religious education, an occasional course on the psychology of religion. Then, in 1954, LPTS brought in Clarence Barton as an instructor to teach a "Clinical Course in Pastoral Counseling," in which students did counseling with mentally and emotionally ill people under Barton's supervision. Courses in the field of pastoral counseling expanded the next year, and in 1957 the Seminary called David Steere, an alumnus who earned his Ph.D. at Union Seminary in New York, to be the Director of Field Education and to teach pastoral counseling. Steere, who taught at the Seminary until 1996 and holds the record for longest service to the Seminary, became renowned in the field and led Louisville Seminary in offering its students an exceptional education in pastoral care.[76]

Shortly after Steere's arrival a new area of study — social ethics — emerged in Group C. Evangelism and mission had been seen as two elements of one mandate to proclaim the gospel to all people. Pratt had taught both mission and evangelism, and the fieldwork of students took them into situations where they were expected to practice communicating the gospel: mission stations, the "colored" missions, Y meetings, and so on. Slowly, field education became separated from efforts at evangelization and, when placed under Steere, more linked to pastoral care and the role of the pastor as administrator. Consequently, the social element of the gospel, which had always been a part of the evangelistic efforts of students (hence the location of many of the missions in the center city), became separated from an identification with evangelism and made its own distinct field of study.[77]

Obviously the civil rights movement played a determining role in the emergence of social ethics and activism as its own area of study, as did the growing acceptance of the social gospel and the theology of Reinhold and H. Richard Niebuhr in their emphasis on the need to combat sin in its systemic as well as personal form. Engagement with the world also received theoretical support from the writings of the late Dietrich Bonhoeffer and such contemporary writers as Harvey Cox and the "death of God" theologians.[78] This movement took institutional form in 1961 when the Seminary

76. See copies of the spring issue of *The Register* for the rapid growth of pastoral counseling as a discipline at LPTS. Hal M. Warheim, "The History of a 'First-Class Dream,'" 56, notes the trend also.

77. This observation regarding the movement of field education from evangelism to pastoral care is found in Horner, King, and Weeks, "Evangelism and Mission," 7.

78. Dietrich Bonhoeffer, *Letters and Papers from Prison* (New York: Macmillan, 1962); Harvey Cox, *The Secular City: Secularization and Urbanization in Theological Perspective*

called Harold Warheim to teach in the area called Christianity and society. He offered courses such as "The Christian Ministry and American Society," which covered the "social structures of city, suburb, town and country in America; a sociological understanding of religion, economics, class, minorities, and other institutions."[79] Other representative courses were "Walter Rauschenbusch and the Social Gospel Movement" and "Christian Social Ethics." Students at LPTS were beginning to learn methods for creating a prophetic ministry for social action.

In their analysis of theological education in the twentieth century, John M. Mulder and Lee Wyatt have written:

> Throughout the twentieth century seminaries gradually replaced these faculty [the self-taught pastor-theologian] with professors with Ph.D.'s from both European and American universities. Such faculty members carried with them the ideals of the modern university, which were sometimes in tension, if not opposition, to the values of the church.
>
> . . . Consequently, not only has the sociological setting of the study of religion changed but also the field itself. Theology has become more broadly defined, dependent on dialogue with other disciplines, and less related to the church. Furthermore, the social sciences in particular have made a deep impression on the theological curriculum, especially in the practical disciplines. Coupled with the expansion of the churches' expectations of ministers, the social sciences have contributed to the vast expansion of the practical area of the curriculum of theological seminaries. Even more important, the social sciences, the history of religions, and historical criticism have raised implicitly and explicitly the degree to which theologians could make claims to transcendent truth.[80]

Those are the kinds of changes Louisville Seminary began to experience in the 1950s, as the study of religion underwent a transition and some of the "old guard" gave way to the next generation of professors. The methods and, as has been shown, even the areas of theological study were substantially different by the end of the 1950s as the social sciences and literary criticism made their impact on education at LPTS.

(New York: Macmillan, 1965); and Thomas J. J. Altizer and William Hamilton, *Radical Theology and the Death of God* (Indianapolis: Bobbs-Merrill Co., 1966).

79. *The Register* 51 (spring 1962): 37. LPTS Archives.

80. Mulder and Wyatt, "The Predicament of Pluralism," 39-40.

The one area where Mulder's and Wyatt's observations seem applicable to Louisville only in part is in the tendency for faculty to identify more with the world of academia than the church. Generally speaking, the faculty at Louisville Seminary in the 1950s and 1960s remained very conscious that they were educating ministers for the church and identified their own work as a ministry of the church. Indeed, many alumni of those years suggest that it was just such a commitment that mitigated those few theological differences that did exist. William Young noted that in the midst of some disagreements over the methodology and content of theology, the faculty felt such loyalty to the church, the Seminary, and the students that the shared commitment positively affected how they related. Norman Horner, a fundamentalist in his youth in Colorado, was afraid of the liberalism of which he had heard in many PCUSA seminaries and believed LPTS would be a safe, conservative choice. He found the faculty relatively moderate, with Rule most conservative and Sherrill and Love probably the most liberal. Toward the end of his seminary studies (in 1938) he broadened his theological and biblical outlook — but no teachers "stomped" on his fundamentalism if they disagreed. Rather, they accepted it and dealt with him gently. He was convinced, in retrospect, that the ties to the PCUS did not make Louisville a more conservative seminary than most in the PCUSA.[81]

George Edwards liked the motto of his student days, "Preaching the ancient gospel to a modern world," because it made a connection of the biblical roots of Christian faith with the context of the modern worldview in which it was to be lived and proclaimed.[82] Horner echoed that approach and summarized the Seminary's stance regarding theological study when he said, "Christian faith can stand the most penetrating kind of examination from all intellectual disciplines, and it must be submitted to such examination if it is to remain the faith of the most thoughtful Christians in this generation. I have also come to see that it is much more important to proclaim the faith than to defend it."[83] In 1961 the Seminary expressed its understanding of theological education when it amended the section of the by-laws which dealt with faculty to add a statement on academic freedom. A faculty member, they wrote, should recognize his or her responsibility to the denominations of which the Seminary was a part and the confessional stance it represented. Within that context, however,

81. Young Interview; Horner Interview.
82. Edwards Interview.
83. Norman Horner, "What Has Happened to the Seminary?" A sermon preached at Central Presbyterian Church in 1968, copy in LPTS Archives. This sermon came, of course, in the midst of the civil rights and Vietnam upheavals in the nation.

it was necessary to "interpret that Gospel in its relation to the broad scope of human knowledge and to the changing conditions and problems of human life. Such freedom is also required for the fulfillment of the Seminary's obligations as a community of scholars to which the Church has reason to look for thoughtful leadership in bringing the minds of men into harmony with the will of God in intellectual integrity."[84] The Seminary, committed to the church and to Reformed theology, was also declaring its responsibility to cast the gospel in terms that would speak to a rapidly changing world.

As the content and method of Louisville Seminary's courses changed, so too did field education. Already in the 1920s and early 1930s Sherrill pushed the field experience beyond mere fieldwork to actual laboratory experience with supervised reflection. Two elements made field education unique at LPTS: it was supervised by the faculty and performed during the school year. Many seminaries only allowed students to work in the field during the summers or an intern year. In 1937 Sherrill reported to the board that the "Junior Field Work" had proved worthwhile in combining the classroom with practical experience. Louisville's reputation in field education was one strong drawing point for prospective students.[85] Enough middler and senior students took preaching positions out of town, leaving on Saturday and returning Sunday night or Monday morning, that Saturday chapel was discontinued in 1937; Saturday classes had ended years before.[86]

Students learned in many ways through their field education. John Fox, class of 1942, remembered working at the Cabbage Patch Settlement House. During a program a group of boys with whom he worked were to act out the parable of the Prodigal Son. The boy playing the elder brother panicked from an attack of nerves just before he went on stage and forgot his lines. Fox told him not to worry and just remember what the elder brother was like and act like that on stage. The boy rushed on stage, and when the servant told him his father was throwing a lavish party for his brother, the boy retorted, "Has that damn skunk came home?" Fox contended that such a rendering of the passage was the equal of any Clarence Jordan translation.[87]

In 1941 the Seminary began to participate in a unique and innovative program of field education. The PCUSA Board of National Missions, the

84. Minutes of the Board (1960-1970), April 11, 1961. LPTS Archives.
85. Young Interview; Minutes of the Board (1920-1939), May 18, 1937.
86. Faculty Minutes (1932-1940), November 4, 1937.
87. Fox in "Life at Louisville Revisited."

Synod of Indiana, New Albany Presbytery, and LPTS, concerned with the future of small churches and the dearth of ministers to serve them, joined together to create the Todd-Dickey Rural Training Parish just across the Ohio River from Louisville. C. Morton Hanna was brought to Louisville to operate the program. One student was placed in each of the twelve congregations of the parish, while Hanna became the moderator of all twelve sessions and directed the student work. In addition to that work, Hanna taught four courses in rural church ministry and, before long, was named director of all fieldwork for the Seminary.

This project had a number of benefits. It allowed for a supervised field experience, which made it truly a clinic of education; it provided a link between Louisville Seminary and every level of the denomination's governing boards (and all invested financially in the Todd-Dickey Parish); it manifested Presbyterian concern for rural churches; it provided a modest income for the Seminary students; it strengthened congregations. Out of this project, more than any other, the Seminary thought of field placement as more than a way for future ministers to earn money and gain some experience. Nor was the program, or field education in general, just for the benefit of the school and the students. The Seminary catalogue stated as the first objective of its field placements the development of the "maximum possibilities of the field served by the students."[88] Fieldwork was understood as the "laboratory phase" of theological education — that is, as field education. It was this approach that made LPTS' field program stand out and for which the Seminary earned a reputation.[89]

The Todd-Dickey Parish became so successful that two more churches were added, and two area ministers became moderators of the sessions. In 1944 supervised field education became a requirement for graduation, although the amount of work necessary was not stated. The requirement was made seven units in 1950; one semester of approved work

88. *The Register* 34 (March 1945): 8. The Seminary anticipated a point the Niebuhr study made a decade later (*The Purpose of the Church and Its Ministry,* 131-32). Field education, he argued, should be a true laboratory where a student experienced and participated in the love of God and neighbor in action that is the goal of the church and of theological education. If students were just practicing or learning how to "do ministry" later, then fieldwork was perverted into a kind of self-love in which the people in the field were just a means to an end. Louisville and other seminaries were no doubt guilty of the charge, but LPTS sought to avoid the trap.

89. See Minutes of the Board (1940-1960), February 4, 1941; *The Register* 31 (March 1942): 30-31, 50; Sanders, *History of Louisville Seminary,* 86; Horner, King, and Weeks, "Evangelism and Mission," 5-6.

equaled one unit, and summer work counted as two. Field Work Practicum, in which students discussed worship, evangelism, polity, administration, ministerial ethics, pastoral work, and pastoral counseling, related the students' field experience very consciously to the content of their biblical and theological education.[90]

Another innovative co-curricular learning experience that was linked to field education started in 1946. That year Pratt and Hanna required all students to hold evangelistic services during Holy Week in the churches they served for field education. A precedent for this had been set as early as 1931 when Pratt required students in the Practicum in Evangelism to do the same thing.[91] Classes were canceled for the week to make the program possible, and faculty members took part in preaching at various student charges. By this time field placements ranged from Louisville to southern Indiana to places in Kentucky and Tennessee that required train travel for the student; in the 1950s student Morton McMillan traveled to southern Alabama. When classes began again after Easter the students reported that 209 people had joined the church by profession of faith, 104 by transfer of letter, and 22 by re-affirmation of faith. The next year there was satisfaction in learning that in one place the African-American and white churches met together. The Holy Week services became a part of the Seminary calendar and persisted into the 1960s. However, the decline of traditional styles of evangelism wrought changes in the methods and expectations of the week. In 1964 the week was described as a "commitment to some evangelistic mission. This has involved such things as preaching, personal visitation, teaching and group work, counseling, and many unique experiences of the church's mission to the world."[92]

As always, Louisville Seminary offered less formal means by which the students could learn. Worship continued to be held in chapel each day. Faculty members usually preached, occasionally relieved by a guest. Periodically the Seminary attended chapel at Southern Baptist Seminary, as when George Buttrick preached there once.[93] Graduates remember that students learned about preaching simply from hearing the finely-crafted

90. Minutes of the Board (1940-1960), Executive Committee, April 26, 1944, and *The Register* 39 (March 1950): 20-21 and 30.

91. *The Register* 20 (January, February, March 1931): 45.

92. *The Register* 53 (spring 1964): 11. For other references to the Holy Week evangelistic work see Faculty Minutes (1940-1951), May 17, 1946, and May 9, 1947; *The Register* 35 (March 1946): 1; and Sanders, *History of Louisville Seminary,* 97.

93. Duncan Interview and Faculty Minutes (1940-1951), March 11, 1943.

homilies of their teachers. Juniors and middlers preached their required sermons in chapel, but even more daunting were the senior sermons, after which the community gathered for analysis and critique, followed by Caldwell's own response in private. George Edwards remembered those post-chapel meetings with fondness and thought that a lot of learning and community were achieved in that setting.[94]

Other learning opportunities were provided. The Mission Day, reduced from one a month to one each semester, remained under the name of Frontier Day through the 1940s and 1950s. The community still heard lectures and held discussions regarding both global and domestic mission in their varied forms of ministry, including ecumenism and social problems. When the World Council of Churches met at Evanston, Illinois, in 1954, the Interseminary Movement, an organization of ministerial students with a special emphasis on mission, met simultaneously; three students from LPTS attended and learned first-hand of the ecumenical movement. Foreman attended a Theological Consultation held at McCormick Seminary and stayed on for the World Council meeting with press credentials from *Presbyterian Outlook*.[95] During the 1954-1955 school year, just after the papacy's proclamation of the doctrine of the assumption of Mary, the students heard a lecture by Father Charles Boldrick, priest at Holy Trinity Catholic Church, on "The Catholic Doctrine of Mary."[96] The late 1940s and early 1950s also saw a series of forums held at the Seminary and organized by the students themselves, in which current events or topics of interest were discussed. The 1948-1949 year covered issues such as the Berlin Crisis, the problems of public schools and teachers, the Kinsey Report, the implications of television and radio broadcasting for the church, and the problem of public housing. The next year there was another forum on American-Soviet relations and also one on religious education in the public schools in which a local rabbi was one of two presenters.[97]

The centennial class (1953) instituted a lecture series that proved to have a lasting effect on Louisville Seminary. The class gift to the Seminary was a pledge of $10 per year for five years by each member of the class to fund the Centennial Class lecture series. The lectures were inaugurated in 1955 with Nels Ferre's presentations on "Christ and the Church," and the

94. See McAtee Interview; Edwards Interview; Duncan Interview; and Mobley and Jones Interview.

95. *The Register* 43 (October 1954): 4.

96. *The Register* 44 (spring 1955): 57. LPTS Archives.

97. Faculty Minutes (1940-1951), October 8, 1948, and *The Register* 39 (March 1950): 49.

famed church historian Roland Bainton lectured the next year on key figures of the Reformation. Among the other lecturers was John Bright, renowned biblical theologian at Union Seminary in Virginia.[98] The Centennial Class lectures marked an advance in the level of those invited to speak on campus. Historically, the lecturers at Louisville Seminary had usually been denominational figures, General Assembly moderators, alumni, or people engaged in a particular missionary endeavor or ministry. Certainly there were those periodically on campus who were leading scholars or exceptional church figures — Kagawa, Speer, and, in 1947, Martin Niemoeller.[99] Still, the Centennial Class lectures brought a new quality of scholarship on campus, and that enabled the Seminary to persuade other lecturers to come for other presentations. In 1958 alone LPTS received Frank Cross, Old Testament scholar at Harvard, Roger Shinn, theologian at Vanderbilt University, and E. Stanley Jones, famous Methodist missionary.[100] The Centennial Class lecture series later became Lecture Week, which evolved into the ongoing Caldwell Lectures. Louisville Seminary has entertained some of the finest Christian thinkers through these lectures, providing students and churches with yet more learning opportunities.

An Institution of the Church

Louisville Seminary always had close and warm relationships with the Presbyterian churches of Louisville, the surrounding area, and throughout the nearby states — especially Kentucky and Tennessee. Although impossible to judge accurately, this was probably more true under Caldwell's presidency than those who preceded him, even the immensely popular Hemphill. Caldwell had both incredible energy that kept him on the road, preaching and recruiting, and the ability to engage people and communicate the Seminary's mission effectively. The presence of students in churches for worship or for field education and the work of the faculty preaching, lecturing, teaching Sunday school, leading conferences in churches or meetings gave a face to the Seminary, especially in the Louisville area, that created a solid relationship of mutual service. Louisville

98. Arthur Depew in "Reflections"; *The Register* 44 (spring 1955): 1; *The Register* 45 (spring 1956): 58; *The Register* 46 (spring 1957): 58; Faculty Minutes (1951-1962), February 15, 1955, and April 7, 1958.

99. *The Register* 36 (March 1947): 48. LPTS Archives. Niemoeller's lecture was "Preaching the Word of God in a World of Tension."

100. *The Register* 48 (spring 1959): 60. LPTS Archives.

Seminary clearly understood itself to be an institution of the Presbyterian church, offering educational opportunities not only to its students but to the church at large.

The faculty continued to offer special classes for laypeople and continuing education events for pastors. Indeed, those programs expanded. In the spring of 1945 Louisville offered five courses for area lay leaders: Old and New Testaments, doctrine, Presbyterianism, and Christian living. Courses were offered the next year also.[101] The Pastor's Institute, sometimes also called the Pastor's Conference, began in 1945 as well, and continued until being replaced by the Centennial Class lectures. This educational event was the one occasion before the formal lecture series when LPTS consistently brought "big-name" scholars on campus. The leaders included George Buttrick, E. T. Thompson, James S. Stewart, Elton Trueblood, and William F. Albright. Attendance at the conference was consistently 125 and above.[102] There were other occasional, less formal educational events offered. *The Register* issue for winter 1959 described an eight-week Bible study for laity based on the Layman's Bible Commentary, led by Edwards, Foreman, Love, and Rhodes; a series of Wednesday Night Lectures during which church leaders came to campus for public presentations; a meeting of the National Convocation on the Church in Town and Country, held under the auspices of the National Council of Churches.[103]

Another way in which Louisville Seminary contributed to the education of the church was through the published scholarship of the faculty. Although books such as Sherrill's *Guilt and Redemption* and *The Struggle of the Soul* set a standard in the field, most LPTS faculty did not produce ground-breaking scholarship. More often the faculty sought to write for the church, bringing the best knowledge of their fields to pastors and laypeople in congregations. One thinks of Sherrill's book with his wife, Helen, *Becoming a Christian: A Manual for Communicant Classes;* Rhodes' serving as associate editor of the Layman's Bible Commentary (for which he wrote an introductory essay and the volume on the Psalms while Foreman, Love, and Winn each contributed a volume); Winn's *You and Your Lifework: A Christian Choice for Youth,* an excellent book on vocation; Love's *The Missionary Message of the Bible;* Foreman's *From This Day For-*

101. Faculty Minutes (1940-1951), January 25, 1945, and May 18, 1945.

102. *The Register* 33 (December 1944): 1; *The Register* 35 (June 1946): 8; Faculty Minutes (1940-1951), November 10 and 24, 1948, and November 9, 1949; *The Register* 37 (June 1948): 4; *The Register* 37 (September 1948): 4; Faculty Minutes (1940-1951), October 4, 1950; and *The Register* 39 (September 1950): 1.

103. *The Register* 48 (winter 1959): 4-5. LPTS Archives.

ward: Thoughts About a Christian Marriage, another collection of articles in *Presbyterian Outlook;* and Chamberlain's *The Meaning of Repentance.*[104] Nor could one fail to note Rhodes' *The Mighty Acts of God,* published in 1964 as part of the PCUS' Covenant Life Curriculum for adult study. Along with Shirley Guthrie's *Christian Doctrine,* it was perhaps the most widely-read book in the history of the PCUS.[105] There were, of course, many others. The faculty found other ways of serving the church in print. In 1946 Chamberlain became an associate editor of the PCUSA journal *The Presbyterian;* Foreman's weekly article in *Presbyterian Outlook* ran beyond his retirement, and beginning in 1948 he was the editor of the International Sunday School lessons which appeared, according to one report, in 1,600 small town newspapers in the U.S. and Canada.[106]

Perhaps the single greatest illustration of this concern of the faculty for the church was the publication in 1958 of *The Church Faces the Isms.* The book grew out of the senior seminar on "isms" and was an effort of the entire faculty. Individuals wrote chapters on the various movements and Rhodes served as editor. The book was, in effect, a microcosm of Louisville's theological stance. Rhodes wrote that the Seminary faculty all took the Bible as their authority in matters of faith and life, and each religious, political, and cultural movement discussed in the book was addressed from that authority as the person could best interpret it. Each chapter introduced the group or topic with a brief historical sketch, then presented its characteristic features, movements within it, a method for addressing it, and tools for further study. The book was a solid introduction to each "ism," providing the reader with the basic ideas and practices of each. The treatments were as fair as the faculty could make them, with no caricatures or exaggerations and no extreme examples representing the group as a whole. The differences between the "ism" and mainstream Protestant

104. Lewis Joseph Sherrill and Helen Hardwick Sherrill, *Becoming a Christian: A Manual for Communicant Classes* (Richmond, Va.: John Knox Press, 1943); Albert Curry Winn, *You and Your Lifework: A Christian Choice for Youth* (Chicago: Science Research Associates, 1963); Love, *The Missionary Message of the Bible* (New York: The Macmillan Co., 1941); Foreman, *From This Day Forward: Thoughts About a Christian Marriage* (Richmond, Va.: Outlook Publishers, 1950); and William Douglas Chamberlain, *The Meaning of Repentance* (Philadelphia: The Westminster Press, 1943).

105. Rhodes, *The Mighty Acts of God* (Richmond, Va.: CLC Press, 1964). This book, exceedingly moderate in its approach to biblical study, was the first introduction for many people in the denomination to the work of historical criticism. An updated revision has been written by W. Eugene March, published in 2000.

106. Minutes of the Board 1940-1960, Executive Committee, January 4, 1946; *The Register* 37 (September 1948): 4.

Breckinridge Hall, Centre College
(Photo courtesy of Centre College)

The Rev. Robert Jefferson
Breckinridge, D.D., LL.D. (1800-1871),
founder of Danville Theological Seminary

Danville Seminary, Constitution Square, in Danville, Kentucky

The Rev. Stuart Robinson (1814-1881),
professor at Danville Seminary and pastor
of Second Presbyterian Church, Louisville.

Second Presbyterian Church, southeast corner of Broadway and Second Streets, Louisville. It was dedicated in September 1874.

Second Street looking north to Broadway. Seminary students met at Second Presbyterian Church. In this photo, the church is located across the street from the horse-drawn trolley. *(Photo from the Fredrick H. Verhoeff Collection, The Filson Club, Louisville)*

Louisville Presbyterian Theological Seminary stood at the corner of First and Broadway Streets for nearly seven decades. The very location of the Seminary in the heart of a large city raised questions for some.

Walter Newman Haldeman

After meeting in the Sunday School rooms of Second Presbyterian Church, LPTS received a gift of property at First and Broadway from W. N. Haldeman

Left: Seminarians gathered for daily chapel in the John J. Harbison Memorial Chapel at East Broadway. *(Caufield and Shook Studio Collection, Ekstrom Library, University of Louisville)*

The Rev Charles Robert Hemphill, D.D., pastor of Second Presbyterian Church (1885), professor at LPTS (1893), and the Seminary's first president (1910-1920). He is considered the chief founder of Louisville Seminary.

Many wanted LPTS in a suburb of Louisville, against the judgment of those who held it should stand downtown. *(Photo by Smylie)*

Dr. Jesse Cotton,
professor of Hebrew.

Dr. Henry E. Dosker (left);
Edward Warren, librarian (right).

East Broadway from Second Presbyterian Church, lower right.
Louisville Presbyterian Seminary was located at 106 East
Broadway just below the Broadway Baptist Church steeple,
upper left. *(Caufield and Shook Studio Collection, Ekstrom
Library, University of Louisville)*

All meals were shared together in the refectory.

Broadway, looking east.

During his first year as president, Frank H. Caldwell and LPTS faced a challenging crisis in the great flood of 1937. The Seminary became a temporary refuge and Red Cross site for many who could not make it to the Highlands. *(Caufield and Shook Studio Collection, Ekstrom Library, University of Louisville)*

Floodwaters reached Second Presbyterian Church. The current on Broadway was so strong that only boats with large motors could navigate it. *(SG Collection, Ekstrom Library, University of Louisville)*

Librarian Ernest White (far left) helped to establish the theological holdings in the Seminary's library.

A 1950s seminar class led by Dr. Andrew K. Rule (bottom right), professor of apologetics and church history from 1927 to 1962.

The 1955-1956 faculty. Left to right, seated: Julian Love Price, William Chamberlain, Frank H. Caldwell, Andrew Rule; standing: Ernest White, L. C. Rudolph, Norman Horner, Kenneth Foreman, C. Morton Hanna, A. B. Rhodes, Harry Goodykoontz.

In 1941, the Todd-Dickey Rural Training Parish in southern Indiana became an integral part of the Seminary's hallmark program in supervised field education.

The seminary experience included emphasis on missions and global awareness. Speakers such as M. A. Thomas (left) from India were invited to the campus.

As more married students enrolled, the Seminary was faced with growing issues of housing and space.

Dora Pierce, who graduated with a Bachelor of Divinity degree in 1961, was the first woman in the school's history to receive a degree.

In the late 1940s, a quartet of students (left to right: Julian Houston, Max Perrow, Roger Williams, John Fredick) sang each afternoon on a devotional program sponsored by the Louisville Council of Churches on WAVE radio. *(Photo courtesy of* The Courier-Journal and Louisville Times, *1949)*

In 1950, LPTS accepted applications for enrollment regardless of a student's race. Snowden Isaiah McKinnon, who was denied entrance into another school, became the first degree-seeking African-American student and the first to receive a degree at LPTS. *(Photo by James N. Keen)*

The Class of 1955. In 1956, LPTS denied admission to qualified students because the school could not accommodate all of them.

Upon learning that I-64 would intersect with the chosen site for the new LPTS campus, President Caldwell secured land overlooking Cherokee Park from the Southern Baptist Theological Seminary. LPTS broke ground on April 11, 1961. *(Photo by James N. Keen)*

Building an entire campus at one time, a monumental achievement in the years following World War II, cost $4.4 million (approximately $21.5 million in 1999 dollars).

The Rev. Charles Robert
Hemphill, D.D.
1910–1920

The Rev. John M.
Vander Meulen, D.D., LL.D.
1920–1930

The Rev. John R.
Cunningham, D.D., LL.D.
1930–1936

The Rev. Frank H. Caldwell, Ph.D., D.D.,
LL.D.
1936–1964

The Rev. Albert Curry
Winn, Th.D., Th.M., B.D.
1966–1973

The Rev. C. Ellis
Nelson, Ph.D., M.A., M.Div.
1974–1981

The Presidents of Louisville Presbyterian Theological Seminary

The Rev. John M.
Mulder, Ph.D., M.Div., D.D.
1981–present

Clockwise from top: main quadrangle from chapel *(Photo by Henry-Blessing, Chicago);* the library *(Photo by James N. Keen);* Milner Lounge in the student center; student Karen Korkles in dorm room *(Photos by Jim Wright).* Ernest White coordinated the move of the library to the new campus. The chapel was constructed in 1962.

The women's movement and the war during the
1960s initiated profound change, growth,
activism, and spiritual hunger among the
Seminary's students and faculty.

The 1975 Women's Caucus meetings included (clockwise from far left) Cheryl Duncan, Mary Edwards, Ann Hickey, Deborah
Block, Mary Gene Boteler, Tina Robb, Linda Chase, Marie Cross, and two students who could not be identified.

Interior of the Frank H. and Fannie W. Caldwell Chapel. The 1982 Caldwell Lectures featured W. R. Reuther. *(Photo by Jim Wright)*

Top: Burton Cooper (far left) leads a small group discussion with students. Middle: Johanna W. H. van Wijk-Bos was the first woman to receive academic tenure on the LPTS faculty. Bottom: A. B. Rhodes (far right) crowds under an umbrella with graduates on a rainy Commencement Day.

The 1978-1979 faculty. Left to right, front row: Ernest White, George Bennett, David Steere, Norman Horner, Harold Nebelsick; middle row: Craig Dykstra, Linda Chase, Tom Jones, Johanna Bos, Clinton Morrison; back row: George Edwards, Lewis Weeks, A. B. Rhodes, Ellis Nelson, Grayson Tucker. Missing from the photo: Burton Cooper, Daniel B. Wessler, Charles Brockwell.

In 1986 Virgil Cruz (right) became professor of New Testament. He was the first tenured and only African-American on the faculty at that time.

Louisville Seminary has become a part of significant contributions to the Louisville community. Below left: Since 1990 LPTS and the University of Louisville have jointly awarded the prestigious Grawemeyer Award in Religion. Right: The Roger Wood Puckett Organ was donated to LPTS in 1985. Bottom: The Seminary celebrated its role in bringing together the Presbyterian Churches.

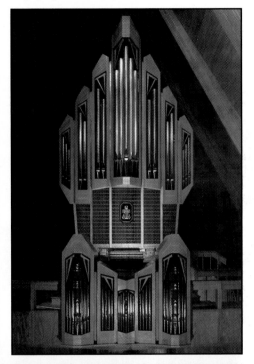

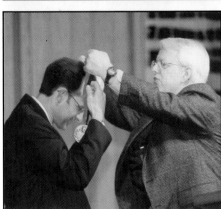

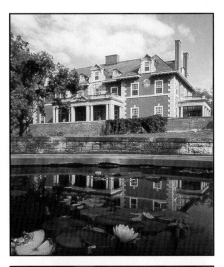

LPTS submitted a bid to purchase Gardencourt, which was up for public auction by the University of Louisville. After winning the bid, LPTS launched a community-wide campaign to fund the restoration of the historic mansion. *(Photo of press conference by Christina Freitag; photo of Gardencourt by John Nation)*

To commemorate the Seminary's sesquicentennial, a fund-raising campaign, "Equipping the Saints," was initiated in 1996. Some of the goals included the renovation of the Winn Student Center *(above, by Jonathan Roberts)*, new pitched roofs on the buildings of the main quadrangle *(below, by Jonathan Roberts)*, and the William R. and Ellen Laws Lodge Retreat and Conference Center *(left, by Stephen Driver)* for continuing and lay education. The Lodge was the first building to be constructed since the campus had been built in 1963.

Right: LPTS students, alumni/ae, and faculty and the community interact with theological scholars at the endowed Caldwell and Greenhoe Lectures series, held during the annual Festival of Theology.
(Photo by Jonathan Roberts)

Left: Professors (left to right) Stephen G. Ray, Jr., Scott C. Williamson, Dale P. Andrews, John M. Mulder. Below left: The Marriage and Family Therapy Program at LPTS is one of four accredited seminary programs in the nation *(Photo by Dan Dry & Associates)*. Below: The unique work of the Center for Congregations and Family Ministries provides resources, practical help, research, and theological vision toward nurturing a life of faith in families.
(Photo by Jonathan Watson)

A Lilly Endowment Inc. Technology Grant helped LPTS to develop a computer lab and integrate technology into teaching and learning in the classroom.
(Photo by Dan Dry & Associates)

Professor Carol J. Cook is one of nine women on a faculty of 22 individuals. *(Photo by Dan Dry & Associates)*

The faculty of 1999. Left to right, front row: David Hester, Patricia Tull, Nancy Ramsay, Johanna Bos; second row: Susan Garrett, Kathryn Johnson, Christopher Elwood, Amy Plantinga Pauw, Scott Williamson, Eugene March; third row: Loren Townsend, Dianne Reistroffer, John McClure, Stephen Ray; fourth row: Marion (Marty) Soards, John Mulder, Milton (Joe) Coalter. Missing from photo: Frances S. Adeney, Dale P. Andrews, J. Bradley Wigger, George Carter. *(Photo by Ralph Homan)*

The Louisville Seminary faculty is distinctive because of its involvement in and service to the church. It is comprised of nationally recognized scholars who minister to students and the church simultaneously.

Above, left: Scott Williamson, Robert H. Walkup Professor of Theological Ethics. Left: W. Eugene March, A. B. Rhodes Professor of Old Testament

Christianity were delineated, and the book offered helpful ways for pastors or church members to respond. This even-handed approach can be seen in Rudolph's chapter on fundamentalism. He asserted that there existed a type of fundamentalist Christianity one might call conservative which is not militant, divisive, or legalistic and remained in conversation with other points of view. He had Rule at hand to offer as proof. Further, fundamentalism had at least one strength broader types of Christianity often lacked: it knew what it believed and judged faith on the authority of Scripture and tradition. Yet it was often too narrow — for instance, in its insistence on interpreting the death of Jesus by the theory of penal substitutionary atonement, drawing on the image of one who accepted punishment (or paid a debt) that humans could not. There were also biblical images of ransom, adoption, and the union of Christ with the believer. "When the point of substitutionary atonement becomes man's recital of what God *must* do to be God or to satisfy justice," Rudolph asserted, "it approaches blasphemy." The book was and continues to be a very useful resource for its readers.[107]

The Seminary faculty served the church not only in their role as scholars but also in their capacity as presbyters. They served as pulpit supplies, Sunday school teachers, moderators of presbytery, synod, and General Assembly, and on committees at all levels of the church. Of course, Louisville alumni served in a variety of ways also. In 1939 the following list of alumni achievement was compiled: 3 had been seminary presidents, 1 (Sherrill) a dean, 11 seminary professors, 7 college presidents, 9 college professors, 9 General Assembly moderators (alumni, former students, and faculty were counted here), and 7 secretaries (executives) with General Assembly boards or executive committees.[108] One can only wonder what the totals would have been twenty or sixty years later. In this area of service one should not fail to note the important role of the library as a place of study for area clergy and laity and the off-campus lending, by mail, offered by the library. Another element of church and Seminary relations developed in the 1950s, when a group of women, mainly from the PCUS synods of Kentucky and Tennessee, approached Caldwell and Horner regarding the possibility of buying a house to serve as a furlough home for missionaries. This was a PCUS seminary tradition, and a house was bought in the Crescent Hill area of Louisville. The women funded it and the Seminary supported it and

107. Rhodes, ed., *The Church Faces the Isms.* Rudolph's discussion of fundamentalism is chapter 3; the quotation (italics original) is from p. 64.

108. *The Register* 28 (June 1939): 1.

served as the treasurer. The house provided a service to the denomination and gave Louisville another resource for education.[109]

The middle decades of the twentieth century marked something of an apex in ecumenism and church unions. Although the two largest Presbyterian denominations in the United States remained separated, they watched other denominations unite and played a role in church cooperation in global Christianity. The World Council of Churches, delayed by World War II, became a reality in 1948. Northern and Southern Methodism, including the Protestant Methodist Episcopal Church, reunited in 1939, later to form the United Methodist Church by merger with the Evangelical United Brethren. The small German Evangelical and Reformed churches joined in the 1930s to form the Evangelical and Reformed Church, which in 1957 merged with the Congregationalist church to form the United Church of Christ. In India, the first union of churches with episcopal and non-episcopal forms of government took place in 1947 with the creation of the United Church of South India.

It was during Caldwell's presidency, and by his active leadership, that Louisville Seminary's dual identity became a factor in the drive for reunion of the PCUSA and PCUS. When the PCUS created its Permanent Committee on Cooperation and Union in 1937, Caldwell was appointed to serve on it and did so until it was disbanded in 1955. Sentiment was growing in the denomination for reunion, and this committee's task was to promote reunion in the denomination and explore the basis on which it might be achieved. Caldwell worked tirelessly for reunion. He was convinced, from his experience at Louisville Seminary and serving PCUSA congregations in Kentucky when first out of seminary, that there was virtually no difference between the PCUSA and PCUS. If you spoke with a Presbyterian you could rarely identify her or his affiliation, he often said.[110]

Louisville Seminary began to portray itself, in contrast to earlier disclaimers, as favoring and playing a role in reunion efforts. Charles Pratt wrote an article for *The Register* in 1939 in which he referred to Jesus' prayer for unity in John 17 and then noted that, from the missionaries' standpoint, church division created a stumbling block to proclaiming the gospel. Drawing on the work of H. Richard Niebuhr in *The Social Sources of Denominationalism,* he bluntly declared that the PCUSA and PCUS

---

109. Ken Hougland Interview, March 17, 1992. LPTS Archives.

110. Fannie Caldwell Interview. Harrison Ray Anderson, pastor of Fourth Presbyterian Church in Chicago, strongly supported reunion and also served on the committee. The Seminary later established a chair in his name in recognition of that work.

should reunite. A member of the PCUS, he laid the blame for failure to do so at the feet of his denomination, arguing that sectionalism, the belief that the PCUS had a distinctive witness, racial attitudes, and the doctrine of the spirituality of the church were all wrong.[111]

The 1946 catalogue asserted that at Louisville Seminary a student would know people from both denominations, know the life and issues in each, and hear and meet leaders of each denomination. "It is difficult for students to graduate from Louisville Seminary with provincial minds and spirits," the catalogue boasted. "The natural impact is toward a Kingdom-of-God vision."[112] Graduates testify to the broadening views their LPTS experience evoked — both through meeting people and, very often, serving as student pastors in congregations of the other denomination. Of course, Louisville was sending alumni into both the PCUS and PCUSA who were disposed to reunion and usually served as active advocates for merger. Al Winn stated the case plainly: ". . . the Seminary was the one counter-argument to the kind of belief that there was no way that the two churches could have belonged together." Beyond its actual connecting of the two churches he believed LPTS served a key symbolic value, perhaps for the South more than the North.[113]

The work for reunion reached its apex in the early 1950s, with a vote finally arranged for the 1955 General Assemblies. The Seminary's advocacy for merger did not preclude an attempt to present both sides of the question fairly; in 1954, for example, the tape of a debate on the issue between L. Nelson Bell, conservative associate editor of the *Southern Presbyterian Journal,* and E. T. Thompson, church historian at Union Seminary and a leader in the reunion effort, was played for the students.[114] With the vote approaching and Louisville Seminary reflecting on 100 years of its own history, the board gave thanks for the merger of the two seminaries in 1901, inasmuch as it was doubtful if either could have survived without the other. "Here we have learned that we are one," the statement continued. "Here we have experienced together the Grace of God as this institution has prepared men to serve our common Lord and Saviour in a divided church. We have come to know that actually we are not two, but one."[115] The PCUSA General Assembly approved reunion, but it failed in the

111. *The Register* 28 (November 1939): 1-7. LPTS Archives.
112. *The Register* 35 (March 1946): 10-12. LPTS Archives.
113. Al and Grace Winn Interview, February 22, 1992. LPTS Archives.
114. Faculty Minutes (1951-1962), March 1, 1954.
115. Minutes of the Board (1940-1969), June 2, 1953.

PCUS. Reunion would have to await more hard labor and a later day for success. Caldwell and LPTS continued the struggle.[116]

The Seminary Ethos

In 1961, as Louisville Seminary moved more fully into modern theological education, a statement of purpose written by the faculty to appear in the catalogue affirmed the original vision of Presbyterian seminaries as "nurser[ies] of vital piety, as well as of sound theological learning."[117] "As an arm of the church the Seminary understands that, without lessening in any way its demands for academic and professional excellence, it must also be in its own place the household of faith and the body of Christ on earth," the faculty wrote. "Therefore its purpose is not finally achieved until it welds students and faculty into a genuine Christian community which by its common life of worship and service aids all its members to grow in grace and edifies the church beyond its wall."[118] The Seminary sought to achieve that goal by engendering a family, even intimate, atmosphere on campus — which was facilitated by the building itself, in which students lived in the same space where classes were taught, faculty had offices, worship was conducted, people ate, the administration worked, and library research was conducted. Alumni and faculty universally speak of the intimacy that existed at the downtown campus between students and faculty and within the student body. Mobley said the personal relationships that developed "would just touch our [hearts]," and people recalled the frequency with which faculty entertained students in their homes — some students would do yard work or odd jobs on faculty homes, visiting with both professor and wife all the while. The Seminary retreat at the beginning of each school year helped build trust with open discussion and worship. The new students learned

116. The ecumenicity of LPTS went beyond the two Presbyterian denominations. Students of other denominations, especially Methodists, were regularly educated at LPTS. Work with local ministerial groups and the Federal (later the National) Council of Churches was a part of faculty service. Caldwell and Horner attended the World Alliance of Reformed Churches meeting in Brazil in 1959 and, in 1961, Caldwell was a delegate to the World Council of Churches meeting in New Delhi, India.

117. The General Assembly of 1810, cited in Steve Hancock, "Nurseries of Piety? Spiritual Formation at Four Presbyterian Seminaries," in Coalter, Mulder, and Weeks, eds., *The Pluralistic Vision: Presbyterians and Mainstream Protestant Education and Leadership,* The Presbyterian Presence Series (Louisville: Westminster/John Knox Press, 1992).

118. Faculty Minutes (1951-1962), April 3, 1961.

that seniors did not have all the answers yet, and that "faculty members can say 'I don't know,' that unity and mutual self-respect can prevail despite varieties of experience and conviction."[119]

The faculty's concern and affection for students were genuine. One year Foreman spent a sabbatical traveling around the world visiting Louisville Seminary graduates working overseas. Paul Love, with whom Foreman spent three days, spoke of the enjoyable visit and noted that Foreman's questions and desire to understand his ministry "spoke of a deep concern for my work and experience."[120] John Dunstan remembered that in 1949, in his first year at LPTS and with a Patterson scholarship, he prepared to withdraw because, with a wife and child, his indebtedness was more than he felt was safe. He could not refuse an offer to take a job in a plant in New Albany, Indiana. When he told Hanna, the field education director asked him what he needed to be able to stay in school. The answer was $500 for his debt and $75 per month. In three days he had it and never knew the source of the money.[121] Mobley and Jones said Caldwell, in addition to his other tasks, was often the Seminary loan officer. When he learned a student was in need, he sent him to the bank for a loan secured with his personal life insurance policy.[122]

Sometimes students surely wished the faculty had been a little less diligent. Late one night in the 1950s a student thought he smelled smoke and called for the fire inspector to investigate. The fire department came out in force. After hours of diligent searching — which included a student climbing through the transom into Goodykoontz's office, knocking over a bookshelf and scattering papers on his desk, putting things back as best he could, and the professor not realizing it had happened because his was a notoriously unkempt office — they found nothing. In the meantime someone had called Hanna, who arrived from his small farm in Jeffersontown dressed in suit and tie just as the excitement abated. He reportedly said, "'Well, I'm dressed and here.' It was about 4:30–5:30 in the morning by then. He said, 'I need to talk to Billy Babbs about his field work.' So, he went and drug the boy out of bed and started talking to him."[123]

119. *The Register* 36 (March 1947): 7. LPTS Archives. Young Interview. For some comments on the intimacy of the downtown campus, see Delia Collins Interview, March 16, 1994; remembrances in "Life at Louisville Revisited" and "Reunion 1993 Reflections"; Fannie Caldwell Interview; Mobley and Jones Interview; Duncan Interview; and Winn Interview.
120. "Reunion 1993 Reflections."
121. "Life at Louisville Revisited."
122. Mobley and Jones Interview.
123. McAtee Interview.

Students also created their own community. Although by the early 1960s some of the group devotional practices, such as evening prayer meetings and mission study groups, no longer existed, bonds were formed in many ways. They all contributed to a Student Benevolence Fund, which was for emergency assistance to students in need, with some of the money going to the Red Cross, Community Chest, and like organizations. The basketball team continued to play and in the late 1940s the Seminary quartet sang each afternoon on a devotional program sponsored by the Louisville Council of Churches on WAVE radio. Christmas parties, involving the entire Seminary community and at which faculty were often roasted, were a large part of Seminary life. Robert Freytag, class of 1953, related that his student charge was the home church of the great Brooklyn Dodger infielder Pee Wee Reese, whom he brought to one of the Christmas parties. It was a big thrill for the Seminary, and Reese later said it put Christmas in its proper perspective for him.[124]

There have only been occasional opportunities in this study to mention another segment of the Seminary community: faculty and student wives. The wives of faculty members took on the duties usually associated with the designation "pastor's wife." The preparations for the entertaining of students in faculty homes fell to them, as did those for events held at the Seminary — parties, dinners, and receptions after lectures or other special occasions. Dinnerware was usually brought from faculty homes. Grace Winn recalled a day just after her husband had joined the faculty when she received a call that she needed to be downtown at the campus for some event, and she should bring her silver. She had no car at home and could not reach Al, so she made the trip on the bus with her silver chest in hand.[125]

This work of the women took organizational form in the Divinity Dames. This group served a number of roles for women on campus. It provided, above all, a support group for young women who were in an experience with their husbands that they could not fully share, partly because their opportunities were limited and partly because their husbands were in an exciting and often overwhelming program of study. The Dames also gave an opportunity for the faculty wives to prepare the young women for life as pastors' wives, for they had all been in that role for at least a few years before their husbands joined the faculty.[126] Classes were also offered

124. "Reunion 1993 Reflections."
125. Winn Interview; see also Ernest White Interview, March 16, 1992.
126. Leonard I. Sweet, *The Minister's Wife: Her Role in Nineteenth-Century American Evangelicalism* (Philadelphia: Temple University Press, 1983), is an interesting study of the

to the women; faculty members frequently offered them biblical and theological courses. The Divinity Dames also planned ministries of their own. Grace Winn remembered teaching low-income women in the city how they could fix economical and healthy meals for their families. The group obviously reflected the traditional norms of the day, but the support and help it provided wives of students should not be discounted.[127]

Louisville Seminary's conviction that it was preparing ministers for the church meant that the faculty took a student's spiritual preparation as seriously as it took his (and, rarely, her) intellectual readiness. The question of non-academic criteria for granting a degree raised by Love earlier was raised again. In 1939 the board informed the faculty that, given the responsibility of presbyteries for ordination, the Seminary's role in judging factors other than academic should be limited. They urged the faculty to continue to mold the moral and spiritual character of students and, in cases of deficiency, to try to persuade a person to forego the ministry. Presbyteries should also be informed of any problems of which the faculty was aware before a person was ordained.[128] Soon after, the faculty made clear that its graduating fellowships would not be granted on academic achievement alone, "but only if he is likewise distinguished for Christian character and promise of usefulness as an evangelical pastor or teacher of religion."[129] Occasionally faculty admonitions were funny: in 1946 the faculty voted to communicate with a student "suggesting that he give more time to sermon preparation and to cultivate the art of saving his money."[130]

At times Louisville narrowed the gate of entry to theological education. In 1938 a Unitarian minister inquired whether or not he could enroll for classes at the Seminary in pursuit of a Th.M. He was welcomed to enroll, although without a B.D. he could not receive the master's degree. Be-

---

understanding of ministers' wives in American Protestantism. Sweet identifies four models of the way women generally understood themselves as wives of clergy in the nineteenth century: Companion, who supported her husband's work; Sacrificer, who gave up her own needs and expected little from her husband at home; Assistant, who helped in the ministry of her husband; and Partner, who built a ministry alongside her husband. Sweet argues that the last two became severely restricted models in the twentieth century because of a host of issues, among them the professionalization of ministry and the identity of Protestantism with capitalist culture (in which women played mainly derivative roles to men in terms of participation in public life). That meant the twentieth-century minister's wife tended to be Companion or Sacrificer.

127. White Interview; Winn Interview.
128. Minutes of the Board (1940-1960), March 29, 1940.
129. *The Register* 31 (March 1942): 60.
130. Faculty Minutes (1940-1951), May 17, 1946.

yond that, the faculty referred to the board the question whether or not this man might be a candidate, given the Seminary's charter; they would gladly allow it if proper to do so. The board ruled that, inasmuch as section one of the constitution said a degree candidate must be either a member of an evangelical church or a person in "full communion with some other Christian Church," a Unitarian could not receive a degree from the Louisville Seminary. Apparently by their standards the Unitarian Church was not Christian.[131] Tom Duncan observed that Seminary attitudes could become self-righteous in defense of the church. In his senior year, when he was student body president, a Seminary student was found at a downtown bus station in a "compromising homosexual position." Duncan said everybody simply knew he had to go. No one raised the question of his future, how he felt, or any other matter about him. He was dismissed, with no apparent pangs on the part of anyone, Duncan included, to his later regret.[132]

Most Seminary disciplinary cases arose around the issue of the consumption of alcohol. In 1944 a student was expelled after admitting to being in a bar and having drinks in Louisville. A week later another student who had been arrested in Union City, Tennessee, on charges of public drunkenness was allowed to receive his degree. He said he was on his way to Memphis, stopped for two drinks in this city where he had been student pastor, and — because he had been up for two nights finishing Seminary work — apparently was uncharacteristically affected by the drinks and fell asleep on a stranger's porch. A fellowship in biblical theology and a strong recommendation by the faculty for a scholarship at Duke University for further study were withdrawn.[133] The problem appeared again periodically in the 1950s, and in 1959 the faculty declared its stance on drinking by Seminary students. Drunkenness was a sign of lack of self-control, which rendered one unfit for the ministry. Social drinking was inadvisable, and the faculty disapproved of it because it was dangerous to the individual and injurious to an effective ministry, for most Presbyterian congregations would oppose it. Drinking further set a poor example for youth and endangered alcoholics. Finally, publicity about seminarians drinking alcohol would be harmful to the LPTS. Students were urged to act accordingly.[134]

An important element in the atmosphere of any educational institution, especially for students, is the staff. Louisville was no exception. The

131. Faculty Minutes (1932-1940), January 13, 1938, and March 3, 1938; Minutes of the Board (1920-1939), February 18, 1939.

132. Duncan Interview.

133. Faculty Minutes (1940-1951), May 9 and 15, 1944.

134. Faculty Minutes (1952-1962), February 10, 1959.

presence and contribution of Bob Veazey, who played the organ at the Seminary until his retirement in the 1950s, has been noted. In 1963 LPTS celebrated the retirement of William Warford, who had been Louisville Seminary's janitor since 1923. He worked hard and served the Seminary well, but generations of students speak of the counsel he dispensed and the hard-won wisdom with which he could speak to those who sought him out. He was a special aspect of life at the downtown campus.[135] Another valued member of the LPTS "staff" was known simply as Mannie; he ran a drug-store across Broadway from the Seminary. McAtee remembered that the students called his place "Abraham's bosom" because Mannie was Jewish. Kind, personable, and sharing, Mannie was a help to untold numbers of students through his lending of money and counsel — and, according to Mobley, the solutions to problems in Hebrew translation.[136]

One aspect of life at the campus on Broadway was having urban life literally at the Seminary's gates. People speak of transients, prostitutes, panhandlers, and alcoholics along the street, and periodic eruptions of vio-lence, even gunfire, just outside the campus. The immediacy of the darker side of life was an important element of the educational experience for many students. McAtee said that, as a young man from small-town Missis-sippi, he would not have traded what he learned of life there for anything.[137]

Although the doctrine of the spirituality of the church remained power-ful in the PCUS, the denomination and its ministers, under the influence of neo-orthodox theology, increasingly asserted the legitimacy of a social minis-try, especially in the PCUSA. During the years from the late 1930s to the 1960s the church's theological reflection gradually caught up with the imme-diacy of LPTS' urban context to lead the school into more social awareness and action. Since thr Seminary was located in Louisville, social awareness meant, above all, confronting racism. Haltingly and with extreme caution be-fore the emergence of the civil rights movement of the 1950s, and with more certainty afterward, Louisville Seminary began to address Jim Crow.

In 1938 the Seminary undertook to train local African-Americans as leaders of classes on the Christian family and extended to them use of the library. It was plainly stated, however, that none of the participants could hold classes in the Seminary buildings or sit in Seminary classes, so that LPTS could "conform to the State Constitution."[138] Just two months later,

135. *The Register* 52 (winter 1963): 6. LPTS Archives.
136. McAtee Interview; Mobley and Jones Interview.
137. McAtee Interview.
138. Faculty Minutes (1932-1940), January 13, 1938.

however, the Southern Interseminary Movement, of which Benfield was an officer, requested that Louisville Seminary house the African-American delegates when the group met in Louisville later that year. The faculty agreed. Presumably, since the guests were not students at the Seminary, they would not be breaking the law.[139]

Neither the faculty nor Caldwell was satisfied with mandated segregation in education. When a student at Louisville, Caldwell attended the 1924 Student Volunteer Movement convention in Indianapolis. As a young man from Mississippi, he was taken aback to learn the meeting was integrated, and then impressed with an African Christian speaker whom he judged the best at the entire convention — better than such notables as Speer, Sherwood Eddy, and John Mott. Caldwell was forced to re-evaluate his belief that African-Americans were inferior to whites and examine his stricken conscience. He began to change.[140] Late in 1944 Caldwell and the faculty sought a way to integrate LPTS, but attorneys told them there was no way legally to do so.[141] At the same time the faculty was offering its classes for lay leaders and they expressed their "profound regret" that the law prohibited them from conducting integrated classes and arranged special courses for African-Americans if enough applied to justify them.[142]

The end of World War II brought increasing opposition to Jim Crow laws. In 1949 Kentucky's Day Law[143] was amended to allow integrated attendance in classes at colleges and universities, but it did not provide for integrated residence on campus. In 1950 an African-American Baptist, Snowden Isaiah McKinnon, was denied admission to Southern Baptist Seminary on the basis of the law and made overtures to Louisville Seminary regarding admission. Caldwell informed the board that he intended to accept applications regardless of a student's race. The board endorsed that course of action.[144] McKinnon did apply and became the first degree-seeking African-American student in the history of Louisville Seminary and the first to receive a degree. Since he was a resident student, LPTS breached the law, although no legal response was made. Students at the

139. Faculty Minutes (1932-1940), March 13, 1938.

140. The story is told in "Liberal Cleric in the South: Frank Hill Caldwell," *New York Times* (April 13, 1966). Photocopy of newsclipping. LPTS Archives. The article appeared on the occasion of Caldwell's election as moderator of the PCUS General Assembly.

141. Faculty Minutes (1940-1951), December 20, 1944, and January 4, 1945.

142. Faculty Minutes (1940-1951), January 25, 1945.

143. The law took its name from Carl Day, the legislator who sponsored the segregation bill in 1904.

144. Minutes of the Board (1940-1960), May 23, 1950.

time remember no public reaction at all, nor did the Seminary work overtly for the complete integration of church and private schools which became Kentucky law in 1954.[145] In the 1955-1956 school year, Charles Henry Johnson, a student from Liberia, developed sickle cell anemia and died. Caldwell contacted the Liberian embassy in Washington, D.C., and the ambassador traveled to Louisville and stayed with the Caldwells. Anne Caldwell remembered that as a rare event in the Cherokee Gardens section of the city, where African-Americans normally came only as servants.[146]

The acceleration of the civil rights movement in the late 1950s led to more deliberate stances by the LPTS community. In 1960 the student body appointed a special committee to study positive means for encouraging integration in Louisville area businesses. This committee proposed, and the student body passed, a statement of concern to be printed in Louisville newspapers. The declaration asserted the incompatibility of Christianity and discrimination, called upon businesses in the area to desegregate their services and places of business, and pledged their support for those who did. The students also drafted a letter of commendation and support that would be sent to businesses that already had or did integrate their facilities.

In a separate action the LPTS students addressed the Executive Board of the YMCA for the Louisville area, which met nearby at Third and Broadway. The students, acknowledging their own sinfulness before God, stated their conviction that the gospel required Christian opposition to segregation and that Christian groups must work for the end of racial separation. Consequently, they urged the board of directors of the YMCA to reverse its stated policy of segregation at all of its locations in the Louisville area. The faculty concurred in all those communications and commended the students' "earnest concern for the realization of Christian race relations."[147]

A year later the faculty went on record as favoring the desegregation of downtown Louisville businesses "at the earliest feasible time," notifying the Mayor's Committee on Integration of their stance. They also sent a letter to the YMCA approving of the desegregation implemented up to that time and urging the board to move to full integration.[148] In 1964 the Seminary community became involved in more direct political action for civil

---

145. "Reunion 1993 Reflections" and Edwards Interview.

146. Anne Caldwell Interview.

147. Faculty Minutes (1951-1962), May 19, 1960.

148. Faculty Minutes (1951-1962), March 19, 1961. The students again voted for desegregation, pledging massive support of businesses that opened their doors to blacks and whites over against the massive resistance to integration practiced by many in the South. "Seminary Times," 6 (April 11, 1961). LPTS Archives.

rights. Classes were dismissed on March 5 so that faculty and students could join an open housing march in Frankfort. Caldwell attended and participated.[149] Newspapers ran pictures of seminarians at the march, which caused a negative reaction in some Presbyterian quarters in Louisville.[150]

Caldwell, as president and primary fundraiser, was naturally sensitive to publicity that might injure the warm relations the Seminary enjoyed with Presbyterians in Louisville and the surrounding region. It was rarely an issue, but occasional episodes like the Frankfort march caught people's attention. In 1958 Love was invited to speak at the Indiana University extension campus at Jeffersonville. When asked to take a loyalty oath to the U.S. he refused, calling it "childish and insulting."[151] The administration of the school then asked Edwards to speak, and he agreed without knowing of either the loyalty oath or the prior offer to Love. When the newspaper ran an article on Love's refusal of the oath, Edwards notified the dean he would not deliver his lecture. Soon thereafter Edwards was to lead a youth program at Harvey Browne Presbyterian Church. Edwards said that Caldwell asked him not to mention the Indiana University affair to the students or any reporters who might seek him out. Caldwell stressed the need for maintaining LPTS' good reputation in the city.[152]

In 1961 the faculty sent a letter to the board expressing its "unqualified confidence in the Christian integrity" of each member of the faculty. They declared that "no member of this faculty is teaching or preaching communism, nor is any of us promoting communist objectives. On the contrary, we are all devoutly concerned with eliminating the social swamps in which communism breeds."[153] Apparently a member of the faculty, probably the highly activist Edwards, had been the target of accusations of communist subversion. These occasional difficulties made Caldwell cautious about the form the Seminary's social witness took. Complaints against the Seminary were but harbingers of more turbulent days ahead.

---

149. Winn's memory is that Caldwell marched in Frankfort, although Caldwell's daughter remembers him keeping a lower profile by staying in the car, so as not to appear that he was "dragging the seminary behind him."

150. Anne Caldwell Interview; Louisville Presbyterian Theological Seminary. Minutes of the Faculty (1962-1967), February 19, 1964, and March 18, 1964. LPTS Archives.

151. The lingering effects of McCarthyism, with its belief that subversives were undermining America's security, accounted for the school's requiring an oath of loyalty to the nation.

152. On this episode see "Seminary Ex-President, Dr. Julian Love, 74, Dies," *Courier-Journal* (May 13, 1969). Newsclipping, LPTS Archives. Edwards, untitled recollections.

153. Faculty Minutes (1951-1962), November 21, 1961.

A New Campus

Shortly after the end of the war it became obvious that the campus was inadequate for the Seminary's needs. The perennial problem of married student housing has been noted, but space for the growing faculty and classrooms was also an issue. In 1956 the Seminary denied admission to qualified applicants because the school could only accommodate fifty-eight new students.[154] There was no room for expansion of the Broadway campus and, equally important, the authorities planned to build a new expressway alongside the Seminary.[155]

Under such constraints the board voted in 1953 to purchase a new site for the Seminary, citing housing, library, and parking inadequacies as the primary reasons for the decision.[156] This move was part of the original plan for the Seminary; in the 1950s churches rapidly sprang up in the suburbs as congregations followed the demographic changes which marked American society.[157] Perhaps for those reasons the board and Seminary personnel did not fully understand what a risky and courageous undertaking they initiated. The purchase of land and raising of money sufficient to erect an entirely new campus required vision and commitment of the highest magnitude, especially given the series of setbacks which arose to impede the completion of the move. It would take ten years following the board's vote to bring the project to fruition.

The process to effect the move, led by Caldwell and board member Frank Anderson, chair of the building committee, got underway with the purchase of a tract of land between Old Cannons Lane and Seneca Park in the eastern part of the city. So great was the affection for the old building that the decision was made to move it block-by-block to the new site to stand as the centerpiece of the new campus. The campaign to fund the purchase of the land and the erection of the new campus began in 1956, with the Louisville phase to raise $1,250,000.[158] By early 1959 the new freeway was ready to move from the planning stage to reality, and the Seminary's move, going steadily but slowly ahead, gained new urgency. The board rescinded the decision to move the building from Broadway, choosing to sell

154. *The Register* 45 (winter 1956): 1-2. LPTS Archives.

155. The expressway — part of the current I-65 — literally passed within fifteen feet of the east side of campus.

156. Minutes of the Board (1940-1960), June 5, 1953.

157. See Hudnut-Beumler, *Looking for God in the Suburbs.*

158. Hudnut-Beumler, *Looking for God;* Executive Committee, October 20, 1953; Faculty Minutes (1951-1962), September 10, 1956.

it as quickly as possible before the value fell any more because of the highway; they would begin construction on Cannons Lane soon. Just one month later, however, Caldwell learned that a new eastern expressway (now I-64) planned by the state would intersect the new site. Pleas all the way to the governor brought no diversion of the highway. Frantic work led to the purchase of the "Norton tract," twenty-one acres of land owned by Southern Baptist Theological Seminary along Cherokee Park, and an adjacent seventeen acres for a total price of $330,000. Finally the Seminary broke ground at the new site at 1044 Alta Vista Road on April 11, 1961. Louisville Seminary was moved from Broadway to the new site just two years later, but even that did not take place easily — a fire in the chapel roof shortly before completion provided one more hurdle to overcome. Finally the move was accomplished and LPTS had roomy and beautiful new accommodations.[159]

The final cost of the new campus was approximately $4,400,000.[160] The Seminary had just over $100,000 remaining in its building fund in 1965, which meant it occupied the new site debt-free and could use the surplus for the three-bedroom apartments still needed.[161] Although no one doubted the necessity of the move from Broadway, given the inadequacy of the building for the Seminary's needs, there was sadness mixed with the excitement of the move. People regretted leaving the old building and wanted desperately for it to be preserved rather than destroyed in urban renewal. There were negotiations with the PCUS Synod of Kentucky to convert the building for use as a retirement home, but the talks bore no fruit. Eventually it was sold to the city for use as part of the Jefferson County Community College for approximately $400,000. It was less than LPTS believed it was worth, but the Seminary was happy the building would be preserved. Its continued use for educational purposes was a bonus. The other drawback to the move, seen more in retrospect, was the loss of immediate contact with urban life, which had until then been one of the advantages of an LPTS education. Still, no one questioned that the move had to happen.[162]

159. Minutes of the Board (1940-1960), January 6, 1959, and November 20, 1959; Executive Committee, February 17, 1959; October 7, 1959; and September 12, 1960; Louisville Presbyterian Theological Seminary Board of Directors, Minutes (1960-1970), April 11, 1961, and June 4, 1963; Executive Committee, June 11, 1962, and December 4, 1962. LPTS Archives. Mobley, "The Administration of Louisville Presbyterian Theological Seminary."
160. That is approximately $21.5 million in 1999 dollars.
161. Those apartments were named Love Hall and Sherrill Hall when built.
162. Minutes of the Board (1960-1970), November 9, 1964, and October 27, 1965; Executive Committee, June 11, 1962. On the necessity and drawbacks of the move, see William

The campus on Alta Vista Road stood as a physical reminder of the impact Caldwell had made on Louisville Seminary. With the move completed, Caldwell chose the end of the 1963-1964 year to sadden the Seminary community with his resignation. He became the executive director of the Presbyterian Foundation, succeeding John Cunningham, whom he had earlier followed into the Seminary presidency.[163]

Caldwell's presidency was remarkable. Elected president at the age of thirty-four, he was the youngest president in the Seminary's history and he held the post for twenty-eight years. He saw the Seminary through the final years of the Depression and World War II, guided the expansion of the faculty after the war, oversaw the first steps into a social ministry and more liberal biblical and theological seminary education, and more than any other person made the new campus a reality.[164] Caldwell was simply a great ambassador for theological education in general, and LPTS in particular, and a denominational leader held in the highest esteem by all. Mobley described him as the Chief Executive Officer, loan officer, scholarship manager, and teacher. "In addition to other duties," he added, "he was also the channel for most money which came to the school; and he became the long range planning chief, and head of the campaign for capital funds, and he also preached on most Sundays."[165] William Ekstrom noted his ability to know the entire Louisville community and his skill at public relations and organization, combined with tremendous energy.[166] His pace, however — especially the endless labor to get the new campus built — had a price; in the last few years at LPTS Caldwell rarely taught. Although his resignation was hard for the Seminary to bear, Caldwell believed it was time to let fresh leadership take the Seminary into a new era. Few could have foreseen how "new" the next few years of the nation's and LPTS' existence would be.

Ekstrom Interview, March 17, 1992; Fannie Caldwell Interview; Delia Collins Interview; Edwards, untitled recollections; Mobley, "The Administration of Louisville Presbyterian Theological Seminary"; Robert Wood Lynn Interview, May 7, 1994; George Newlin Interview, May 9, 1992. LPTS Archives.

163. Minutes of the Board (1960-1970), Executive Committee, June 4, 1964.

164. John M. Mulder, "Memorial Minute: Frank H. Caldwell." 1987. LPTS Archives.

165. Mobley, "The Administration of Louisville Presbyterian Theological Seminary."

166. Ekstrom Interview.

· V ·

A VERY STRONG SENSE OF COMMUNITY

The Presidencies of Albert Curry Winn
and C. Ellis Nelson, 1965-1981

W hen Frank Hill Caldwell resigned from the presidency, Louisville Seminary had come through the trying days of the Depression and World War II and was enjoying the relative calm of the 1950s. Julian Price Love was named acting president, a position he held for more than a year until Albert Curry Winn was elected and assumed office on February 1, 1966. Winn had taught at Stillman College, the PCUS' historically African-American school in Tuscaloosa, Alabama, prior to his call to LPTS in 1960 to succeed Foreman in doctrinal theology. Winn's tenure as president — from 1966 to 1973 — coincided with the worst years of national upheaval over civil rights and the war in Southeast Asia. Seminaries across the nation, including LPTS, participated in and felt the impact of the sociopolitical battles of those years, and it fell to Winn to guide the Seminary through the difficulties they entailed. In addition, the demographics of the students preparing for ministry began to shift dramatically and the content and methodology of theological education changed even more radically than it had in the late 1950s. In the midst of all this Louisville Seminary had to carry on with its work.

Winn's resignation and the arrival of Ellis Nelson in 1974 brought another crisis to address. By the early 1970s deficit spending, gone at LPTS for years, returned, as it had in seminaries throughout the nation during these years.[1] Nelson perceived that his first and paramount goal would be

1. See Badgett Dillard, "Financial Support of Protestant Theological Education" (Ed.D. thesis, Indiana University, 1973), and Anthony Ruger, *Lean Years, Fat Years: Changes*

to rein in spending, which required, in part, reduction of staff and faculty. It was painful for both Nelson and the Seminary community to do so, but the realities of Seminary finances were undergoing a shift that can be fully grasped only in retrospect. It would take hard decisions to address the new situation. However, Nelson's presidency was not limited to financial problem solving; during his tenure the Seminary community began to formulate a vision of a renewed purpose for Louisville and to chart a way into the future. There were great forces of change, both internal and external, in theological education through the 1960s and 1970s. Under Winn and Nelson the Seminary weathered numerous storms and emerged in a position to move ahead once again.

The Turbulence of the Civil Rights and Anti-War Movements

The previous chapter recounted the support for integration of businesses that prevailed among the faculty and students by the early 1960s. By the mid-1960s the issue had become desegregation of residential neighborhoods through open housing ordinances and enforcement. In 1967 the faculty voted to commend three members of the Board of Aldermen who voted for an open housing bill, and the mayor for the "position he finally took" regarding the legislation.[2] Desegregation of housing was only fitfully achieved, of course, and so court-ordered busing became necessary in 1974 to effect integration of the public schools. The faculty acknowledged the problems with busing and admitted the value of neighborhood schools; yet the benefits of integrating education surpassed these drawbacks. "We also recognize that pupil transportation can cause fears, confusion, inconvenience, or resistance and so we affirm the need of a ministry of reconciliation through constructive, compassionate, affirmative action."[3] Faculty and student support exceeded the passing of resolutions, as in the 1964 march in Frankfort. Periodically people engaged in acts of civil disobedience and were jailed briefly for their actions — including George Edwards and Harold Warheim on one occasion. Edwards recalled one student who,

---

in the Financial Support of Protestant Theological Education (Auburn, N.Y.: Auburn Theological Seminary, 1994).

2. Minutes of the Faculty (1962-1967), April 12, 1967. LPTS Archives.

3. Minutes of the Faculty (1971-1979), May 28, 1974.

in Gandhian fashion, entered into a period of fasting to promote the cause of civil rights and open housing.[4]

Despite involvement in various elements of the civil rights movement, it was the war in Vietnam that was responsible for spurring the most continual, fervent, and widespread acts of protest by the faculty and students. As with civil rights, there was unanimity of opinion among the faculty and, apparently, the student body regarding the immorality of the nation's involvement in the war. The only real question had to do with the form and the extent of protest that individuals deemed appropriate and in which they felt comfortable participating. It was a time in the Seminary's history when students saw the faculty's faith in action and were able to relate to them outside the classroom — an opportunity both students and faculty felt was important.[5] That joint action became an integral part of theological education at LPTS as well as at other seminaries around the nation.[6]

The various social protests of the Vietnam years were far too numerous to chronicle here. The first harbinger of the turmoil to come was a 1965 faculty resolution sent to President Lyndon Johnson, Kentucky's senators, and Louisville's congressional representative in Washington. U.S. military escalation had just begun in Vietnam, and the resolution expressed doubt regarding American policy and urged the nation to call "an international conference on Southeast Asia, that conference to include Communist China."[7] As the fighting began and then intensified, so did the opposition. Faculty and students regularly participated in and led weekly vigils organized by the Louisville peace activists at the Federal Building for the duration of the war. Nor was the activism limited to Louisville. A group traveled to Washington, D.C., for a demonstration that included a silent vigil in the Capitol. Daniel Wessler and others from LPTS were arrested when they refused to leave the building.[8]

---

4. George Edwards Interview.

5. Burton Cooper Interview, March 13, 1993; Syngman Rhee, a Korean student just before this time who became a campus minister at the University of Louisville, mentioned this element of education also. Syngman Rhee Interview, June 21, 1994. See also Daniel Wessler Interview.

6. For the antiwar movement in general, see Charles DeBenedetti and Charles Chatfield, *An American Ordeal: The Antiwar Movement of the Vietnam Era* (Syracuse, N.Y.: Syracuse University Press, 1990). For a treatment of some of the Christian involvement in that movement see Mitchell K. Hall, *Because of Their Faith: CALCAV and Religious Opposition to the Vietnam War* (New York: Columbia University Press, 1990).

7. Faculty Minutes (1962-1967), February 10, 1965.

8. Wessler Interview.

The faculty and students, separately and jointly, continued to pass resolutions and express themselves through a variety of communications to media or public figures. Moratorium Day, which was observed annually around the U.S. by opponents of the war, became a part of Seminary life, inspiring professors to cancel classes in favor of some act of protest. Once crosses were placed in the new Seminary quadrangle to represent the deaths of soldiers and civilians in Vietnam. On another occasion the Seminary supported a Meal of Reconciliation at a local Presbyterian church, the proceeds of which went to provide relief for war victims in South and North Vietnam.[9] When the fighting spread beyond Vietnam to Laos and Cambodia, the faculty appointed Winn, Clinton Morrison (who was academic dean at the time), and Harold Nebelsick (professor of doctrinal theology) to represent the Seminary at a meeting of the Churchmen's Emergency Committee on Cambodia in Washington. Faculty and students received permission to leave classes on May 6 to engage in some form of protest and education on the issue, and then on May 12 the faculty approved a student petition granting those who desired to work full-time to end the U.S.' military involvement in Southeast Asia to cease their academic work for the remainder of the semester with the instructor either granting a grade for work completed or giving the student until September 15 to complete the course requirements.[10]

The Vietnam War provoked more than protest against the killing itself and the use of the military in international relations. It also prompted an evaluation of some of the social dimensions of military service and the draft. The selective service system allowed for any number of exemptions, or deferments, from military service, and college students, clergy, and seminary students were all among those whose service was deferred.

It became obvious to many that American combatants were disproportionately represented by those who did not have the means, financial or otherwise, to obtain a deferment. There emerged a growing sentiment that

9. Edwards Interview; Faculty Minutes (1962-1967), January 4, 1967.

10. Faculty Minutes (1967-1971), May 4, 1970, and May 12, 1970. For a sampling of statements and activities surrounding the war see the following in the LPTS Archives: Faculty Minutes (1962-1967), January 4, 1967; January 9, 1967; February 1, 1967; and March 13, 1967; Faculty Minutes (1967-1971), May 29, 1969; October 6 and 8, 1969; Faculty Minutes (1971-1979), May 1, 1972; May 8, 1973; "Anti-Draft Group Gets Support," *The Louisville Times* (May 8, 1969); "War Foe Refused Hearing at School Board Meeting," *The Courier-Journal* (September 24, 1968); "Minister Leads 50 in Picketing," *The Louisville Times* (March 26, 1966); and "Quakers, Louisville Presbyterians Visit Capital to Lobby Against War," *The Courier-Journal* (May 8, 1970).

the draft law should be changed to alleviate, or at least mitigate, those inequities. Some in the religious community believed that the ministerial deferment allowed the believer to avoid facing the hard decisions about war in general, and the Vietnam War in particular, that were necessary to stop it. If the deferment were eliminated, then clergy and seminarians would be forced either to declare themselves conscientious objectors or live with the reality of military service — as did every other eligible Christian, Jew, Muslim, or other religious adherent. Why should clergy be treated differently from any other believer?

In 1967, recognizing this situation, a joint student-faculty Social Action Committee undertook a study with a view to preparing a recommendation regarding military service. As the committee did its work, a resolution before the entire student body that the 4-D (ministerial student deferment) classification be abolished by the government was defeated. The committee could reach no decision regarding a recommendation for the students and faculty. The faculty adopted the stance that the draft should be abolished altogether, with the nation relying on an all-volunteer force. Until then, the college deferment should be reconsidered, it said, and clergy and seminarians classified with graduate students and professionals. Students, on the other hand, voted in favor of the seminary classification. It has been suggested that a significant number of students enrolled in seminaries, Louisville included, to avoid the draft. Although many faculty at the time believed such students were few in number at LPTS, one wonders if the student vote reflects that element.[11]

Less than two years later a group called Seminary Students Concerned about the War and the Draft, consisting of students from Louisville and Southern Baptist Seminaries, wrote a paper in which they denounced the war for diverting energy, imagination, and money from solving problems such as hunger and education; for international policy dominated by a strategy of military threat or intervention; and for the injustices of the selective service system. The group called for a volunteer army, but they did not call for the abolition of special classification for seminarians, although it was implied in their criticism of the draft system as a whole. The group received the support of most of the faculty at LPTS.[12]

Although the end of the war certainly brought a reduction in the social activism of the Seminary community, social concern and action did not disappear. George Edwards played a national role in the movement to

11. Faculty Minutes (1967-1971), December 4, 1967; Burton Cooper Interview.
12. Faculty Minutes (1967-1971), May 7, 1969.

grant amnesty to draft resisters; the control and reduction of nuclear arms — in the public eye due to the Strategic Arms Limitations Talks (SALT) and agreements — drew Seminary attention for years. Boycotts supporting the United Farm Workers and protesting the restoration of the death penalty also caught the Seminary's attention. In the attempt to help people learn strategies to move beyond protest to effective social change, Warheim and three students organized a three-day training event for social and political action they called the Institute of Social Justice. One hundred church and community leaders from the eastern half of the United States attended, led by twelve staff people in workshops. Public lectures were delivered by Jesse Jackson and Ralph Nader.[13]

To no one's surprise, fervent opposition to the war and support for civil rights negatively affected the Seminary's relationship to many in the city, to local Presbyterian churches, and to the PCUS and UPCUSA. The new Seminary campus had attracted church people in a number of ways; in 1965 the board learned that the Seminary had hosted two presbytery meetings, ten synod committee meetings, ten special luncheons, twenty-five ministerial associations meetings, two "schools for young pastors," and given tours to five hundred visitors.[14] Such contact with church people and Presbyterians in the region enabled the Seminary to build on the good reputation it had established. But that solid relationship suffered as the social and political activism of members of the Seminary community accelerated. The influence of the ultraconservative John Birch Society in some local churches only exacerbated the problem.[15] Much of the controversy swirled around Edwards, although many in the Seminary community took action that was very public — some going so far as to be arrested.

Edwards had been one of only three known conscientious objectors from the PCUS during World War II, giving alternative service. Among other assignments, he served as one of the "guinea pigs" on whom malaria tests were run by the military. At war's end he went with the American Friends' Service Committee work groups, doing reconstruction work in Italy. His studies at Louisville and then at Duke University did nothing to reduce his conviction that war and injustice should elicit nothing but opposition from Christians, and he became very zealous in his work for civil rights, nuclear disarmament, and American international policy that was

13. Hal M. Warheim, "The History of a 'First-Class Dream,'" 53.

14. Minutes of the Board (1960-1970), April 27, 1965.

15. This point is made by a number of those interviewed. See especially Davis Young Interview. The Strathmoor Presbyterian Church was particularly affected by the John Birch Society.

not dependent on military intervention. Edwards' wife, Jean, shared his convictions, and together they took a leading role in developing one of the strongest chapters of the pacifist Fellowship of Reconciliation in the nation; they later served on its national board. Edwards played a very public role in the various phases of the civil rights struggle in Louisville, particularly during the antiwar movement. He was often in the newspapers, sometimes with a picture. He was thus a lightning rod during the storm of criticism that descended on LPTS from those who disagreed with either the stance or methods — or both — of the war's opponents.[16]

In 1967 the board directed its president, Lyman Dawson, to tell people who voiced concern over Seminary participation in protests that the board had discussed the issue and that church sessions were invited to send representatives to Louisville Seminary to talk with members of the board. On April 25 of that year the board appointed a committee of board members, faculty members, administrators, and students to "discuss the tension between political activity and institutional loyalty" and to propose principles and guidelines for the Seminary community.[17] Their action suggests that local churches had already begun to react against the Seminary's antiwar stance; these reactions would only accelerate as the war escalated. George Newlin, on the board at the time, understood that there were periods during which Henry Mobley, board president after Dawson, received as many as six calls a day from people complaining about some resolution or action by someone at the Seminary.[18] Winn, Horner (dean until his departure in 1968), and members of the board who lived in the Louisville area spent countless hours meeting with church sessions or receiving people at the Seminary to explain the necessity of maintaining academic freedom and the rights of conscience regardless of the popularity of someone's stance.

16. Tom Duncan, a classmate of Edwards' at Southwestern College, said he always appreciated his commitment to pacifism, even if he did not always agree. Edwards did not have to become a conscientious objector during the war — he was in the ministerial curriculum in college and could have received a deferment, but did not believe he could do so while others were facing death. He also notes that Edwards was known around the Seminary as one person to whom students could turn with any problem, any time of day or night, and many students were devoted to him. Duncan Interview. Ellis Nelson, who became president after most of the Vietnam turmoil had died down, also spoke well of Edwards' commitment, even though he did make it more difficult for the president and board to raise money. But he said that Edwards often took stands that, perhaps as long as ten years later, would be proven correct or at least gain more widespread backing.

17. Minutes of the Board (1960-1970), April 25, 1967.

18. George Newlin Interview, May 9, 1992.

Of course the denominational press covered the Seminary's activism; the conservative *Presbyterian Journal* in particular pointed to protests and arrests as symbols of the liberalism and lack of respect for authority that were so prominent in society and had lodged in the Presbyterian church as well.[19] The publicity definitely had an impact on Seminary fortunes. In 1967 the enrollment of PCUS students dropped very precipitously.[20] Giving from churches and individuals dropped. Some churches were reluctant or unwilling to make themselves available as field education sites.[21] Edwards said that even Peace Presbyterian Church, a predominantly African-American church that he and his family had helped organize, opposed his anti-war work because military careers provided one of few ready means of improvement to men in the black community.[22]

The intensity of feeling evoked by the war and the problems with which Louisville Seminary had to deal were epitomized at the Seminary commencement of 1967. The graduating class selected Edwards to preach the baccalaureate sermon. When he finished reading the Scripture lesson, fourteen men rose en masse to read a statement of protest. Ben Johnson, a member of Second Presbyterian Church, proclaimed that they only stood as a serious matter of conscience, believing that Edwards' biblical and theological positions were inconsistent with the standards of the PCUS and that his conduct on public matters was unbecoming a minister and seminary professor. The senior class rose in opposition to the statement, and Winn moved to the pulpit, declaring that the group had made their declaration without interruption and that the service would continue. The protesters left. As if he had known the protest was coming, Edwards said in his sermon:

> The church, the ministry, and the institutions of the church, including this seminary, stand today under the tests of freedom. The shrill cries of the racists, the nationalists, the Birchers, and the anticommunists

19. See, for example, "The Louisville Story," *Presbyterian Journal* 31 (June 21, 1972): 9-11, 20. The article described the work of LPTS alumnus Terence Davis, who worked for a civilian review board to deal with police brutality in the city of Louisville. The journal cited charges that his work was linked to the Southern Christian Education Fund, called a Communist-front organization, and Carl Braden, whom the *Journal* called at least pink, if not red. An entire series of Seminary involvements in protests and contacts with people designated leftists was recorded in the article.

20. Minutes of the Board (1960-1970), October 10, 1967.

21. McAtee made this point in particular about congregations in Transylvania Presbytery.

22. George Edwards, untitled recollections.

are raised in every corner where the Christian faith seeks its unhampered application. . . . Where we are exempted from the defamation and attacks of this reaction, it is evidence that the church lies under suburban captivity and purchases its peace at the price of justice and human rights.[23]

Interviewed later, Winn defended Edwards' freedom to act according to the dictates of his conscience. He added that, although some board members disliked his activism and disapproved of his relationship with the Southern Christian Education Fund (considered by some a Communist front — Edwards was not a member, but periodically cooperated in some civil rights work), none doubted Edwards' dedication as a Christian and his loyalty as a citizen of the United States.[24]

Winn's comments demonstrate the mediating role he played between the Seminary and the public and, at times, between the board and the students and faculty. Winn opposed the Vietnam War and approved of many of the forms of protest taken by members of the Seminary community. In 1968 he addressed the General Assembly of the PCUS and challenged the commissioners to consider what it meant to love one's neighbor when that neighbor is Vietnamese, or Negro, or a white segregationist.[25] Periodically Winn himself participated in some protest; Edwards remembered he once was pictured in the newspaper marching with a group from Louisville and Southern Baptist Seminary to Bellarmine College for a teach-in regarding the war. The questions surrounding Vietnam were very personal to Winn: he had three sons who struggled with their consciences regarding military service.[26] More than any other he spent countless hours explaining Louisville's position to concerned individuals and sessions. Burton Cooper, who joined the faculty in 1970, was thoroughly impressed with Winn, recalling him as "unpretentious, very intelligent, [and] very concerned about curricular matters and theological education." His social conscience attracted Cooper as it did so many others.[27] As important as the Seminary's good relationship to the church was, Winn would not preserve it at the expense of his own conscience and freedom or those of others.

Winn and the board bore the responsibility for managing the school

---

23. The story is told in "Louisville Seminary Worship Disrupted by Protesters," *Presbyterian Survey* 57 (July 1967): 36-37.

24. "Worship Disrupted," 36-37.

25. "Seminary Leader Stirs Assembly," *Dallas Morning News* (April 24, 1966).

26. Edwards Interview.

27. Cooper Interview.

financially, of course, and so sought to find a way to minimize the fiscal side effects that were an unavoidable result of the protests. In 1968 the board adopted the American Association of University Professors' 1940 "Statement of the Principles of Academic Freedom and Tenure." The statement declared that professors should be free to speak as citizens but should also realize that their words could lead people to judge not only them but also the schools where they taught. The Seminary board said that, by extension, the same was true of actions. All constituencies of the Seminary should respect the position of others. Faculty and students should remember the importance of support (financial and otherwise) of friends, and those friends should remember that a seminary without freedom would not be the laboratory of intellectual honesty it was intended to be. The board would be clear to those outside of Louisville Seminary that their defense of freedom and divergent viewpoints did not necessarily equal endorsement and that it was not their place to prescribe for others the appropriate response of faith to God. It was proper, however, for the board to "make clear that actions and associations of members of the Seminary community can and do provoke criticism of the institution, create considerable ill will, lower morale, and diminish resources necessary to the Seminary's health and welfare."[28]

Duncan recalled that some members of the board were "aghast" at some of the actions people took — especially Edwards — although he did not think there were attempts to have Winn restrict the witness of anyone. He thought some clergy on the board believed Winn, Edwards, and the others were making the witness which they felt they could not make, while a number of lay members simply could not understand why a person would act in such a way that harm came to Louisville Seminary.[29] William F. Ekstrom, dean in the School of Arts and Sciences at the University of Louisville, had great respect for the board and said he never knew a board as congenial or dedicated as was the one at LPTS. He once found himself in the position of having his office picketed by college students (with assistance from Edwards) by day, then going at night to meetings with church sessions as a member of the LPTS board to defend the right of protest.[30]

28. Minutes of the Board (1960-1970), April 23, 1968.
29. Thomas Duncan Interview.
30. William Ekstrom Interview, March 17, 1992. For examples of board attempts to address differences with faculty and students, see Minutes of the Board (1960-1970), October 13, 1969, and Minutes of the Board and Executive Committee (February 1971–July 1977), October 9-10, 1972.

Ekstrom was one of many who believed Winn was central to maintaining order and the operation of the school through those years, as he was fair to all sides and able to understand both the students and the church members whom they offended. "I think Al [Winn] handled this very well," Ekstrom asserted. "He let the students know that there were limits that had to be placed upon [the] kinds of things they could do. And, they had to have some respect for the attitudes of the people in the local churches who did not share their point of view. It was a matter of walking a very fine line."[31] And even as he walked this line he built bridges of understanding with the board. Looking back it is difficult to describe the maelstrom that was Louisville Seminary in the 1960s — when different constituencies struggled constantly with each other over the meaning of faith, the ethical implications of the gospel, the Christian's political role and relationship to war, and the morality of American policy in Southeast Asia. But Winn was at the center of it all, and it is due in large part to his efforts that Louis Weeks found many congregations still interested in the Seminary and its students in the early 1970s.[32]

Changes to the Curriculum and Seminary Governance

The social situation in which the church, and consequently the seminaries, found itself in the 1960s led to internal changes at LPTS. The first had to do with the curriculum, which, with minor adjustments, had remained the same into the mid-1960s. One of the consequences of the exciteme●: and willingness to entertain new ideas of the period was continual evaluation of how better to equip people for ministry.[33] Winn, in his address "Teaching Theology in the Age of Secularity," given at his inauguration as professor of doctrinal theology, said that it was not enough simply to impart the Calvinist past to students, as had often been the case in previous generations. Now it was important to acquaint future pastors not only with the great ideas of the past but also with different contemporary

31. Ekstrom Interview.

32. Louis Weeks Interview, March 15, 1993. Edwards notes today that, despite those difficult days, he has positive memories of the board and friendships with individual members such as Alan Steilberg and Morgan Roberts. For an example of Horner's defense of the rights of conscience and academic freedom see a sermon he preached at Central Presbyterian Church in 1968, "What Has Happened to the Seminary?" LPTS Archives.

33. Wessler in particular noted that new courses, new teaching methods, and various experiments were implemented. Wessler Interview.

schools. Pastors needed to be theologians, to form their own theological stances and to be able to think theologically about life — their own, their parishioners', and the world's.[34]

In 1967 Louisville Seminary implemented a new curriculum to embody that understanding of theological education. Morrison noted that this was a time of extensive, even radical, curriculum revision at seminaries all over the U.S. LPTS took a rather cautious approach, but nonetheless participated in a national trend.[35] Faculty minutes show that it took a number of years to settle on the new plan. Winn sat on the committee, which was very unusual for a president; toward the end it was led by Hal Warheim as the chair of the Library, Curriculum, and Schedule Committee.[36] Warheim later described the new curriculum as dialogical, growing out of the meeting of the world and church in the great struggles of the day. Samuel Keen, for instance, taught "Philosophy *and* Christian Faith," and Warheim taught "Christianity *and* Society."[37]

The curriculum aimed for four goals in preparing ministers to be theologians and meet the world. First was independence, based on the reality that ministers are not in classrooms following seminary, but must be independent learners for life. For this reason required courses were minimal; students would create their course of study almost wholly out of electives. The expectation was that learning would happen through their own reading in the library.

Second, the curriculum aimed for integration of theory and practice. The only two required courses addressed problems students would confront in ministry and, through team-teaching, would "call upon the various disciplines to dialogue with each other and to demonstrate their relevance to practical problems."

Third, the school sought more competence in the traditional disciplines. To graduate, students were required to pass an examination in each of the three areas of study at LPTS: Bible, History and Theology, and Pastoral Theology. Since the curriculum was elective, preparation for those tests would be by the students, selecting their own classes and doing independent study. Students had the option of completing two area exams and passing eighteen hours of coursework in the third.

34. Albert C. Winn, "Teaching Theology in the Age of Secularity," *The Register* 54 (winter 1965): n.p. LPTS Archives.

35. Clinton Morrison Interview.

36. See Faculty Minutes (1962-1967). Cooper commented on the involvement of Winn in academic matters of every sort, even as president. Cooper Interview.

37. Warheim, "First-Class Dream," 34.

The final goal was specialization by students in one area of ministry. The domination of the curriculum by electives made this possible, but it was also hoped that in the final semester students in the top one-fourth of their class would take no classes in order to pursue an in-depth research project in an area of specialization.[38] As Cooper remarked, the curriculum was based on the premise that individuals knew their own educational needs better than anyone else could.

The new curriculum had a relatively short lifespan; it was eliminated in 1972, though parts of it remained. The students themselves did not like it in many cases; they found that they needed more guidance than it provided. It was too much, perhaps, to expect students to make the theological connections between fields of study, integrate the content of different disciplines, and then apply that to the world and their pastoral situations all on their own. The faculty, too, grew convinced that the curriculum was not working, mainly due to the difficulties it placed on them. The key to students' finding their way successfully through the course of study was close and good advising, which either placed tremendous claims on the time of the faculty or, as sometimes happened, was inadequately done. Even more, the heart of the system was the area examinations, on which a student's graduation completely depended. If the tests were not satisfactory, the results for the student's life were disastrous, and so the faculty felt great pressure to pass a student if at all possible.[39]

Thus in 1972 Louisville Seminary instituted a more conventional course of study. The requirement was that a student would take eighteen hours in each of the three areas of study, with the remainder of hours (approximately half) elective. The faculty later referred to this curriculum as the "political curriculum," for everyone on the faculty had at least one course that met a core distribution requirement, ensuring that each teacher would have at least one class with a large number of students. The primary element retained from the previous curriculum was a required statement of faith in the senior year. The student presented to two faculty members from different areas his or her own credo, demonstrating not only the student's beliefs but their "implications for ministry and the intellectual and

38. "Report of the President to the Fall Meeting of the Board of Directors, Louisville Presbyterian Theological Seminary, October 25, 1966," 4. Folder "Report of the President, 1966," Box "President's Office, 1966-1967," LPTS Archives. *The Register* 57 (spring 1968): 30-32. *The Register* 60 (spring 1971): 9, described the aims of the curriculum as "The policy of independent study, a high degree of election of courses, and tutorial, team, and field teaching."

39. Cooper Interview; Warheim, "First-Class Dream," 45.

social context in which they were made." (This final, "dialogical" portion was seldom realized in fact, Warheim believed.)[40]

If the curricular reform of 1967 reflected the freedom and engagement of the world by the church that marked the 1960s, the governance of the Seminary grew out of the anti-authoritarian and egalitarian atmosphere of the day. Duncan held that the Seminary atmosphere would have been very different under Winn than Caldwell even without the 1960s. Caldwell always gave the sense that he was in charge — not in an oppressive or inappropriate way, but more in the manner he managed and directed affairs at the institution. Winn, he said, had a much more laissez-faire style that allowed people to work issues out on their own. Neither was authoritarian; it was rather a matter of the approach each took to his work.[41] Ekstrom also noted the egalitarian nature of LPTS. The faculty tended to be very open with students and strove for a sense of equality with one another. The difference between the salaries of full and assistant professors was intended to be comparatively small (consequently, compared to similar seminaries Louisville's pay for full professors tended to be lower, and pay for assistant professors higher).[42] In this setting the students and some faculty began to seek a change in the governance of LPTS to give students — who were, after all, graduate students — a greater role in decision-making. Again, Winn's interest in such matters resulted in his service on the committee charged with developing a proposal.

The new system was introduced gradually, beginning in 1971 and reaching its full form three years later.[43] With periodic adjustments, the same plan governs the Seminary today. It replaced the traditional pattern of faculty autonomy in academic matters and administrative autonomy in other institutional affairs with a system in which students and staff played a role. The central entity in the plan was the Academic Council, comprised of the president, the dean, all faculty holding the rank of assistant professor or above, and student representatives elected by the student body. The council dealt with all academic matters of Louisville Seminary — all degree programs, lectures, continuing education, and so on. There were Seminary Committees (all with student and some with support staff mem-

40. Warheim, "First-Class Dream," 48.

41. Duncan Interview.

42. Ekstrom Interview. Weeks notes that the intention of egalitarianism was not always realized in fact. When he arrived in 1970 he found some full professors paid almost twice what he received.

43. See Minutes of the Board (1960-1970), April 6-7, 1970, and Minutes of the Board (February 1971–July 1977), April 19, 1971.

bers) that addressed other areas of community life: recruitment and admissions, worship, community affairs, and student affairs. These committees were authorized to take action, and the Academic Council could approve or veto those actions but not amend them.

The third major body of governance was the Forum. Moderated by a student, the Forum met monthly, bringing together the entire Seminary community (students, faculty, and staff) to deal with any issue brought forward. Decisions of the Forum went to the Academic Council for referral to a committee. The only responsibilities the faculty retained for themselves alone were those internal to it — such matters as election of representatives to the board, recommendation of candidates for graduation to the board, and tenure and promotion decisions. The moderator of the Forum and one other student sat on the board, with voice but no vote, in order to promote communication and understanding between the two groups.[44] Governing the Seminary in this way not only gave students significant input into decisions regarding the life of LPTS; it promoted communication, understanding, and a sense of empowerment not only for students but for those who worked as staff at Louisville Seminary. It was a unique step beyond the traditional structure in which the student government existed apart from the faculty and administrative decision-making process, involving all the community in a more egalitarian and trust-building system.[45]

A More Diverse Student Body

The 1960s and 1970s brought a new level of diversity to LPTS. That diversity existed in the student body, the faculty, theological study, and programs. The continuing enrollment of large numbers of married students became less of a problem with the building of Love-Sherrill Hall. And while there was a slight decline in the number of Master of Divinity (M.Div., the degree which replaced the B.D.) students in the mid-1960s and early 1970s, reflecting a national trend, the Seminary generally maintained an average of 150 students. The onset of civil rights and antiwar ac-

44. Minutes of the Board (February 1971–July 1977), April 7-8, 1975.
45. Craig Dykstra, who taught at LPTS from 1977-1984, and Ekstrom, referred specifically to the unique nature of the LPTS plan, and Laverne Alexander and Gloria Bryant — registrar and secretary in the office of development, respectively — comment on the openness and good feeling the system provides for staff. Ekstrom Interview; Craig Dykstra Interview, May 6, 1994; Gloria Bryant Interview, March 16, 1994; and Laverne Alexander Interview, March 1993.

tivism coincided with a precipitous drop in the enrollment of students from the PCUS. For example, of 105 full-time M.Div. students in 1973-1974, only 16 were PCUS, 75 were UPCUSA, and the remainder hailed from other denominations. (By this time there were union presbyteries, made up of congregations from both denominations, so it is sometimes difficult to judge students accurately; nonetheless the imbalance is evident enough.)[46] It was clear that LPTS, which in many ways had long manifested its Old School roots and had the typically conservative atmosphere of a southern seminary, had undergone a shift. Already in 1966 Horner reported that M.Div. students for the year came from twenty-eight states, making LPTS the least regional of all the PCUS seminaries and equal to most of the UPCUSA seminaries.[47] Winn remembered that one year Louisville Seminary had more students from California, and more states represented, than Princeton Seminary. The school was not as provincial as one might have thought.[48]

Without doubt the most far-reaching change in the student body was the rapid growth in the numbers of women. Until this time the ministry had been a profession associated exclusively with men. Women were barred from ordination in the PCUSA until 1956 and until 1964 in the PCUS, and it was not until the emergence of modern feminism that women began to attend seminary in significant numbers. A few women graduated from Louisville following Dora Pierce (Louise Farrior, a member of the PCUS, which made her rare, and Jean Willis were in the class of 1967), but they were only a trickle foretelling the flood of women to come. Beginning in 1969 each entering class had four and occasionally five women until 1973 and 1974, when the number was eight, and then in 1975 eighteen women began seminary study. This last group was out of a total class of forty-four, which meant they constituted forty percent of the entering class. Those percentages, or higher, have remained the rule at LPTS. Women were in theological education and, more importantly, the ministry, to stay.

The presence of so many women in new roles on campus naturally prompted changes and created tensions. The Divinity Dames, which had provided support and help for seminary wives in more traditional ways

46. C. Ellis Nelson, "Report of the President to the Fall Meeting of the Board of Directors, Louisville Presbyterian Theological Seminary, October 14-15, 1974." Copy in author's possession. See also Minutes of the Board (1960-1970), November 9, 1964, for another illustration of the trend.
47. Minutes of the Board (1960-1970), October 25, 1966.
48. Al Winn Interview.

and with traditional assumptions, ended with the close of the 1969-1970 school year. In the fall of that year the LPTS Women's Organization formed. Like the Dames it served as a support group for women, but also offered a variety of interest groups in which women — both students and wives — could participate. Some of those were in areas one would identify with traditional women's roles (decorating or sewing, for instance), but others offered other forms of self-expression — drawing and painting — or social involvement. One group, led by Blanche Cooper, wife of Professor Burton Cooper, studied Kate Millett's *Sexual Politics* and called itself a "Women's Lib" group.[49] Feminism began to make itself known on campus.

The experiences of women students, who were pioneers in creating a new place in the church for women, were varied. The faculty accepted the presence of women as candidates for the degree and for ordination willingly. There was precedent for it in the few who came during the 1960s. Except from a handful of male students, the women felt little overt opposition.

The real issues were that all too often people had trouble figuring out how women would fit in to campus life and a kind of insensitivity to the concerns, needs, and new perspectives women brought to campus. The lone woman on the faculty was Catherine Gunsalus, professor of church history, who was also ordained (the first ordained woman most students had met). Some of the women had children, and arranging day care became an issue for which they pushed. Of course, the references to God and human beings were constantly couched in male language, which the women, and some men, resented the more they became aware of the way in which that language excluded and oppressed them. Women often found that to administrators and faculty they sometimes "all looked alike" and were called by each other's names. One woman reported that she was told by a person in the field education office that she should be prepared to go into Christian education if she hoped to receive a call to a church; that comment, even if meant to suggest the hard reality of the day, did not imply that the Seminary would work to help place her in a different call. On another occasion an administrator was reported to have responded to a question about the male-oriented nature of a Seminary brochure with, "In this day of pantsuits, who can tell the difference?" Some churches resisted receiving women as student workers in field education. On one student's first Sunday in her church, a woman addressed the pastor of the church —

49. "Seminary Times," 16 (September 21, 1970). LPTS Archives.

with the student present, greeting parishioners — with the words, "We don't need that little girl up there."[50]

In the face of resistance, or misunderstanding and insensitivity, women tried to support one another and work toward change. The Women's Organization provided one such means of support. In 1971 a group began to publish a mimeographed newsletter titled "Liberation Notes." The paper intended to "present women's liberation to the seminary community; to provide resources and information regarding women; and to become a consciousness-raising agent."[51] It mainly provided information or quotations about women's rights from other sources, addressed issues as they arose on campus, and told of opportunities for women in the Louisville area to meet together to promote each other in their feminism. "Liberation Notes" was relatively short-lived, replaced in the spring semester of 1972 by "What Every Seminary Woman Wants to Know." This newsletter served the same role as its predecessor, and its writers hoped that all the women of the Seminary community, not just students, would read it and play a part in addressing the place of women on campus. Change came slowly, so in 1974 a group of women formed the Women's Caucus to replace the moribund Women's Organization, again to be a support group but also to provide a united voice through which they could address the administration, faculty, and other students.

What were the concerns of the Women's Caucus? There were many, but a few were constant and foremost. First, women wanted the Seminary community and the church to embrace the use of inclusive language when speaking of God and humanity. The importance of inclusive language lay not only in the recognition that women constituted fully one-half the human race and that many felt excluded and rendered invisible by male referents, but also in the theological implications of language. People made sense of reality, they asserted, by the use of symbols, of which language is primary. If the references to God and people were always, or even predominantly, in male terms, then God and society would also be understood in male terms. The saying developed, "If God is male, then the male is God." It was a matter not only of liberating women for the right to make choices about their lives, but about expanding the ways in which God and God's relationship to creation were conceived.

Second, women believed it was important that there be a strong fe-

---

50. See Jane Krauss-Jackson Interview, May 16, 1994; Mary Gene Boteler Interview, February 25, 1999; "Liberation Notes," 1 (November 6, 1971). LPTS Archives.

51. "Liberation Notes," 1 (August 30, 1971). LPTS Archives.

male presence on the faculty. Women professors would serve as important models for women students as they formed their own pastoral identities and, as faculty, would more likely be sensitive to the concerns and needs of women students.

Third, women worked to have the school develop what one might call "women's courses." As feminism informed the study of theology, church history, the Bible, and religion and personality, the contributions and role of women in Christianity which had been largely ignored by the male scholarly community became more fully known. The place of women in Scripture was given an entirely new assessment. Courses could be developed which would give new credence to women as leaders and shapers of faith.

A final concern was placement in a pastoral call following graduation. The Seminary's record on this score proved good. Studies eventually showed that most women did not have much difficulty securing the initial call out of seminary. The greater problem occurred when a woman sought to move to a second church, when the apparatus of the seminary placement system was absent. Change in none of these areas came easily, but the presence and work of women definitely wrought deep changes in theological education and the church.[52]

Another group the Seminary naturally sought to bring on campus for the purpose of greater diversity was African-Americans. Their inclusion had become a goal of mainline seminaries everywhere, and Winn, partly because he had taught at Stillman College, made it a priority at LPTS. The effort met with some success, as a few students enrolled and graduated, but never to the extent the Seminary community had hoped. Even the addition of Arvin Sexton, an African-American recruitment officer, failed to produce the hoped-for results.[53] Of course, the Presbyterian church remained predominantly white, and many African-Americans entering the ministry wanted to study at traditionally black institutions such as Howard Divinity School in Washington, D.C., or the Interdenominational Theological Center in Atlanta. The Seminary continued to search for ways to increase the racial ethnic presence on campus.[54]

52. In an interesting footnote to the story of women's ordination in the church, Caldwell and Winn were the ministers presiding at what was probably the first communion served entirely by women elders in the PCUS — and definitely the first at Montreat Conference Center. The occasion was the Presbyterian Women's Conference at Montreat in 1966. Newsclipping from *Christian Observer* (August 23, 1966). LPTS Archives.

53. Winn Interview.

54. See, for example, Faculty Minutes (1967-1971), June 5, 1970.

In a related area, the Seminary continued to receive, periodically, international students, primarily from Korea and the African nations. Winn developed a concern over their study in the U.S. — not because he doubted their ability to become acclimated to Western language and culture, but because he worried about the Westernization of developing countries. He found that the students who came often chose to stay in the U.S. to enjoy the comfort and higher standard of living it offered. And those who went home often did so with an approach to faith influenced by Western culture. Winn speculated that it might be better to focus on raising the level of theological education in other nations so that the preparation for ministry could take place in the context in which people lived.[55]

After women, perhaps the group of students who made the most impact on Seminary life were those usually referred to as "second-career" students. Second-career students did not become a large percentage of the Louisville Seminary student body until later in Nelson's presidency, but the presence of more students who were not only married (or divorced) but had children and were leaving behind the security of a job in order to incur sizeable debt in answering a call to ministry presented new challenges to the Seminary administration. Although not bringing the challenges to theological and social traditions that women and ethnic minority students did, second-career students presented the school with the very practical issues of more children on campus, a need for more housing, a new set of emotional needs toward which the faculty and administration had to be sensitive, and problems of financing an increasingly expensive education.

Of course, not every change that took place was for the better. As the Seminary began to recognize the importance of applying the gospel to social and political issues in the civil rights and antiwar movements, some perceived a decline in personal and communal devotion. Student study and prayer groups had become almost non-existent, although certainly students prayed on their own and groups were formed on occasion.[56] Chapel services were reduced to two per week, and attendance rarely reached the levels for which the faculty and administration hoped. There were exceptions, of course; some students attended services very regularly. But Cooper noted that the student body never, from the time he joined the faculty

---

55. Winn Interview.

56. Nelson, "Report of the President to the Fall Meeting of the Board of Directors, 1974," notes that for the 1973-1974 school year two informal prayer groups were begun by students.

in 1970, participated widely in worship on campus. He attributed that in part to the idea in the 1960s that the life of faith was one of action, and also to the traditional Presbyterian low church tradition. The students expressed a strong interest in biblical and theological study, but not in the drama of the liturgy.[57] Weeks added that the antiestablishment sentiments so prevalent in the 1960s — and the church was one of the establishments — must have played a role as well.[58]

Students were also becoming somewhat less concerned with evangelism. The Easter Period for Special Church Service existed through the late 1960s, but little or no direct evangelistic work was conducted and by 1970 it was gone altogether. Involvement in the social problems of the world was seen as a form of proclaiming the gospel, and the growing pluralism of American society, the spread of the belief that non-Christians would not spend eternity being tormented in hell, the understanding of faith in gradualist and psychological categories, and the decline of mass evangelism in favor of person-to-person evangelism led, for many, to a loss of the ability to invite others to faith. Presbyterians as well as other mainstream Protestants seemed uncomfortable declaring their faith, fearing that a statement of their own belief might put off others. What one study concluded about global mission work suggests the state of evangelism as well: "Presbyterian foreign mission efforts have largely discarded the methods (and the verbiage) of the turn of the century. But newer, more collaborative and complex relationships with partner churches are difficult to communicate and fewer devote themselves to the attempts to do so."[59]

The way in which Louisville Seminary experienced community changed over these years, but that was primarily a function of the new campus. Instead of having a campus contained on an approximately one-half-acre plot of land, the Seminary spread out over two spacious hills. The dormitory was separated from the dining room, bookstore, and lounge facilities in the student center; the administration building held the faculty offices and classrooms; married housing was across a small valley to the east. Those with fond memories of the downtown campus perceived a loss of closeness on the new one. There may indeed have been a difference in

57. Cooper Interview.
58. Weeks Interview. Benton Johnson, "From Old to New Agendas: Presbyterians and Social Issues in the Twentieth Century," in Coalter, Mulder, and Weeks, *The Confessional Mosaic,* touches on developments of this nature.
59. Horner, King, and Weeks, "Evangelism and Mission," 2. See Coalter's treatment of developments in evangelism in "Presbyterian Evangelism: A Case of Parallel Allegiances Diverging," in Coalter, Mulder, and Weeks, *The Diversity of Discipleship.*

the degree of community, but evidence suggests there was a difference in kind as well.

To compensate for these changes, there were occasions built into the Seminary schedule to bring people together for fellowship. Following each chapel service a coffee hour convened in the student union at which faculty, staff, and students gathered informally. Lunch brought together people from all segments of the Seminary. Faculty continued to entertain students in their homes, although less frequently than in the past. There was a closeness across many Seminary boundaries. Students, reflecting the informality of the 1960s and 1970s, often called professors by their first names, without intending disrespect, and the faculty for the most part received the practice without any resentment. Weeks believed the absence of a faculty lounge contributed greatly to the interaction and relationship of faculty and students. There were efforts to make the staff a part of Seminary life also, as seen in their inclusion in the governance plan. When the board planned to raise faculty salaries $500 in 1965, the faculty voted to "strongly recommend" to the executive committee that "as much as $300. or $500. of these increases be used to raise further the salaries of the Seminary's maintenance staff."[60] Laverne Alexander, as registrar, had a singular relationship to both administration, faculty, and students, and always believed Louisville Seminary was "the church at work."[61]

The Seminary family did fight, of course, and family fights are among the worst. It also had a difficult time integrating married students and their spouses, who lived across the valley, into its life. But by and large, according to Craig Dykstra, the campus was a true community — especially to the students and faculty. He observed:

> It was a faculty that I thought worked exceedingly well together. I've never been in a place quite like it. The cooperation with one another, the sense of having a common task . . . as a body who had a common, shared responsibility for teaching the Christian faith, the Christian ministry to the student. While the curriculum was broken up into various disciplines . . . [they were] places of special expertise, but not areas in which nobody else could enter.
>
> . . . [The lunch room gave] a very, very strong sense of community. That was very important for the learning environment. I spent a lot of time and a lot of faculty spent a lot of time in individual conversations

60. Faculty Minutes (1962-1967), May 15, 1965.
61. Alexander Interview.

with students of everything going on in their lives. I think it was a place for me where I was able to be a pastor-theologian-scholar myself — to be a minister in that place for students.[62]

A More Diverse Faculty

The faculty underwent significant turnover during Winn's presidency. In 1966 Daniel Wessler was called to teach worship and communication (replacing Kenneth Phifer, who taught homiletics from 1959 to 1965) and Grayson Tucker to work in the field education office (teaching church administration and evangelism) and allowing David Steere to spend more time teaching. 1968 saw the addition of Clinton Morrison as dean and professor of New Testament, and Harold Nebelsick as professor of doctrinal theology. Louis Weeks was hired to teach church history in 1969, and Catherine Gunsalus joined him in 1970. That same year David Jobling began teaching biblical hermeneutics, and Samuel Keen resigned and was replaced in philosophical theology by Burton Cooper. William Eichelberger, finally, was hired to teach Christian ethics in 1973. By the time Winn resigned later that year, over half of the full-time faculty had been hired during his seven-year presidency. Excluding visiting and adjunct professors, there had been an average of more than one hiring per year. Nelson inherited, then, a relatively young and established faculty, and made only three hires during his presidency. In 1977 Linda Chase, an alumna of Louisville, was named instructor and Director of Field Education (Steere held a faculty appointment alone and Tucker had become dean in 1976). The same year Craig Dykstra arrived to teach Christian education (Goodykoontz retired in 1975) and Johanna van Wijk-Bos joined the faculty in Old Testament following Mauser's resignation in 1977.

The addition of so many new faculty, most of whom received their post-graduate education in the late 1950s and 1960s, brought an unprecedented diversity to Louisville Seminary. Catherine Gunsalus became the first woman called to the faculty. She was popular with students and had the faculty's respect, but she departed at the close of the fall 1973 semester to teach at Columbia Seminary. Marilyn Massey served as an adjunct in church history, but Linda Chase was the next woman hired as a full-time faculty member with significant administrative responsibilities. She re-

---

62. Dykstra Interview. For some other comments on this see, among other interviews, Nelson, Weeks, and Wessler.

signed to enter into pastoral ministry. Van Wijk-Bos, who arrived in 1977, was the first woman to make her career at LPTS and was the only one on the faculty at the end of Nelson's presidency.

Both board and faculty believed it was important to include African-Americans on the faculty. The first to be called was William Eichelberger, during Winn's presidency, and his stay at Louisville was brief. The school tried to fill this gap with periodic visiting professors and adjuncts (Howard Thurman as the former and Cyprian Davis, a Roman Catholic religious who taught ancient and medieval church history, as the latter), but on the whole, like most other mainstream Protestant schools, remained unrepresentative of significant segments of the population of American church and society.

More noticeable was the diversity of the theology and methodological approaches held by the faculty. Although there had been hints of change already at the end of Caldwell's presidency with the growth of pastoral counseling and the addition of people like George Edwards and Samuel Keen, the additions of the 1960s and 1970s ended what Warheim called the "theological and moral consensus" of the Louisville faculty.[63] The faculty now represented a variety of approaches to theology and biblical studies — indeed, a variety of theologies — and teaching methods. Even more, there were different lifestyles and relationships to the church. People observed that the contemporary theological scene was a "shattered spectrum" of competing methods and emphases with no coherent center around which the whole could hinge.[64] According to John Mulder and Lee Wyatt, pluralistic tendencies in theological education displaced a distinct Reformed identity at many Presbyterian seminaries: "A majority of faculty and students continued to be Presbyterian," they noted, "but theological education became an ecumenical and increasingly cross-cultural exploration of the nature of Christian faith and witness."[65] Although that state of affairs was probably less true at Louisville than at some other seminaries, the uniformly moderate Calvinism that one traditionally found in the faculty at the Seminary gave way to a more diverse group of ideas. Winn himself was aware of the shift taking place and made it a goal of the hiring process.[66]

The growing diversity of the faculty coincided with its ongoing

63. Warheim, "First-Class Dream," 35.

64. Lonnie D. Kliever, *The Shattered Spectrum: A Survey of Contemporary Theology* (Atlanta: John Knox Press, 1981).

65. John Mulder and Lee Wyatt, "The Predicament of Pluralism," 63.

66. Winn Interview. Virtually everybody who knew the Seminary in the 1950s remarked about the theological change at the Seminary.

professionalization, and led to some concern regarding the constituency to which faculty should feel loyalty. Winn felt that a consequence of new developments in graduate study and theological diversity was that faculty could feel a greater sense of fealty to the profession and to the "scholarly guild" of which each was a member than to the church and its needs.[67] Clinton Morrison believed that hiring policies in seminaries were becoming more like those in graduate divinity schools — that is, based on candidates' scholarly ability rather than their church commitment and understanding of ministry. The question was raised: How does an institution or an instructor decide what a student needs to know to be prepared for church ministry?[68] Simply put, pastor-theologian was no longer the primary identity for most members of the faculty.

Despite these changes, though, the Louisville Seminary faculty continued to understand itself as engaged in a ministry of and to the church. A few teachers were not ordained, and a handful did not make the institutional church a part of their life of faith. But most did, and most had served as pastors of congregations, even if only for a short time. In their classes they discussed the relevance of certain academic issues to the life of the church; outside the classroom they continued to fill pulpits, teach Sunday school classes, speak to church groups, and write for denominational publications. They also served on any number of committees or work groups of the General Assemblies. Winn chaired the committee that wrote "A Declaration of Faith" for the PCUS, and Daniel Wessler led the one that produced a new worship directory for the UPCUSA. When Norman Horner left LPTS in 1968 he returned to global mission with the Middle East Council of Churches in Lebanon.

After discussions with faculty and students, the board adopted in 1969 a new statement of purpose which declared the primary goal of the Seminary to be the "task of preparing men and women for participation in the continuing ministry of Jesus Christ in the world." The Seminary saw four main components in meeting that goal: a curriculum of traditional disciplines in "dialogue" with the practice of ministry; a "community of scholars uniting faculty and students" which should lead the church in thinking and planning how best to communicate the gospel in the current context (and offer the church constructive criticism); responsible participation in the work for social justice; and concern for one another within the Seminary community. The result was to be a seminary that maintained

67. Winn Interview.
68. Morrison Interview.

the Presbyterian tradition in its curriculum but was also informed and en-
riched by the ecumenical movement.[69] In fact, although there was an emphasis on social justice and sensitivity to the ways in which ministry was
shaped by the context of modern life, in many ways the statement evidenced its lineage back to the purpose of Danville Seminary: preparing individuals to be ministers in the church. The means for doing so changed,
and there were a few who understood that goal in other than traditional
terms and may even have dissented from it. In essence, however, Louisville
Seminary, in its faculty, students, and staff, remained committed to education for the life of the church.[70] What tensions were occasioned by new developments in theological studies manifested themselves mainly in three
disciplines — women's studies, biblical and theological studies, and homiletics — as well as in the case of one particular course.

First was women's studies. Women were gradually coming to feel that
their concerns were being addressed by the Seminary; this was due in large
part to courses on women in the church (both historically and in the present), to feminist interpretation of the Bible, and to attention given to the
ways in which women's liberation could impact theology and the church. In
the late 1960s and early 1970s, however, all of these were new fields of research. Male professors had had little exposure to them and could not, at
any rate, understand what it meant to be a woman in American society and
the church. Gunsalus offered the first course at LPTS on women and the
church, and after her departure Massey, as an adjunct professor, offered another, simply called "Christianity and the Women's Movement."[71]

But their departures left the Seminary without a woman on the faculty, and the Women's Caucus petitioned the board in 1976 to make hiring
a woman a priority. In a well-argued statement the women applied each
part of the Seminary mission statement to their concern: First, the mission
statement said Louisville would teach the traditional disciplines in dialogue with current experience; that made a woman faculty member imperative because without one there were no models of women in theology or
pastoral experience to help interpret what women students learned. Second, the Seminary was to offer the church constructive criticism, and the
place of women in the church was a central challenge and could not be
properly addressed without the help of a faculty member. Third, it was to

69. Minutes of the Board (1960-1970), October 13, 1969.
70. Wessler noted that the question of how the Seminary should relate to local presbyteries in the oversight of candidates for ministry continued to perplex the faculty. Does the
Seminary only educate, or play a greater role in the overall faith formation for ministry?
71. Catalogue (1975-1976), 40. LPTS Archives.

teach responsible participation in social struggle; the liberation of women was without doubt one of these. Finally, LPTS was to provide worship and mutual pastoral concern for all of its community; that was impossible for women students without any women faculty, counselors, or leaders in worship and liturgy. The students proposed two classes for a woman to teach: "The New Woman: Her Roles and Identities, Meaning for Ministry," and "The History of Women in Theology."[72] Johanna van Wijk-Bos was called the next year, but it was a few years before "women's" courses became a part of the curriculum, and longer still before feminist analysis became a regular part of Seminary study.

Much more controversial than the need for women on the faculty was the question of language. Most women and many men found consistent use of male referents or images for God and humanity offensive and exclusionary (not to mention ignorant of the fact that there were myriad images of God in the Bible that were either female or gender-neutral). Some, however, defended the old terminology, asserting that words like "man" did include all people, male and female, when used to designate the human race, and that referring to God as "he," "Father," and so on, was biblical and that everyone should realize that God transcended gender. Arguments over the issue raged within the student body, within the faculty, and between the two groups. In February 1977, the Academic Council adopted a policy recommending "that the seminary community adopt use of Wholistic Language in all official publications, chapel services, classrooms and lectures," and slowly the community generally reached agreement that this was just.[73] Van Wijk-Bos remembered that by the early 1980s the issue had been decided regarding references to humankind; most people avoided exclusive language. But language about God, with its more direct theological and biblical implications, remained an unresolved issue.[74]

A second area of tension existed in the approaches of faculty to biblical and theological study. Edwards remained the most extreme biblical critic over against the more moderate and traditional Rhodes and Morrison.[75] Deeper differences, which spilled over more into the classroom, ex-

72. Minutes of the Board (February 1971–July 1977), April 26-27, 1976.
73. "Seminary Times," 22 (February 18, 1977). LPTS Archives.
74. Johanna van Wijk-Bos Interview, April 17, 1994.
75. A great asset to biblical studies was completed, under Rhodes' supervision, in 1975: the Lemon Collection, with some additions, received a home in the library. Mrs. J. H. Horn provided funding for equipping the museum and her daughter, Mildred Horn, made possible the acquisition of a photographic replica of the Isaiah scroll found at Qumran in 1947. It was mounted on a cylinder so that it could be viewed in its completeness.

isted in theology. Nebelsick was an adherent of the neo-orthodox theology of Karl Barth. On the other hand, Cooper, the philosophical theologian, was one of those who applied the work of process philosophers such as Alfred North Whitehead and Charles Hartshorne to Christian thought; this process theology was innovative and often discarded or redefined traditional theological concepts. The theological discussions raised by the differences between the two professors helped students formulate their own stances — and the two men maintained a good personal relationship despite their disagreements. When Nebelsick died unexpectedly of a heart attack, Cooper asserted that Louisville Seminary lost its one real draw for more conservative students, although Nebelsick would not be considered at all conservative in some ways.[76]

Homiletics was a third area of debate. Since the Protestant Reformation, Reformed worship had centered on the Word read and proclaimed, with a de-emphasis on visual and dramatic elements of worship and the emotions they evoke. In the United States that tradition combined with revivalism and the necessary simplicity of frontier worship to create a generally low-church atmosphere in the Presbyterian denominations. But in the 1960s mainstream Protestantism began to experience a liturgical renewal that incorporated the traditions of others. Phifer promoted that trend in his 1965 book *A Protestant Case for Liturgical Renewal*.[77] He noted the poverty of American Presbyterian worship with its single appeal to the intellect by an emphasis on the sermon. What Christian faith required, he argued, was a worship that reached and called forth the totality of human being. He then suggested resources from which Presbyterians might draw to enrich their own worship, including Catholicism, especially in the wake of the Second Vatican Council; Reformed thinkers such as John W. Nevin; and the modern ecumenical movement.[78] The Seminary experimented with different styles of worship, including liturgical dance, as early as 1964 while continuing to emphasize the teaching of preaching in the classoom.[79]

Wessler, who succeeded Phifer in 1965, emphasized the entire context of worship in his teaching of homiletics. He prompted students to consider the variety of means by which the gospel was communicated in wor-

76. Cooper Interview.

77. Kenneth G. Phifer, *A Protestant Case for Liturgical Renewal* (Philadelphia: The Westminster Press, 1965).

78. Phifer, *Liturgical Renewal*.

79. "Leotards and Letter Sweater Part of Service," *Courier-Journal* (December 6, 1964).

ship, and how a sermon fit into that setting. A new class that he offered, "Sacraments, Rites, and Ordinances of the Church," represented this understanding of how one might appeal to the whole being in worship, not just the intellect, and explored the incorporation of practices that had fallen out of favor in most Reformed worship — times of contemplative prayer, for example, or singing the psalter in responsive form under the leadership of a cantor. That course became required in area C, alongside a course in basic preaching. Rather than teach homiletics in a more traditional manner, as had Caldwell and Phifer, in which students were guided in sermon structure, the use of illustrations, and oration, Wessler's way of "teaching homiletics was to try to help people find out who they were," as Cooper expressed it. In short, it was a very non-directive pedagogy.

John McClure has shown that there was a widespread movement in Presbyterianism away from preaching as an assumed authoritative endeavor for expounding Scripture to a more democratically conceived exercise in relevancy during this period.[80] LPTS reflected that development. Some students sought more leadership in developing their preaching craft and in 1979 petitioned the board to create a chair of homiletics alongside Wessler's work in communication and worship — which all acknowledged he taught very well. When Louisville experienced another faculty expansion in the 1980s a preaching chair was established in honor of Caldwell.[81]

Another debate arose over a particular course developed by Wessler. He received a grant from the Lilly Endowment to develop a course in spiritual discipline and formation which was called "Life Springs." The practice of spiritual discipline had not yet made many inroads into the thinking of mainstream Protestantism, so the course introduced ideas and practices which seemed odd, or even questionable, to some. The course made use of art and visual stimuli, contemplative techniques drawn from other Christian traditions and even other religions, and group exercises to explore a life of prayer. The aim of the course was to lead students in exploring their own faith experiences and to cultivate a life of prayer. Inasmuch as Chris-

80. John McClure, "Changes in Authority, Method, and Message of Presbyterian (UPCUSA) Preaching in the Twentieth Century," in Coalter, Mulder, and Weeks, eds., *The Confessional Mosaic*.

81. For some indication of the developments in worship and preaching see *The Register* 56 (spring 1967): 34-35, and 57 (spring 1968): 49-51; Cooper Interview; Duncan Interview; "Board and Executive Committee Minutes, September 2, 1977–December 28, 1979," April 23-24, 1979. These minutes are unbound. LPTS Archives; Weeks Interview; and Minutes of the Faculty (1971-1979), March 22, 1979. LPTS Archives.

tian faith existed within the corporate body of Christ, Life Springs also discussed means of building faith within local congregations. Students who participated in the course unanimously spoke of its value, and not all who wanted to enroll could be admitted. Yet the eclectic nature of the resources and content of the course raised a question for some, as Dykstra observed: "Is there a way of teaching a Reformed spirituality rather than letting spirituality get, the way some people saw it, unhooked from the tradition of which this Seminary is a part and what you ought to be teaching?"[82] A secondary issue in the discussion was the co-teaching in the class of Wessler's wife, Jen — raising questions of who had authority to teach at the Seminary, and who was to give that authority.[83]

These debates that arose at LPTS in the 1970s illustrate the new developments occasioned by the diversity emerging on campus and the tensions they caused. Cooper characterized LPTS as a seminary that was pluralistic in what it offered students, providing a range of viewpoints and, although moderately liberal overall, a place that accepted conservatives. Students had the freedom to explore theologically and to develop their own points of view.[84]

Curricular developments in mission also deserve mention. When Horner resigned in 1968, no one was called to replace him. The Seminary planned to have visiting professors from the global church teach a course in mission every few semesters, and initially some top people were called for that role. For example, in 1972, J. Russell Chandran, principal of Bangalore Theological Seminary, who was a leader of Indian Christianity and active in the World Council of Churches, was visiting professor. After 1973, however, mission courses disappeared from the curriculum and the Seminary's legacy of promoting interest in and study of the global church was interrupted.

Expanding Programs

During these days of change the Seminary also began to offer more programs of study. The Th.M. degree, an academic degree that allowed a person to spend a year studying a particular topic, had drawn many students to LPTS over the years. In the 1960s, however, few ministers sought that

82. Dykstra Interview.
83. Wessler Interview.
84. Cooper Interview.

degree and seminaries began to develop Doctor of Ministry (D.Min.) programs. The D.Min. was a professional degree that allowed ministers to focus on single areas of ministry during short residencies, develop programs in their congregations to apply their studies, and write a thesis to demonstrate their findings. Louisville Seminary began its D.Min. program in 1973, and by 1976 seventy-five students were pursuing the degree.[85] The proposal raised questions among the faculty, who feared that some might go through the program simply to put "Dr." in front of their names. They resolved to approve only of a quality program that required hard work of its students — at least in part because the D.Min. also placed an increased teaching load on them.[86]

Other degree possibilities offered people a range of educational options. The school developed a Master of Arts in Religion program, a two-year degree with a concentration in either Bible or theology. In an attempt to make theological education ever more relevant to social need, LPTS created double-competency programs. The first was a combined degree in social work at the University of Louisville, and the second combined theological study with studies in law. This latter was the first at any theological school in the nation. Finally, Louisville established a Th.M. in Pastoral Care. Over four years a student earned an M.Div. and the master's degree with intensive work in pastoral counseling, and received accreditation from the American Association of Pastoral Counselors and the Association for Clinical Pastoral Education.[87]

Resources available to students expanded when the Seminary helped form two consortia of schools in the area. The effort grew out of a study by the Association of Theological Schools that held that there were too many seminaries and divinity schools in the nation, and that most would soon experience serious financial problems. The study urged the creation of consortia by theological institutions to share resources and facilities and the cooperation of those schools with nearby universities. (It was at this time that such efforts as the Graduate Theological Union in the San Francisco-Berkeley area began.) In the Louisville area, Kentuckiana Metroversity was a cooperative effort between colleges, universities, and seminaries in the city to share facilities and programs. The key benefit proved

85. Minutes of the Board (February 1971–July 1977), April 10-11, 1972; "Life at Louisville Seminary," Catalogue (1977-1978), 99-101.

86. Winn Interview.

87. See Catalogue (1976-1977), 22-23; *The Register* 58 (spring 1969): 27; *The Register: Programs of Double Competence. Supplement to Catalog Issue, 1969/1970* 58 (fall 1969); *The Register* 59 (spring 1970): 23-25; and Winn Interview.

to be free access to and borrowing privileges in libraries. The Theological Education Association of Mid-America (TEAM-A) brought together Louisville Seminary, Southern Baptist Seminary, Lexington Theological Seminary, Asbury Theological Seminary, and St. Meinrad Seminary in Indiana to share in the task of theological education. All the schools put in place a January term (J-term), during which students were encouraged to take a class at one of the other schools, thus fostering understanding between the institutions and denominations represented.[88] These arrangements widened the scope of the cooperation that existed historically between Louisville Seminary and Southern Baptist Seminary. Students often took classes at both institutions and periodically faculty moved back and forth for teaching. In the 1990s the two schools electronically linked their catalogue of holdings and the Baptist seminary made its new recreation facility available to the LPTS community. TEAM-A and Kentuckiana Metroversity made that kind of relationship possible with the other area schools, albeit to a lesser degree.

Winn's Departure

The extensive changes in Seminary life and education, the energy required to deal with the turbulence of the Vietnam era, and the administrative responsibilities of the presidency led Winn to resign at summer's end in 1973.[89] Not only had the seven years of his presidency been difficult for him professionally, but they had created strains on his family as well. Thomas Duncan, on the board at the time, believed few other people could have pulled LPTS through those years as well as Winn had done. He was a Christian who led by example.[90] On the occasion of his departure he received an eloquent and heartfelt tribute from Goodykoontz:

> Serving in very difficult days when theological education was undergoing tremendous changes and when our national life was torn by the

88. On Metroversity and TEAM-A see "Report of the President to the Spring Meeting of the Board of Directors, Louisville Presbyterian Theological Seminary, April 14-15, 1969," 11-12. Folder "Report of the President 1966," Box "President's Office, 1966-1967," LPTS Archives; Minutes of the Board (1960-1970), Executive Committee, November 26, 1968; Ekstrom Interview; and Wessler Interview. The double-competency programs received their impetus from this same effort.

89. Minutes of the Board (February 1971–July 1977), June 7, 1973.

90. Duncan Interview.

civil rights struggle and the Vietnam War, he gave statesmanlike guidance to the Seminary which enabled the Seminary to weather the many storms of the sixties and come to the new decade revitalized and still true to her ancient purpose of teaching men and women to proclaim an ancient gospel to a modern world.

. . . Courageous in his convictions, charitable in his dealings with all people, demanding excellence from himself and calling forth excellence from others, he was pastor of the Seminary family, teacher of both faculty and students, and respected churchman throughout our two denominations.[91]

Nelson Faces the Seminary's Financial Problems

Upon Winn's departure the Seminary called Ray Kearns as interim president for the 1973-1974 year. Kearns had served the church in a variety of ways: as university pastor at the University of Nebraska, as director of adult work for the Board of Christian Education of the PCUSA, as pastor of Broad Street Presbyterian Church in Columbus, Ohio, and most recently with Inter-Church Relations for the UPCUSA. His service in theological education came as a member of the McCormick Theological Seminary board from 1961-1970. The search committee settled on C. Ellis Nelson, well-known Christian educator and professor at Union Theological Seminary in New York, as the new president beginning in 1974. He had a particularly formidable challenge to meet upon his arrival. The 1970s presented seminaries and small colleges across the nation with a dilemma that had an impact, in its own way, as difficult as the civil rights and antiwar movements: the challenge of finding the money to provide the education for which the institutions existed.

Studies have shown that religious giving patterns have shifted dramatically since approximately 1965, primarily marked by growing percentages of money given to ministries of congregations and to non-denominational causes (food pantries, for example) close to home over against giving to denominations or national entities, a trend one person referred to as "localism."[92] That meant the Presbyterian denominations, their judica-

91. Minutes of the Board (February 1971–July 1977), October 15-16, 1973.
92. Robin Klay, "Changing Priorities: Allocation of Giving in the Presbyterian Church in the U.S.," in Coalter, Mulder, and Weeks, eds., *The Organizational Revolution: Presbyterians and American Denominationalism*, The Presbyterian Presence Series (Louisville: Westminster/John Knox Press, 1992).

tories, and their national entities, such as the Council of Theological Seminaries, had less money to give to seminaries. To project slightly beyond the years under consideration in this chapter, Kenneth Hougland, business manager at LPTS, observed that at his arrival in 1969 approximately forty percent of the budget came from the PCUS and UPCUSA denominationally; at his retirement in 1986 that percentage had fallen to ten.[93] Nelson noted some trends in giving to Louisville Seminary at the end of his first year: alumni/ae giving had risen rapidly, up from $3,000 in 1968-1969 to $36,000 in 1973-1974. Giving from "friends" — that is, church members with an interest in theological education — had fallen, and giving from congregations remained stagnant. Support from the Council of Theological Seminaries and judicatories was dropping.[94] When combined with the other major economic factor affecting Seminary funding — growing inflation, especially in energy costs — the danger to the school's financial standing was clear.[95] And there were any number of other financial pressures on the school: for example, faculty and staff salaries had to rise and tuition and student costs were raised, but often that resulted not in increased income, but more expense in student aid.

When Nelson arrived as president in 1974 Louisville Seminary had overspent its budget three years in a row, with the amount of the deficit growing each year. The impact of the decrease in giving had become clear. For example, the board anticipated that the budget for 1971-1972 would be nine percent higher than 1970-1971, necessitating a $70,000 withdrawal from the League of Support reserve fund to meet expenses.[96] Even though the endowment grew approximately $600,000 in Nelson's first year, he asserted that "these generous legacies under ordinary circumstances would provide enough added income to take care of inflation. But inflation and increased costs are going up faster than the added income from endowment, so we will have a deficit in our budget this year."[97] In

93. Kenneth Hougland Interview, March 17, 1992.

94. C. Ellis Nelson, "Report of the President to the Fall Meeting of the Board of Directors, Louisville Presbyterian Theological Seminary, October 14-15, 1974." Copy in author's possession.

95. For studies of the financial context which theological educational institutions faced after the 1950s, see Badgett Dillard, "Financial Support of Protestant Theological Education" (Ed.D. thesis, Indiana University, 1973), and Anthony Ruger, *Lean Years, Fat Years: Changes in the Financial Support of Protestant Theological Education* (Auburn, N.Y.: Auburn Theological Seminary, 1994).

96. Minutes of the Board (February 1971–July 1977), April 19-20, 1971.

97. Nelson, "Report of Louisville Presbyterian Theological Seminary, 1974-1975." Copy in author's possession.

all, LPTS used $260,000 of endowment capital to balance the budget from 1971-1975; after that Nelson closed each year in the black.[98] It was important to break the "psychology of deficit spending," he argued, for the school was "foreclosing our future."[99] Nelson had seen Union Seminary in New York prolong just such a financial pattern and then experience a very painful series of austerity measures that included releasing seven faculty members at one time. The outflow of money at Louisville had to stop, he was convinced, and difficult decisions made before even harsher steps would be necessary to place the Seminary on firm financial footing.[100]

Nelson sought to cut the cost of operating the Seminary. It was inevitable before he arrived that the year 1974-1975 would be in the red, and he could not avoid that. In his second year, however, the budget was projected to be about $1,200,000, of which he hoped to cut $120,000 — that is, one-tenth.[101] Nelson's first grant, soon after his arrival, was from the Lilly Endowment to retain an outside team to review the administrative structure and level of performance at LPTS. This turned out to be a fortuitous way of doing the review for relations within the Seminary, for when cuts came he had not made the choice of who would be let go alone, nor could it be thought the choices were arbitrary. Out of that review three positions were to be eliminated. First was the position of Long Range Planning and Deferred Gifts, a job filled by Herbert Chase, who lived three months per year in Harrodsburg, Kentucky, and the remainder of

98. That was approximately a $730,000 reduction in the endowment in 1999 dollars.

99. Nelson, "Notes for Future Historians Regarding the 1974-1981 Period in the Life of Louisville Presbyterian Theological Seminary," 13-14. Copy in author's possession. George Newlin, chair of the investment committee, remembered a meeting with faculty and students during a period of cutbacks to balance the budget. A student asked, in all honesty, if the Seminary already had $25,000 in deficit spending that year (as projected), why not go to $100,000? "And it turned out it was a very fortunate question that he asked," Newlin noted, "because that managed to get across . . . to the students and the faculty that were there that it really wasn't a question of money versus people. It was people versus people — people now versus people later." George Newlin Interview, May 9, 1992.

100. Dykstra, now with the Lilly Endowment, noted that a seminary president is one of the most difficult jobs in education. The key problem is that there is no natural constituency for giving except alumni/ae, and their resources are limited. Church members do not naturally or quickly identify the seminary as an object of giving, because few have any immediate experience of it at all — unlike college, which any number may have attended. And few people think of having a son or daughter attend there. In short, a seminary president is always building a group of supporters.

101. Minutes of the Board (February 1971–July 1977), Executive Committee, May 9, 1975.

the year in Palm Beach, Florida. The position did not generate enough giving to justify its continuation.[102] Second was the Director of Recruiting and Admission.[103]

Unlike those two jobs, Nelson's decision to close the office of the Dean of Students provoked a hue and cry from students and some faculty. Nelson remembered that when the administrative review team had been on campus, no students had attended an open meeting with them and, consequently, were surprised that student services were being cut. George Bennett, who held the post, was also on the Area C faculty and a bit eccentric. For a period he kept a pet monkey in his office and was given to propelling himself around campus on roller skates. Bennett was also very popular with students, and student and faculty reaction proved sufficiently persistent that, following a board meeting which involved "lengthy discussion" of the issue, the administration decided to maintain the Dean of Students office.[104] Two or three cuts in support staff were made, and Nelson managed to finish 1975-1976 in the black.

The other area for cuts in personnel was in the faculty. In 1975 the faculty offered to take a reduction in salary to help end deficit spending.[105] Fortunately, reductions in faculty personnel were achieved without releasing established, tenured members. As noted, Gunsalus' position was filled for two years by Massey as a full-time adjunct. After 1975 and well into the 1980s, part-time adjuncts taught ancient and medieval church history. Jobling, whose position in biblical hermeneutics became a luxury with two Old Testament and two New Testament professors, received a terminal contract by virtue of a faculty vote not to extend him an offer of tenure for the 1975-1976 year. He was not replaced.[106]

The third faculty dismissal proved difficult. In the 1973-1974 school year the faculty voted not to recommend tenure for Eichelberger, making 1974-1975 his last year at LPTS. Eichelberger was not the most popular teacher, and he held only the Master of Arts. Unfortunately, Kearns, in-

---

102. Mobley, "The Administration of Louisville Presbyterian Theological Seminary"; and Minutes of the Board (February 1971–July 1977), Executive Committee, May 23, 1972, and January 17, 1975.

103. Minutes of the Board (February 1971–July 1977), Executive Committee, October 9, 1972; Nelson Interview.

104. Minutes of the Board (February 1971–July 1977), April 7-8, 1975; Nelson Interview; and Mobley, "The Administration of Louisville Presbyterian Theological Seminary."

105. Faculty Minutes (1971-1979), May 30, 1975.

106. Minutes of the Board (February 1971–July 1977), Executive Committee, June 12, 1975; Nelson Interview.

terim president when that decision was made, had no experience in academic matters of this sort and did not officially inform Eichelberger that his contract with the school would end at the close of the spring 1975 semester. When Nelson became president, Eichelberger approached him and asked what he should do. He was given a contract for one more year, 1975-1976.

Arvin Sexton, the Director of Recruiting and Admissions who was released from the administration, was African-American. The African-Americans of Louisville were very sensitive to the low numbers of people of color at the Seminary, despite people's protestations that the Seminary wanted to change that. Now it appeared to them that Nelson was firing the only African-American on the faculty because he wrote the actual terminal contract. It looked very much like discrimination to those outside the Seminary. Nelson said that he was later told that, had the Seminary retained Jobling on the faculty that spring, a suit would have been filed on Eichelberger's behalf. Jobling's dismissal made it easier to explain that the cut was made for academic and economic reasons. Still, the episode understandably strained Louisville Seminary's relationship with Presbyterian African-Americans, and the battle over employment of Bennett and Eichelberger made Nelson's first year very stressful.[107]

There were other means for saving expenses, and everyone at the Seminary contributed to the effort during the 1970s. Special steps were taken by Kenneth Hougland, business manager, and Charles Redmon, director of maintenance. Many people credited Hougland with tremendous skill as an organizer and for his ability to make things run efficiently. Indeed, he deserves much of the credit for steering Louisville Seminary through the austerity measures of the 1970s and constantly monitoring the cost of keeping the physical plant in operation. One of the great cost increases in those years came from energy. Hougland suggested to Redmon that they try removing one-half of the light bulbs in the Seminary classrooms and workplaces to see if they could lower the use of electricity and still have enough light. It worked, to great benefit. Redmon remembered that fuel oil rose from eight cents per gallon to almost one dollar. The campus, built long before either the depletion of resources or inflation became concerns, had two fuel oil boilers for the main buildings on the quadrangle. Redmon converted one for natural gas, lower in price, to heat the buildings, keeping the other for fuel oil in case there was a need for an al-

107. Nelson Interview; Minutes of the Board (February 1971–July 1977), October 14-15, 1974, and January 17, 1975.

ternate source of fuel. Steps like these saved significant amounts of money over the years.[108]

Nelson took steps to do more than reduce costs. Already during Winn's presidency people realized that the Seminary needed to increase the endowment constantly and cultivate more annual giving. A number of personnel changes were made with that development in mind, particularly the arrivals of Andrew Newcomer as vice president and Arthur Depew as Director of Development in the early 1970s. Depew's departure led to a new vice president, Thomas Laird Jones, who again carried responsibility for development. The job descriptions of these officers reflected the conviction that Louisville Seminary needed an aggressive program to increase the endowment. George Newlin, longtime board member, noted that when he joined the board in the early 1960s denominational giving accounted for approximately forty percent of the Seminary's budget and the endowment no more than ten percent. Those numbers were shifting significantly by the end of Nelson's presidency.[109]

Changing the Board of Directors and Investment Management

Two main programs were undertaken in addition to soliciting gifts for the institution to address the changing reality of Seminary funding. First was the make-up of the board of directors. The LPTS board, like that of most seminaries, had historically been comprised of ministers of large churches with some wealthy and faithful lay members. In Louisville's case, the lay members were mainly from the city and involved in either law or banking. The executive committee consisted of people in the immediate area, almost by necessity until the 1960s, because of the difficulties of bringing in people from distant locations for important but brief meetings that were sometimes held on short notice. Changes to that pattern of board membership had begun under Winn but accelerated under Nelson; the number of clergy members began to decline, and the added lay members reflected a wider geographical distribution. That brought more people on the board who had the potential to give or raise more money for the school. Part of

108. For the contribution of Hougland and Redmon see Redmon Interview; Minutes of the Board (1960-1970), April 14, 1969; Winfrey Blackburn Interview, 1994; and Nelson Interview.

109. Newlin Interview.

the impetus for change came from realignment to synods in the region caused by the creation of union presbyteries and synods, and changes to the board provided one way to increase the endowment.[110]

The second means by which the administration sought growth in the endowment was a more aggressive investment practice. The Seminary had long placed responsibility for the management of its endowment with local banks, the officers of whom were generally faithful Presbyterians who gave long and diligent service to the Seminary by serving on its board and supporting it liberally with their money. Those managers, and the board generally, were cautious, even conservative in the investment of the endowment. In 1964, for instance, the endowment yielded $161,500, which represented a 3.8% return on the endowment. When the downtown campus was sold and the money came into hand in 1966, the entire $400,000 was put in treasury bills at a little below 5.5%.[111]

Newlin, who was an investment manager, served on the finance committee of the board and began, under Winn, slowly to move the institution toward a portfolio that would yield more earnings. Sensitive to the faith and service of the Louisville bankers to the school, and aware that suggested changes could be seen as criticism of their handling of the funds, he very cautiously and with political acumen led LPTS into a more diverse and aggressive investment practice. The first step was simply to move more money out of lower-yield vehicles such as bonds into stocks. Under Nelson, Newlin prepared a presentation for the board in which he showed the returns the Seminary endowment was receiving over against the yields possible in a different investment scenario, complete with graphs and hard facts that were the result of solid research on his part. The board could not argue with the facts and decided to diversify its endowment much more than they had ever done and to monitor the performance of the managers of the various elements of the portfolio and reward those performing well with a larger share of the endowment.

All involved in this process later spoke of the great spirit with which J. Van Dyke Norman, board member since 1971 and president of First National Bank, where most of the Seminary's money had been placed, supported the change in policy and responded with higher yields on the money the board left in the bank's care. The board eventually began a new

110. Hougland Interview; Nelson Interview; Minutes of the Board (February 1971–July 1977), October 15-16, 1973; and Minutes of the Board (September 2, 1977–December 28, 1979), Executive Committee, October 10-11, 1977.

111. Minutes of the Board (1960-1970), November 9, 1964, and Executive Committee, December 2, 1966.

practice in the use of the annual income from the investment, so that a significant percentage of the yield was added to the capital.[112] Partly as a result of new gifts and partly as a result of this new strategy the endowment
grew 116% (from approximately $5 million to approximately $11 million)
during Nelson's presidency.[113] The importance of the endowment made itself clear in the finance committee's report to the executive committee of
the board in 1980, as Nelson was preparing to retire. He observed that
Louisville Seminary was not operating with a deficit and the investments
were doing well, but that inflation continued at such a rate that, all things
being equal (that is, no increase in investment yield, tuition, or annual giving) the Seminary would need to raise $1 million per year for the endow-
ment to keep pace. That made no allowance for new programs, new buildings, or even building maintenance.[114]

Two other developments during these years deserve note. A campaign
throughout the Synod of the Mid-South conducted on behalf of Columbia
and Louisville Seminaries added approximately $2.5 million to the LPTS en-
dowment, part of which eventually supported the Paul Tudor Jones Chair in
Church History. Then, near the end of Nelson's presidency, the Synod of the
Mid-South polled its members for opinions of the most important tasks in
which the synod should be engaged. To the surprise of many, theological education emerged as the top priority. The Seminary immediately proposed
working with the synod on that idea, and a plan emerged that was a forerunner of the later Theological Education Fund of the reunited denomination.
Congregations were asked to pledge two percent of their previous year's
budget, 25% of which would remain in the synod to help fund ministers' continuing education, and 75% of which the synod would divide between Columbia (28%) and Louisville (72%). This plan, formally approved after Nelson's departure, had a number of advantages that were not directly financial.
People at LPTS liked the plan because it linked together all of the theological
education of a minister from seminary to post-ordination, was easy for congregations to understand, allowed the Seminary to count on a certain
amount of money without having to invest time and resources to raising it,
and tied churches and members to Louisville Seminary as they perceived
theological education as a component of their ministry and responsibility.[115]

112. Winn Interview; Blackburn Interview; Hougland Interview; Newlin Interview;
Minutes of the Board (February 1971–July 1977), October 11-12, 1971.

113. Nelson, "Notes for Future Historians," 19.

114. Minutes of the Board (1980-1992), Executive Committee, October 13-14, 1980.
LPTS Archives.

115. Nelson Interview; and Minutes of the Board (1980-1992), April 14-15, 1980.

Looking to the Future

Nelson believed that tying congregations and individual Presbyterians more closely to the Seminary was important for LPTS' future. When his presidency began, Nelson and his wife, Nancy, saw the ongoing effects of the Vietnam years in the relative absence of local Presbyterians visiting and using the campus. Nancy began to work on that issue, primarily with the women's groups of area churches. She invited women to meet on campus, entertained them in the president's home, and arranged for students to give tours. The results were so positive that Nelson received a Lilly Endowment grant to pay for a formal structure in the institution to expand the work. Frances Dorris, wife of the pastor at Second Presbyterian Church, worked full-time organizing the project. The aim of the work was to "act in the area of public relations and gifts."[116] The program was called Friends of the Seminary. Dorris traveled in the supporting synods interpreting the work of Louisville Seminary, still primarily to women's groups, and entertained women on campus.

When the grant money was exhausted, the program was cut back to what the Seminary could fund on its own. Betty Goodykoontz, wife of the former professor, operated it part-time and was later succeeded by Susan Helms. The Friends project was so successful in convincing women of the importance of theological education that presidents of presbyterials (the women's organizations at the level of presbytery) traveled to LPTS at their own expense to learn more closely the work done there and receive help in interpreting the Seminary to churches in their presbytery. The Friends project eventually focused on donating money to provide book scholarships for LPTS students, and has been perpetuated as the Bookends program at the Seminary today. It proved very important not only for restoring good will in Louisville Seminary's relationships with area Presbyterians but also as a boost to annual giving at a time when denominational support was falling.[117]

The attempt to reestablish good relations with the church did not grow solely out of financial concerns. Nelson had a clear vision of what he understood theological education in a seminary, as opposed to a school of religion, should be. That understanding turned on the traditional center of LPTS' self image: the church. "I have tried to make the case that the seminary is not merely one good cause among many causes of the church," Nel-

116. Faculty Minutes (1971-1979), December 2, 1976.
117. Nelson Interview; Nelson, "Notes for Future Historians."

son wrote. "Rather, the seminary is the first institution the church has to establish and maintain in order to have properly educated ministers. . . . But this is not a one-way proposition. American history can also be used to show that, when a seminary no longer serves the church that founded it, the seminary withers away or merges with another school. My usual way of saying this is that 'Louisville Seminary has only one client — Presbyterian congregations.'"[118] This emphasis on the Seminary's awareness of educating ministers for church vocation resulted in a new approach to teaching that involved students, faculty, ministers, and laypeople.

Nelson had served on the faculty at Union Seminary in New York with Robert Wood Lynn, both in Christian education. Their interest was in discerning the ways that congregations develop and shape the faith of their members.[119] Nelson left for Louisville at about the same time Lynn accepted a position coordinating the religion program for the Lilly Endowment. The latter suggested that Louisville Seminary submit a proposal that the Seminary study and put into practice their faith formation understanding as a part of theological education. Nelson appointed a committee of faculty to develop the proposal. The grant was awarded, and so began LPTS' pilot project, called Congregation-Based Ministry in Christian Education. Craig Dykstra was called to the faculty to teach Christian education and to coordinate and nurture the program as it grew.

The project funded sixteen students in their field education for one year. Students, the pastors of the churches, faculty, and sometimes members of a lay committee met every other Monday for the entire morning. There were reading assignments and projects to be done in the church. The first semester was primarily a congregational study to determine the dynamics and patterns of behavior in the congregation. In the second semester the student and congregation created a program with an educational goal appropriate to the congregation that could continue after the student's departure. Class meetings included devotional reading, verbatim reports of student-pastor and student-member discussions, and relating the experience to classroom work.

Congregation-Based Ministry was similar to the practica Sherrill

118. Nelson, "Notes for Future Historians," 14. One could argue that God is the Seminary's sole "client" to serve, but Nelson might retort — staying with the metaphor — that congregations are the client and God the founder and chief executive officer. Morrison was among those who noted Nelson's clear sense of purpose for LPTS and his ability to communicate it to others. Morrison Interview.

119. This was reflected in Nelson's *Where Faith Begins* (Atlanta: John Knox Press, 1971).

had taught forty years before, but more thoroughly involved the congregation in the educational and reflective process itself. The administration admitted that it was an expensive program for Louisville, even with the Lilly funding, for it was team-taught and required a large commitment of time and energy by faculty. However, its impact on students and the Seminary's way of thinking about theological education was deep.[120] Weeks, who team-taught the first course with Dykstra, described this as embodying the direction Nelson gave to LPTS with its emphasis on congregations. "The idea of teaching for the church and teaching in the church and getting church people to collaborate on the curriculum," he observed, "but keeping it in a highly structured environment in which there is no slacking on academic rigor" was characteristic of Nelson's vision.[121] Nor did the emphasis fall only on the local church. The Seminary became the site of the PCUS and UPCUSA Joint Office of Worship, giving a concrete reality to the link to the denominations, and the women of the church built a new furlough home on the Seminary campus. Members of the global church often stayed there, and eventually a relationship developed with the Overseas Ministries Study Center that helped fund LPTS students who desired to study abroad for a year.[122]

Tucker, who succeeded Morrison as dean in 1976, proved himself an astute administrator. Despite differences of opinion within the faculty, he facilitated cooperation and helped them advance the educational endeavor of the Seminary. Tucker encouraged faculty to use their imaginations in devising exciting ways to prepare people for ministry. Weeks became known for his embodiments of key people in the church's history during class presentations; he further pioneered in the use of case studies in theological education and used them effectively in his courses. Others tried innovative techniques and developed new courses.

Louisville Seminary continued to serve the local and national church through its programs of continuing education. A variety of learning opportunities had long marked the Seminary's outreach; what had begun as the Centennial Class lectures eventually became the Caldwell Lectures to

---

120. See Dykstra Interview for a very thorough description of the program and fuller discussion of the breadth of influence it had on the Seminary.

121. Weeks Interview. Weeks, always interested in innovative teaching methods, taught in the program for two years; others followed. There were other avenues of this approach apart from Congregation-Based Ministry: a special course on preaching and worship and one on person-to-person evangelism are examples.

122. On the Joint Office of Worship see Wessler Interview. On the furlough home see Hougland Interview.

honor the former president, to which were added the Greenhoe Lectures in the 1967-1968 school year.[123] In the late 1970s Tom Jones, as vice president, coordinated continuing education programs, and upon his departure in 1979 that responsibility fell to Dykstra. Looking to strengthen the Seminary's relationship with the churches, LPTS created the Lay Institute of Theology under Weeks' leadership, designed to attract local church people to classes offered by current or emeritus faculty. That program eventually came under continuing education. Aiming to serve ministers in their continuing education needs, the Seminary also initiated a program of Reflectimes which involved independent reading and a series of seminar meetings over four or five days. Continuing education was set more firmly in the institutional structure of Louisville Seminary and took on an even higher profile.[124]

The final way Nelson began to position Louisville for the future was by securing money from foundations. Wessler said that Nelson supported the faculty in a way Winn had not and could not. He encouraged faculty members to think of research projects or programs they would like to pursue and gave them ideas for writing grant proposals to fund them because the Seminary budget obviously could not sustain those extra expenditures. Weeks said it gave the Seminary a broader vision of itself and its possibilities, leading faculty in particular to think more "expansively."[125] Nelson opened up the world of foundations to Louisville Seminary, and the funding for "Life Springs," Congregation-Based Ministry, and the Friends of the Seminary have already been noted.

Two other grants were important firsts. Nelson secured a grant from the Arthur Vining Davis Foundation to purchase Louisville Seminary's first computer system. The proposal included instructional workshops for employees and the development of hardware and software fashioned for the small educational institution. What LPTS developed was called the Louisville Computer Concept and was eventually adopted by approximately ten seminaries and some small colleges. Thus the Seminary not only became more efficient but took a lead in computerization at small schools.[126] Then, when it came time to expand the library, Nelson was able to persuade the Kresge Foundation to grant $200,000 for the project. Total foundation

123. For the extent to which LPTS sought to educate the church, including even distance learning, see *The Register* 54 (spring 1965): 11.

124. See Dykstra Interview and Nelson, "Report of the President, October 14-15, 1974."

125. Wessler Interview and Weeks Interview.

126. Nelson Interview and Hougland Interview.

funding for the library addition eventually reached $325,000.[127] With denominational funding falling precipitously by the 1980s, foundation money relieved strains on the budget and made possible special projects and building that would have been very difficult otherwise. When Nelson retired, Louisville Seminary had received over $955,000 in grants during his seven-year presidency, not counting those for the library.

When Louisville reached the close of the 1980-1981 school year it had weathered yet another difficult period in its history. The nature of theological education had changed; the faculty had gone through a significant transition; students were very different (both in attitudes and demographics); the civil rights and anti-war movements had made their impact; and a financial crisis had been averted. Although the presidents had provided the leadership which made survival possible — and brought LPTS to a vital state by the end of Nelson's tenure — every segment of the institution's constituency had played its part. The Seminary was poised to move toward the new millennium.

127. Nelson Interview; Minutes of the Board (September 2, 1977–December 28, 1979), Executive Committee, March 5, 1979; and Nelson, "Notes for Future Historians," 19.

• VI •

A BRIDGE INSTITUTION

The Presidency of John M. Mulder, 1981-Present

B y the time C. Ellis Nelson retired in 1981, Louisville Seminary had re-
gained a level of stability it had not enjoyed in fifteen years. The school
was prepared financially to move into a new era — an era that would be
marked by changes in society, in mainstream Protestantism, in theological
education, and in the Seminary itself. Economic developments, continued
erosion of denominational identity, reduction in denominational funding,
ongoing shifts in the nature of the student body, the final reunion of the
two Presbyterian denominations to which LPTS was related, and the reality of global Christianity were all to affect the educational enterprise at the
Seminary. Maintaining its vision in the face of these changes would require
creativity, imagination, and leadership — qualities which, fortunately, defined LPTS' administrators and faculty.

A More Diverse Seminary

It was not readily apparent who should succeed Nelson. Indeed, the search
committee was at a standstill when Craig Dykstra mentioned a young professor of American church history at Princeton whom he thought would
make a good choice as president. John M. Mulder was his name, and on his
thirty-fifth birthday he accepted the presidency of Louisville Seminary. Despite his youth, Mulder brought a variety of experiences to the task. He had
edited the student paper at Hope College, learned about the business world
in a summer job as a reporter for the *Wall Street Journal,* and had been associate editor of *Theology Today.* Beyond those experiences, he was a person

with organizational skills, a creative mind, and insight into contemporary mainstream Protestantism and the ways in which a seminary could serve the church. Ekstrom said that Mulder was "deeply concerned about the health and well-being of the Presbyterian Church and the Reformed tradition, and its public significance and impact."[1] A number of initiatives undertaken at Louisville Seminary since 1981 reflected that concern.[2]

After a period of relative stability during the Nelson years, the faculty underwent extensive turnover and expansion in the 1980s and 1990s — so much so that by 2000 the only faculty member remaining from the beginning of Mulder's presidency was Johanna van Wijk-Bos. The diversity for which the Seminary had previously striven became more of a reality. A number of women joined the faculty: Nancy Ramsay in pastoral care; Kathryn Johnson in church history (the position vacated by Gunsalus now restored ten years hence); Amy Plantinga Pauw in theology; Patricia Tull and Susan Garrett in biblical studies; Dianne Reistroffer as Director of Graduate Studies and professor of ministry and eventually dean; Frances Adeney in evangelism and mission; and Carol Cook in pastoral care and counseling. At the turn of the millennium there were eight women serving full-time on the faculty. Although these women's scholarly interests and work were not limited to women's concerns or feminist interpretation, they provided a strong and consistent female perspective to the life and work of the campus. Van Wijk-Bos, not particularly concerned with many women's issues when she first arrived at Louisville Seminary, became a committed feminist.[3]

Issues important to women remained visible on campus. In 1984 the Women's Caucus again presented the faculty with a resolution on inclusive language; the faculty endorsed it but acknowledged that academic freedom forbade their dictating the speech used by students or faculty.[4] Although speech about humankind became generally inclusive on campus, language about God was less so. Over time the Women's Caucus became less active

1. William Ekstrom Interview, March 17, 1992.

2. Morgan Roberts Interview, April 29, 1994, noted Mulder's fundraising ability and attributed it in large measure to his pastoral style of meeting with people. Roberts believed strongly that fundraising was a form of stewardship and, therefore, constituted a very pastoral matter in seminary life.

3. Johanna van Wijk-Bos Interview, April 17, 1994. Bos's feminism was illustrated by her participation in an ecumenical Reimagining Conference celebrating the United Nations' Decade with Women and exploring feminist insight into faith, and by books such as *Reimagining God: The Case for Scriptural Diversity* (Louisville: Westminster/John Knox Press, 1995) and *Reformed and Feminist: A Challenge to the Church* (Louisville: Westminster/John Knox Press, 1991).

4. Minutes of the Faculty (1982-1986), October 23, 1984. LPTS Archives.

and more of a support group, its activist role taken up by Feminists at LPTS (FALPTS). In the early 1990s a Women's Center, given institutional standing through oversight by the Gender and Ministry Committee, was created to hold resources and provide women a place to meet.[5]

The Seminary still suffered difficulty in attracting people of color to the faculty. Upon George Edwards' retirement in 1986, Virgil Cruz became professor of New Testament. Cruz was the first tenured and the only African-American on the faculty. When he neared retirement in the mid-1990s, the Seminary, frustrated by its inability to hire other people of color, conducted what were, in effect, affirmative action searches. Those efforts brought, in the space of two years, three African-Americans to the campus: Dale Andrews in homiletics, Scott Williamson in ethics, and Stephen Ray in philosophical theology. Again, as was true with the women, these scholars were by no means limited to African-American interests or approaches to their fields, but their unique perspectives were highly beneficial to their students. These three faculty also highlighted the denominational diversity that had come to characterize the LPTS faculty. The African Methodist Episcopal Church, American Baptist Church, Evangelical Lutheran Church in America, United Church of Christ, and United Methodist Church were among those represented as the twentieth century drew to a close.

Virgil Cruz embodied the attempt of Louisville Seminary to create a place in which the liberal and conservative (or evangelical) elements within Presbyterianism might discuss their different approaches to faith and begin to find common ground. Of course, the Seminary had been quite conservative in its Calvinism for much of its history, but since the 1960s it had grown more liberal theologically and in its involvement in social justice issues. But it remained more moderate in its liberalism than some people imagined. Morrison and Rhodes were cautious in their biblical scholarship and, while certainly well informed of current methods, would be considered moderate. Nebelsick was conservative in that he had a deep concern for traditional Reformed theology, liberal in his concern for a number of social justice issues, and far from evangelical in his personal style. So while LPTS welcomed more conservative students and offered them a place to explore their own faith, it did not present any evangelical models for them or provide an evangelical approach to biblical or theological study.

The situation typified two realities that emerged during the 1980s. First, the greatest division in Protestantism existed not between denomi-

5. Van Wijk-Bos Interview; Robert Reed Interview, March 13, 1994.

nations, as had once been the case, but between liberal and conservative Protestants within and across denominational lines. That is, a conservative Presbyterian had more in common with a conservative Episcopalian or Methodist than with a liberal Presbyterian.[6] Second, for various reasons, the student body at LPTS (and other seminaries) had become more conservative than those who passed through in the 1960s and 1970s. Given these circumstances Mulder (and to an extent Nelson before him) believed the Seminary could (and should) begin to play a role in bridging the differences between the two groups by intentionally bringing the evangelical perspective to campus in the form of professors who could articulate it for the community. Cruz, who became a leader of Presbyterians for Renewal, was one such evangelical. When mission and evangelism were restored to the curriculum in the late 1980s, Darrell Guder, with a wide variety of experiences that included work with Young Life in Germany, brought an evangelical stance to his substantial scholarship and teaching. Amy Plantinga Pauw (who was reared in the more conservative Christian Reformed Church) and John McClure both earned degrees from the evangelical Fuller Theological Seminary. They consequently understood and had a respect for the evangelical stance and spoke occasionally to evangelical groups in an attempt to build the Seminary's and the denomination's relationship with them. Dale Andrews, ordained in the African Methodist Episcopal Zion Church, and Frances Adeney, who called herself evangelical despite areas of disagreement with many others who claimed that name, broadened the evangelical presence on campus. David Wood, who joined the administration as associate director of the Louisville Institute in 1998, held a bachelor's degree from Oral Roberts University and the M.Div. from Gordon-Conwell Theological Seminary, which clearly gave him an understanding of evangelical Christianity. By the 1990s, then, the faculty at Louisville Seminary displayed a diversity previously unseen in its history.

The trends in student diversity evident in the 1970s accelerated through the remainder of the century. Women continued to enroll in seminaries and divinity schools in record numbers; at LPTS their numbers ap-

6. Any number of studies discuss this situation, but perhaps it is most clearly documented and explicated in Robert Wuthnow, *The Restructuring of American Religion: Society and Faith Since World War II* (Princeton: Princeton University Press, 1988). I am aware that the terms "liberal" and "conservative" are imprecise and problematical. I use them here in the belief that they have a common enough parlance to be useful and that liberals and conservatives resemble obscenities: we may not be able to define them but we know them when we see them.

proached fifty percent of the student body. The movement toward greater numbers of second-career students persisted as well. Attracting people of color remained a difficult task for the Seminary but, as we shall see, programs with that goal in mind eventually began to bear fruit. The denominational, racial, and gender diversity on campus reached new highs.

Scholarship in Service of the Church

Given the personal and theological variety of the students and faculty — which reflected the growing pluralism of the nation — the possibility existed for LPTS to evolve into small factions of area interests and competing visions. Perhaps the greatest challenge for the community was to find a unified and unifying vision for itself. Indeed, it was necessary if the Seminary was to serve as a bridge within the denomination, especially between the left and right.[7] The vision around which the Seminary leadership wanted to center the community was its traditional one: an institution called into being by the church and existing for the education of ministers and serving the church.[8]

Much of the responsibility for promoting a common vision for the Seminary fell to the academic deans. Louis Weeks succeeded Grayson Tucker soon after Mulder's arrival, and the two church historians worked well together. The former promoted the expectation of academic excellence for the Seminary community. Having served in Zaire as a missionary between his graduation from Union Seminary in Virginia and earning his doctorate at Duke University, he stressed a concern for Louisville Seminary's relationship to the church and for missions. Gene March, A. B. Rhodes Professor of Old Testament, served the Seminary in numerous roles, including acting president during a Mulder sabbatical. His impact on Seminary life was so positive that he was made dean when Weeks retired. He brought a special emphasis on Jewish-Christian understanding to campus. The vision of these two leaders in curriculum, cross-cultural programs, promotion of international studies, and service to the church was invaluable for the development of LPTS.

7. John Kuykendall, who served on the board during the 1980s, noted the necessity of building a diverse but truly cohesive faculty, and believed Mulder had been able to do that.
8. Mulder himself articulated this as his hope for LPTS, and in 1996 believed the Seminary, most importantly the faculty, was committed to that calling. John M. Mulder, "Reflections on 15 Years: Louisville Presbyterian Theological Seminary, 1981-1996," 4. LPTS Archives.

The faculty published at a level of scholarship unprecedented for the school. Of course, the school's tradition of scholarly publication stretched as far back as the work of Robert J. Breckinridge in the 1860s, but faculty output in the 1980s and 1990s reached a new height.

In biblical studies, Marty Soards published widely and gained an international reputation for his New Testament research.[9] His accomplishments earned him editorships with the *Journal of Biblical Literature* and *The New Interpreter's Bible.* Johanna van Wijk-Bos published such works as *Ezra, Nehemiah, and Esther* in the *Westminster Bible Companion* and *Re-Imagining God: The Case for Scriptural Diversity.*[10] Susan Garrett wrote *The Demise of the Devil: Magic and the Demonic in Luke's Writing* and *The Temptations of Jesus in Mark's Gospel* and served on a variety of committees in the Society of Biblical Literature.[11] Patricia Tull's *Remember the Former Things: The Recollection of Previous Texts in Second Isaiah* advanced the method of understanding the Bible through a study of the use of texts within Scripture itself.[12] She also served as the co-chair of the Formation of the Book of Isaiah Group of the Society for Biblical Literature and wrote the 2001-2002 Horizons Bible Study for Presbyterian Women on Esther. Gene March, keenly interested in Jewish-Christian relations and the Middle East, published *Israel and the Politics of Land: A Theological Case Study* and an updated revision of *The Mighty Acts of God.*[13] He also contributed the commentary on Haggai to the *New Interpreter's Bible.*

The Area B faculty were also productive. Harold Nebelsick published the culmination of years of work in the relationship between theology and

9. His work included *The Apostle Paul: An Introduction to His Writings and Teaching* (New York: Paulist Press, 1987); *The Passion According to Luke: The Special Material of Luke 22* (Sheffield: JSOT Press, 1987); *The Speeches in Acts: Their Content, Context, and Concerns* (Louisville: Westminster/John Knox Press, 1994); *Scripture and Homosexuality: Biblical Authority and the Church Today* (Louisville: Westminster/John Knox Press, 1995); and *First Corinthians,* New International Biblical Commentary Series (Peabody, Mass.: Hendrickson Publishers, 1999).

10. Johanna W. H. van Wijk-Bos, *Ezra, Nehemiah, and Esther* (Louisville: Westminster John Knox Press, 1998); *Re-Imagining God: The Case for Scriptural Diversity* (Louisville: Westminster John Knox Press, 1995).

11. Susan R. Garrett, *The Demise of the Devil: Magic and the Demonic in Luke's Writing* (Minneapolis: Fortress Press, 1989); *The Temptations of Jesus in Mark's Gospel* (Grand Rapids, Mich.: Wm. B. Eerdmans Publishing Co., 1998).

12. Patricia Tull Willey, *Remember the Former Things: The Recollection of Previous Texts in Second Isaiah* (Atlanta: Scholars Press, 1997).

13. W. Eugene March, *Israel and the Politics of Land: A Theological Case Study* (Louisville: Westminster/John Knox Press, 1994) and *The Mighty Acts of God* (Louisville: Westminster John Knox Press, 2000).

science in three books prior to his death.[14] Cooper wrote *Why, God?*, an exploration of suffering from a process theology perspective.[15] Pauw's work earned her editorial positions with the Columbia Reformed Theology Series and the Yale Press edition of *The Works of Jonathan Edwards*. Weeks published his history of *Kentucky Presbyterians* and released a series of books of case studies for the study of religion and faith issues. He also, along with Joe Coalter and John Mulder, coordinated and edited the seven-volume *The Presbyterian Presence* series and a follow-up book, *Vital Signs: The Promise of Mainstream Protestantism*.[16] Kathryn Johnson wrote a number of articles, particularly on the experience of women in the monastic tradition and the history of biblical interpretation. Christopher Elwood published *The Body Broken: The Calvinist Doctrine of the Eucharist and the Symbolization of Power in Sixteenth-Century France*, a study of the impact of the French Reformed understanding of the sacrament on ecclesiastic and political power.[17]

Nor did the faculty in practical theology lag in its scholarship. David Steere established himself as a leading figure in the field of pastoral counseling, a reputation solidified by his publications.[18] Nancy Ramsay authored chapters in edited volumes and published *Pastoral Diagnosis: A Resource for Ministries of Care and Counseling* and edited (with John McClure) *Telling the Truth: Preaching About Sexual and Domestic Violence*.[19] She served on the editorial board and later co-edited the *Journal of Pastoral Theology*. Craig Dykstra published *Vision and Character: A Christian Educator's Alternative to Kohlberg*.[20] His scholarly abilities were fur-

14. See his *Theology and Science in Mutual Modification* (New York: Oxford University Press, 1981); *Circles of God: Theology and Science from the Greeks to Copernicus* (Edinburgh: Scottish Academic Press, 1985); and, posthumously, *The Renaissance, the Reformation and the Rise of Science* (Edinburgh: T and T Clark, 1992).

15. Burton Z. Cooper, *Why, God?* (Atlanta: John Knox Press, 1988).

16. Milton J Coalter, John M. Mulder, and Louis B. Weeks, *Vital Signs: The Promise of Mainstream Protestantism* (Grand Rapids, Mich.: William B. Eerdmans Publishing Co., 1996).

17. Christopher Elwood, *The Body Broken: The Calvinist Doctrine of the Eucharist and the Symbolization of Power in Sixteenth-Century France* (New York and Oxford: Oxford University Press, 1999).

18. See, for example, his *Bodily Expressions in Psychotherapy* (New York: Brunner/Mozel, 1982) and *Spiritual Presence in Psychotherapy: A Guide for Caregivers* (New York: Brunner/Mozel, 1997).

19. Nancy J. Ramsay, *Pastoral Diagnosis: A Resource for Ministries of Care and Counseling* (Minneapolis: Fortress Press, 1998); Ramsay and John S. McClure, *Telling the Truth: Preaching About Sexual and Domestic Violence* (Cleveland, Ohio.: United Church Press, 1998).

20. Craig R. Dykstra, *Vision and Character: A Christian Educator's Alternative to Kohlberg* (New York: Paulist Press, 1981).

ther confirmed by his eventual appointment as Vice President for Religion at the Lilly Endowment. David Hester served the Seminary and the wider scholarly community as director of the Grawemeyer Award in Religion. He also co-edited, with Thomas P. Holland, *Building Effective Boards for Religious Organizations: A Handbook for Trustees, Presidents, and Church Leaders*.[21] Brad Wigger wrote *The Texture of Mystery* and served as consultant to the Lilly Endowment on a number of projects, in addition to directing LPTS' Center for Congregations and Family Ministries.[22] John McClure published, among other works, *The Four Codes of Preaching: Rhetorical Strategies* and *The Roundtable Pulpit: Where Leadership and Preaching Meet*.[23] He also served on the editorial board of the journal *Homiletic*. Darrell Guder added *Be My Witnesses: The Church's Mission, Message, and Messengers*.[24] Tucker produced *A Church Planning Questionnaire: Manual and Discoveries from 100 Churches* to assist congregations in identifying congregational dynamics.[25] Clearly the Seminary faculty was prolific and scholarly. The additions to the faculty as the twentieth century drew to a close held promise for continuing contributions to every field of theological study.

One drawback to such wide-ranging scholarship was that some people believed that contemporary seminary faculties were too defined by their professional and scholarly identities and stood too far removed from the realities of and concern for church life. But LPTS did not disregard the church. Virtually all faculty spent large amounts of time filling vacant pulpits, teaching in a variety of settings, and serving on presbytery and denominational committees.[26] Nancy Ramsay, for example, served on the com-

21. David C. Hester and Thomas P. Holland, eds., *Building Effective Boards for Religious Organizations: A Handbook for Trustees, Presidents, and Church Leaders* (San Francisco, Calif.: Jossey-Bass, 2000).

22. J. Bradley Wigger, *The Texture of Mystery: An Interdisciplinary Inquiry into Perception and Learning* (Lewisburg, Pa.: Bucknell University Press, 1998).

23. John S. McClure, *The Four Codes of Preaching: Rhetorical Strategies* (Minneapolis: Fortress Press, 1991); *The Roundtable Pulpit: Where Leadership and Preaching Meet* (Nashville: Abingdon Press, 1995).

24. Darrell L. Guder, *Be My Witnesses: The Church's Mission, Message, and Messengers* (Grand Rapids, Mich.: Wm. B. Eerdmans Publishing Co., 1985).

25. Grayson L. Tucker, *A Church Planning Questionnaire: Manual and Discoveries from 100 Churches* (Louisville: Grayson L. Tucker, 1982).

26. Mulder himself, who tabulated the church-related service of the faculty in 1998, was surprised at the amount of time the faculty was so involved because it had never been systematically documented in its entirety. John Mulder Interview, October 8, 1998. No survey of those activities could begin to exhaust the work of the faculty on behalf of the denomi-

mittee to write the new "A Brief Declaration of Faith" for the reunited denomination. Mulder chaired the committee to create a new seal for the denomination; his companion book, *Sealed in Christ: The Symbolism of the Seal of the Presbyterian Church (U.S.A.)* proved very popular. Weeks' study books *To Be a Presbyterian* and *The Presbyterian Source* were used across the denomination in educational settings. Gene March accepted the responsibility for writing the weekly Sunday school Bible lesson which appeared in *Presbyterian Outlook* and provided help to countless teachers in congregations. Faculty wrote for the *Proclamation* series to aid pastors who preached from the lectionary and for women's groups studies such as *Horizons*.

The Seminary also strove to embody the community of the church in its own life, thus maintaining an important element of its tradition. Seminary dinners, picnics, informal discussions, and other activities drew together students, faculty, and staff (and families of all), for sharing and fellowship. Instances of help for students in need continued to abound. The entire community raised money and offered support as students confronted difficulties — from the need to fly home in times of family bereavement, to meeting expenses for extraordinary medical need, to more common financial and emotional problems. On one occasion, a student wrote a check for $1,000 to help two other students who were struggling to meet medical expenses.[27] The Seminary sought never to forget that it existed as an institution of the church and provided a living laboratory of preparation for ministry.

Louisville Seminary continued to address controversial issues arising out of the differences of faculty interests and approaches, and out of the issues confronting society and the church. Generally speaking, however, this was done in a less public and activist way; as in the nation at large, that day had passed. Van Wijk-Bos believed the Seminary was at its best when dealing with difficult topics, as did Morrison. They thought LPTS did a commendable job of creating an open forum of ideas as befits an educational institution.[28] When the National Council of Churches released an inclusive language lectionary for use in the churches, the Seminary provided a

---

nations of which they were a part. Nor could it be fair to those whose contributions remained inadequately mentioned. Even the most cursory reading of the dean's report to the board of trustees through the 1980s and 1990s bespeaks the level of church participation by the LPTS faculty.

27. This last gift, in 2000, was given by the student on the condition of anonymity, indicating even further the unselfish nature of the LPTS community. Electronic mail from John M. Mulder, January 25, 2000.

28. Van Wijk-Bos Interview; Clinton Morrison Interview, March 16, 1993.

panel discussion between two faculty favoring its use and two opposed, with a question and answer period. Van Wijk-Bos remembered it as very open and helpful. The ordination of homosexuals in the Presbyterian Church became very divisive. There were presentations on the topic, although not simultaneously in an open forum. Though Edwards had retired by the time the issue was presented on campus, he had argued previously against the use of Scripture passages such as the destruction of Sodom and Gomorrah and Romans 1 to designate homosexuality a sin and, consequently, he supported the ordination of gays and lesbians. Marty Soards in New Testament offered an opposing view: that a study of Scripture precluded the propriety of ordination (although he argued against any other discrimination against homosexuals in church or society).[29] Those who favored ordination brought Edwards on campus to speak in reply. While there was a great deal of dialogue, van Wijk-Bos did not think the topic was handled as well as discussion of the lectionary.[30]

One of the first and most obvious means of working toward the goal of educating ministers for the church was revision of the 1973 curriculum, which gave students exposure to the various areas of knowledge and practice of ministry through its distribution of requirements, but lacked the integrative structure necessary to unify them. The faculty grew concerned about this specialization of knowledge and learning by the late 1970s but seemed unable to find a way to move to action.[31] Warheim summed up the feelings of many when he wrote that the trend in theological education at LPTS, which was taking place at other seminaries as well, "led to a faculty of specialists presiding over autonomous and often insulated pieces of specialized skill and knowledge, an unintegrated curriculum, and a fragmented professional consciousness in the Seminary's graduates. This trend has eroded the faculty's historical modeling function, compartmentalized learnings, and often produces a professional style in which one ministerial function such as counseling is done in a manner which may not complement and, indeed, often contradicts what is done in others."[32]

---

29. Soards' comments eventuated in a book, *Scripture and Homosexuality: Biblical Authority and the Church Today* (Louisville: Westminster/John Knox Press, 1995). Edwards' book was *Gay/Lesbian Liberation: A Biblical Perspective* (New York: Pilgrim Press, 1984).

30. See "Sexism, Racism, and Homophobia Task Force," April 19, 1991, manuscript copy, LPTS Archives; and van Wijk-Bos Interview.

31. I remember conversations with Cooper and Dykstra over lunch regarding this issue, occasioned by the very helpful experience of writing my senior statement of faith which brought together various areas of study in my mind.

32. Hal Warheim, "The History of a 'First-Class Dream,'" vi.

Mulder identified curriculum as an area in need of attention early in his presidency.[33]

Change also resulted from developments in the 1960s and 1970s which were external to the Seminary.[34] There was a decline in denominational identity within mainstream Protestantism and less theological and biblical preparation among students compared to those generations of students who attended seminary through the 1950s. This was true for a number of reasons. First, the baby boom generation swelled the ranks in state-run colleges and universities, drastically reducing the percentages of those educated in denominational colleges. Fewer students came to seminary from Presbyterian schools or had collegiate preparation for theological study. The decline of biblical and theological study in Sunday schools also contributed to this change in the preparation of students for seminary study. Further, an increasing number of students decided for ministry not out of experiences they had within Presbyterian church structures but through para-church groups such as Young Life, Campus Crusade for Christ, or some non-denominational group on their college campus. This led to a more conservative student body generally at Louisville Seminary, and one that had less grounding in Reformed theology, Presbyterian worship and governance, and the traditions of Reformed biblical study.

Compounding that situation was the continuing growth of second-career students preparing for ministry. Their areas of study in college rarely included theology or Bible, but they came to seminary out of deep commitment and often at great sacrifice. "The Presbyterian Presence," an in-depth study of Presbyterianism in the twentieth century conducted by Mulder, Louis Weeks, and Milton J (Joe) Coalter, showed that the contemporary situation was marked by a clear weakening of Presbyterian identity as a denomination and a theological tradition. Robert Wuthnow asserted, "By all indications, Presbyterians have not only been diminishing in numbers but have also experienced an erosion in the social and cultural boundaries that have set them off from other denominations [and, he might have added, the surrounding culture] in the past."[35] Edward

33. Faculty Minutes (1982-1986), August 27, 1982.

34. The "Report of the Special Committee to Study Theological Institutions," PCUSA *GAM*, 1993, showed that the factors were societal and affected all seminaries. Among the issues affecting the preparation of ministers the report named pluralism, the difficulty of stating a coherent theological rationale of ministerial education, the level of student preparation for theological study, the decline of denominational identity, and financial pressures.

35. Robert Wuthnow, "The Restructuring of American Presbyterianism: Turmoil in

Farley and Benton Johnson also demonstrated that decline in theology and behavior.[36]

The faculty decided to revise the curriculum to create a course of study that would attempt to provide integrative learning and a solid grounding in the Reformed tradition. They worked diligently in its creation, coordinated and guided by Weeks as dean. The initial hope was to develop foundational courses taught by one member from each area of the curriculum. When that proved unrealistic for a number of logistical reasons, the faculty scaled back its vision to create foundational courses within each of the three areas of study. They would be team-taught and strive to integrate the content of the disciplines within each area. Some of the insights gained from the Congregation-Based Ministry helped in this process, and the new curriculum was finally instituted in 1990.[37] Area A developed Scripture I and II, which in effect became an Old and New Testament sequence led by a professor from each of those areas. Area B created Church History and Theological Studies (CHATS), which surveyed key theological doctrines and issues in their historical development, with special attention to the Calvinist tradition. Area C had more difficulty developing a core course but eventually built an introductory one in practical theology.

These courses met four days a week; presentations by professors alternated with seminars in which students summarized readings and discussed essential ideas. Weeks remarked that he could see students' thinking skills developing before his eyes. Interaction between professors and their classes spilled over into other areas of campus life.[38] Others noted the benefit of the foundational courses in the ability of a teacher to assume a shared body of knowledge by students in upper-level courses and in providing a sequential learning process over against the previous (relatively) random collection of credits.[39] Some felt that the elusive and difficult goal of helping students integrate their knowledge and think theologically

One Denomination," in Coalter, Mulder, Weeks, eds., *The Presbyterian Predicament: Six Perspectives,* The Presbyterian Presence (Louisville: Westminster/John Knox Press, 1990).

36. Edward Farley, "The Presbyterian Heritage as Modernism: Reaffirming a Forgotten Past in Hard Times," and Benton Johnson, "On Dropping the Subject: Presbyterians and Sabbath Observance in the Twentieth Century," in Coalter, Mulder, Weeks, eds., *Presbyterian Predicament.* See also part of this discussion on the LPTS campus in "Louisville Presbyterian Theological Seminary Long-Range Plan, 1985." LPTS Archives.

37. Craig Dykstra Interview, May 6, 1994.

38. Weeks Interview, March 15, 1993.

39. Van Wijk-Bos Interview; Reed Interview.

about ministry was not fully met, although the small-group sections in foundations courses provided some reflective link to field education.

Curricula never meet all needs, of course, and students and faculty sought further refinements in 1998: two more required courses in Bible, regular courses in spirituality (suggesting that, in some ways, Wessler had been ahead of his time with "Life Springs"), and a required course in polity.[40] With the faculty additions and the new curriculum, Louisville Seminary emerged as an institution that was academically stronger than it perhaps had ever been. Steere believed the faculty of the 1990s stronger than the one under which he had studied in the 1950s.[41]

During the 1980s and 1990s the library entered a new stage of modernization and growth. Milton J Coalter assumed leadership of the library on Ernest White's retirement and instituted significant changes. He completed the transition of the library's holdings to the Library of Congress classification system, bringing Louisville Seminary into conformity with other college and seminary libraries. Building on White's efforts to make the volume of the collection suitable for a seminary "of the first class," Coalter ensured that the holdings continued to increase rapidly. Most important, Coalter brought computer technology to the LPTS library. The card catalog was placed on computer and linked electronically to that of Southern Baptist Seminary, which in turn had connections to libraries around the nation. Coalter's election as president of the American Theological Library Association for 1998-1999 attested to the quality of his leadership, as did his selection by the Lilly Endowment to create a web site providing information on their research grants in religious studies.

Further Changing the Administration and Finances

Mulder also set out to build on Nelson's efforts to make Louisville Seminary stronger administratively and financially. The dominant impetus for the changes he instituted was the changing pattern of financial support for seminaries across the nation. With the increasing dependence of seminar-

---

40. Minutes of the Board and Executive Committee (1993-present), Academic Affairs Committee, October 24, 1996. LPTS Archives. With the new curriculum LPTS made another change that many other seminaries had adopted — introductory Hebrew classes were taken in the summer, before the regular school year, and Greek was taught in the January term.

41. David Steere Interview, May 15, 1994.

ies on endowment performance and annual giving, some aspects of Seminary administration needed revision.

Over time the composition of the board of directors (by this time renamed the board of trustees) changed.[42] Mulder drew from studies of boards of directors funded by the Lilly Endowment, and a grant from Lilly enabled LPTS to begin a program of board education for effective seminary leadership. Consequently, changes to the board and its work received full discussion and approval by the board itself.

Accelerating the trend begun under Nelson, the Seminary moved to a board of predominantly lay members, with a general goal of having two-thirds laity and one-third clergy. The administration required that every person offered a seat be a committed Christian, an active member of a Presbyterian church, and willing to learn about and work diligently for theological education. In the process of those changes the board's membership became more diverse; women constituted approximately 40% of the board and African-Americans approximately 15%. Board members represented all regions of the nation, with an expected concentration from the Seminary's natural constituency in Middle America. People asserted that the board was as intelligent, committed, and faithful in its work as it had ever been.[43]

A predominantly lay membership on the board created a new set of needs for Louisville Seminary. The laity, unlike the clergy, generally had no first-hand knowledge of theological education or of seminary life. And the decrease in numbers of clergy members might, it was feared, reduce one of the Seminary's natural points of contact with the church and the "tall steeple" leadership that had, historically, been a mainstay of support for seminaries; fortunately, this potential problem was averted through the work of lay board members from those churches. Too, there were those who worried that even if contact with large and wealthy congregations were maintained in the midst of the changes, the needs and roles of smaller churches and their pastors would be neglected.[44] Others feared too much "secularization" of the Seminary's thinking. William Young believed LPTS could use "more theological language, especially that which relates to Christian stewardship, when talking with prospective donors." Too often he per-

42. The head of the board, formerly titled "president," had been changed to "chairman." During Mulder's presidency it became "chair" and, finally, "moderator."

43. On the changing composition of the board see Kenneth Hougland Interview, March 17, 1992; Anne Caldwell Interview, February 27, 1993; Thomas Duncan Interview, March 23, 1992; John Kuykendall Interview, May 20, 1994; Henry Mobley and Paul Tudor Jones Interview, April 26, 1992.

44. See especially Duncan Interview.

ceived excessive "fund raising parlance" in financial campaigns and believed LPTS would "do better with donors and among ourselves to keep
our primary focus on the Christian character of giving, rather than the
'professionalese' that frequently characterizes major church campaigns."[45] But others held that the development staff, especially by the late
1990s, was doing a fine job of casting its appeals for giving in the theological language of stewardship.

The lay board members had to become important interpreters of the
Seminary and its mission to the church. To fill that role effectively in turn
required that they be educated. Mulder undertook that task and pursued it
with vigor. He received a grant from the Lilly Endowment for a program of
board development that involved a retreat with educational modules.[46]
Board meetings included a devotional component and a presentation high-
lighting some element of theological education. For instance, at the spring
1982 meeting Al Winn, Catherine Gunsalus Gonzalez, and Bruce Robertson spoke on theological education; and at the fall 1983 meeting there was a
panel discussion by six international students at LPTS.[47] Mulder, reading
widely in ecclesiastical and secular literature and journals, provided a
steady stream of reading material for board members on the state of the
church, the relationship of the church to the world, and developments and
challenges for theological education. Board members became more familiar with theology and theological education and learned to think more
theologically about their life and work.

The board was more knowledgeable regarding Seminary life and
more involved in planning the life of Louisville Seminary than had been
the case since the early twentieth century when it was comprised mainly of
ministers who lived a short distance away.[48] With the concentration on the
forces pressing in on theological education from within and without came
an emphasis on long-range planning in a more formal and consistent way
than had been the case in the past. The board identified areas of growth
they hoped to see, directions in which LPTS should move, and especially
the means for financing the future. The key to the process lay in the strategic nature of the planning. Reed described it as a process in which the
board did not simply outline a series of steps to be taken and a timetable

45. William Young Interview, May 4, 1994.
46. Mobley said that this idea was first planted in Lynn's mind at Lilly by Nelson, and
that Lynn then passed it on to Mulder.
47. Minutes of the Board (1980-1992), April 19-20, 1982, and October 17-18, 1983.
48. For the effect of Mulder's program on the board see particularly Reed Interview
and Anne Caldwell Interview.

within which to achieve them, but rather established goals with enough re-visiting of them and flexibility in their pursuit that people could react to new opportunities or changes in the "environment" to good advantage.[49]

Essentially, Louisville Seminary decided that it had to do a better job of interpreting itself and its mission to the church and to potential donors. That inevitably led to new administrative structures and staff to conduct the public relations and development work necessitated by the new situation. These years at LPTS were marked, as they were at most seminaries and colleges, by a growth in the size of the administration. When Thomas Jones left at the end of C. Ellis Nelson's tenure, development received greater emphasis and Frank Penick was hired as Vice-President for Development by Nelson. Nelson also hired Joe Suitor as Director of Planned Giving; he was succeeded by Anne Caldwell, who was appointed by Mulder. Penick's departure led to the hiring of Dennis Riggs, who resigned in a few years to be succeeded by Larry Hitner.[50]

This trend of enlarging administration was accelerated by constant advancements in technological equipment in the library and administration building. The staff grew in other ways: Bennett's resignation eventually led to a division of his tasks into Director of Admissions and a Dean of Students, and during the 1990s a Director of Graduate Studies oversaw the Master of Theology, Doctor of Ministry, and continuing and lay education programs.[51] Of course, the need for more development and public relations staff was not the sole impetus for growth at Louisville Seminary. The replacement of positions reduced during the Nelson administration accounted for some of the additions. Computerization of the campus required skilled operators to manage the technology. Nor did Seminary relations grow out of proportion to other areas of the budget. The faculty also expanded, and compensation for all areas of the Seminary community rose. The single largest increase in the budget was for student aid.[52] In short, Louisville Seminary's growth did not seem out of proportion to its need or inappropriate to meet its mission for theological education.

Changes to the board and administration became necessary because the financial trends that became evident during Nelson's presidency continued and accelerated. Inflation, rising costs, and the drop in funding

49. Reed Interview.

50. Minutes of the Board (1980-1992), April 14-15, 1980; Anne Caldwell Interview; Dennis Riggs Interview, May 16, 1994.

51. Mulder, "Reflections on 15 Years," 9-10.

52. Dykstra thought the issue of fundraising and staffing in small theological institutions was a "great dilemma" for them. Dykstra Interview.

from traditional sources all made the importance of raising and managing the endowment even more important.[53] Mulder's work on the *Wall Street Journal* and his independent reading made him a knowledgeable and active participant in these efforts. The development office was also effective in its work — Riggs saw his duty as more than fundraising, which he defined as asking for money for a particular need. Development, he believed, presented an ethos of the institution to donors in such a way that they felt they were meeting both their own and the institution's needs. Development cultivated ongoing support. Riggs also sensed that he gave development a higher and better profile on campus, so that faculty and students perceived it as a responsible part of Seminary life and work, and not a distasteful task that someone had to do to pay the bills.[54] Through management of the endowment, the remarkable performance of the stock market in the 1980s and 1990s, new gifts solicited, and bequests (many of which were the result of Caldwell's work two and three decades before), the endowment grew incredibly from almost $11 million at the start of Mulder's presidency to approximately $68 million by 2000.[55]

Expansion of programs and personnel, rising costs, and maintenance of and additions to the campus required that kind of growth in the endowment — the income from which provided approximately forty-five percent of the budget by the late 1990s. One area of need was particularly disturbing: student expense. Tuition and living costs rose alongside other expenses, and some students left the Seminary with an indebtedness of anywhere from $10,000 to $20,000. Some who came to seminary directly from college brought undergraduate debts to compound their burden, and second-career people had less time to repay their loans on ministers' salaries and jeopardized their retirement.[56] Louisville Seminary took this problem very seriously and consequently devoted more of the budget to student aid for both tuition and housing costs. The Seminary adopted the goal of providing its education tuition-free to those who demonstrated financial need, and this goal was achieved by the mid-1990s.[57] In 1996

53. See Ruger, *Lean Years, Fat Years.*

54. Riggs Interview.

55. Minutes of the Board (1993-present), Finance and Administration Committee, April 25, 1997.

56. See Minutes of the Board (1980-1992), April 30–May 1, 1984; Executive Committee, April 24, 1997; and Laverne Alexander Interview.

57. Minutes of the Board (1993-present), Executive Committee, April 24, 1997. The first study of seminary student indebtedness was done by LPTS. Dean of Students Steve Hancock directed the study, funded with a grant from the Lilly Endowment.

Mulder noted that since 1981 the LPTS budget had grown 136%. Over the same period total financial aid rose 217%, but grants-in-aid (those based on financial need) by 460% — the most of any item in the Seminary's budget. The Seminary had also been able to establish a series of academic merit scholarships for incoming students (the Patterson had been the only one until then), which attracted quality students and relieved their expenses.[58] The endowment for those scholarships relieved pressure on the rest of the budget as well.

A new step taken to help raise money was special campaigns to honor some key people in Louisville Seminary's life, especially by endowing professorships, something out of practice at LPTS since the 1930s. At the close of his presidency Nelson had completed a campaign to endow the Arnold Black Rhodes Chair in Old Testament; its namesake not only gave almost four decades of service to the school but had also been a teacher of the church through his publications and countless lectures. Rhodes was a beloved and popular teacher, perceptive counselor, and model for generations of students. (At the close of the 1990s the Seminary also established a memorial garden for ashes behind Caldwell Chapel to honor Lela Rhodes, manager of the bookstore for many years and *de facto* pastoral counselor for untold numbers of students.)[59]

Upon his arrival Mulder began a campaign to establish the Harrison Ray Anderson Chair in Pastoral Counseling and Frank H. Caldwell Chair in Preaching. The purpose was to commemorate the work of the two great leaders of the reunion efforts in their respective denominations before a new vote for reunion was taken in 1983. That vote would provide good publicity and impetus for the fundraising, and the campaign would again highlight the Seminary's unique role in Presbyterianism.[60]

Other chairs followed: the William A. Benfield Chair of Evangelism and Mission, first filled by Guder and then Adeney;[61] the Paul Tudor Jones

58. Mulder, "Reflections on 15 Years," 6-8.

59. Minutes of the Board (1993-present), Finance and Administration Committee, April 21, 1995.

60. Minutes of the Board (1980-1992), Executive Committee, January 21, 1982; letter of Mulder to the board, January 29, 1982. Mulder, who had grown up in Chicago's Fourth Presbyterian Church under Anderson's ministry, was able to draw on that relationship to help reach the $750,000 needed for that chair.

61. Mission study had finally returned to LPTS when Arch and Margaret Taylor retired from work in Japan and taught a course while living in the Furlough Home, followed by Horner in his retirement. Faculty Minutes (1979-1982), November 17, 1981, and Catalogue (1986-1988), 74.

Chair in Church History, held by Weeks and then Kathryn Johnson; the Robert H. Walkup Chair in Theological Ethics, held by Scott Williamson; the Henry P. Mobley Professorship in Doctrinal Theology, held by Amy Plantinga Pauw; and the Second Presbyterian Church Chair in Christian Education, filled by J. Bradley Wigger. At the turn of the millennium the Independent Presbyterian Church honored its founding pastor, Henry Morris Edmonds, with a Professorship in Pastoral Ministry. The Seminary also established the Dora E. Pierce Chair in Bible, first filled by Johanna van Wijk-Bos. Edwards' retirement in 1985 brought the George R. Edwards Peacemaking Lectureship, appropriately inaugurated by Richard Deats of the Fellowship of Reconciliation, whose lecture was titled "The Legacy of Martin Luther King Jr. for Our World Today."[62] When the dormitory was remodeled, it was named for Leland D. Schlegel, long-time board member who had helped bring the new campus to fruition and took a keen interest in the buildings and grounds. The renovation was made possible through a generous gift from his widow, Evelyn Schlegel. To commemorate Louisville Seminary's sesquicentennial, the "Equipping the Saints" campaign was undertaken with a goal of $43 million. The first public phase began in 1996, to remodel the Winn Student Center and put pitched roofs and covered entryways on the Winn Center, Nelson Hall, and the White Library.[63] In all these campaigns the Seminary staff proved astute in securing grants from individuals and foundations.

The Winn Center restoration illustrated another important characteristic of development since 1981: alumni and alumnae development. This emphasis, too, had begun under Nelson. Alumni and alumnae could provide the ministerial link to the denomination and congregations affected by the reduction of clergy on the board. The financial gifts of alumni and alumnae were important, not so much in the amount given but in the numbers who provided support.[64] Much more important, however, was that ministers touched lives in churches and could communicate the work of LPTS to Presbyterians most effectively. Ministers remained a most powerful influence in a candidate's selection of a seminary; ministers represented the Seminary in the church; and ministers, though their own ability to give was limited, could identify potential donors for the development office. Naming Louisville Seminary in their wills was one way the graduates

62. Catalogue (1986-1988), 32.

63. Minutes of the Board (1993-present), October 28, 1995.

64. When applying for grants, for instance, foundations ask what percentage of alumni/ae contribute to the support of an institution.

could give to the Seminary, and it provided an example for others.[65] Nelson had Depew work very hard on annual giving from alumni and alumnae.[66] Mulder continued that and made the alumni and alumnae board a more active participant in Seminary life and planning. The alumni and alumnae board received the same reading material as did the board. The Winn Center remodeling was supported by a financial campaign among the Seminary's graduates.

In the face of seismic shifts in theology, denominational realities, economics, the Seminary ethos, and society, Louisville Seminary succeeded in strengthening itself financially and academically.

Toward a National Seminary

At the same time that Louisville Seminary was solidifying itself, other steps were being taken which opened new possibilities for programs, expanded the Seminary's work, and established its reputation once again in the city and began to give the Seminary a national profile it had not enjoyed previously. Some events were planned; other opportunities arose providentially and had to be seized.

The first huge effort came to fruition when the PC(USA) General Assembly in Biloxi, Mississippi, voted to make Louisville the site for the Presbyterian Center, the national offices of the reunited denomination. The defeat of reunion by the PCUS General Assembly in 1955 had not ended efforts in that direction. The PCUSA united in 1958 with the United Presbyterian Church in North America, creating the United Presbyterian Church in the United States of America (UPCUSA). In the early 1970s the PCUS and UPCUSA began to form union presbyteries and synods, almost all of which existed in the former border states of the Civil War. Finally, in 1983, another vote was taken on reunion with both General Assemblies meeting in Atlanta, Georgia, and this time it passed. Caldwell was given the privilege of making the motion for reunion at the PCUS General Assembly. A location committee was created to select a city as the site for the national headquarters of the reunited denomination and make a recommendation to the General Assembly. The decision was made that the headquarters would be in neither Atlanta or New York City, the locations for the PCUS and UPCUSA, respectively, but elsewhere.

65. Riggs Interview; Young Interview.
66. Ellis and Nancy Nelson Interview, April 25, 1992.

When the announcement was made that the denominational offices might be moved, it was suggested to Mulder that Louisville make a bid. He hesitated at the suggestion, knowing that putting together a proposal would require a lot of work and community effort. Further, from LPTS' vantage he knew that people often had a negative image of the bureaucratic center of a denomination and that the Seminary would undoubtedly be identified with that to some extent. On the other hand, reunion had taken away Louisville Seminary's most distinctive point of identity — bridging the two denominations. Having the offices in Louisville would give the Seminary a different identity, one that would provide national recognition. He judged that the headquarters would undoubtedly attract some students, which it did. Further, it would provide new field education experiences for students, which would add an interesting perspective to their preparation for ministry and would bring in people who could be valuable resources for LPTS. Finally, he knew that the city of Louisville had been close to securing a number of major business relocations to the city but had not been the final choice for any of them. Mulder thought bringing the Presbyterian Center to Louisville would be a boost for civic morale.[67]

Mulder suggested the possibility of developing a proposal to David A. Jones, founder of the major health-care insurance provider Humana and an active Presbyterian. He liked the idea and an invitation was issued. However, Louisville was not considered for the second round of the selection process. Jones, who had a lot of energy for the idea and was a zealous promoter of the city of Louisville, asked Mulder if the gift of a building in which to house the Center might sway the committee. Jones owned the Belknap buildings on the Ohio River in downtown Louisville, and he was willing to donate one of them to the denomination — and thus the Belknap family name continued to play a role in LPTS' history. Mulder knew it would make a difference but could not get Louisville's proposal back before the committee. He suggested to Jones that they wait to see the final recommendation the committee would make to the General Assembly. In January 1987, Kansas City, Missouri, was named as the relocation committee's choice; Mulder learned only after the General Assembly that neither a building nor a final plan for the move to Kansas City had been determined. Mulder then suggested that Louisville supporters simply make their offer, complete with the gift of the Belknap building, and see what happened. The proposal made its way to the meeting of the General Assembly Council in March, where it landed like a bombshell with its offer of a $6 million

67. Most of the story here is based on Mulder Interview.

facility. The relocation committee's choice remained Kansas City, but the reaction from the Council gave the Louisvillians momentum to mount a campaign to persuade the General Assembly that Louisville was the better choice.

Mulder asserted in retrospect that what appeared to many from the outside as an orchestrated movement with him at the helm was, in fact, a relatively chaotic series of initiatives which different people led and he and Grayson Tucker, to a degree, coordinated. Tucker did much of the planning, organizing, and legwork of the effort. Weeks and Cruz developed support among the area's racial-ethnic communities; others at the Seminary spent time on the effort as well. Educational, religious, civic, business, and political leaders from around the city also participated. An executive at the *Courier-Journal* asked if it would be helpful to have its newspapers in Biloxi, so during the General Assembly the paper ran stories each day on the Presbyterian move, the General Assembly, and the city's hard work to lure the Center to Louisville and then flew thousands of copies to Biloxi. The Hillerich and Bradsby Company sent miniature Louisville Sluggers to distribute. Louisville people spoke before the Budget Committee, which would make the recommendation of a location to the General Assembly as a whole. On June 3, prior to the General Assembly, Winfrey P. Blackburn, the Seminary's attorney and a figure in the city's arts community, organized a "Destination Louisville" rally which featured an ecumenical array of Louisville ecclesiastical leaders and political figures. The rally was taped and shown to the General Assembly.

All the hard work succeeded; the Budget Committee determined that relocation to Louisville would save the denomination $21.5 million. The commissioners approved the choice. All told, the relocation efforts brought the city together, gave LPTS a heightened profile in the entire community, and fortuitously engendered good will which played a role in the subsequent financial campaign for the purchase and renovation of the Gardencourt estate. It also put Louisville Seminary in the denominational spotlight.[68]

Remarkably, on the very day that the General Assembly approved Louisville as the location for its headquarters the Seminary's attorneys closed on the purchase of the Gardencourt estate adjacent to the campus. The grounds of the estate contained a lovely mansion and gardens designed by the sons of the famed landscape architect Frederick Law Olmsted, the creator of Central Park in New York City. The University of

68. See Mulder Interview and Winfrey Blackburn Interview, May 15, 1994.

Louisville owned the estate, but years of disuse had resulted in its deterioration. The Seminary had long expressed an interest in purchasing Gardencourt; doing so would give LPTS room for expansion and protection from development alongside the campus. In 1987 the university placed the estate up for auction because state law prohibited a sale without public notice and open bidding, and the Seminary decided to bid. The board authorized its representative to bid up to $2 million, but was outbid by Mrs. Helen Rechtin Combs, who bought Gardencourt for $2.2 million to develop lots on the property. For personal reasons she decided it was not an opportune time for such an investment and Louisville Seminary approached her regarding her plans for the estate. They secured it for $2.25 million.

The committee to conduct the campaign to fund the purchase and restoration of Gardencourt was chaired by David A. Jones, Baylor Landrum, and Malcolm Chancey. Riggs, Vice-President for Development at the time, knew Louisville well and pitched the campaign to save Gardencourt as an architectural resource to the city's constituents. In presenting the project to the city the Seminary made three points. First, LPTS was an educational institution that had served Louisville continuously for 130 years without asking its citizens for any assistance. Second, the Seminary was preserving and restoring Gardencourt, which contained a major portion of Louisville's arts heritage (the city orchestra, opera, and ballet all had their origins in Gardencourt). That meant that Louisville Seminary was saving a property central to Louisville's quality of life and which its patrons of the arts knew well. Finally, LPTS was preserving the facility for the greater good of the community. The campaign slogan became "Recovering the Past for the Sake of the Future." It was an effective appeal, bolstered by the good will fostered by the success of bringing the denominational headquarters to the city. Norma Porterfield remembered that on the day of the public announcement of the campaign, which took place in the home, part of the ceiling of one porch crashed in the middle of the news conference. No one could doubt the renovation was necessary after that.[69]

The campaign eventually raised $7.7 million, of which $5.7 was raised in the city of Louisville with very few corporate gifts. The final cost of purchase and restoration was almost $6.5 million, and the difference of $1.2 became the maintenance endowment for the house and grounds. The Gardencourt campaign proved remarkably efficient. Only $7,698 (0.1% of the total raised) of the pledges were written off as uncollectible, and the

---

69. Norma Porterfield Interview, March 13, 1993.

campaign expenses were only $95,400 (1.25% of the total raised).[70] The renovations received an award for historic preservation.

The purchase and renovation of Gardencourt and the upkeep and improvements to the Alta Vista campus as it reached its thirtieth year highlighted the growing importance of the development office, facilities department, and finance officers at the Seminary. Kent Jones, Catherine Dawson, and Pat Cecil, successors to Hougland as Vice-President for Finance, worked with Tim Williams, head of facilities, to oversee a far-reaching series of construction and renovation projects without over-reaching the budget.

The acquisition of Gardencourt allowed necessary expansion for Louisville Seminary. The growing faculty and administration left no more space in Nelson Hall, and classrooms were at a premium. Gardencourt provided new office space, classrooms, and offered a variety of spaces for public functions, a lecture auditorium and a formal reception space among them. It could not be denied that spreading the campus, especially faculty offices, even further made the maintenance of community more of a challenge, but neither could it be denied that LPTS needed the new space Gardencourt provided. Even so, the Seminary's continued growth necessitated the erection of a new academic building, with the hope that it would be completed in time for the sesquicentennial celebration. Reed thought that the purchase of Gardencourt perfectly illustrated the importance of the Seminary's strategic planning process. Louisville Seminary had identified physical growth as a need of the school but had not made any plans for it in 1987. The strategic plan in place in 1987 was flexible enough that when the opportunity to purchase Gardencourt presented itself, the institution was able to say to the community that both the city and Seminary needed to preserve this property. He further asserted that it took strength and vision by the Seminary to make it happen, given the enormity of the financial undertaking.[71] Louisville Seminary's acquisition of Gardencourt and its headquarters effort were major factors in restoring its standing in Louisville to levels it had not seen since before Vietnam.

Three other projects, more planned, helped give Louisville Seminary a national reputation as a center for research. Mulder, Weeks, and Coalter secured a grant in 1987 from the Lilly Endowment for a major study of

70. On the Gardencourt purchase and campaign see especially Riggs Interview and Minutes of the Board (1993-present), Development Committee, October 24, 1997. See also Minutes of the Board (1980-1992), Executive Committee, April 22, 1987, and June 5, 1987; Mulder Interview; Ekstrom Interview; and Blackburn Interview.

71. Reed Interview.

Presbyterianism in the twentieth century. The three coordinated a group of more than sixty scholars and pastors to research various aspects of Presbyterian life: theology, higher education, theological education, stewardship, social ethics, and governance, to name but a few. Coalter, Mulder, and Weeks made a number of presentations on the project and its meaning for the church, as did some of the research team. The primary result of the project was a series of seven books, The Presbyterian Presence: The Twentieth-Century Experience. Many of the cultural, social, and theological forces that led to the metamorphosis of mainstream Protestantism were described. The Presbyterian Church, in effect, became a case study of the genus. The study was well known in the denomination, although the reaction to its findings was mixed in many quarters: some people believed the study was overly critical of the denomination and a number of directions the church had taken. Regardless, The Presbyterian Presence was a significant and thought-provoking study for the entire denomination.

LPTS also secured money from the Lilly Endowment to establish the Louisville Institute for the Study of Protestantism and American Culture (later shortened to the Louisville Institute). With James W. Lewis as the director, the Institute offered grants and stipends for scholars doing research in American Protestantism. As the name change suggested, eventually projects studying the interplay of culture and various forms of Christianity in the nation were funded. The Institute later established grants for research involving congregations, pastors, and denominations in yet another endeavor to bridge the gap between the academy and the pew. The Institute enjoyed such success that an associate director, David Wood, joined the staff in 1998 and expanded programs, such as sabbaticals, with pastors. By January 2000, the Louisville Institute had made a total of 581 grants to 514 different grantees (individuals and institutions), at a total of just over $9.8 million. The work of grant recipients resulted in sixty-four books and many more articles. Further, the Institute convened five national conferences on a variety of issues important to the contemporary church, such as "The Future of Denominationalism," "Practicing Christian Faith," and "The Money Problem: A Conference on Financing American Religion."[72] Louisville Seminary became a nationally-known center for promoting research.

Another undertaking which gave Louisville Seminary a national reputation was establishing the Louisville Grawemeyer Award in Religion. A

72. Source for these statistics is an electronic mail message from James Lewis, director of the Institute, February 14, 2000.

Seminary trustee, H. Charles Grawemeyer was a member of Highland Presbyterian Church and later of Central Presbyterian Church. A self-made millionaire, Grawemeyer wanted to make philanthropic use of his money, but he preferred promoting education and scholarship by some other means than simple donations to institutions such as LPTS and the University of Louisville. Using the Nobel Prizes as a model, he struck on the idea of rewarding significant achievement in creative thinking. The first four awards he developed were in music, education, world order, and religion. He said, "Our hope is, our reason to exist, if you want to call it that, is that through the award we can bring attention to the outstanding ideas" — and, by recognizing them, help them have an impact on the world.[73] The award program profited from the administrative work of Gene March and, subsequently, David Hester and Susan Garrett. Sponsored and adjudicated jointly by LPTS and the University of Louisville, the Grawemeyer Award in Religion has become a prestigious recognition in religious studies.[74]

Bridge to the Future

With the Seminary in a strengthened position for theological education, it was ready to move into the future making a greater impact on the life of the church. Joyfully, reunion had left LPTS without its traditional distinctive role in the denomination. With what could Louisville Seminary replace its former identity and carve out a place in Presbyterian life? The Seminary decided to build on what had always been its strength: preparing men and women for ministry in the church. The Seminary would sharpen its focus on educating for the church, which was its tradition and greatest asset from the earliest years. The metaphor which embodied that renewed emphasis was that of the bridge, first suggested by Tucker during the movement for the Presbyterian Center. "The image of the bridge is helpful in

73. Charles Grawemeyer Interview, March 13, 1993. LPTS Archives. A fifth award in psychology was added in 2000.

74. Recipients of the award through 2000 were E. P. Sanders for his work on Jesus and Judaism; John H. Hick for his study of human responses to the transcendent; Ralph Harper for his study *On Presence: Variations and Reflections;* Elizabeth A. Johnson for her analysis of God's mystery in feminist theology; Stephen L. Carter for his work in religion in American public life; Diana L. Eck for her work in religious pluralism; Larry L. Rasmussen for his study on environmental theology; Charles Marsh for his work on the civil rights movement in Mississippi; and Jürgen Moltmann for his work on Christian eschatology.

thinking about our future," Mulder wrote. "Bridges connect land and people who would otherwise be separated. Bridges help people travel over
dangers and difficulties. Bridges suggest stability but also promote communication and change. Louisville Seminary has an opportunity to make a
unique theological and ecclesiastical contribution by being a 'bridge' institution."[75]

The attempt to bridge liberal and conservative factions in the church
has been noted. More at issue was the effort to help Presbyterians focus on
the local congregation where faith was formed and ministries of members
lived out — in short, where most church members identified with faith and
being Presbyterian.[76] In the process it was hoped that LPTS could play a
role in revitalizing the church. The campaign to build a residence for short-
term study, named the William R. and Ellen Laws Lodge, for graduate and
continuing and lay education programs demonstrated a major commitment of resources, thought, and energy to that emphasis, as had the earlier
expansion of lay education into the Lay Institute. To help fulfill that purpose, the Lodge was available to congregations, the Presbyterian Center,
and community groups for retreats and study.

Another attempt to develop a relationship with congregations was
the President's Roundtable. The Roundtable brought back to life, in a different form, the Friends of the Seminary program. Formed in the late
1990s, it brought pastors and, predominantly, laypeople to campus to provide another format for conversation between the Seminary and the pew.
Mulder believed by 2000 that the group provided valuable insights for
LPTS in preparing students for ministry.[77]

Two degree programs grew out of the goal of serving as a revitalizing
agent for the church. The Seminary created a Master of Arts in Christian

75. Mulder, "Louisville Presbyterian Theological Seminary: The Challenge of the
1990s," in Minutes of the Board (1980-1992), October 20-22, 1991.

76. Analysis of contemporary Christianity, the religious attitudes and needs of people
in American culture, and how the church might respond is widespread. Most prominent are
Robert Wuthnow, *The Restructuring of American Religion: Society and Faith Since World
War II* (Princeton: Princeton University Press, 1988); Wuthnow, *Christianity in the Twenty-
first Century: Reflections on the Challenges Ahead* (New York and Oxford: Oxford University
Press, 1993); Wuthnow, *The Struggle for America's Soul: Evangelicals, Liberals, and Secularism*
(Grand Rapids, Mich.: Wm. B. Eerdmans, 1989); Wade Clark Roof and William McKinney,
American Mainline Religion: Its Changing Shape and Future (London and New Brunswick,
N.J.: Rutgers University Press, 1987); and Dean R. Hoge, Benton Johnson, and Donald A.
Luidens, *Vanishing Boundaries: The Religion of Mainline Protestant Baby Boomers* (Louisville,
Ky.: Westminster/John Knox Press, 1994).

77. Electronic mail from Mulder, January 25, 2000.

Education, which met with some success but was eventually cancelled because of changing denominational requirements in Christian education. Even more, the Master of Arts in Marriage and Family Therapy, pioneered by David Steere, met a real need for those interested in pastoral counseling. Steere had moved the field education program ahead at LPTS by his emphasis on the supervisor's role in a student's field placement. Further, he had established a reputation as a leader in the area of pastoral counseling, especially in group therapy. There was a need, he felt, for pastors and pastoral counselors with special training in marriage and family therapy, given that such counseling constituted a major portion of a person's counseling ministry. He led the way in establishing this new program with a concentration in family dynamics, and it grew quickly after its inception in the early 1990s. It was one of only four such programs in the United States. Loren Townsend, who directed marriage and family therapy programs while serving pastorates in Arizona and Georgia, assumed leadership of the program following Steere's retirement, and was succeeded by Sheri Ferguson, who had years of experience in the field and had taught at the University of Louisville.

As the Seminary leadership continued to think about ways to understand congregations and their impact on faith, they learned that a number of organizations — the Alban Institute leading among them — were doing good work and training in congregational understanding and ministry. However, with the exception of the evangelical James Dobson's "Focus on the Family," little was being done in mainstream Protestant circles to help congregations support families in their faith development and family ministries in churches. Consequently, in 1997 LPTS established its Center for Congregations and Family Ministries to support and promote research in that area. The center was facilitated by a seed grant from the Lilly Endowment, then supported by the creation of the Second Presbyterian Church (Louisville) Chair in Christian Education. J. Bradley Wigger, called to fill that chair, very effectively led and built up the program. After just one year the Seminary leadership judged that the program successfully met a need in congregations to minister with families and help them transmit Christian faith from one generation to the next. As part of that emphasis on congregational ministry the Seminary also assumed responsibility for editing and publishing the journal *Family Ministry: Empowering Through Faith*.

Louisville Seminary's administration and faculty knew that a seminary's greatest impact comes through its graduates as they lead congregations in faith and ministry. Therefore, as the century drew to a close LPTS established a new program for its own students, which focused on the Bible and spiritual formation. The initiative sought to address the decline in biblical literacy in American society and American Christianity and the contemporary search for meaning, often called spirituality or spiritual formation. The Seminary expanded its graduation requirement in Bible and established the Dora E. Pierce Professor of Bible; van Wijk-Bos filled that position. March taught what had once been called "English Bible" and "Biblical Theology"; that is, the emphasis fell on Bible content and theological themes in Scripture, as opposed to exegetical questions. In addition, March helped students make use of the Bible for personal growth in faith and discipleship. The grant provided a strengthening of the program in Area A and added another component as the faculty in biblical studies worked to implement the goals of the program.

Further, the Seminary created the position of Director of Vocational Formation. Garnett Foster, a woman who had served several congregations in Christian education and as pastor and been assistant director of the McCormick Seminary D.Min. program, first held the post. She developed programs for spiritual discipline and formation for the students, with particular emphasis on how the Bible informs personal and communal piety. Students also received guidance in building a pastoral identity and identifying their skills for ministry. Given that knowledge, seminarians could then begin to understand their role as leaders of congregations in faith and discipleship and as leaders in the larger church. The Bible and Spiritual Formation programs even included a module of continuing education for selected graduates to help them, during their first three years out of seminary, make the transition from the training they learned at seminary to its application in the congregations they served. Louisville Seminary clearly took its role as an institution of the church very seriously.[78]

The most important reality facing Christianity in the United States at the turn of the twenty-first century was that the faith was growing most rapidly in the southern hemisphere. Christians in the U.S. were beginning to acknowledge that, globally, the church would no longer necessarily think and act in theological categories determined by European tradition. At the same time, demographers noted a similar trend in the population of the U.S. Early in the new century people of color — people of African, Hispanic, Asian, and Arabic birth or descent — would surpass in number those of European ancestry in the nation.

---

78. This program, like "Life Springs," reflected a growing emphasis on personal spiritual formation in theological education after the 1960s. See Cherry, *Hurrying Toward Zion,* 235-37.

Louisville, intent on preparing its students for those realities, took steps to bridge the diversity that had become the dominant reality of the world and nation. The Ministry Across Cultures program, led by deans Weeks and March, created intentional settings for students to learn how they could understand cultural settings different from their own and feel more comfortable entering into ministry in them. Study tours abroad were offered, students were given the opportunity to study overseas, international students were more actively sought to have their own multi-cultural experiences and enrich LPTS by their presence, and faculty received financial support for study abroad. The faculty themselves brought a variety of international and global ministry experiences to their tasks. Van Wijk-Bos was from the Netherlands; Weeks had served as a missionary in Africa; Elwood had been headmaster of a school in Kenya; Ramsay taught at St. Paul's United Theological College in Kenya during a sabbatical; Dale Andrews had conducted study tours to Latin America; March and Tull led groups to Israel for study; Cook had taught in Taiwan; and Adeney had taught in Indonesia and Southeast Asia. Another important element in building cultural awareness for students were course offerings in world religions, a component missing from the Seminary's curriculum since the decline of mission studies. In the 1970s Rabbi Chester Diamond taught an annual one-hour course in the practices and rites of Judaism. In the 1980s similar courses in Islam and Buddhism and Hinduism appeared. By the 1990s there were three-hour offerings in those religions each year. Student trips to synagogues in the city took place several times each year. A course, "Reading the Bible after the Holocaust," was offered occasionally and brought Holocaust survivors on campus to speak to the class.[79]

In addition to global awareness, the Seminary realized there were differences to bridge domestically as well. The affirmative action hiring of African-Americans helped to promote that, as did the formation of a Cultural Diversity Committee initially chaired by Scott Williamson. At the same time that LPTS wanted to strengthen its curriculum within the Reformed tradition, it wanted to reflect the ecumenical reality within which ministers had to work; for instance, studies showed that fewer than fifty percent of Presbyterians had been reared in a Presbyterian church. The Seminary had long had a significant number of Methodist students, and courses in Methodist polity and history addressed the needs of those students. In the 1990s similar courses were offered for Baptist students.

---

79. Cherry, *Hurrying Toward Zion,* 64-69, discusses the widespread movement to "globalization" in theological education beginning in the 1980s.

A big step in the direction of both ecumenism and racial diversity came in the form of agreements with the bishops of the regional jurisdictions of the African Methodist Episcopal Church, the African Methodist Episcopal Zion Church, and the Christian Methodist Episcopal Church, historically African-American denominations. All three officially recognized Louisville Presbyterian Theological Seminary as the recommended seminary for their candidates and ordained ministers from their regional bodies. Those agreements resulted in a wider denominational variety on campus and increased the number of African-American students at the Seminary. Field education placements in a variety of cultural settings became more intentional.[80]

Louisville Seminary approached its sesquicentennial year with perhaps better health than it had ever enjoyed in its history. There was a solid financial foundation, exemplary faculty, challenging and complete curriculum, and a vision for serving the church. Mulder's leadership had helped LPTS reach that point; however, he did not do it alone, and the success Louisville Seminary enjoyed during his presidency was also due to the factors that had always made the Seminary a special place — dedicated and hard-working members of the board, committed and intelligent faculty, students responding to God's call for ministry, and a supporting constituency, all intent on making it possible for the Seminary to serve God and the church. As Louisville Seminary reaches its sesquicentennial anniversary, those same qualities and resources will carry it into the future.

80. See *The Mosaic of Louisville Seminary* 5 (fall 1998) for a description of this movement.

CONCLUSION

Louisville Seminary reaches its sesquicentennial year able to celebrate a rich history and ready to fulfill a vision for the future. The Seminary has not been without its struggles, problems, and setbacks. But it has always tried to fulfill its mission to prepare men and women for ministry.

The Seminary, even in its earliest years at Danville, has reflected the influence of any number of internal and external forces. When new ways of understanding reality challenged old patterns of thought, LPTS answered with conservative Reformed theology and biblical criticism, only later to appropriate the insights offered by the disciplines of philosophy and science. The emergence of the city prompted Louisville Seminary to develop a response to urban needs. The Seminary slowly but eventually and vigorously participated in the social struggles of society. Through its dual denominational identity the Seminary had a very influential role in Presbyterian reunion. Norman Horner, who came to LPTS with a fundamentalist's approach to faith, succinctly stated the Seminary's stance toward the world of which it was a part: "Christian faith can stand the most penetrating kind of examination from all intellectual disciplines, and it must be submitted to such examination if it is to remain the faith of the most thoughtful Christians in this generation. I have also come to see that it is much more important to proclaim the faith than to defend it."[1]

As it has sought to remain relevant to a changing world, Louisville Seminary has done so as a means to serve the church. From Robert

---

1. Norman Horner, "What Has Happened to the Seminary?" 5. A sermon preached at Central Presbyterian Church in Louisville, Kentucky, in 1968. LPTS Archives.

CONCLUSION

Breckinridge's first descriptions of the unique nature of theological education to Julian Price Love's question of the basis on which a person was to be graduated from LPTS to the most recent emphases on ministry in congregations, Louisville Seminary has understood itself as an institution existing to serve the church. Instinctively, and usually self-consciously, LPTS has understood what H. Richard Niebuhr wrote of education almost fifty years ago:

> [E]ducation is so closely connected with the life of a community that queries about the aims of teaching and learning cannot be answered unless ideas about the character and purposes of the society in which it is carried on are clarified first of all. . . . [A] school is never separable from the community in which it works, whose living tradition it carries on, into which it sends citizens and leaders involved with that tradition and committed to the social values.[2]

For Louisville Seminary, that community has always been, first and foremost, the church. May the Seminary never lose that focus, for it is the people who sit in pews and struggle to be faithful who need ministers prepared to preach the ancient gospel to this modern world.

An educational institution requires countless resources to weather the years. Facilities, faculties, students, financial assets, and supporters are key ingredients to a successful school. Those kinds of resources, to a lesser or greater degree, lend themselves to analysis, description, and interpretation. It is more difficult to capture those elements of institutional life that give a school its unique spirit. What was it like to be a student? How did people relate on a daily basis? How did the administration and faculty get along? How did people feel about one another? That is to say, what was the ethos of the place? In his final report to the dean as he approached retirement, Burton Cooper offered some words to the Board of Trustees which suggest some of the atmosphere of learning and preparation for ministry which marked Louisville Seminary and its predecessor institutions:

> I love teaching, and the activities that accompany it, and I discovered that relatively early in my adult life. What I did not know, and had to learn, was the depth of the symbiosis between a teacher and the institution in which he or she teaches. That I could sustain my love of teaching all these years, that I could finally achieve a profound understanding of

2. Niebuhr, *The Purpose of the Church and Its Ministry: Reflections on the Aims of Theological Education* (New York: Harper and Brothers, 1956), 1-2.

242

what it means to be a teacher, that the quality of my teaching could steadily better itself, all this was possible because of the character and dynamics of this institution and the people who make it up. I am very grateful to my faculty colleagues who are supportive and intellectually stimulating and who have become much more than colleagues to me; and to my students who are wonderfully sincere and serious in understanding and living their faith and ministry; and to the administrators and supportive staff who are so determined to minimize bureaucracy and to keep our working relations personal and caring; and to the Board, of course, who, even in difficult moments, or should I say, especially in difficult moments, have never failed to exercise anything but just, caring and wise use of the powers and responsibilities designated to them.

It must be obvious by now that this is a love letter as well as a letter of thanks, let alone a report on my activities. But it is mainly a letter of thanks to you, the Board. Thank you for sustaining my call to this school, and thank you for sustaining the spirit of this school. And finally, thanks be to God.[3]

---

3. Quoted in Gene March, "Report of the Dean of the Seminary to the Board of Trustees, Louisville Presbyterian Theological Seminary. April, 1997." LPTS Archives.

TRUSTEES: DANVILLE, 1853-1893

Missing trustees from 1861-1867; no catalogues for these years could be found (Civil War) and the information was not in the General Assembly Minutes for these years.

Names marked with * might have served prior to 1867.

Allen, Herman H.
  1860-??

Barbour, James*
  1856-??, 1867-1874, 1877-1890

Barrett, John G.*
  1867-1876

Beatty, Ormond*
  1867-1890

Berryman, J. S.
  1853-1855

Boyle, J. T.*
  1853-??, 1867-1872

Breckinridge, Robert J.*
  1853-??, 1867-1871

Breckinridge, William L.*
  1853-??, 1867-1876

Brooks, W. C.
  1853-1857

Caldwell, Charles
  1853-??

Cheek, J. A.
  1886-1901

Craig, John G.
  1872-1901

Curry, D. J.
  1887-1901

Curtis, J. P.
  1853-??

Denny, George*
  1867-1897

Duke, William
  1859-??

Simpson, John A.
1892-1901

Sutherland, R. R
1897-1901

Temple, J. B.
1881-1886

Temple, John B.
1857-1859

Thompson, William
1853-1857

Warren, L. L.
1872-1881

Welsh, George W.*
1860-??, 1867-71, and 1872-1901

Wherritt, W. H.
1885-1886

Wiseman, Gavin E.
1872-1901

Yerkes, S.
1868-1870 and 1887-1901

Young, John C.
1853-1857

Young, W. C.
1889-1896

BOARD OF DIRECTORS: DANVILLE
THEOLOGICAL SEMINARY, 1853-1901

Names marked with * also served on the new LPTS of KY Board of Directors when it was formed.

Alexander, S. R.
  1853-1854

Alexander, T. T.
  1863-1872

Allen, Herman H.
  1866-1898

Allen, Richard H.
  1865-1867

Anderson, Albert
  1853-1855

Anderson, S. J. P.
  1853-1858

Anderson, W. C.
  1853-1856

Appersen, R.
  1873-1877

Archibald, George D.
  1869-1870

Archibald, J. H.
  1853-1854

Armstrong, J. M.
  1889-1892

Armstrong, S. H.
  1853-1859

Averill, William H.
  1882-1885

Avery, B. F.
  1863-1872

Baird, E. T.
  1858-1864

Baird, S. J.
  1853-1854

Baker, H. C.
  1895-consolidation

Barbour, James
  1854-1867 and 1885-1891

Barbour, John
1900-consolidation

Barnett, Joseph
1853-1856

Barrett, John G.
1863-1876

Barry, Thomas
1853-1854

Bartlett, P. Mason
1875-1889

Beatty, Ormond
1854-1867 and 1870-1891

Berryman, J. S.
1853-1855

Birch, George W.
1871-1878

Blackburn, J. I.*
1898-consolidation

Blake, J.
1853-1854

Blayney, J. McClusky*
1898-consolidation

Boardman, S. W.
1892-consolidation

Boyd, Wilson P.
1860-1866

Braddock, J. S.
1865-1867

Brank, R. G.
1858-1867

Breckinridge, R. J.
1866-1870

Breckinridge, William L.
1856-1862 and 1864-1875

Brooks, James H.
1855-1863

Brown, James
1858-1860

Browne, W. B.
1864-1867

Bryce, W. E.*
1898-consolidation

Buell, W. P.
1853-1855

Bull, Samuel C.
1872-1882

Bullock, Jos. J.
1853-1862

Bullock, Thomas W.
1855-1864

Burt, J. C.
1853-1855

Burt, N. C.
1863-1867

Butler, Zebulon
1855-1860

Caldwell, Robert F.
1858-1868

Camp, E. H.
1869-1871

Carter, C.
1858-1864

Chamberlain, A. E.
1866-1867

Chamberlain, N.
1864-1867

Cheek, Francis J.*
1896-consolidation

Chiles, L. T.
1891-1895

Christie, Robert
1874-1886

Cleland, Thomas H.
1862-1892

Cochran, Andrew M. J.
1894-consolidation

Cochran, W. P.
1854-1856

Coe, J.
1853-1856

Coffey, A.
1853-1854

Collier, James R.
1888-1896

Colmery, W. W.
1865-1867

Condit, John B.
1863-1867

Condit, W. C.
1869-1871 and 1885-consolidation

Coons, J. F.
1866-1867 and 1869-1871

Cooper, Jacob
1865-1867

Cortelyou, Thomas F.
1858-1868

Coulter, David
1862-1865

Cowan, J. F.
1853-1854

Craig, L. Green
1864-1867

Crawford, John M.
1873-1874 and 1875-1889

Crothers, S. D.
1866-1868

Curry, Daniel J.
1864-consolidation

Deadrick, D. A.
1853-1856

Denny, George
1865-1894

Dickerson, A. E.
1862-1865

Dickerson, Archer C.
1871-1892

Dickey, D. D.
1864-1867

Doak, D. G.
1854-1857

Doak, William S.
1877-1883

Downton, William A.
1872-1873

Dwelly, J. T.
1895-consolidation

Edgar, John T.
1853-1860

Edwards, Jonathan
1853-1855

Ernst, William
1860-1865 and 1869-1870

Ewing, J. W.
1854-1857

Findlay, S. B.
1853-1856

Fishback, George
1864-1867

Forman, Ezekiel
1857-1865

Fulton, William S.
1896-consolidation

Gamble, H. R.
1853-1854

Goodloe, William O.
1886-consolidation

Gray, John H.
1853-1864

Green, Lewis W.
1857-1864

Grundy, A. J.
1884-consolidation

Grundy, Robert C.
1853-1866

Gurley, P. D.
1853-1854

Halsey, L. J.
1853-1854

Hamilton, S. M.
1891-1894

Hays, J. S.
1861-1866

Hays, John H.
1873-1874

Henderson, Thomas
1855-1864

Hendrick, J. T.
1854-1857

Hendrick, James P.
1886-1899

Hendrick, W. J.
1891-1894

Hendricks, J. P.
1866-1867

Herbener, J. H.
1894-1896

Hibben, Samuel E.
1856-1867

Hill, W. W.
1853-1864

Hobson, B. M.
1857-1863

Hogue, A. A.
1862-1867

Hopkins, James
1853-1866

Hoyt, Thomas A.
1860-1863

Hudson, J.
1853-1856

Humphrey, E. W. C.
1890-consolidation

Humphrey, Edward P.
1869-1888

Hutchinson, Charles
1876-1891

January, A. M.
1869-1870

Jennings, William B.
1896-1898

Johnstone, Robert A.
1865-1869 and 1874-1886

Jones, John
1878-1886

Kemper, Hugh E.
1856-1859 and 1870-1872

Kerr, A. H.
1853-1855

Keys, J. F.
1853-1854

Kinkead, J. B.
1872-1873 and 1874-1875

Kinnaird, William H.
1870-1885

Laird, Samuel
1853-1858

Lamar, Thomas J.
1880-1888

Landes, J. I.
1872-1893

Landes, Joseph L.
1869-1870

Landis, J. I.*
1897-consolidation

Landis, R. W.
1863-1870

Lapsley, James T.
1864-consolidation

Lapsley, R. A.
1854-1863

Leavitt, H. H.
1865-1867

Lewis, G. W.
1864-1866

Lord, Willis
1854-1855

Loving, H. V.
1887-1888, 1889-1900

Lyle, Henry C.
1877-1887, 1888-1889, and
1901-consolidation

Lyle, J. K.
1855-1872

Lyle, John A.
1853-1866

Marshall, Glass
1857-1867

Marshall, Louis
1853-1859

Marshall, Robert
1855-1858

Matthews, A. E.
1862-1865

Maxwell, John C.
1862-1895

McCampbell, James
1870-1872

McCullough
1856-1867

McInnis, R.
1853-1862

McKeage, John
1854-1860

McKee, J. L.
1864-1868

McMillan, J. P.
1865-1867

McMullen, Robert B.
1853-1857 and 1860-1863

Minnis, John B.
1894-1896

Mitchell, J.
1853-1864

Mitchell, William
1853-1858

Monroe, B.
1857-1860

Montgomery, J.
1857-1863

Montgomery, T. J.
1853-1858

More, E. Anson
1866-1868

Morrison, George
1864-1868

Mutchmore, S. A.
1862-1865

Neeley, J. B.
1853-1864

Neff, William H.
1882-1885

Nelson, A. B.
1885-consolidation

Nesbitt, John H.
1871-1877

Niccolls, Samuel J.
1865-1869 and 1870-1872

Norton, George W.
1876-1881

Paxton, J. D.
1853-1856

Penick, Buford M.
1864-1873

Penick, E. Y.
1880-1882

Perkins, George R.
1863-1866

Perkins, W. O. N.
1860-1863

Pope, Curran
1855-1864

Porter, E. H.
1853-1862

Prather, William
1857-1868

Pratt, E. Perkins
1870-1886

Preston, C. A.
1865-1867

Price, Daniel B.
1853-1860

Putnam, A. W.
1853-1856

Quisenberry, R. T.
1901-consolidation

Ramsey, R. G.
1901-consolidation

Randolph, J. C.
1867-1876

Rankin, Alexander
1869-1871

Reed, George J.[1]
1879-1893

Reid, George J.[1]
1874-1879

Reynolds, J.
1853-1855

Rhea, J. J.
1896-1901

Richardson, William
1857-1863

Roberts, W. C.*
1899-consolidation

Robertson, Gilbert H.
1872-1873

Rochester, Charles
1858-1864

Rodes, R.
1867-1868

Rutherford, Edwin H.
1861-1862

Sampson, William
1862-1865

Scarborough, W. W.
1862-1867

1. Reed and Reid could possibly be the same person; both names are from Columbia, Ky.; spelling changed in the catalogs.

Schenck, A. V. C.
1853-1860

Scott, John W.[2]
1870-71, 1874-77, 1880-89

Scott, Isaac W.[2]
1871-1874 and 1877-1880

Scott, William M.
1856-1860

Shryock, L. B. W.
1870-1871

Simpson, James
1862-1865

Simpson, John A.
1893-consolidation

Smith, Alexander
1854-1857

Smith, Charles W.
1853-1854

Smith, H. N.
1853-1854

Smith, J. Addison
1861-1864

Smith, J. K.
1897-1898

Smith, James
1854-1862

Smith, Kilburn W.
1894-1897

Smith, Luther
1859-1862

Stanton, Robert L.
1870-1871

Steele, Samuel
1853-1864

Stevenson, David
1856-1858

Stonestreet, James
1853-1857

Strahan, F. G.
1853-1865

Sturgis, Frederick E.
1883-1886

Sutherland, R. R.
1893-consolidation

Temple, O. P.
1892-1894

Thompson, Henry P.
1871-?

Thompson, John
1859-1862

Thomson, E. W.
1889-1891

Thomson, S. H.
1874-1879

Thorpe, J. D.
1853-1860

Todd, John
1853-1862

Todd, L. B.
1889-consolidation

Torrence, William
1873-1885

Trimble, William J.
1892-1900

Trussell, F. Baker
1881-1901

Waddell, John N.
1855-1858

2. J. Scott and I. Scott could possibly be the same person.

Wade, Nehemiah
1862-1867

Walker, L. Faye
1879-1901

Waller, Maurice
1891-consolidation

Warren, E. L.
1897-consolidation

Warren, H. C.*
1900-consolidation

Warren, L. L.
1865-1884

Washburn, W. P.
1876-1879

Watson, John
1857-1863

Wayland, A.
1853-1855

Welsh, George W.
1862-1890

West, James N.
1859-1862

West, Nathaniel
1869-1870

West, Thomas E.
1856-1856

Wherritt, W. H.
1885-consolidation

White, J. J.
1856-1862

Whiteman, Lewis
1859-1862

Williams, S. R.
1864-1870

Williams, William
1854-1857

Willitts, A. A.
1886-1889

Willoughby, J. W. C.
1889-1897

Wilson, E. S.
1863-1866

Wilson, S. R.
1853-1854

Wiseman, Gavin E.*
1874-consolidation

Wiseman, John
1863-1866

Wood, George T.
1867-1876

Worrall, J. M.*
1874-1880

Worrall, John M.
1860-65 and 1871-??

Yantis, John L.
1856-1865

Yerkes, Stephen
1869-1870

Young, Archibald
1854-1857

Young, John C.
1857-1857

Young, John C.
1867-1869

Young, William C.
1871-1872 and 1888-1896

BOARD OF DIRECTORS: LOUISVILLE PRESBYTERIAN THEOLOGICAL SEMINARY OF KENTUCKY, 1893-1901

The seminary's name was changed to LPTS in 1927.

Andrew, S. J.
1893-1894

Barbee, Joshua
1899-1901

Blanton, L. H.
1893-1902

Bullitt, T. W.
1893-1895

Cannon, J. F.
1894-1901

Dobyns, W. R.
1893-1920

Dyke, Jacob Van
1894-1899

Evans, H. C.
1893-1894

Gorin, M. G.
1893-1901

Graham, William
1893-1901

Grant, W. T.
1893-1901

Harbison, James J.
1898-1906

Hunter, J. G.
1893-1919

Irvine, William
1893-1911

Lyons, J. S.
1893-1901

McClintic, W. S.
1893-1899

McElroy, I. S.
1895-1905

Neel, S. M.
1893-1916

Nourse, W. L.
1893-1901

Pollock, William
1899-1901

Ruffner, S. T.
1893-1901

Sumrall, J. K.
1893-1901

Trenholm, G. A.
1893-1899

Vandiver, C. H.
1899-1901

Veech, R. S.
1893-1898

Wallace, A. A.
1893-1899, 1901-1919

Willis, T. F.
1899-1901

Young, Bennett H.
1893-1919

BOARD OF DIRECTORS: LOUISVILLE PRESBYTERIAN THEOLOGICAL SEMINARY, 1901-PRESENT

Names marked with * served on Board prior to 1901 at LPTS of KY — see Board of Dir. 1893-1901.

Names marked with ** served on Board prior to 1901 at Danville — see Board of Dir. 1853-1901.

Abbott, Eugene F.
  1906-1938

Abernethy, R. S.
  1939-1943

Adams, Ann Greer
  1988-present

Agnew, Robert
  2000-present

Airey, Donald L.
  1967-1975

Albright, Edwin W.
  1954-1961

Alexander, David
  1966-1969

Allen, C. E.
  1956-1962

Anderson, Frank C.
  1942-1965

Anderson, Olof, Sr.
  1926-1931

Anderson, Peter R.
  1989-present

Andrews, Mark J.
  1946-1953

Bachmann, Albert
  1935-1965

Bandeen, James G.
  1989-1993

Barnes, Barbara Z.
1990-present

Barr, J. McFerran
1959-1970

Barret, James R.
1905-1925

Beasley, W. S.
1932-1960

Benfield, William A.
1949-1958

Bickel, George R.
1953-1980

Blackburn, J. I.**
1901-1914

Blanton, L. H.*
1893-1902

Blayney, J. McClusky**
1901-1908

Bosch, F. W. A.
1935-1955

Brigham, Harold F.
1934-1955

Broecker, T. H.
1956-1965

Bronaugh, W. H.
1948-1954

Brooks, John M.
1917-1920

Brown, Ralph A.
1946-1955

Bryce, W. E.**
1901-1904

Burr, Borden
1942-1952

Bush, Benjamin J.
1917-1957

Caldwell, Frank H.
1939-1964

Callen, Samuel
1919-1927

Campbell, Stuart C.
1931-1954

Cannon, John F.
1954-1960

Carl, William Joseph III
1988-present

Carpenter, J. B.
1927-1947

Carroll, Herbert
1985-1999

Carson, Chas. C.
1923-1929

Carson, H. V.
1921-1924

Carter, James L.
1997-present

Cassels, S. J.
1926-1941

Castner, Charles B.
1939-1954

Cheek, F. J.**
1901-1923

Chess, Marcia (Mrs. Walter)
1976-1984

Clark, Robert P.
1968-1973

Coleman, A. J.
1966-1974

Comfort, C. Ransom
1950-1956

Cook, Joseph C. Jr.
1991-present

Courtenay, Walter R.
1962-1965

Cousley, David
1998-present

Croft, Timothy Lent
1990-1995

Crowe, William
1933-1955

Crowell, John M.
1953-1963, 1965-1975

Cunningham, J. R.
1929-1937

Currie, Armand
1950-1977

Currie, Stuart D.
1949-1954

Curry, A. B.
1923-1932

Dale, W. Andrew
1923-1924, 1931-1932

Dale, Mrs. Wm. Andrew
1960-1969

Dallas, A. E.
1943-1959

Davis, Finis
1969-1985

Davis, James I.
1977-1983

Davis, John J.
1925-1946

Davis, Wallace M.
1932-1943

Dawson, Lyman L.
1957-1967

Diehl, Charles E.
1923-1925, 1929-1955

Dinning, J. Donald
1957-1968

Dobyns, W. R.*
1893-1920

Dobyns, William Ray
1923-1931

Donaho, Joe B.
1980-1987

Dorris, W. Glenn
1982-1989

Dugan, Jeane
1995-1998

Duncan, Thomas C.
1964-1976

Duncan, W. G.
1919-1929

Ekstrom, William F.
1965-1993

Elliott, William M.
1932-1935

Elwang, W. W.
1919-1920

Ernst, Richard P.
1924-1934

Ervin, John N.
1904-1941

Fant, Anthony
1999-present

Fisher, Dale H.
1979-1995

Fleming, W. S.
1924-1929

Fogartie, A. F.
1927-1939

Force, Jill L.
1989-1997

Forrester, Alexander M.
1930-1944

Frantz, George A.
1943-1947

Frierson, J. Burton
1959-1972

Friesen, Mary Lou
1995-present

Frist, Carol
2000-present

Fulton, John A.
1964-1987

Fulton, R. E.
1922-1926

Gabbard, Elmer E.
1929-1930, 1935-1947

Gammon, E. G.
1925-1927

Gamon, Robert I.
1927-1943

Ganfield, W. A.
1915-1920

Gates, Charles D.
1917-1920

Gillespie, R. T.
1922-1924

Gillingham, Clinton H.
1922-1932

Gilmore, W. Russell
1942-1956

Glasgow, S. M.
1922-1924

Gouwens, Teunis E.
1942-1949

Grawemeyer, H. Charles
1983-1989

Green, E. M.
1901-1926

Greene, Walter R.
1983-1984

Greenhoe, Dewey R.
1955-1967

Gregory, James M.
1960-1963

Gregory, W. Voris
1920-1929

Grubbs, Susan Faurest
1997-present

Guerrant, W. B.
1935-1939

Hall, Arthur R.
1962-1970

Hall, B. Frank
1942-1948

Halliday, Janet W.
1997-present

Harbison, John J.
1898-1906

Harper, W. V.
1966-1972

Harrod, William W.
1996-2000

Hartman, J. Reed
1953-1964

Haskins, L. Owsley
1941-1964

Hawley, Robert C.
1965-1967

Hemingway, George R.
1927-1939

Herrmann, Jesse
1943-1947

Hill, J. J.
1904-1906

Hinitt, F. W.
1904-1915

Hoagland, Laurance
1994-present

Hobart, Mrs. James L.
1970-1971

Hoge, Charles E.
1909-1919

Hoge, Peyton H.
1901-1940

Hoge, S. French
1919-1936

Houston, Julian L.
1967-1981

Howard, A. J.
1931-1942

Hubbard, George T.
1949-1960

Hulst, Anton Ver
1920-1921

Humphrey, Alexander P.
1901-1917

Hunter, J. G.*
1893-1919

Irvine, William*
1893-1911

Irwin, W. Francis
1911-1916

Jay, Helen Sears
1985-1996

Jetton, R. J.
1932-1946

Johnson, William Monte
1947-1954

Jones, Paul Tudor
1969-1984

Jones, Walk III
1984-1998

Karsch, Robert F.
1960-1974

Kerr, John E.
1920-1934

King, Clarence
1948-1959

Kramer, Wayne R.
1997-present

Kubik, J. Fred
1989-present

Kuykendall, John W.
1982-1990

Lacy, J. H.
1925-1941

Landis, J. I.**
1901-1907

Landrum, Baylor Jr.
1987-1995

Lang, George S.
1939-1954

Layman, James E.
1981-1989

Lee, W. Howard
1960-1967

Leith, Hugh
1920-1921

Lemon, Brainard
1923-1929

Leyburn, G. L.
1901-1904

Lingle, Walter L., Jr.
1957-1962

Logan, C. Sumpter
1994-present

Logan, J. V.
1917-1920, 1924-1930

Lynn, Robert Wood
1990-1995

Lyons, J. S.
1906-1915

Lyons, Pitser M., III
1980-1982

MacLeod, Donald C.
1920-1923

Mann, Horace N. Jr.
1991-present

Marcotte, Henry
1930-1935

Martin, Mrs. Robert B.
1958-1966

Mathes, Frank A.
1954-1958

McCabe, Mrs. John
1958-1980

McCallie, S. J., Jr.
1944-1947

McCluer, Franc L.
1938-1947

McDowell, J. Q. A.
1909-1922

McElroy, I. S.*
1895-1905

McIlhaney, B. I.
1947-1949

McLeod, Robert Lee, Jr.
1938-1951, 1954-1956, 1965-1966

McMillan, Toney D.
1990-present

Melvin, M. E.
1931-1933

Merkel, Virginia (Ginger)
1998-present

Millard, W. John
1946-1966

Miller, Clyde W.
1966-1989

Miller, Dixie Sayre
1984-1996

Miller, Shackelford
1901-1924

Minter, Steven A.
1975-1976

Mobley, Henry P.
1960-1992

Moffett, H. M.
1926-1927

Montgomery, R. Ames
1924-1926

Morton, W. W.
1936-1949

Mount, C. E.
1954-1967

Mourning, G. H.
1911-1924

Mulder, John M.
1982-present

Nash, Margaret
1979-1991

Neel, S. M.*
1893-1916

Nelson, C. Ellis
1975-1981

Nelson, Frank A.
1921-1944

Nesbit, John B., Jr.
1974-1982

Newlin, George W.
1958-1994

Nichols, Martha Clay (Macie)
1993-present

Nicol, M.P.
1954-1961

Norman, J. V. Jr.
1970-1982

Nunemacher, F. C.
1902-1911

Ogden, Dunbar H.
1919-1922, 1924-1926

Olert, Frederick H.
1937-1951

Olert, John, Jr.
1951-59, 1964-86

Patterson, Merle C.
1958-1959

Patterson, P. Andrew
1983-1987

Patton, James R.
1974-1977

Pelgrim, J. Carlton
1924-1935

Pence, James H.
1963-1970

Petersen, James
1985-1990

Phifer, William E., Jr.
1944-1949

Pike, Hezzie B.
1955-1965

Ping, Charles
1996-present

Pleune, Peter H.
1930-1961

Pratt, Chas. H.
1922-1924

Price, John W.
1924-1925

Reed, Robert L.
1986-present

Regen, William M.
1961-1970

Reid, O. L.
1916-1920

Reuss, Lloyd E.
1985-present

Reynolds, Chas. L.
1914-1917

Reynolds, R. S.
1923-1931

Rhea, Thomas C.
1959-1980

Rich, Norma
1982-1995

Ridings, Dot S.
1992-present

Roberts, F. Morgan
1970-present

Roberts, W. C.
1901-1903

Rodes, Joe M.
1967-1976

Ross, Norma
2000-present

Rushton, J. Frank
1922-1925

Ryan, Mike
1995-present

Samuel, E. L.
1901-1908

Sanders, Robert S.
1922-1953, 1955-1964

Schlegel, Leland D.
1954-1978

Sellers, Richard M.
1961-1962

Settle, W. E.
1907-1924

Shelton, Barret C.
1952-1956

Singer, Paris
1956-1959

Smith, Robert M.
1962-1974

Sommers, M. O.
1967-1969

Spalding, J. Greig
1957-1974

Speed, Thomas
1901-1902

Steilberg, H. Alan
1967-present

Stein, Luther R.
1949-1957

Stevenson, Miss Jane
1972-present

Stimson, Edward W.
1947-1953

Stites, John
1902-1938

Stoess, Milton
1966-1974

Stuart, Marion F.
1953-1957

Sutterlin, Fred J.
1942-1961

Swallow, Isaac F.
1923-1942

Thomas, Carl O.
1969-1970

Thompson, H. H.
1930-1946

Thompson, John H.
1963-1964

Thompson, Robert C.
1983-1988

Todd, James A. Jr.
1997-present

Todd, James Ross
1908-1918

Trabue, W. D.
1930-1931

Turck, Charles. J.
1932-1938

Unruh, Henry
1972-1975

Van Keuren, E. B.
1955-1958

Van Winkle, F. D.
1930-1939

Vander Meulen, J. M.
1915-1917, 1925-1931

Vander Veen, Richard F.
1990-1994

Walker, Henry A.
1924-1930

Walker, Lynn R.
1919-1921

Walker, William G.
1976-1984

• *Appendix B* •

FACULTY: DANVILLE THEOLOGICAL
SEMINARY, 1853-1901

NAME	POSITION	DATE
Archibald, George D.	Prof. of Church Government and Pastoral Theology	1870-1872 and 1874-1878
Archibald, George D.	Prof. of Sacred Rhetoric; Church Government; Pastoral Theology	1878-1883
Beatty, Ormond	Prof. of Historical Theology	1886-1887
Beatty, Ormond	Prof. of Apologetics; Mediaeval and Modern Church History	1887-1889
Beatty, Ormond	Prof. of Mediaeval and Modern Church History	1889-1890
Breckinridge, Robert J.	Prof. of Exegetic, Didactic and Polemic Theology	1853-1869
Crawford, Clarence K.	Tutor in Hebrew	1887-1889
Crawford, Clarence K.	Prof. of Hebrew and Old Testament History	1889-1890
Crawford, Clarence K.	Prof. of Old Testament Exegesis; History and Archaeology	1890-1892

Crawford, Clarence K.	Prof. of Old Testament Languages and Exegesis; Biblical Antiquities	1892-1901
Edwards, Jonathan	Prof. of Didactic and Polemic Theology	1877-1881
Ely, John C.	Prof. of Homiletics	1897-1899
Hays, John S.	Prof. of Biblical and Ecclesiastical History	1874-1883
Humphrey, Edward P.	Prof. of Biblical and Ecclesiastical History	1853-1866
Johnson, William H.	Prof. of New Testament Literature and Exegesis	1897-1901
Johnson, William H.	Prof. of the Study of the English Bible	1899-1900
Landis, Robert W.	Prof. of Church Government and Pastoral Theology	1867-1869
Martin, Claude B. H.	Prof. of Didactic and Polemic Theology	1886-1887
Martin, Claude B. H.	Prof. of Systematic Theology	1890-1892 and 1899-1901
Martin, Claude B. H.	Prof. of Systematic and Pastoral Theology	1887-1889
Martin, Claude B. H.	Prof. of Systematic Theology and Study of the English Bible	1889-1890, 1892-1899, and 1900-1901
McKee, John L.	Prof. of Homiletics and Pastoral Theology	1886-1887
McKee, John L.	Prof. of Old Testament History; Exegesis of the English Bible; Homiletics	1887-1889
McKee, John L.	Prof. of Pastoral Theology and Elocution	1889-1892

McKee, John L.	Prof. of Elocution and Mission Work	1892-1896
McMullin, Samuel H.	Prof. of Biblical and Ecclesiastical History	1870-1872
Reaser, Joseph G.	Instructor of Oriental and Biblical Literature	1853-1857
Redd, John W.	Prof. of Biblical Greek and New Testament History	1887-1890
Rice, Nathan L.	Prof. of Didactic and Polemic Theology	1874-1877
Robinson, Stuart	Prof. of Church Government and Pastoral Theology	1856-1858
Smith, Joseph T.	Prof. of Church Government and Pastoral Theology	1860-1861
Stanton, Robert L.	Prof. of Church Government and Pastoral Theology	1863-1866
Sutherland, Robert R.	Prof. of Pastoral Theology	1896-1897
West, Nathaniel	Prof. of Biblical and Ecclesiastical Theology	1868-1870
West, Nathaniel	Prof. of Didactic and Polemic Theology	1870-1873
Worrall, John M.	Prof. of Ecclesiastical History and Church Government; Study of the English Bible	1890-1892
Worrall, John M.	Prof. of Biblical and Ecclesiastical History; Church Government	1892-1899
Worrall, John M.	Prof. of Homiletics; Pastoral Theology; Church Government	1899-1901
Yerkes, Stephen	Prof. of Biblical and Oriental Literature	1857-1869
Yerkes, Stephen	Prof. of Biblical Literature and Exegetical Theology	1869-1887

Yerkes, Stephen	Prof. of Biblical Literature and Exegetical Theology; Ancient History; Church Government	1887-1890
Yerkes, Stephen	Prof. of Biblical Literature and New Testament Exegesis	1890-1892
Yerkes, Stephen	Prof. of New Testament Literature and Exegesis	1892-1896
Young, William C.	Prof. of Homiletics, Theoretical and Practical	1889-1892
Young, William C.	Prof. of Homiletics and Pastoral Theology	1892-1896

FACULTY: LOUISVILLE PRESBYTERIAN THEOLOGICAL SEMINARY OF KENTUCKY, 1893-1901

The seminary's name was changed to LPTS in 1927.

NAME	POSITION	DATE
Beattie, Francis R.	Prof. of Systematic Theology; Apologetics	1893-1901
Browne, A. Oscar	Instructor of Music	1898-1899
Dabney, R.L.	Lecturer on Christian Ethics	1894-1895
Deggendorf, J. E.	Instructor of Music	1895-1897
Gallaber, T. F.	Instructor of Music	1899-1900
Hawes, Thompson M.	Prof. of Elocution	1893-1901
Hemphill, Charles R.	Prof. of New Testament Exegesis	1893-1901
Lyons, John S.	Prof. Pro Tem of Homiletics	1898-1899
Marquess, William Hoge	Prof. of Old Testament Exegesis; English Bible; Biblical Theology	1893-1901

Faculty: Louisville Seminary, 1893-1901

Muller, Edwin	Adjunct Prof. of Church History; Church Polity	1893-1895
Muller, Edwin	Prof. of Church History; Church Polity	1895-1901
Stapleford, Clement A.	Instructor in Music	1894-1895
Witherspoon, Thomas Dwight	Prof. of Homiletics; Pastoral Theology; Biblical Introduction	1893-1901

FACULTY: LOUISVILLE PRESBYTERIAN THEOLOGICAL SEMINARY, 1901-PRESENT

NAME	POSITION	DATE
Adeney, Frances Screnock	William A. Benfield Jr. Associate Prof. of Evangelism and Global Missions	1999-present
Aleshire, Daniel O.	Visiting Prof. of Christian Education	1985-1986
Andrews, Dale P.	Assistant Prof. of Homiletics and Pastoral Theology	1998-2000
Andrews, Dale P.	Frank H. Caldwell Assistant Prof. of Homiletics and Assistant Prof. of Homiletics and Pastoral Theology	2000-present
Archibald, Bruce	Adjunct Prof. of Clinical Pastoral Education	1977-1978
Arnold, William	Adjunct Prof. of Clinical Pastoral Education	1973-1977
Averitt, James Williams	Instructor in Polity	1961-1962
Averitt, James Williams	Instructor in Methodist Polity	1962-1969

Faculty: Louisville Presbyterian Seminary, 1901-Present

Barnes, Barbara	Adjunct Prof. of Homiletics	1996-1998
Barnes, J. Mark	Adjunct Prof. of Speech Practicum	1994-1996
Barnes, J. Mark	Adjunct Prof. of Homiletics	1996-1998
Barton, Clarence Y.	Instructor in Pastoral Counseling	1954-1964
Barton, Clarence Y.	Instructor in Pastoral Theology	1964-1966
Beattie, Francis R.	Prof. of Apologetics; Systematic Theology	1901-1906
Benfield, William A.	Instructor in Hebrew and Old Testament	1940-1941
Benfield, William A.	Assistant Prof. of Hebrew and Old Testament	1941-1943
Benfield, William A.	Prof. of Hebrew and Old Testament	1943-1944
Benfield, William A.	Prof. of Practical Theology	1944-1950
Benfield, William A.	Instructor in Homiletics	1951-1957
Bennett, George F.	Instructor in Pastoral Theology	1964-1966
Bennett, George G.	Adjunct Prof. of Pastoral Theology	1966-1971
Bennett, George G.	Adjunct Prof. of Pastoral Care and Counseling	1978-1984
Blackwood, Andrew W.	Prof. of Biblical Introduction; English Bible; Biblical Theology	1925-1929
Blanton, Judy	Adjunct Prof. of Pastoral Care and Counseling	1993-1995
Blanton, Judy	Adjunct Prof. of Marriage and Family Therapy	1995-1996
Blanton, Judy	Adjunct Prof. of Pastoral Care and Counseling	1996-1998

273

APPENDIX B

Bosch, Frederick W. A.	Lecturer in English Bible; Biblical Introduction	1930-1931
Bowman, Locke E.	Adjunct Prof. of Christian Education	1974-1978
Boyle, John H.	Instructor in Pastoral Care	1957-1964
Boyle, John H.	Instructor in Pastoral Theology	1964-1967
Brachlow, Stephen	Adjunct Prof. of Spiritual Formation	1995-1996
Breslin, Charles	Visiting Prof. of Philosophical Theology	1977-1978
Briner, Lewis A.	Visiting Prof. of Worship	1984-1986
Brockwell, Charles W., Jr.	Visiting Prof. of Methodist Studies	1978-1992
Brockwell, Charles W., Jr.	Prof. of Church History and Wesleyan Studies	1993-1997
Brockwell, Charles W., Jr.	Adjunct Prof. of Methodist Studies	1997-1998
Brown, Milton P.	Instructor in Biblical Theology	1953-1954
Buckwalter, Georgine	Adjunct Prof. of Field Education	1994-Present
Byrd, James	Visiting Prof. of Speech	1978-1984
Cabaniss, James Allen	Instructor in New Testament Greek	1934-1935
Caldwell, Frank Hill	Prof. of Homiletics	1930-1964
Caldwell, Frank Hill	Prof. Emeritus of Homiletics	1974-1987
Carter, George D., Jr.	Associate Prof. of Pastoral Ministry	1986-1990
Carter, George D., Jr.	Prof. of Pastoral Ministry	1992-1993
Carter, George D., Jr.	Prof. of Ministry	1993-Present

Carter, Marie	Adjunct Prof. of Pastoral Counseling	1996-Present
Cater, Douglas G.	Instructor in New Testament Greek	1953-1954
Catron, Janice	Adjunct Prof. of Biblical Theology	1989-1991
Chase, Linda D.	Instructor in Church and Ministry	1977-1982
Chamberlain, William Douglas	Associate Prof. of New Testament Exegesis	1928-1930
Chamberlain, William Douglas	Prof. of New Testament Exegesis	1930-1958
Coalter, Milton J, Jr.	Librarian and Assistant Prof. of Bibliography and Research	1985-1988
Coalter, Milton J, Jr.	Librarian and Associate Prof. of Bibliography and Research	1988-1991
Coalter, Milton J, Jr.	Librarian and Prof. of Bibliography and Research	1991-Present
Comerford, Jane Ann	Adjunct Prof. of Pastoral Counseling	1994-Present
Conning, Gordon R.	Instructor in Old Testament Exegesis	1935-1937
Cook, Carol	Assistant Prof. of Pastoral Care and Counseling	2000-Present
Cooper, Burton Z.	Associate Prof. of Philosophical Theology	1970-1975
Cooper, Burton Z.	Prof. of Philosophical Theology	1975-1998
Cooper, Burton Z.	Prof. Emeritus of Philosophical Theology	1998-Present
Cotton, Jesse Lee	Prof. of Old Testament Exegesis	1910-1919

Cotton, Jesse Lee	Prof. of Old Testament Exegesis; Hermeneutics; Sociology	1919-1932
Cotton, Jesse Lee	Prof. of Old Testament Exegesis	1932-1935
Cotton, Jesse Lee	Prof. Emeritus of Old Testament Exegesis	1935-1937
Crawford, Ernest G.	Instructor in New Testament Greek	1946-1947
Crawford, Clarence K.	Prof. of Old Testament Exegesis	1901-1909
Cross, Marie	Adjunct Prof. of Entering Ministry Effectively	1994-1998
Cruz, Virgil	Prof. of New Testament	1986-1995
Cruz, Virgil	Prof. Emeritus of New Testament	1995-Present
Cully, Kendig Brubaker	Visiting Prof. of Anglican Studies	1978-1981
Cummins, John	Adjunct Prof. of Music	1991-1996
Cunningham, John Rood	Prof. of Pastoral Theology	1930-1936
Cunningham, John Rood	Prof. of Church Polity	1932-1936
Cunningham, John Rood	Prof. of American Church History	1934-1936
Daniel, Glover A.	Instructor in New Testament Greek; Music	1925-1926
Daniel, Glover A.	Assistant Prof. in New Testament Exegesis	1927-1928
Davis, Father Cyprian	Visiting Prof. of Historical Theology	1979-1983
Davis, Father Cyprian	Adjunct Prof. of Historical Theology	1986-1988
Davis, Father Cyprian	Adjunct Prof. of African-American Studies	1996-1997
Diamond, Rabbi Chester	Adjunct Prof. of Judaism	1994-Present

Dosker, Henry E.	Prof. of Church History	1903-1919
Dosker, Henry E.	Prof. of Church History; Pastoral Theology; Missions	1919-1924
Dosker, Henry E.	Prof. of Church History; Pastoral Theology	1924-1926
Duncan, Thomas C.	Instructor in New Testament Greek	1944-1945
Duncan, Franklin	Adjunct Prof. of Clinical Pastoral Education	1973-1976
Durham, Roger L.	Adjunct Prof. of Pastoral Care and Counseling	1994-1995
Durham, Roger L.	Adjunct Prof. of Field Education	1995-1998
Dykstra, Craig	Assistant Prof. of Christian Education	1977-1981
Dykstra, Craig	Associate Prof. of Christian Education	1981-1984
Edwards, George Riley	Instructor in New Testament Greek	1949-1951
Edwards, George Riley	Instructor in Bible	1956-1958
Edwards, George Riley	Prof. of New Testament	1958-1985
Edwards, George Riley	Prof. Emeritus of New Testament	1985-Present
Ehrman, Fred	Adjunct Prof. of German	1998-1999
Eichelberger, William L.	Associate Prof. of Christian Social Ethics	1972-1975
Elliott, William M.	Assistant Prof. in Church History; Homiletics	1929-1930
Elwood, Christopher L.	Assistant Prof. of Historical Theology	1996-2000
Elwood, Christopher L.	Associate Prof. of Historical Theology	2000-Present

Faucette, James R.	Adjunct Prof. of Pastoral Theology	1969-1971
Fedyszyn, Stan	Adjunct Prof. of Preaching	1996-1997
Ferguson, Sheri	Adjunct Prof. of Counseling and Marriage and Family Therapy	1998-Present
Foley, Grover Ellis	Visiting Prof. of Doctrinal Theology	1966-1967
Fontenot, Nancy	Adjunct Prof. of Pastoral Counseling	1988-Present
Foreman, Kenneth Joseph	Prof. of Doctrinal Theology	1947-1960
Foreman, Kenneth Joseph	Prof. Emeritus of Doctrinal Theology	1960-1966
Fowlkes, Mary Ann	Visiting Prof. of Christian Education	1985-1986
Fry, James Arthur	Instructor in Pastoral Care	1957-1958
Gannaway, Bruce	Adjunct Prof. of Evangelism and Mission	1997-1998
Garber, Paul L.	Instructor in New Testament Greek	1936-1937
Garrett, Susan R.	Prof. of New Testament	1995-Present
George, Timothy	Visiting Prof. of Early Church History	1983-1985
Goatley, David Emmanuel	Adjunct Prof. of Theology	1995-1996
Goetz, Thomas	Adjunct Prof. of Music	1996-Present
Golden, Edward S.	Instructor in Pastoral Care	1956-1957
Goodykoontz, Harry Gordon	Prof. of Christian Education	1950-1975
Goodykoontz, Harry Gordon	Prof. Emeritus of Christian Education	1976-1998

Faculty: Louisville Presbyterian Seminary, 1901-Present

Gouwens, Tevnis E.	Instructor in Homiletics	1940-1941
Groves, Walter A.	Prof. of Doctrinal Theology	1942-1946
Guder, Darrell	William A. Benfield Jr. Prof. of Evangelism and Global Missions	1991-1997
Gunsalus, Catherine Lee	Associate Prof. of Historical Theology	1969-1973
Hammond, Trey	Adjunct Prof. of Urban Ministry	1998-1999
Hancock, Steve	Adjunct Prof. of Advanced Homiletics	1988-1991
Hanna, Charles Morton	Instructor-Supervisor of Rural Church	1941-1949
Hanna, Charles Morton	Prof. of Rural Church	1949-1962
Hanna, Charles Morton	Prof. of Pastoral Leadership	1950-1962
Hanna, Charles Morton	Prof. Emeritus of Pastoral Leadership and Rural Church	1961-1964
Hassan, Riffat	Visiting Prof. of Islam	1981-1986
Hassan, Riffat	Adjunct Prof. of Islam	1986-1988
Hassan, Riffat	Adjunct Prof. of Hinduism and Buddhism	1988-1993
Hassan, Riffat	Adjunct Prof. of Buddhism, Hinduism, and Islam	1994-1998
Hassan, Riffat	Adjunct Prof. of Islam	1998-1999
Hawes, Thompson M.	Associate Prof. of Practical Theology	1901-1919
Hay, Edward C.	Instructor in New Testament Greek	1947-1949
Haynes, Douglas	Adjunct Prof. of Biblical Languages	1994-1997

Hemphill, Charles R.	Prof. of New Testament Exegesis; Practical Theology	1901-1919
Hemphill, Charles R.	Prof. of Religious Education	1919-1921
Hemphill, Charles R.	Prof. of Homiletics	1919-1923
Hemphill, Charles R.	Prof. of New Testament Exegesis; Church Polity	1919-1930
Hemphill, Charles R.	Prof. Emeritus of New Testament Exegesis; Church Polity	1930-1932
Henry, Alexander	Instructor in New Testament Greek	1930-1934
Hester, David	Associate Prof. of Christian Education	1986-1990
Hester, David	Prof. of Christian Education	1990-Present
Hockenberry, Judy	Adjunct Prof. of Polity	1999-Present
Hockenberry, Kenneth J.	Adjunct Prof. of Speech	1997-2000
Hockenberry, Kenneth J.	Adjunct Prof. of Preaching	2000-Present
Holladay, James	Adjunct Prof. of Evangelism	1997-Present
Horner, Norman Aste	Prof. of Missions	1949-1951
Horner, Norman Aste	Associate Prof. of Missions and Evangelism	1951-1955
Horner, Norman Aste	Prof. of Missions and Evangelism	1955-1965
Horner, Norman Aste	Prof. of Ecumenical Mission and Evangelism	1965-1968
Horner, Norman Aste	Adjunct Prof. of Missions	1986-1987
Horner, Norman Aste	Prof. Emeritus of Missions	1987-1997
Houchins, Jerry	Adjunct Prof. of Polity	1994-1997
Hunter, Joseph L.	Instructor in New Testament Greek	1945-1946

Hyde, James A.	Adjunct Prof. of Pastoral Care/ Counseling and Family Therapy	1995-1996
Jamison, A. Leland	Instructor in New Testament Greek	1935-1936
Jenkins, Finley D.	Acting Prof. of Systematic Theology; Apologetics; Ethics	1920-1921
Jobling, David Kenneth	Assistant Prof. of Hermeneutics	1970-1972
Jobling, David Kenneth	Assistant Prof. of Interpretation	1972-1975
Jobling, David Kenneth	Associate Prof. of Interpretation	1975-1976
Johnson, Kathryn L.	Assistant Prof. of Historical Theology	1984-1996
Johnson, Kathryn L.	Paul Tudor Jones Associate Prof. of Historical Theology	1996-1998
Johnson, Kathryn L.	Prof. of Historical Theology and Paul Tudor Jones Prof. of Church History	1999-Present
Johnson, Robert I.	Instructor in Public Speaking; Music	1926-1928
Jones, Jameson M.	Instructor in New Testament Greek	1937-1939
Jones, Thomas Laird	Adjunct Prof. of Church and Ministry	1977-1980
Kaylor, Robert David	Instructor in Greek	1956-1957
Keen, Samuel McMurray	Associate Prof. of Philosophy and Christian Faith	1962-1968
Keen, Samuel McMurray	Prof. of Philosophy and Christian Faith	1968-1969
Kendrick, Leslie Smith	Adjunct Prof. of Pastoral Counseling	1999-Present
Kerr, Hugh Thomson, Jr.	Instructor in Doctrinal Theology	1936-1937

Kerr, Hugh Thomson, Jr.	Associate Prof. of Doctrinal Theology	1937-1940
Kipp, John	Adjunct Prof. of New Testament	1994-1996
Knowles, Joseph W.	Instructor in Pastoral Counseling	1953-1954
Knox, S. J.	Visiting Prof. of Church History	1967-1968
Krauss-Jackson, Jane	Adjunct Prof. of Practical Theology	1994-1996
Kuhns, Mary J.	Adjunct Prof. of Professional Issues and Ethics	1999-Present
Kyle, Melvin Grove	Permanent Lecturer on Archaeology	1929-1933
Larsen-Wigger, Jane	Adjunct Prof. of Basic Preaching	1999-Present
Laws, William Roberts, Jr.	Instructor in New Testament Greek	1942-1943
Leggett, John P.	Adjunct Prof. of Homiletics	1994-1995
Lentz, John	Adjunct Prof. of Pastoral Care and Counseling	1994-1999
Lewis, James W.	Adjunct Prof. of American Religious History	1997-Present
Lile, R. Kenneth	Adjunct Prof. of Homiletics	1995-1996
Lindsey, Carolyn	Adjunct Prof. of Pastoral Care and Counseling	1994-1997
Love, Julian Price	Lecturer in English Bible; Biblical Introduction	1929-1931
Love, Julian Price	Prof. of English Bible; Biblical Introduction	1931-1939
Love, Julian Price	Prof. of Biblical Theology	1931-1965
Love, Julian Price	Prof. Emeritus of Biblical Theology	1965-1970

Lyons, John Sprole	Prof. Pro Tem of Homiletics	1906-1907
Lytch, Carol	Adjunct Prof. of Congregational Studies	2000-Present
Malone, Whit	Adjunct Prof. of Homiletics	1995-1997
March, W. Eugene	Arnold Black Rhodes Prof. of Old Testament	1982-Present
Marquess, William Hoge	Prof. of Biblical Introduction; English Bible; Biblical Theology	1901-1911
Martin, Claude B. H.	Prof. of Church History	1901-1909
Mason, Richard	Adjunct Prof. of Chemical Dependency	1997-1998
Massey, Marilyn C.	Adjunct Prof. of Historical Theology	1974-1976
Mauser, Ulrich Wilhelm	Associate Prof. of Biblical Theology	1964-1968
Mauser, Ulrich Wilhelm	Prof. of Biblical Theology	1968-1977
Maxwell, Glenn	Instructor in Doctrinal Theology	1940-1942
McAllister, J. Gray	Acting Prof. of Old Testament Exegesis; English Bible	1909-1910
McAllister, J. Gray	Acting Prof. of Biblical Introduction; English Bible; Biblical Theology	1910-1911
McAllister, J. Gray	Prof. of Biblical Introduction; English Bible; Biblical Theology	1911-1925
McAllister, J. Gray	Prof. of Public Speaking	1919-1920 and 1921-1925
McAtee, William	Adjunct Prof. of Town and Country Ministry	1999-Present

McClure, John S.	Assistant Prof. of Preaching and Worship	1986-1991
McClure, John S.	Associate Prof. of Preaching and Worship	1991-1994
McClure, John S.	Frank H. Caldwell Prof. of Preaching and Worship	1994-1998
McClure, John S.	Frank H. Caldwell Prof. of Homiletics and Liturgics	1999-2000
McClure, John S.	Henry Morris Edmonds Prof. of Ministry and Prof. of Preaching and Worship	2000-Present
McGill, S. W.	Instructor in Church Efficiency	1922-1923
Meek, Gavin	Adjunct Prof. of Town and Country Ministry	1996-1999
Mohns, Edward A.	Instructor in New Testament Greek	1926-1927
Morrison, Clinton Dawson, Jr.	Prof. of New Testament	1968-1990
Morrison, Clinton Dawson, Jr.	Prof. Emeritus of New Testament	1990-Present
Mortonstout, Donna	Adjunct Prof. of Methodist Studies	1994-1996
Mulder, John M.	Prof. of Historical Theology	1981-Present
Murphy, Bonneau P.	Instructor of Methodist Students in Pastoral Theology and Methodist Discipline	1946-1948
Murray, J. J.	Visiting Prof. of Homiletics	1957-1959
Myers, Marcia	Adjunct Prof. of Town and Country Ministry	1999-Present
Myers, William R.	Visiting Prof. of Christian Education	1982-1983 and 1984-1985

Faculty: Louisville Presbyterian Seminary, 1901-Present

Myers, William R.	Adjunct Prof. of Christian Education	1986-1988 and 1990-1993
Myers, William R.	Adjunct Prof. of Youth Ministry	1988-1989
Nebelsick, Harold P.	Prof. of Doctrinal Theology	1968-1989
Nelson, C. Ellis	Prof. of Christian Education	1974-1981
Nelson, C. Ellis	Prof. Emeritus of Christian Education	1981-Present
Nelson, C. Ellis	Adjunct Prof. of Christian Education	1986-1988
Newman, Carey	Adjunct Prof. of Jesus in History and Tradition	1998-1999
Oates, Wayne E.	Visiting Prof. of Pastoral Counseling	1977-1978
Ogden, Dunbar H.	Acting Prof. of Apologetics	1919-1920
Ogden, Robert F.	Instructor in Hebrew and Old Testament	1938-1940
Old, Hughes O.	Visiting Prof. of Worship	1984-1986
Oliver, Allen	Adjunct Prof. of Pastoral Care and Counseling	1993-1995
Oliver, Allen	Adjunct Prof. of Pastoral Care and Family Therapy	1995-1997
Patterson, Louis Dale	Adjunct Prof. of Methodist Studies	1989-1993
Pauw, Amy Plantinga	Assistant Prof. of Doctrinal Theology	1990-1994
Pauw, Amy Plantinga	Associate Prof. of Doctrinal Theology	1994-1998
Pauw, Amy Plantinga	Henry P. Mobley Jr. Prof. of Doctrinal Theology	1998-Present
Phifer, Kenneth G.	Prof. of Homiletics	1959-1965

Phifer, Kenneth G.	Visiting Prof. of Homiletics	1984-1985
Pleune, Peter H.	Instructor in Church Polity; Pastoral Theology	1936-1940
Pons, Jacques	Visiting Prof. of Old Testament	1986-1988
Pratt, Charles H.	Prof. of Missions and Evangelism	1924-1927 and 1928-1944
Pratt, Charles H.	Prof. of Pastoral Theology	1928-1930
Pratt, Charles H.	Prof. of Church Polity; Pastoral Theology	1940-1944
Pratt, Charles H.	Prof. of Missions	1944-1948
Ptomey, K. C.	Visiting Prof. of Preaching	1985-1986
Ragland, Amanda	Adjunct Prof. of Pastoral Care and Counseling	1994-1998
Ragland, Jack	Adjunct Prof. of Pastoral Care and Counseling	1994-1998
Rainbow, Jon	Adjunct Prof. of Pastoral Care and Counseling	1994-1997
Ramsay, Nancy Jean	Assistant Prof. of Pastoral Theology	1983-1988
Ramsay, Nancy Jean	Associate Prof. of Pastoral Theology	1988-1992
Ramsay, Nancy Jean	Prof. of Pastoral Theology	1992-1996
Ramsay, Nancy Jean	Harrison Ray Anderson Prof. of Pastoral Theology	1996-Present
Ray, Stephen	Assistant Prof. of Theology and Philosophy	1999-Present
Reistroffer, Dianne	Assistant Prof. of Ministry	1998-Present
Rhodes, Arnold Black	Instructor in New Testament Greek	1939-1941

Rhodes, Arnold Black	Associate Prof. of Old Testament	1944-1949
Rhodes, Arnold Black	Prof. of Old Testament	1949-1982
Rhodes, Arnold Black	Prof. Emeritus of Old Testament	1982-Present
Rightmyer, James	Adjunct Prof. of Music for Pastors	1988-1991
Ritchie, Jeff	Adjunct Prof. of Evangelism and Mission	1996-1998
Ritchie, Megan	Adjunct Prof. of Field Education	1998-1999
Robbins, Thomas D.	Adjunct Prof. of Pastoral Care and Counseling	1994-1995 and 1996-1999
Robbins, Thomas D.	Adjunct Prof. of Marriage and Family Therapy	1995-1996
Roberts, F. Morgan	Visiting Prof. of Preaching	1985-1986
Rodgers, Alex	Adjunct Prof. of Methodist Studies	1993-1994
Rudolph, L. C.	Instructor in Church History	1954-1957
Rudolph, L. C.	Assistant Prof. of Church History	1957-1958
Rudolph, L. C.	Prof. of Church History	1958-1969
Ruffin, Jac C.	Instructor in New Testament Greek	1943-1944
Rule, Andrew Kerr	Prof. of Church History; Apologetics	1927-1961
Rule, Andrew Kerr	Prof. of Apologetics and Ethics	1961-1962
Rule, Andrew Kerr	Prof. Emeritus of Church History and Apologetics	1962-1974
Russell, Walter L.	Instructor in Polity	1956-1961
Sackman, Robert	Adjunct Prof. of Town and Country Ministry	????-1992
Salmon, John Mellersh	Assistant Prof. of Biblical Studies	1963-1966

Salmon, John Mellersh	Associate Prof. of Biblical Studies	1966-1969
Sapp, Willard D.	Adjunct Prof. of Pastoral Care and Counseling	1988-1991
Shaw, Angus R.	Acting Prof. of Systematic Theology	1919-1920
Sherrill, Lewis J.	Prof. of Religious Education and Young People's Work; Church Efficiency	1924-1928
Sherrill, Lewis J.	Prof. of Religious Education; Church Efficiency	1928-1944
Sherrill, Lewis J.	Prof. of Religious Education	1944-1949
Simmons, Paul D.	Adjunct Prof. of Theological Ethics	1996-1999
Skaggs, Bruce	Adjunct Prof. of Pastoral Care and Counseling	1988-1997
Smith, Alexa	Adjunct Prof. of Homiletics	1994-1999
Smith, Alexa	Adjunct Prof. of Preaching	2000-Present
Soards, Marion L.	Prof. of New Testament Studies	1990-1993
Soards, Marion L.	Prof. of New Testament	1993-Present
Steere, David Alden	Assistant Prof. of Pastoral Leadership	1957-1961
Steere, David Alden	Associate Prof. of Pastoral Theology	1961-1966
Steere, David Alden	Prof. of Pastoral Theology	1966-1975
Steere, David Alden	Prof. of Pastoral Care	1975-1991
Steere, David Alden	Prof. of Pastoral Care and Counseling	1991-1996
Steere, David Alden	Prof. Emeritus of Pastoral Care and Counseling	1996-Present

Stone, Nathan J.	Instructor in Hebrew	1929-1930
Street, T. Watson	Instructor of New Testament Greek	1941-1942
Stroble, Paul	Adjunct Prof. of Methodist Studies	1994-1999
Stroble, Paul	Adjunct Prof. of United Methodist Ecclesiology	1999-2000
Temple, Elwood L.	Instructor in Biblical Archaeology	1934-1935
Thom, Robert Dayer, Jr.	Instructor in New Testament Greek	1951-1953
Thurman, Howard	Visiting Prof. of Spiritual Resources and Disciplines	1967-1968
Townsend, Loren	Associate Prof. of Pastoral Care and Counseling	1996-2000
Townsend, Loren	Prof. of Pastoral Care and Counseling	2000-Present
Trower, J. Joseph	Instructor in New Testament Greek	1954-1956
Tucker, Grayson L., Jr.	Associate Prof. of Church Administration	1966-1971
Tucker, Grayson L., Jr.	Prof. of Church Administration	1971-1984
Tucker, Grayson L., Jr.	Prof. of Church Administration and Evangelism	1984-1988
Tucker, Grayson L., Jr.	Harrison Ray Anderson Prof. of Pastoral Ministry	1987-1988
Tucker, Grayson L., Jr.	Prof. Emeritus of Church Administration and Evangelism	1988-Present
Tucker, Grayson L., Jr.	Harrison Ray Anderson Prof. Emeritus of Pastoral Theology	1988-Present

Tull, Patricia Kathleen (Patricia Willey until 1998)	Assistant Prof. of Old Testament	1994-1998
Tull, Patricia Kathleen (Patricia Willey until 1998)	Associate Prof. of Old Testament	1998-Present
Van Wijk-Bos, Johanna W. H.	Assistant Prof. of Old Testament	1977-1981
Van Wijk-Bos, Johanna W. H.	Associate Prof. of Old Testament	1981-1986
Van Wijk-Bos, Johanna W. H.	Prof. of Old Testament	1986-Present
Van Wijk-Bos, Johanna W. H.	Dora E. Pierce Professor of Bible	2000-Present
Vander Meulen, John M.	Prof. of Sunday School; Young People's Work; Church Efficiency	1920-1921
Vander Meulen, John M.	Prof. of Religious Education; Young People's Work; Church Efficiency	1921-1922
Vander Meulen, John M.	Prof. of Religious Education; Young People's Work	1922-1924
Vander Meulen, John M.	Acting Prof. of Homiletics	1923-1924
Vander Meulen, John M.	Prof. of Homiletics	1924-1930
Vander Meulen, John M.	Prof. of Doctrinal Theology	1930-1936
Ward, Michael	Adjunct Prof. of Town and Country Ministry	1994-1996
Warheim, Harold Mervin (Hal)	Associate Prof. of Christianity and Society	1962-1979
Warheim, Harold Mervin (Hal)	Prof. of Christianity and Society	1979-1995
Warheim, Harold Mervin (Hal)	Prof. Emeritus of Christianity and Society	1996-Present

Faculty: Louisville Presbyterian Seminary, 1901-Present

Webb, Robert Alexander	Prof. of Apologetics; Systematic Theology	1908-1919
Weeks, Louis B., III	Assistant Prof. of Historical Theology	1970-1975
Weeks, Louis B., III	Associate Prof. of Historical Theology	1975-1979
Weeks, Louis B., III	Prof. of Historical Theology	1979-1988
Weeks, Louis B., III	Paul Tudor Jones Prof. of Church History	1988-1994
Weisenbeck, Jude	Adjunct Prof. of Ecumenism	1997-1998
Wessler, Daniel Bayne	Associate Prof. of Homiletics	1966-1968
Wessler, Daniel Bayne	Associate Prof. of Worship and Communication	1968-1971
Wessler, Daniel Bayne	Prof. of Worship and Communication	1971-1984
Wessler, Daniel Bayne	Visiting Prof. Emeritus of Worship and Communication	1984-1986
Wessler, Daniel Bayne	Prof. Emeritus of Worship and Communication	1984-Present
Westmoreland, Kathryn Barlow	Adjunct Prof. of Gerontology	1994-Present
Weston, Beau	Adjunct Prof. of American Christianity	1994-1996
Whaling, Thornton	Prof. of Systematic Theology; Apologetics; Ethics	1921-1927
Whaling, Thornton	Prof. of Systematic Theology; Ethics	1927-1929
Whaling, Thornton	Prof. Emeritus of Systematic Theology; Ethics	1929-1939
White, Ernest Miller	Librarian and Prof. of Bibliography and Research	1965-1985

White, Ernest Miller	Librarian and Prof. Emeritus of Bibliography and Research	1985-1998
Wigger, J. Bradley	Second Presbyterian Church Assistant Prof. of Christian Education	1997-2000
Wigger, J. Bradley	Second Presbyterian Church Associate Prof. of Christian Education	2000-Present

Willey, Patricia Tull — *see* Patricia Tull

Williams, Aubrey	Adjunct Prof. of Ethics	1996-1999
Williamson, Scott C.	Assistant Prof. of Theological Ethics	1997-1998
Williamson, Scott C.	Robert H. Walkup Assistant Prof. of Theological Ethics	1998-Present
Winn, Albert Curry	Prof. of Doctrinal Theology	1959-1974
Winn, Albert Curry	Prof. Emeritus of Systematic Theology	1981-Present
Woolever, Cynthia	Adjunct Prof. of Urban Ministry	1998-1999
Worrall, John M.	Prof. Emeritus of Practical Theology	1901-1913
Yeager, Beth	Adjunct Prof. of Basic Preaching	1995-1997
Yeager, Beth	Adjunct Prof. of Homiletics	1997-1999
Yeager, Beth	Adjunct Prof. of Basic Preaching	1999-Present

ADMINISTRATORS: DANVILLE
THEOLOGICAL SEMINARY, 1853-1901

The only catalogues on file for Danville (and that are known to exist) are:

1853-54 through 1860-61
1874-75 through 1882-83
1886-87 through 1887-88
1889-90 through 1897-98
1899-1900 through 1900-1901

The missing years could be due to the Civil War (1861-1865) and reconstruction and the lack of professors (1883-1886 the only professor was Dr. Yerkes).

NAME	POSITION	DATE
Robert Jefferson Breckinridge	Controlling Spirit — founding father	1853-1869
Stephen Yerkes[1]	Controlling Spirit	1869-1896
J. A. Jacobs	Treasurer	1853-1857
B. T. Milton	Business and Financial Agent	1857-1858
William J. McKnight	Business and Financial Agent	1858-1860

1. "Dr. Yerkes was Dr. Breckinridge's right-hand man, and, upon the death of the latter, he became the controlling spirit in the Seminary." Quote from: *History of Louisville Presbyterian Theological Seminary, 1853-1953*, by Robert Stuart Sanders.

Heman H. Allen	Business and Financial Agent	1860-?
Robert A. Johnstone[2]	Financial Agent	?-1879
George D. Archibald[3]	Financial Agent	1879-?
George W. Welsh, Jr.[4]	Financial Agent/Treasurer	?-1901

2. The 1874-75 catalogue lists Johnstone as the financial agent.
3. The 1882-83 catalogue lists Archibald as the financial agent.
4. The 1886-87 catalogue lists Welsh as the financial agent.

ADMINISTRATORS: LOUISVILLE PRESBYTERIAN THEOLOGICAL SEMINARY OF KENTUCKY, 1893-1901

The seminary's name changed to LPTS in 1927.

NAME	POSITION	DATE
Rev. William Hoge Marquess	Chairman of the Faculty — acting head (until 1910)	1893-1901
Rev. Edwin Muller	Secretary of the Faculty or Clerk of the Faculty	1893-1901
Rev. F. R. Beattie	Intendant	1893-1901
Mr. W. T. Grant	Treasurer	1893-1901
Rev. T. D. Witherspoon	Librarian	1893-1898
Rev. F. R. Beattie	Librarian	1898-1899
Rev. Charles R. Hemphill	Librarian	1899-1901

ADMINISTRATORS: LOUISVILLE PRESBYTERIAN THEOLOGICAL SEMINARY, 1901-PRESENT

NAME	POSITION	DATE
Akers-Bell, Leah	Director of Admissions	1986-1991
Alexander, LaVerne	Registrar	1971-1999
Avera, Robert	Food Service Manager	1970-1975
Barnes, Barbara	Director of the Office of Information	1983-1984
Barrow, Suzanne H.	Director of Food Services	1990-1994
Barrow, Suzanne H.	Food Service Manager	1994-1996
Beard, Sandy Jo	Dining Room Supervisor	1979-1988
Beard, Sandy Jo	Director of Food Services	1988-1990
Beattie, Francis R.	Chairman of the Faculty	1902-1903
Beattie, Francis R.	Intendant	1901-1906
Benfield, William A., Jr.	Clerk of the Faculty	1941-1942
Benfield, William A., Jr.	Vice President	1944-1949

Administrators: Louisville Presbyterian Seminary, 1901-Present

Bennett, George F.   Associate Dean for Student   1971-1972
                            Affairs

Bennett, George F.   Associate Dean   1972-1974

Bennett, George F.   Dean of Students   1974-1984

Bennett, George F.   Director of Admissions   1982-1983

Bradley, Leah Ellison   Acting Director of Alumni/ae Re-   1997-1998
                            lations and the Annual Fund

Breland, Mrs. Robert E.   Director of Public Relations   1969-1971

Brockwell, Charles, Jr.   Director of Graduate Studies   1993-1997

Brown, Tommy   Audio-Visual Coordinator   1987-1991

Brown, Karen Shafer   Director of the Annual Fund   1992-1993

Burke, Ted G.   Director of Food/Dining Services   1996-present

Caldwell, Anne S.   Director of Planned Giving   1982-1991

Caldwell, Frank Hill   President   1936-1964

Campbell, A. B.   Business Manager   1960-1969

Carter, George D., Jr.   Director of Field Education   1988-present

Carter, George D., Jr.   Director of Clinical Pastoral Edu- 2000-present
                            cation

Cecil, Patrick A.   Vice President for Finance   1998-present

Chamberlain, Dorthea   Dining Room Supervisor   1975-1977

Chase, Linda   Director of Field Education   1977-1982

Chase, Herbert S.   Vice President for Deferred   1973-1975
                            Giving

Coalter, Milton J, Jr.   Library Director   1985-present

Conn, Miss Louise   Acting Librarian   1928-1931

Conn, Miss Louise   Librarian   1931-1944

Conn, Miss Louise	Assistant Librarian	1944-1956
Cornelison, John J.	Financial Secretary	1915-1917
Cotton, Jesse Lee	Clerk of the Faculty	1920-1926
Cotton, Jesse Lee	Registrar	1922-1924
Crawford, Clarence K.	Librarian	1901-1902
Crawford, Clarence K.	Chairman of the Faculty	1903-1904
Crawford, Clarence K.	Chairman of the Faculty	1907-1908
Cunningham, John Rood	President	1930-Mar. 1, 1936
Dawson, Cathy	Vice President for Finance	1993-1998
Dawson, Cathy	Vice President for Seminary Relations	1998-present
Depew, J. Arthur	Vice President for Development	1969-1976
Depew, J. Arthur	Consultant for Development	1976-1977
Dorris, Frances	Director of Special Projects	1977-1979
Dosker, Henry E.	Clerk of the Faculty	1904-1905 and 1906-1908
Dosker, Henry E.	Chairman of the Faculty	1905-1906 and 1909-1910
Duncan, Thomas C.	Special Assistant in Development	1987-1989
Dykstra, Craig R.	Director of Continuing Education	1979-1983
Fels, G. Leonard	Director of Public Relations	1949-1953
Fels, G. Leonard	Business Manager	1949-1953
Ferguson, Sheri	Director of Louisville Seminary Counseling Ministry	1998-present
Foster, Garnett	Director of Vocational and Spiritual Formation	1999-present

Garland, Diana	Director of the Family Ministry Project	1996-1998
Goodykoontz, Betty	Director of Special Projects	1979-1983
Gray, David	Director of Academic Programming	1999-present
Gray, David	Registrar	1999-present
Hagan, Mrs. Percy	Assistant to Business Manager	1954-1956
Hammond, Claude E.	Director of Communications	1998-1999
Hancock, Stephen C.	Dean of Students	1984-1991
Hanna, C. Morton	Supervisor of Field Work	1944-1961
Hawley, Mrs. Ralph J.	Registrar	1965-1971
Hayes, Ruth	Registrar	1958-1965
Heck, Miss Nancy	Registrar	1954-1958
Helm, Susan M.	Director of Special Projects	1983-1984
Helm, Susan M.	Director of Office of Friends	1985-1993
Hemphill, Charles R.	Secretary	1901-1902
Hemphill, Charles R.	Clerk of the Faculty	1902-1904
Hemphill, Charles R.	Chairman of the Faculty	1904-1905 and 1908-1909
Hemphill, Charles R.	President	1910-1920
Hemphill, Charles R.	Director of Religious Work	1920-1924
Hemphill, Charles R.	Dean	1920-1930
Hemphill, Charles R.	Dean Emeritus	1930-1932
Hennessy, William D.	Associate Librarian and Cataloger	1969-1983
Hicks, David	Audio-Visual Coordinator	1985-1987

Hills, Richard L.	Director of Deferred Giving	1970-1971
Hitner, Larry	Vice President for Development	1992-1998
Hofmann, Oliver K.	Assistant to the President	1979-1980
Hofmann, Oliver K.	Director of the Office of Information	1980-1983
Holden, Phyllis	Director of Public Relations	1975-1976
Horner, Norman A.	Acting Dean	1953-1955
Horner, Norman A.	Dean	1955-1968
Hougland, Kenneth R.	Business Manager and Treasurer/ Vice President of Business	1969-1987
Hubert, Jim	Director of Admissions	1991-2000
James, Mrs. D. C.	Assistant to Business Manager	1953-1954
Jones, Thomas L.	Vice President	1977-1980
Jones, Kent	Vice President for Finance and Administration	1987-1993
Kearns, Raymond V., Jr.	Acting President	1973-1974
Kirchhubel, Margaret C.	House-Mother	1949-1964
Kirkby, Mrs. T. M.	House-Mother	1946-1949
Kiser-Lowrance, Will	Interim Director of Field Education	1982-1983
Lewis, James W.	Executive Director of the Louisville Institute	1991-present
Lewis, Mary Ann	Dining Room Supervisor	1978-1979
Lindsey, Carolyn	Dining Room Supervisor	1977-1978
Love, Julian Price	Acting President	1964-1965
Luce, Mrs. Thomas P.	Food Service Manager	1968-1969

Lytch, Carol	Research Fellow for Family Ministry Project	1996-1999
Lytch, Carol	Coordinator for Theological School Programs for Strengthening Congregational Leadership	1999-present
Mapes, Kathryn	Coordinator of Academic Support Services	2000-present
March, W. Eugene	Director of Continuing Education	1985-1987
March, W. Eugene	Director of Doctor of Ministry Program	1987-1988
March, W. Eugene	Director of Advanced Programs	1988-1990
March, W. Eugene	Assistant to the President	1988-1993
March, W. Eugene	Director of Advanced Studies	1990-1992
March, W. Eugene	Dean	1993-1999
Marquess, William Hoge	Chairman of the Faculty	1901-1902
Marquess, William Hoge	Clerk of the Faculty	1905-1906 and 1908-1909
Marquess, William Hoge	Chairman of the Faculty	1906-1907
Marsh, Martha (Marti)	Comptroller	1985-present
Marsh, Martha (Marti)	Director of Accounting and Management Services	1977-1985
Mason, Alvin	Maintenance Supervisor	1967-1971
Matthews, Mrs. Carl S.	House-Mother	1934-1946
Meeker, Andy	Director of the Annual Fund	1993-1997
Melloan, Donna	Dean of Students	1992-present
Melton, E. Dale	Database Administrator for Seminary Relations	2000-present
Melton, Michelle E.	Director of Communications	1999-present

Miller, Lisa P.	Facilities Programming Coordinator/Manager	1992-1997
Miller, Lisa P.	Director of Marketing and Special Events	1998-present
Miller, Newton B.	Director of Buildings and Grounds	1982-1990
Miller, Newton B.	Coordinator for Special Projects	1991-1992
Morris, Angela	Reference Librarian	1999-present
Morrison, Clinton	Dean	1969-1976
Mulder, John M.	President	1981-present
Nelson, C. Ellis	President	1974-1981
Newcomer, Andrew E.	Vice President	1967 or 68-1972
Owensby, Emma Sue	Director of Public Relations	June 1-Aug. 1, 1976
Parse, Marguerite O.	Matron	1927-1934
Penick, Frank W.	Vice President for Development	1981-1988
Pfangle, Robert F.	Director of Junior Field Work	1936-1937
Ping, Mrs. Charles J.	Registrar	1951-1954
Politinsky, Allison Bell	Director of the Office of Communications	1992-1998
Porterfield, Norma R.	Director of the Office of Information	1987-1992
Pratt, Charles H.	Clerk of the Faculty	1926-1927
Pratt, Charles H.	Director of Religious Work	1924-1938
Ragland, Amanda W.	Director of Louisville Seminary Counseling Ministry	1997-1998
Ragsdale, Don	Associate Vice President for Seminary Relations	1998-present

Ramsay, Nancy	Director of Field Education	1983-1988
Redmon, Charles	Supervisor of Buildings and Grounds	1971-1981
Reistroffer, Dianne	Interim Dean	1999-2000
Reistroffer, Dianne	Director of Graduate Studies	1998-present
Reistroffer, Dianne	Dean and Vice President for Academic Affairs	2000-present
Richardson, Susan	Assistant Library Director for Technical Services	1988-1995
Richardson, Susan	Technical Services Librarian	1986-1988
Richey, Rebecca Smith	Acting Director of Continuing and Lay Education	1999-present
Riddick, John Carleton	Associate Director of Field Education	1969-1970
Riddick, John Carleton	Director of Student Affairs	1970-1971
Riggs, C. Dennis	Vice President for Development	1988-1992
Rudolph, L. C.	Assistant to the President	1954-1960
Rudolph, L. C.	Executive Associate	1960-1961
Rule, Andrew K.	Clerk of the Faculty	1927-1955
Sexton, Arvin L.	Director of Admissions and Recruiting	1973-1975
Sharer, Jack	Systems Director	1992-present
Sharp, Douglas G.	Director of Publications	1973-1976
Sherrill, Lewis J.	Assistant Dean	1929-1930
Sherrill, Lewis J.	Acting President	1936
Sherrill, Lewis J.	Dean	1930-1950
Shippey, Kim	Director of Alumni/ae Relations and the Annual Fund	1998-present

Steere, David A.	Director of Field Education	1961-1973
Steere, David A.	Associate Director of Field Education	1973-1977
Steere, David A.	Director of Clinical Training	1977-1996
Stemme, Suzanne	Director of the Office of Information	1984-1987
Sudduth, Miss Emily H.	Matron	1902-1927
Suitor, Joseph N.	Deferred Gifts Officer	1981-1982
Suitor, Joseph N.	Director of Planned Giving	1980-1981
Sutton, Walter C.	Director of Public Relations	1976-1980
Terry, Barbara W.	Assistant Library Director for Technical Services	1995-1999
Terry, Barbara W.	Associate Library Director	1999-present
Tesorero, Barbara Evans	Director of Continuing and Lay Education	1987-1992
Thompson, French W.	Extension Secretary	1917-1918
Thomson, E. A.	Business Manager	1953-1960
Totten, W. D.	Maintenance Engineer	1963-1967
Totten, Mrs. W. D. (Zenobia)	Business Office Manager	1966-1977
Townsend, Loren	Director of Marriage and Family Therapy Program	1997-2000
Townsend, Loren	Director of Clinical Training and Marriage and Family Therapy	1996-1997
Tucker, Grayson L., Jr.	Associate Director of Field Education	1968-1973
Tucker, Grayson L., Jr.	Director of Field Education	1973-1977
Tucker, Grayson L., Jr.	Dean	1976-1983

Tucker, Grayson L., Jr.	Interim Dean of Students	1991-1992
Van Kleeck, Liz	Librarian for Academic Computing Support	1998-present
Vander Meulen, John M.	President	1920-1930
Vander Meulen, John M.	Vice President	1930-1935
Vaught, David	Director of Public Relations	1976-1976
Warren, Edward L.	Librarian	1902-1927
Warren, Edward L.	pro tem Intendant	1906-1907
Warren, Edward L.	Intendant	1907-1927
Warren, Edward L.	Librarian Emeritus	1927-1931
Webb, Robert Alexander	Clerk of the Faculty	1909-1917
Weeks, Louis B.	Dean	1983-1993
West, Charles R.	Computer Operator	1985-1987
White, Ernest M.	Librarian	1944-1985
White, Ernest M.	Clerk of the Faculty	1955-1972
White, Ernest M.	Seminary Archivist	1987-1998
Wigger, J. Bradley	Director of the Center for Congregations and Family Ministries	1997-present
Wilder, Mrs. Windsor D.	Registrar	1950-1951
Willey, Frank	Director of Seminary Relations	1994-1997
Williams, Tim	Director of Campus Facilities	1990-present
Williams, Dolly	Director of Child Development Center	1987-1992
Winn, Albert Curry	President	1965-1973
Witherspoon, Miss Mattie	Assistant Librarian	1922-1929

Witherspoon, Miss Mattie	Bursar	1922-1953
Witherspoon, Miss Mattie	Librarian	1927-1928
Witherspoon, Miss Mattie	Intendant	1927-1949
Wood, David J.	Associate Director of the Louisville Institute	1998-present
Young, J. William, Jr.	Assistant to the President	1960-1966

• *Appendix D* •

PRESIDENTS OF THE ALUMNI/AE ASSOCIATION, 1907-PRESENT

An Association of the Alumni of the Seminary was formed during the closing exercises in May, 1907.

Clarence K. Crawford 1907-08	W. H. Hopper 1916-17
Clarence K. Crawford 1908-09	W. H. Hopper 1917-18
Clarence K. Crawford 1909-10	W. H. Hopper 1918-19
John Little 1910-11	W. H. Hopper 1919-20
John Little 1911-12	Harry S. Hudson 1920-21
Julian S. Sibley 1912-13	Harry S. Hudson 1921-22
Alfred A. Higgins 1913-14	Harry S. Hudson 1922-23
Cary R. Blain 1914-15	Walter A. Hopkins 1923-24
Paul H. Moore 1915-16	Walter A. Hopkins 1924-25

Walter A. Hopkins
1925-26

J. B. Carpenter
1926-27

T. Duke Williams
1927-28

T. Duke Williams
1928-29

C. A. Ray
1929-30

C. A. Ray
1930-31

C. A. Ray
1931-32

John W. Carpenter
1932-33

John W. Carpenter
1933-34

John W. Carpenter
1934-35

G. F. Bell
1935-36

G. F. Bell
1936-37

G. F. Bell
1937-38

J. Russell Cross
1938-39

J. Russell Cross
1939-40

J. Russell Cross
1940-41

Angus N. Gordon
1941-42

Angus N. Gordon
1942-43

Angus N. Gordon
1943-44

Paul M. Watson
1944-45

Edwin N. Rock
1945-46

G. Dewey Kimbel
1946-47

G. Dewey Kimbel
1947-48

G. Dewey Kimbel
1948-49

R. J. Hunter
1949-50

R. J. Hunter
1950-51

Glover A. Daniel
1951-52

Glover A. Daniel
1952-53

Glover A. Daniel
1953-54

Donald V. Morse
1954-55

Donald V. Morse
1955-56

Donald V. Morse
1956-57

Grayson L. Tucker, Jr.
1957-58

Grayson L. Tucker, Jr.
1958-59

Thomas L. Jones
1959-60

Thomas L. Jones
1960-61

No Alum. Assoc. listed for 1961-66

Carl E. Mills
1966-67

William H. Poore
1968-69

Joseph B. Mullin
1969-70

Edward H. Mesta
1970-71

No Alum. Assoc. listed for 1971-76

John Kirstein
1975-76

James Wilbanks
1976-77

John A. Kirstein
1977-78

Jim Wilbanks
1978-79

Jim Wilbanks
1979-80

Jim Wilbanks
1980-81

Thomas D. Kennedy
1981-82

James B. Wilbanks
1982-83

T. Morton McMillan
1983-84

Linda D. Chase
1984-85

L. Dale DePue
1985-86

Cecil Albright
1986-87

Dave MacDonna
1987-88

Ann Reed Held
1988-89

Ann Reed Held
1989-90

Earl Underwood
1990-91

Mary Gene Boteler
1991-92

Mary Gene Boteler
1992-93

Kevin Killion
1993-94

Kevin Killion
1994-95

Duane Aslyn
1995-96

Duane Aslyn
1996-97

Mary Wright
1997-98

Robert Agnew
1998-99

Robert Agnew
1999-2000

BIBLIOGRAPHY

Archival Material

Seminary Publications

Annual Catalogues of Danville Theological Seminary, Danville Theological Seminary Papers, Centre College Archives.

Annual Announcements of Louisville Presbyterian Theological Seminary, 1893-1901, Louisville Presbyterian Theological Seminary Archives.

Annual Announcement of the Presbyterian Theological Seminary of Kentucky, 1901-1911, Louisville Presbyterian Theological Seminary Archives.

Catalogues, 1971-Present. Louisville Presbyterian Theological Seminary Archives.

Danville Quarterly Review. Danville Theological Seminary Papers, Center College Archives.

"Life at Louisville Seminary." Louisville Presbyterian Theological Seminary Archives.

"The Mosaic." Louisville Presbyterian Theological Seminary Archives.

The Register. 1912-1971. Louisville Presbyterian Theological Seminary Archives.

"Seminary Times." Louisville Presbyterian Theological Seminary Archives.

Minutes

Minutes of the Board of Directors and Executive Committee, 1893-Present. Louisville Presbyterian Theological Seminary Archives.
Minutes of the Faculty, 1893-Present. Louisville Presbyterian Theological Seminary Archives.

Other

All materials in this section are found in the Louisville Presbyterian Theological Seminary archives unless otherwise noted.

"Addresses Delivered at the Inauguration of the Professors in the Danville Theological Seminary, October 13, 1853." Cincinnati: T. Wrightson, 1854. Danville Theological Seminary Papers, Centre College Archives.
"Addresses Delivered at the Inauguration of Rev. Jonathan Edwards, D.D., L.L.D., as Professor of Didactic and Polemic Theology in Danville Theological Seminary, April 17, 1878." Danville, Ky.: 1878. Danville Theological Seminary Papers, Centre College Archives.
"And the Wall Came Tumbling Down." *Louisville Times* (January 20, 1970). Newsclipping.
"Anti-Draft Group Gets Support." *Louisville Times* (May 8, 1969). Newsclipping.
Beattie, Francis R. "Apologetics: Outline of Lectures." 1899.
"The Bitter Scroll," vols. 1-3. 1974.
[Caldwell, Frank H.]. "Educating for a More Effective Ministry." Ca. 1940.
Caldwell, Frank H. "Louisville Seminary Looks Around and Ahead." Ca. 1940.
————. "Notes on the Louisville Flood." Manuscript, 1937.
Christian Observer. (August 23, 1966). Clipping.
"Court of Appeals of Kentucky. Fall Term, 1944."
Dinning, J. Donald, to Albert C. Winn. June 7, 1966.
Dosker, Henry E., Jesse L. Cotton, and Edward L.Warren. "To the Members of the Presbyterian Church (U.S.A.) Louisville." November 6, 1915.
Edwards, George R. Untitled Recollections of Louisville Presbyterian Theological Seminary. 1993. In the author's possession.
Horner, Norman. "What Has Happened to the Seminary?" A sermon preached at Central Presbyterian Church in Louisville, Kentucky, 1968.
Horner, Norman, Kim Smith King, and Louis Weeks. "Evangelism and Mission at Louisville Seminary." Unpublished manuscript.

Hougland, Kenneth. "Comments from Campus Tour." Copy in author's possession.

"Inaugural Services of John M. Worrall as Professor of Ecclesiastical History and Church Government." Danville, 1893. Danville Theological Seminary Papers, Centre College Archives.

"Leotards and Letter Sweater Part of Service." *The Courier-Journal.* December 6, 1964. Newsclipping.

"Liberal Cleric in the South: Frank Hill Caldwell." *New York Times.* April 13, 1966. Photocopy of newsclipping.

"Liberation Notes."

Little, John. Material Prepared by Rev. John Little for a book of history of the Presbyterian Colored Missions. Ca. 1936. Presbyterian Community Center Papers, University Archives and Records Center, University of Louisville.

"The Louisville Presbyterian Seminary and Proposed Consolidations of Presbyterian Seminaries." Ca. 1943.

"Louisville Presbyterian Theological Seminary Long-Range Plan, 1985."

"Minister Leads 50 in Picketing." *Louisville Times.* March 26, 1966. Newsclipping.

Mobley, Henry P. "The Administration of Louisville Presbyterian Theological Seminary, 1930s to the 1990s." Draft manuscript, ca. 1992. Copy in author's possession.

Mulder, John M. "Reflections on 15 Years: Louisville Presbyterian Theological Seminary, 1981-1996."

Nelson, C. Ellis. "Notes for Future Historians Regarding the 1974-1981 Period in the Life of Louisville Presbyterian Theological Seminary."

"New Mood Strikes Local Seminarians." *Louisville Times.* May 22, 1972. Newsclipping.

"Plan of the Danville Theological Seminary, under the care of the General Assembly of the Presbyterian Church in the United States of America." Louisville: Morton and Griswold, 1854. Danville Theological Seminary Papers, Centre College Archives.

"The Presbyterian Theological Seminary of Kentucky," 1901-1902. Information flyer. Danville Theological Seminary Papers, Centre College Archives.

"Quakers, Louisville Presbyterians Visit Capital to Lobby Against War." *The Courier-Journal.* May 8, 1970. Newsclipping.

"Rev. Dr. Wilson's Reply to the Address of Rev. Dr. E. P. Humphrey." Reprint in Danville Theological Seminary Papers, Centre College Archives.

Rule, Andrew K. "Introduction to Apologetics." Class notes of Thomas A. Schafer, ca. 1941.

Bibliography

"Seminary Ex-President, Dr. Julian Love, 74, Dies." *The Courier-Journal.* May 13, 1969. Newsclipping.

"Seminary Leader Stirs Assembly." *The Dallas Morning News.* April 24, 1966. Newsclipping.

"Sexism, Racism, and Homophobia Task Force." April 19, 1991. Manuscript.

"Superwoman: That's Donna Maier, Attorney, and Full-Time Seminary Student." *Louisville Times.* May 22, 1973. Newsclipping.

"Survey. U.S. Seminaries Works' Committee." 1942. Manuscript copy.

"To the Presbyterian People of Kentucky." Reprint in Danville Theological Seminary Papers, Centre College Archives.

"Tucker, Grayson. "A Church Planning Questionnaire."

Vander Meulen, John M., and Andrew K. Rule, "First Semester Course in Modern Tendencies in Theology (Liberal)." Manuscript(s) of lectures. 1930s.

Vander Meulen, John M. "A Review of the Past Ten Years of the Louisville Presbyterian Seminary, 1920-1930."

"War Foe Refused Hearing at School Board Meeting." *The Courier-Journal.* September 24, 1968. Photo of newsclipping.

Warheim, Hal M. "The History of a 'First-Class Dream' (Facts and Fantasies about Curriculum at Louisville Presbyterian Theological Seminary, 1853-1981)." Manuscript copy in author's possession.

"What Every Seminary Woman Wants to Know."

"Where and How at the Seminary." N.p., 1923. Promotional pamphlet written by students.

"Women of the Cloth." *Louisville Times.* September 28, 1971. Newsclipping.

Interviews

Alexander, Laverne. March 14, 1993.

Blackburn, Winfrey. May 15, 1994.

Bos, Johanna. April 17, 1994.

Boteler, Mary Gene. February 25, 1999.

Bryant, Gloria. March 16, 1994

Caldwell, Fannie. February 2, 1992.

Caldwell, Anne. February 27, 1993.

Collins, Delia. March 16, 1994.

Cooper, Burton. March 13, 1994.

Duncan, Thomas. March 23, 1992.

Dykstra, Craig. May 6, 1994.

Edwards, George and Jean. March 16, 1993.

Ekstrom, William. March 17, 1992.

Franklin, McCoy. May 4, 1994.

Goodykoontz, Harry and Betty. March 16, 1992.

Grawemeyer, Charles. March 13, 1993.

Horner, Norman. April 23, 1993.

Hougland, Kenneth. March 17, 1992.

Krauss-Jackson, Jane. May 16, 1994.

Kuykendall, John. May 20, 1994.

Lynn, Robert Wood. May 7, 1994.

McAtee, William. May 17, 1994.

March, Eugene. August 18, 1999.

Marcum, Virginia. May 16, 1994.

Mobley, Henry, and Paul Tudor Jones. April 26, 1992.

Morrison, Clinton. March 16, 1993.

Nash, Marjorie. May 3, 1994.

Nelson, Ellis and Nancy. April 25, 1992.

Newlin, George. May 9, 1992.

Olert, John. March 15, 1992.

Penick, Frank. April 24, 1993.

Porterfield, Norma. March 13, 1993.

Redmon, Charles. March 16, 1994.

Reed, Robert. March 13, 1994.

Rhee, Syngman. June 21, 1994.

Rhodes, Arnold Black and Lela. May 9, 1992.

Riggs, Dennis. May 16, 1994.

Roberts, Morgan. April 29, 1994.

Steere, David. May 15, 1994.

Steilberg, Alan. March 15, 1993.

Stevenson, Jane. May 14, 1994.

Tucker, Grayson and Cate. March 15, 1993.

Weeks, Louis. March 15, 1993.

Wessler, Daniel and Jen. January 30, 1993.

White, Ernest. March 16, 1992.

Winn, Al and Grace. February 22, 1992.

Young, William. May 4, 1994.

Secondary Literature

The American Organist 20 (February, 1986): 52-53.

"An Inquiry into the True Doctrine of Human Society, Civil Government, the

Magistracy, and the Citizen, as Revealed by God, with Special Reference to the State of Public Affairs in America." *Danville Quarterly Review* 3 (March, 1863): 1-38.

Cherry, Conrad. *Hurrying Toward Zion: Universities, Divinity Schools, and American Protestantism.* Bloomington and Indianapolis: Indiana University Press, 1995.

"The Civil War: — Its Nature and End." *Danville Quarterly Review* 1 (December, 1861): 639-72.

"Consolidation of the Kentucky Seminaries." *Christian Observer* 89 (May 29, 1901): 26-28.

"Consolidation of the Presbyterian Institutions in Kentucky." *Christian Observer* 89 (April 17, 1901): 2.

Currie, Thomas White, Jr. *Austin Presbyterian Theological Seminary: A Seventy-Fifth Anniversary History.* San Antonio: Trinity University Press, 1978.

Dillard, Badgett. "Financial Support of Protestant Theological Education." Ed.D. thesis, Indiana University, 1973.

"Discourse of Dr. R. J. Breckinridge Delivered on the Day of National Humiliation, January 4, 1861, at Lexington, Kentucky." *Danville Quarterly Review* 1 (June, 1861): 319-41.

"Educational Movements in Kentucky and Missouri." *Christian Observer* 89 (May 1, 1901): 3.

Evans, Alice Frazer, Robert A. Evans, and David A. Roozen, eds. *The Globalization of Theological Education.* Maryknoll, N.Y.: Orbis Books, 1993.

"The General Assembly." *Christian Observer* 89 (May 29, 1901): 2-3.

"The General Assembly of 1862, of the Presbyterian Church in the United States of America." *Danville Quarterly Review* 2 (June, 1862): 301-70.

Groves, Walter A. "A School of the Prophets at Danville." Reprint copy from the *Filson Club History Quarterly.* Vol. 27, 223-46. Danville Theological Seminary Papers, Centre College Archives.

Handy, Robert T. *A History of Union Theological Seminary in New York.* New York: Columbia University Press, 1987.

Hudnut-Beumler, James. *Looking for God in the Suburbs: The Religion of the American Dream and Its Cities, 1945-1965.* New Brunswick, N.J.: Rutgers University Press, 1994.

"The Late General Assembly — Church and State," *Danville Quarterly Review* 1 (September, 1861): 498-534.

"Life at Louisville Revisited." October, 1992. A book of alumni/ae remembrances.

Little, John. "Our Colored Work." *Christian Observer* 89 (December 25, 1901): 9-10.

"The Louisville Story." *Presbyterian Journal* 31 (June 21, 1972): 9-11, 20.

Marsden, George M. *Reforming Fundamentalism: Fuller Seminary and the New Evangelicalism*. Grand Rapids, Mich.: William B. Eerdmans, 1987.

McElroy, I. S. *The Louisville Presbyterian Theological Seminary*. Charlotte, N.C.: The Presbyterian Standard Publishing Co., 1929.

Miller, Howard. "Seminary and Society: A Case Study of Their Interrelationship. David Leander Stitt and Austin Presbyterian Theological Seminary, 1945-1971." A Report Submitted to the Lilly Endowment, 1987.

Minutes of the General Assembly of the Presbyterian Church in the United States of America.

Minutes of the General Assembly of the Presbyterian Church in the United States.

"The New Gospel of Rationalism." *Danville Quarterly Review* 1 (September, 1861): 365-89.

Niebuhr, H. Richard. *The Purpose of the Church and Its Ministry: Reflections on the Aims of Theological Education*. New York: Harper and Brothers, 1956.

"Our Country — Its Peril — Its Deliverance." *Danville Quarterly Review* 1 (March, 1861): 73-115.

Philips, J. Davison. *Time of Blessing, Time of Hope: Columbia Theological Seminary, 1976-1986*. Decatur, Ga.: Columbia Theological Seminary, 1994.

"The Relation which Reason and Philosophy Sustain to the Theology of Revelation." *Danville Quarterly Review* 1 (March, 1861): 24-54.

"The Relative Doctrinal Tendencies of Presbyterianism and Congregationalism in America." *Danville Quarterly Review* 1 (March, 1861): 1-23.

"Report of the Special Committee to Study Theological Institutions." *Minutes of the Presbyterian Church in the United States of America*. Louisville, Ky.: Office of the Stated Clerk, 1993.

"Reunion 1993 Reflections." A collection of remembrances by alumni/ae.

Richards, J. McDowell. *As I Remember It: Columbia Theological Seminary, 1932-1971*. Decatur, Ga.: Columbia Theological Seminary Press, 1985.

Ruger, Anthony. *Lean Years, Fat Years: Changes in the Financial Support of Protestant Theological Education*. Auburn, N.Y.: Auburn Theological Seminary, 1994.

Sanders, Robert Stuart. *History of Louisville Presbyterian Theological Seminary, 1853-1953*. Louisville, Ky.: Louisville Presbyterian Theological Seminary, 1953.

Selden, William K. *Princeton Theological Seminary: A Narrative History, 1812-1992*. Princeton: Princeton University Press, 1992.

Sellers, Ovid R. *The Fifth Quarter Century of McCormick: The Story of the Years 1929-1954 at McCormick Theological Seminary*. Chicago: McCormick Theological Seminary, 1955.

Sweet, Leonard I. *The Minister's Wife: Her Role in Nineteenth-Century American Evangelicalism*. Philadelphia: Temple University Press, 1983.

"The Secession Conspiracy in Kentucky, and its Overthrow: with the Relations of both to the General Revolt." *Danville Quarterly Review* 2 (June, 1862): 221-47.

Thompson, Ernest Trice. *Presbyterians in the South*. 3 vols. Richmond, Va.: John Knox Press, 1973.

"The Union and the Constitution." *Danville Quarterly Review* 3 (September, 1863): 345-70.

"The Union and the Constitution. No. II." *Danville Quarterly Review* 3 (December, 1863): 539-68.

Walther, James Arthur, ed. *Ever a Frontier: The Bicentennial History of the Pittsburgh Theological Seminary*. Grand Rapids, Mich.: Wm. B. Eerdmans Publishing Co., 1994.

Weeks, Louis B. *Kentucky Presbyterians*. Atlanta: John Knox Press, 1983.

Wheeler, Barbara G., and Edward Farley, eds. *Shifting Boundaries: Contextual Approaches to the Structure of Theological Education*. Louisville: Westminster/John Knox Press, 1991.

Selected Works of the Louisville Seminary Faculty

Beattie, Francis. *The Presbyterian Standards: An Exposition of the Westminster Confession of Faith and Catechisms*. Richmond, Va.: Presbyterian Committee of Publication, 1896.

———. *Radical Criticism: An Exposition of the Radical Critical Theory Concerning the Literature and Religious System of the Old Testament Scriptures*. New York: Fleming H. Revell Co., 1894.

Bos, Johanna W. H. van Wijk. *Ezra, Nehemiah, and Esther*. Louisville: Westminster/John Knox Press, 1998.

———. *Reformed and Feminist: A Challenge to the Church*. Louisville: Westminster/John Knox Press, 1991.

———. *Re-Imagining God: The Case for Scriptural Diversity*. Louisville: Westminster/John Knox Press, 1995.

Breckinridge, Robert J. *The Knowledge of God, Objectively Considered, Being the First Part of Theology Considered as a Science of Positive Truth, Both Inductive and Deductive*. New York: R. Carter and Brothers, 1858.

———. *The Knowledge of God, Subjectively Considered, Being the Second Part of Theology Considered as a Science of Positive Truth, Both Inductive and Deductive*. New York: R. Carter and Brothers, 1859.

Caldwell, Frank H. *Preaching Angles*. Nashville: Abingdon Press, 1954.

Chamberlain, William Douglas. *The Meaning of Prayer.* Philadelphia: The Westminster Press, 1953.

————. *The Meaning of Repentance.* Philadelphia: The Westminster Press, 1943.

Coalter, Milton J. *Gilbert Tennant, Son of Thunder: A Case Study of Continental Pietism's Impact on the First Great Awakening in the Middle Colonies.* New York: Greenwood Press, 1986.

Coalter, Milton J, and Virgil Cruz, eds. *How Shall We Witness? Faithful Evangelism in a Reformed Tradition.* Louisville: Westminster John Knox Press, 1995.

Coalter, Milton J, John M. Mulder, and Louis B. Weeks, eds. *The Presbyterian Presence: The Twentieth-Century Experience.* 7 vols. Louisville: Westminster/John Knox Press, 1990-92.

————. *Vital Signs: The Promise of Mainstream Protestantism.* Grand Rapids, Mich.: William B. Eerdmans Publishing Co., 1996.

Cooper, Burton Z. *The Idea of God: A Whiteheadian Critique of St. Thomas' Concept of God.* The Hague: Martinus Nijhoff, 1974.

————. *Why, God?* Atlanta: John Knox Press, 1988.

Dykstra, Craig R. *Vision and Character: A Christian Educator's Alternative to Kohlberg.* New York: Paulist Press, 1981.

Edwards, George R. *Jesus and the Politics of Violence.* New York: Harper and Row, 1972.

————. *Gay/Lesbian Liberation: A Biblical Perspective.* New York: Pilgrim Press, 1984.

Elwood, Christopher. *The Body Broken: The Calvinist Doctrine of the Eucharist and the Symbolization of Power in Sixteenth-Century France.* New York and Oxford: Oxford University Press, 1999.

Foreman, Kenneth J. *From This Day Forward: Thoughts About a Christian Marriage.* Richmond, Va.: Outlook Publishers, 1950.

————. *God's Will and Ours: An Introduction to the Problem of Freedom, Foreordination, and Faith.* Richmond, Va.: Outlook Publishers, 1954.

————. *Identification: Human and Divine.* Richmond, Va.: John Knox Press, 1963. (These were the Warfield Lectures at Princeton for 1962.)

————. "What is the Bible?" in Balmer H. Kelly, ed., *Introduction to the Bible.* vol. 1 *The Layman's Bible Commentary.* Richmond, Va.: John Knox Press, 1959.

Garrett, Susan R. *The Demise of the Devil: Magic and the Demonic in Luke's Writing.* Minneapolis: Fortress Press, 1989.

————. *The Temptations of Jesus in Mark's Gospel.* Grand Rapids, Mich.: William B. Eerdmans Publishing Co., 1998.

Goodykoontz, Harry G. *The Minister in the Reformed Tradition.* Richmond, Va.: John Knox Press, 1963.

Guder, Darrell L. *Be My Witnesses: The Church's Mission, Message, and Messengers.* Grand Rapids, Mich.: William B. Eerdmans Publishing Co., 1985.

Hester, David C., and Thomas P. Holland, eds. *Building Effective Boards for Religious Organizations: A Handbook for Trustees, Presidents, and Church Leaders.* San Francisco, Calif.: Jossey-Bass, 2000.

Horner, Norman A. *Cross and Crucifix in Mission: A Companion of Protestant-Roman Catholic Missionary Strategy.* Nashville: Abingdon Press, 1965.

———, ed. *Protestant Crosscurrents in Mission: The Ecumenical-Conservative Encounter.* Nashville: Abingdon Press, 1968.

Keen, Samuel. *Apology for Wonder.* New York: Harper and Row, 1969.

Kerr, Hugh T., and John M. Mulder, eds. *Conversions: The Christian Experience.* Grand Rapids, Mich.: William B. Eerdmans Publishing Co., 1983.

Lewis, James W., and James P. Wind, eds. *American Congregations.* 2 vols. Chicago: The University of Chicago Press, 1994.

Lewis, James. W. *The Protestant Experience in Gary, Indiana, 1906-1975: At Home in the City.* Knoxville: The University of Tennessee Press, 1992.

Love, Julian Price. *The First, Second, and Third Letters of John, The Letter of Jude, The Revelation to John.* Richmond, Va.: John Knox Press, 1960. Vol. 25 in *The Layman's Bible Commentary.*

———. *The Gospel and the Gospels.* Nashville: Abingdon-Cokesbury Press, 1953.

———. *How to Read the Bible.* Rev. ed. New York: The Macmillan Co., 1959.

———. *The Missionary Message of the Bible.* New York: The Macmillan Co., 1941.

March, W. Eugene. *Israel and the Politics of Land: A Theological Case Study.* Louisville: Westminster/John Knox Press, 1994.

Mauser, Ulrich. *Christ in the Wilderness: The Wilderness Theme in the Second Gospel and Its Basis in the Biblical Tradition.* Naperville, Ill.: A. R. Allenson, 1963.

———. *Gottesbild and Menschwerdung: Eine Untersuchung zur Einheit des Alten und Neuen Testamenten.* Tübingen: Mohr, 1971.

McClure, John S., ed. *Best Advice for Preaching.* Minneapolis: Fortress Press, 1998.

———. *The Four Codes of Preaching: Rhetorical Strategies.* Minneapolis: Fortress Press, 1991.

———. *The Roundtable Pulpit: Where Leadership and Preaching Meet.* Nashville: Abingdon Press, 1995.

McClure, John S., and Nancy J. Ramsay, eds. *Telling the Truth: Preaching about*

Sexual and Domestic Violence. Cleveland, Ohio: United Church Press, 1998.

Morrison, Clinton. *Analytical Concordance to the Revised Standard Version of the New Testament.* Philadelphia: The Westminster Press, 1979.

Mulder, John M. *Sealed in Christ: The Synbolism of the Seal of the Presbyterian Church (U.S.A.).* Louisville: Presbyterian Publishing House, 1991.

———. *Woodrow Wilson: The Years of Preparation.* Princeton: Princeton University Press, 1978.

Nebelsick, Harold P. *Circles of God: Theology and Science from the Greeks to Copernicus.* Edinburgh: Scottish Academic Press, 1985.

———. *The Renaissance, the Reformation and the Rise of Science.* Edinburgh: T & T Clark, 1992.

———. *Theology and Science in Mutual Modification.* New York: Oxford University Press, 1981.

Nelson, C. Ellis. *Don't Let Your Conscience Be Your Guide.* New York: Paulist Press, 1978.

Phifer, Kenneth G. *A Protestant Case for Liturgical Renewal.* Philadelphia: The Westminster Press, 1965.

Ramsay, Nancy J. *Pastoral Diagnosis: A Resource for Ministries of Care and Counseling.* Minneapolis: Fortress Press, 1998.

Rhodes, Arnold B. *The Book of Psalms.* Richmond, Va.: John Knox Press, 1960. Vol. 9 in *The Layman's Bible Commentary.*

———, ed. *The Church Faces the Isms.* Nashville and New York: Abingdon Press, 1958.

———. *The Mighty Acts of God.* Richmond, Va.: CLC Press, 1964.

Rudolph, L. C. *Francis Asbury.* Nashville: Abingdon Press, 1966.

———. *Hoosier Zion: The Presbyterians in Early Indiana.* New Haven: Yale University Press, 1963.

Sherrill, Lewis J., and Helen H. Sherrill. *Becoming a Christian: A Manual for Communicant Classes.* Richmond, Va.: John Knox Press, 1943.

Sherrill, Lewis J. *Guilt and Redemption.* Richmond, Va.: John Knox Press, 1945.

———. *The Rise of Christian Education.* New York: The Macmillan Co., 1944.

———. *The Struggle of the Soul.* New York: The Macmillan Co., 1951.

Soards, Marion L. *The Apostle Paul: An Introduction to His Writings and Teaching.* New York: Paulist Press, 1987.

———. *First Corinthians.* New International Biblical Commentary Series. Peabody, Mass.: Hendrickson Publishers, 1999.

———. *The Passion According to Luke: The Special Material of Luke 22.* Sheffield: JSOT Press, 1987.

———. *Scripture and Homosexuality: Biblical Authority and the Church Today.* Louisville: Westminster John Knox Press, 1995.

———. *The Speeches in Acts: Their Content, Context, and Concerns.* Louisville: Westminster/John Knox Press, 1994.

Steere, David A. *Bodily Expressions in Psychotherapy.* New York: Brunner/Mozel, 1982.

———. *Spiritual Presence in Psychotherapy: A Guide for Caregivers.* New York: Brunner/Mozel, 1997.

———. *The Supervision of Pastoral Care.* Louisville: Westminster/John Knox Press, 1989.

Tucker, Grayson L., Jr. *A Church Planning Questionnaire: Manual and Discoveries from 100 Churches.* Louisville: Grayson L. Tucker, 1982.

———. *Person-to-Person Evangelism: A Model of Sharing God's Good News Through Personal Experiences.* Good News Series. New York: UPCUSA Evangelism Program, 1979.

Vander Meulen, John M. *The Faith of Christendom: A Series of Studies on the Apostles' Creed.* Richmond, Va.: Presbyterian Committee of Publication, 1936.

———. *Getting Out of the Rough.* New York: George H. Doran Co., 1926.

Webb, Robert Alexander. *Christian Salvation: Its Doctrine and Experience.* Richmond, Va.: Presbyterian Committee of Publication, 1921.

———. *The Christian's Hope: Its Doctrine and Experience.* Richmond, Va.: Presbyterian Committee of Publication, 1921.

———. *The Theology of Infant Salvation.* Richmond, Va.: Presbyterian Committee of Publication, 1907.

Weeks, Louis and Carolyn, and Robert A. and Alice F. Evans. *Casebook for Christian Living: Value Formation for Families and Congregations.* Atlanta: John Knox Press, 1977.

Weeks, Louis B. *A New Christian Nation.* Faith of Our Fathers Series. N.p.: A Consortium Book, 1977.

———. *The Presbyterian Source: Bible Words that Shape a Faith.* Louisville: Westminster/John Knox Press, 1990.

Weeks, Louis B., Ronald C. White, and Garth M. Russell, eds. *American Christianity: A Case Approach.* Grand Rapids, Mich.: William B. Eerdmans Publishing Co., 1986.

Wessler, Daniel B. and M. Jenelyn. *The Gifts of Silence.* Atlanta: John Knox Press, 1976.

Whaling, Thornton. *Jesus and Christian Doctrine.* Richmond, Va.: Presbyterian Committee of Publication, n.d.

———. *Science and Religion Today.* Chapel Hill, N.C.: The University of North Carolina Press, 1929.

Wigger, J. Bradley. *The Texture of Mystery: An Interdisciplinary Inquiry into Perception and Learning.* Lewisburg, Pa.: Bucknell University Press, 1998.

Willey, Patricia Tull. *Remember the Former Things: The Recollection of Previous Texts in Second Isaiah.* Atlanta: Scholars Press, 1997.

Winn, Albert C. *The Acts of the Apostles.* Richmond, Va.: John Knox Press, 1960. Vol. 20 in *The Layman's Bible Commentary.*

———. *The Worry and Wonder of Being Human.* Richmond, Va.: Covenant Life Curriculum Press, 1966.

———. *You and Your Lifework: A Christian Choice for Youth.* Chicago: Science Research Associates, 1963.

INDEX

The Sociology
of Katrina